BOHN'S STANDARD LIBRARY.

———

THE

LIFE OF COLONEL HUTCHINSON,

AND THE

SIEGE OF LATHOM HOUSE.

GEORGE BELL & SONS

LONDON: YORK ST., COVENT GARDEN
NEW YORK: 66 FIFTH AVENUE, AND
BOMBAY: 53 ESPLANADE ROAD
CAMBRIDGE: DEIGHTON BELL & CO.

Colonel Hutchinson.

MEMOIRS

OF THE

LIFE OF COLONEL HUTCHINSON

GOVERNOR OF NOTTINGHAM CASTLE AND TOWN.

WRITTEN BY
HIS WIDOW LUCY.

EDITED
FROM THE ORIGINAL MANUSCRIPT BY THE REV. JULIUS HUTCHINSON.

TO WHICH IS PREFIXED
THE LIFE OF MRS. HUTCHINSON

WRITTEN BY HERSELF.

ALSO AN ACCOUNT OF
THE SIEGE OF LATHOM HOUSE

DEFENDED BY THE COUNTESS OF DERBY AGAINST
SIR THOMAS FAIRFAX.

The Naval & Military Press Ltd

in association with

The National Army Museum, London

Published jointly by

The Naval & Military Press Ltd

Unit 10 Ridgewood Industrial Park,
Uckfield, East Sussex,
TN22 5QE England

Tel: +44 (0) 1825 749494
Fax: +44 (0) 1825 765701

www.naval-military-press.com
www.military-genealogy.com
www.militarymaproom.com

and

The National Army Museum, London

www.national-army-museum.ac.uk

Printed and bound in Great Britain by
CPI Antony Rowe, Chippenham and Eastbourne

*In reprinting in facsimile from the original, any imperfections are inevitably reproduced
and the quality may fall short of modern type and cartographic standards.*

ADVERTISEMENT.

———

THE LIFE OF COLONEL HUTCHINSON embraces the history of a period which, whether considered in a literary or in a political point of view, is unquestionably one of the most remarkable in the British annals. It relates the transactions of an age when Cromwell and Hampden acted, and when Laud and Strafford suffered. The circumstances of this eventful era of our domestic history could not fail to rouse into strong and continued action the respective leaders of the monarchal and republican parties, and to inspire men with qualities proportioned to the gigantic interests which surrounded them, as well as to the momentous principles then at stake. Of the course of policy pursued, and the character of those who took part in this political and religious conflict, there will, however, **continue** to prevail decided and lasting divisions of opinion.

In no work tnat has come down the stream of time will be found such a vivid and distinct picture of the antagonism and mortal strife of the Civil Wars of the seventeenth century, as in the Memoir of the Governor of Nottingham Castle. It is the biography of an unpledged politician and independent man—a man of sterling integrity and steady enthusiasm, carried forward by an excess of honourable and lofty principle, and presenting to future ages a great and noble manifestation of human character in a time of political commotion and danger.

That such a work as the Life of Colonel Hutchinson should have excited so much attention and interest, as to have passed rapidly through three editions within four years after its first appearance in 1806, can be no matter of surprise. The amiable authoress, from being a personal witness of the scenes she so vividly describes, was enabled to trace the true springs and motives of the actions of the leading characters of this stormy period, and to give them the animation, the individuality, and the distinctness of real life. Possessing a taste of the purest and most elevated order, this affectionate tribute of respect to the memory of her husband and her own genius, is writ'fn with all the spirit and raciness of our native idiom, and with all the flexibility and felicitous ease which remind us of her amiable contemporary—the venerable Isaak Walton.

The present volume contains the whole of the valuable notes and additions of the Rev. Julius Hutchinson, the original editor, and is now presented to the public at about one-sixth of its original price. The orthography and punctuation, which, as the former editor justly complains, were at the period when Mrs. Hutchinson wrote, in a most unsettled state, have in the present edition been carefully revised. A few obsolete words and minor defects of phraseology have been sparingly altered for those of modern usage, and to render the work more complete and useful to the reader, chronological dates and references, with a General Index, have been added. These improvements were suggested by the writer of an able article in the Edinburgh Review (vol. xiii.), in a notice of the first edition, and have been made with scrupulous attention to retain, in all its vigour, the antique simplicity and delightful quaintness of the style of the authoress, which forms one of the greatest charms of the work.

THE SIEGE OF LATHOM HOUSE will be found a fit sequel and accompaniment to the foregoing work, being

" one of those remnants of history," to use the words of
Lord Bacon, " which have escaped the shipwreck of time."
It is singularly valuable as an historical narrative, as displaying the chivalrous valour and heroic spirit of the Countess of Derby, and as delineating with perfect accuracy
the plots and incidents connected with this memorable siege.

H. G. B.

YORK STREET, *November* 20, 1845.

PREFACE.

IT is conceived to be necessary, for the satisfaction of the public, to prefix to this work some account of the manuscripts from which it has been printed, and of the manner in which they came into the hands of the editor; which we shall accordingly do, interweaving therewith such subsequent information as we have been able to collect respecting the families and descendants of Colonel and Mrs. Hutchinson.

The memoirs of the Life of Col. Hutchinson had been seen by many persons, as well as the editor, in the possession of the late Thomas Hutchinson, Esq. of Owthorpe, in Nottinghamshire, and of Hatfield Woodhall, in Hertfordshire; and he had been frequently solicited to permit them to be published, particularly by the late Mrs. Catharine Maccaulay, but had uniformly refused. This gentleman dying without issue, the editor, his nephew, inherited some part of his estates which were left unsold, including his mansion-house of Hatfield Woodhall. In the library he found the following books, written by Mrs. Lucy Hutchinson. 1st. The Life of Colonel Hutchinson, 2d. A book without a title, but which appears to have been a kind of diary made use of when she came to write the Life of Colonel Hutchinson. 3d. A Fragment giving an account of the early part of her own life. This book clearly appears to have been Mrs. Hutchinson's first essay at composition, and contains, besides the story of her life and family, several short copies of verses, some finished, some unfinished, many of which are above mediocrity. And, 4th. Two books treating entirely of religious subjects; in which, although the fancy may be rather too much indulged, the judgment still maintains the ascendancy, and sentiments of exalted piety, liberality, and benevolence, are delivered in terms apposite, dignified, and perspicuous.

These works had all been read, and marked in several places with his initials, by Julius Hutchinson, Esq., of Owthorpe, the father of the late Thomas Hutchinson, Esq., just mentioned, and son of Charles Hutchinson, Esq., of Owthorpe, only son of Sir Thomas Hutchinson by his second wife, the Lady Catharine Stanhope. Lady Catharine Hutchinson lived to the age of 102, and is reported to have retained her faculties to the end of her life. Some remarks made by the above-mentioned Julius Hutchinson, which will be found in their proper places in the body of the work, are declared by him to have been communicated by his grandmother Lady Catharine; and as this lady dwelt in splendour at Nottingham, and had ample means of information; as there is only one instance wherein the veracity of the biographer is at all called in question, and even in this, it does not appear to the editor, and probably may not to the reader, that there was sufficient ground for objection; the opposition and the acquiescence of her grandson and herself seem alike to confirm the authenticity and faithfulness of the narrative.

Colonel Hutchinson left four sons, of which the youngest only, John, left issue two sons; and there is a tradition in the family, that these two last descendants of Colonel Hutchinson emigrated, the one to the West Indies or America, the other to Russia; the latter is said to have gone out with the command of a ship of war given by Queen Anne to the Czar Peter, and to have been lost at sea. One of the female descendants of the former the editor once met with by accident at Portsmouth, and she spoke with great warmth of the veneration in which his descendants in the new world held the memory of their ancestor Colonel Hutchinson. Of the daughters little more is known than that Mrs. Hutchinson, addressing one of her books of devotion to her daughter, Mrs. Orgill, ascertains that one of them was married to a gentleman of that name.

The family of Mr. George Hutchinson likewise became extinct in the second generation.

Charles Hutchinson, only son of Sir Thomas Hutchinson by Lady Catharine Stanhope, married one of the daughters and co-heiresses of Sir Francis Boteler, of Hatfield Woodhall, Herts; which family being zealous royalists, and he solicitous to gain their favour, (which he did so effectually, as in the end to obtain nearly their whole inheritance,) it is pro-

bable that he gave small encouragement or assistance to the
elder branch of the family while they suffered for their republican sentiments ; on the contrary, it is certain that he purchased of Mrs. Hutchinson and her son, after the death of
Colonel Hutchinson, their estate at Owthorpe, which, joined
to what his father had given him, and what he obtained by
his marriage, raised him to more opulence than his father
had ever possessed ; and he seems not to have fallen short of
him in popularity, for he represented the town of Nottingham
in parliament from the year 1690 (being the first general
election after the accession of King William) till his death.

His son Julius returned into that line of conduct and connexions which was most natural for one of his descent, for
he married Betty, daughter of Colonel Norton, of Wellow,
of the well-known patriotic family of that name in Hamp-
shire, and whose mother was a Fiennes. He seems to have
bestowed a very rational and well deserved attention upon the
writings of Mrs. Hutchinson, and there is a tradition in the
family, that although he had many children of his own, he
treated with kindness and liberality the last descendants of
his uncle, and assisted them with money to fit them out for
their emigration. The editor has seen a written memorandum
of his, expressing his regret at hearing no more of them after
their departure.

From the circumstance of these, the only grandchildren of
Colonel Hutchinson, standing in need of this pecuniary assistance, from the mention Mrs. Hutchinson makes of her
husband's debts, and from an expression contained in that
book which she addresses to her daughter. Mrs. Orgill,
desiring her not to depise her advice though she sees her in
adversity, it is highly probable that, even after selling her
husband's estates, the sum to be divided left each member of
the family in strait circumstances.

The affection and well-merited esteem with which Mrs.
Hutchinson speaks of her brother Sir Allen Apsley, will excite an interest in the reader to know what became of him
and his posterity ; the short pedigree subjoined will show,
that by two marriages, and by the death of his grandson in
his minority, the family of Apsley entirely merged in the
noble family of Bathurst, who have adopted the name Apsley
a their second title ; there are five or six of the family of

Apsley entombed in Westminster Abbey, near to the entrance of Henry the Seventh's Chapel.

Having traced the manuscript from the hands of the writer to those of the editor, in such a manner as to establish its authenticity beyond all doubt; the next, and that not a less important point, is to remove those objections which may be raised against the tendency of a work of this nature, and to show that the assumption of any evil tendency is groundless.

That avowed predilection for a republican government, which is conspicuous in this history, as it was in the lives of the persons who are the principal subjects of it, may perhaps give a momentary alarm; but a little reflection will dissipate it. At the time when Colonel Hutchinson first entered on the great theatre of life, the contest was just begun between the partizans of the divine right of the sovereign, and the indispensable obligation of the subject to a passive obedience and nonresistance, on one side; and the assertors of the claims of the people to command, through their representatives, the public purse, the freedom of debate in parliament, and the responsibility of ministers, on the other. When the sword, the *ratio ultima regum*, the *last appeal of kings*, was resorted to by the former, and the latter gained the victory, they very naturally adopted the republican system, as concluding, that persons holding such opinions as the princes of the House of Stuart and their adherents did, would never concede to them their franchises, but with a full intention to resume them, whenever they should recover power enough to attempt it with success. The event fully justified this conclusion,* and it is now evident to all, that the only thing which could ever give this nation permanent tranquillity, and put an end to those heartburnings which either openly or covertly had existed even from the time of the Norman conquest, was an explicit compact between king and people, which took its date indeed from the revolution in 1688, but obtained its consummation at the fortunate accession of the house of Brunswick, when the title of the monarch, and the rights of the people, became identified and established on one common basis. Of this truly may be said,

> Quod optanti Divum permittere nemo
> Auderet, volvenda dies en attulit ultrò.— *Virg. Æn.* **ix. 6, 7.**

* In the reigns of Charles II. and James II.

What to his vot'ry not a God dared promise,
Revolving years spontaneously produced.

No one will pretend that such an occasion was within the reach of human foresight; of course the only remedy then attainable was applied to the disorder of the state. Upon a fair review of the contest it will be seen, that what the tory and the courtier of the present day, the friend or even the flatterer of kingly power admits as axioms, were the grand desiderata of the whig and the patriot of those times; and that what were then cried out upon as daring encroachments, now pass as the most moderate and unquestioned claims. Not to deceive ourselves then with words, nor attach our minds to names instead of things, although the government under which we prosper be termed Imperial; yet the greater part of the legislative power resting with the people, and the executive being vested in a chief magistrate, who is under so many limitations that he seems placed in that situation very much more for the common weal, the public benefit, than his own ease or advantage, it must be allowed to come up to Colonel Hutchinson's favourite idea of a republic for all beneficial purposes, and would assuredly be not less acceptable to him, for that the hereditary succession would be found to repress that effervescence of individual ambition which was the study and the labour of his life to keep down. Possessing himself, but finding not in others, the virtue worthy of and essential to a republic, he would gladly have taken shelter under a well-limited monarchy, and of such a one he would unquestionably have been a loyal subject, a vigorous assertor.

The Puritanism which appears in the story, and actuated the conduct of Colonel Hutchinson all through life, may be accounted for on almost a similar ground with his predilection for a republic.

The puritanic turn of thought and style of expression had been adopted by the vindicators of religious freedom and right of inquiry, with whom the champions of civil liberty naturally made common cause. Divinity as a science was a study then in vogue, and seems to have tinctured the conversation and writings of the greater part of society.* In this Mr. Hutch-

* From the practice of dragging religion or religious phraseology into the service of politics, none, not even the king, was exempt, who, making a speech to his small army in the year 1642, to animate them, tells them they will have none to encounter but rebels, most of them *Brownists*, *Anabaptists*, and *Atheists!* who would destroy both church and commonwealth.

inson had been encouraged by his father, whose library subsisted at his family seat of Owthorpe till about the year 1775,
and contained a vast number of folio volumes of polemical
divinity.   A study environed with many dangers! and which
led Colonel Hutchinson into whatever errors he was guilty of.
On another hand, the ministers of the established church in
those times preached up the prerogative in all its extravagance,
and endeavoured to establish, jointly and inseparably, implicit
faith in, and unqualified obedience to, the church and king
(still giving the church the precedency); whilst the laymen
of their party practised, and even professed, a total dissolute-
ness of life; so that those who were slaves in principle were
libertines in practice, while those who were deemed rebels by
the court, and latitudinarians by the hierarchy, were rigorists
in religion and morality.

   This contrariety produced a constant and incessant opposition, augmented the vehemence of antipathy, fortified prejudice, and seemed almost to justify bigotry.*   But from this
(bigotry) we are bound to exculpate Colonel Hutchinson.
The Independents, to whose party, if a man of so much candour and liberality can be said to be of any party, he belonged,
proceeded upon that principle, which, however general soever
it ought to be, is however unfortunately very uncommon, of
allowing to all that liberty of conscience they demanded for
themselves.   Accordingly, they began by desiring only an
act † to be passed " for taking away all coercive power, authority, and jurisdiction, from bishops, extending to civil
penalties," &c.   It was not till after they saw the extreme
pertinaciousness of the king to retain the bishops as instruments at a future opportunity for remounting his system of
arbitrary sway, and that " the prelatical party about him prevailed with him to refuse an accommodation, and hazard his
crown and life, rather than diminish their greatness and power
to persecute others," that they insisted on the abolition of
the order.‡   It was quite a different party, that of the rigid
Presbyterians, and peculiarly their ministers, " who cried out

   * The flower of the French democrats avoided all such inconsistency
and paradox, by discarding at once their king, their God, and their morality.
   † Articles of the army, Rushworth, vol. vii. p. 731.
   ‡ The words of Whitelocke, p. 340, where he regrets that the king's
chaplains prevailed with him beyond the parliament's commissioners or his
own judgment.

against the tyranny of the bishops only that they might get the power into their own hands, and, without the name, might exercise the authority* of popes." That instead of this power being irrevocably and immoveably established over us, we are now governed by the mildest church discipline in the universe, we owe to these Independents! Colonel Hutchinson in particular, if he had lived in times like ours, " when bishops and ministers desire only to be helpers,† not lords over the consciences of God's people," would either have been a conforming member of the church of England, or at most have only dissented from it in few things, and that with modesty and moderation. For it is well worthy of notice, that after having suffered provocation and persecution from catholic, episcopalian, and presbyterian, when power came into his own hands he treated all with lenity, and to the worthy persons of all sects and parties extended his protection.

We have next to consider a part of the conduct of Colonel Hutchinson, which will be the most generally blamed, and is the least capable of defence, the condemnation of Charles the First. To speak of the justice of such a measure in a legal point of view would be a mockery ; nothing but the breaking up of the very foundations of the state, and a war of its elements, could let in the possibility of such a procedure. Amidst the tempest and darkness which then involved the whole political horizon, it savours of presumption to decide what measures were right, expedient, or even necessary : this much alone may safely be asserted, that the king and his friends during the contest, and still more after it was virtually ended by the battle of Naseby, maintained such a conduct as rendered his destruction inevitable : but the remark of Whitelocke, p. 363, seems no less just than ingenious : " that such an irregular and unheard of business should have been left to that irregular set of men—the army, who urged it on." They, however, were determined to throw the odium on others, or at least draw others in to share it.

Be it as it may, though some may blame, many more will pity a man such as Colonel Hutchinson, who found or con-

* Vide Letter of Irving, laird of Drum, and his appeal to Colonel Overton : Whitelocke, p. 526.

† Words of Cromwell in his letter to the Scots ministers : Whitelocke, p. 473.

ceived himself reduced to the cruel alternative of permitting all that system of liberty, civil and religious, to the establishment of which he had devoted all his faculties, and was ready to sacrifice his existence, to be risked upon the good faith of a man whose misfortune it was, to say no worse, to be environed by designing and ambitious persons, who rendered all his virtues abortive, and made all afraid to trust him, or of signing a sentence which has since been called a murder, and the undergoing it a martyrdom ! at any rate, it would be highly ungracious and ungrateful in us, while we enjoy in our well-balanced constitution, the benefits derived to us from the virtue, the energy, the sufferings, and even the faults of our ancestors, to pass a severe censure on their conduct ; for it will hardly be denied, that the remembrance of his father's fate influenced James the Second to yield so easy and bloodless a victory to his opponents, and leave them to settle the constitution amidst calm and sober councils. On the contrary, we are bound to ascribe many of the oversights of those first founders of our liberties, to a precipitancy forced on them by urgent circumstances, to cast a veil over their imperfections, and cherish their memory with thankfulness.

So much having been said for the purpose of obviating misapprehension as to the effect of this work, it may be further expected that some merit or utility should be shown, to justify the editor in presenting it to the public notice. Being not the child of his brain and fancy, but of his adoption and judgment, he may be supposed to view it with so much the less partiality, and allowed to speak of it with so much the more freedom.

The only ends for which any book can reasonably be published are to inform, to amuse, or to improve : but unless many persons of highly reputed judgment are mistaken as well as ourselves, this work will be found to attain all three of them. In point of amusement, perhaps novelty or curiosity holds the foremost rank ; and surely we risk little in saying that a history of a period the most remarkable in the British annals, written one hundred and fifty years ago by a lady of elevated birth, of a most comprehensive and highly cultivated mind, herself a witness of many of the scenes she describes, and active in several of them, is a literary curiosity of no mean sort.

As to information, although there are many histories of the

same period, there is not one that is generally considered satisfactory; most of them carry evident marks of prejudice or partiality; nor were any of those which are now read written at or near the time, or by persons who had an opportunity of being well acquainted with what was passing, except that of Clarendon. But any one who should take the pains, which the Editor has done, to examine Clarendon's State Papers, would find therein documents much better calculated to support Mrs. Hutchinson's representation of affairs than that which he himself has given. Mrs. Hutchinson writing from a motive which will very seldom be found to induce any one to take so much trouble, that of giving her children, and especially her eldest son, then about to enter on the stage of life, a true notion of those eventful scenes which had just been passing before her eyes, and which she well judged must be followed by others not less interesting to the same cause and persons, will surely be thought to have possessed both the means and the inclination to paint with truth and correctness: in effect, she will be seen to exhibit such a faithful, natural, and lively picture of the public mind and manners, taken sometimes in larger, sometimes in smaller groups, as will give a more satisfactory idea to an observant reader than he will any where else discover. He will be further pleased to see avoided the most common error of historians, that of displaying the paradoxical and the marvellous, both in persons and things. But surely the use of history being to instruct the present and future ages by the experience of the past, nothing can be more absurd than a wish to excite and leave the reader in astonishment, which instead of assisting, can only confound his judgment. Mrs. Hutchinson, on the contrary, has made it her business, and that very successfully, to account by common and easy causes for many of those actions and effects which others have left unaccounted for, and only to be gazed at in unmeaning wonder; or, in attempting to account for them, have employed vain subtilty or groundless conjecture. She has likewise not merely described the parties in the state by their general character, but delineated them in *their minute ramifications*, and thus enabled us to trace the springs and discover the reasonableness of many of those proceedings which had hitherto seemed incongruous and inconsistent. Many of these instances will be pointed out in the notes as the passages arise.

But the greater merit shall appear in this work as a history, the greater will be the regret that the writer did not dedicate more of her attention to render it complete and full, instead of summary.

However, the most numerous class of readers are the lovers of biography, and to these it has of late been the practice of historians to address themselves, as Lyttleton in his Life of Henry the Second, Robinson of Charles the Fifth, Roscoe of Leo the Tenth, and many minor writers. Perhaps the prevalence of this predilection may be traced to the circumstance of the reader's thus feeling himself to be, as it were, a party in the transactions which are recounted. A person of this taste will, it his hoped, here have his wishes completely gratified; for he will, in fancy, have lived in times, and witnessed scenes the most interesting that can be imagined to the human mind, especially the mind of an Englishman; he will have conversed with persons the most celebrated and extraordinary, whom one party represent as heroes and demigods, the other as demons, but whom, having had opportunity to view close at hand, he will judge to have been truly great men, and to have carried at once to a high degree of perfection the characters of the warrior, the politician, the legislator, and the philosopher; yet to have had their great qualifications alloyed by such failings, and principally the want of moderation, as defeated their grand designs. He will have accompanied the hero of the tale, not only through all the ages of life, but through almost every situation in society, from the lowest that can become noticeable, which Mrs. Hutchinson calls the *even ground of a gentleman;* to the highest which his principles permitted him to aspire to, that of a counsellor of state, in a large and flourishing republic; he will have seen him mark each with the exercise of its appropriate grace and virtue, and so completely to have adapted himself to each department, as to appear always to move in the sphere most natural to him: and, finally, to have maintained so steady a course through all the vicissitudes of prosperity and adversity, as enabled him, though he could neither control the conduct of his coadjutors, nor stem the fluctuating tides of fortune or popular opinion, yet to preserve for himself not only the great and inexhaustible resource of a good conscience, but even the unanimous esteem of the great assembly of the nation, when they agreed in no other thing; he will no doubt be

sensible that such a character is rare, but he will perceive
such a consistency and harmony of parts as to make him
deem the whole easy of belief, and conclude that such an one
would be even more difficult to feign than to find: he will
hence be led to concur with us in asserting, that it is much
more efficacious and conducive to improvement and to the
advancement of morality thus to hold forth a great example
in real life, and to elicit principle from practice, than first to
feign a sentiment, and then actions and events to support it,
as has been done both by ancients and moderns, from the
Hercules of Prodicus to the Grandison of Richardson.   Nor
has the skill and attention of our author been confined to
the portraying of her principal character, she has equally
succeeded in the delineation of the subordinate ones; so that
whenever their speeches or actions are brought afresh before
our view, we need not that they should be named in order to
recognize the personage; and both in this department, and in
that of the development of the intrigues which she occasionally lays open to us, we shall acknowledge the advantage
of her adding to the vigour of a masculine understanding,
the nice feeling and discrimination, the delicate touch of the
pencil of a female.

As to the style and phraseology, there are so few prose
writings of a prior or coeval date now read, that we should
be at a loss to point out any which could have served her for
models, or us for a standard of comparison; nor does it so
much appear to us to bear the stamp of any particular age,
as by its simplicity, significancy, and propriety, to be worthy
of imitation in all times.   Some expressions will be found
that are uncommon, or used in an uncommon sense, but they
are such as are justified by classical propriety, and, had her
book been published, would probably have been adopted and
brought into general use.

We conclude with expressing a confident hope, that the
public will find this memoir to be such as we first announced
it,—a faithful image of the mode of thinking in those days
of which it treats, an interesting and new specimen of private
and public character, of general and individual biography;
and that recommended as it comes by clearness of discernment, strength and candour of judgment, simplicity, and
perspicuity of narrative, pure, amiable, and Christian morality, sentiments at once tender and elevated, conveyed in

.anguage elegant, expressive, and classical, occasionally embellished with apposite, impressive, and well supported figures, it will be found to afford pleasure and instruction to every class of readers.

The ladies will feel that it carries with it all the interest of a novel, strengthened with the authenticity of real history; they will no doubt feel an additional satisfaction in learning, that though the author added to the erudition of the scholar, the research of the philosopher, the politician, and even the divine, the zeal and magnanimity of a patriot; yet she descended from all these elevations to perform, in the most exemplary manner, the functions of a wife, a mother. and mistress of a family.

LIFE OF MRS. LUCY HUTCHINSON,

WRITTEN BY HERSELF.

A FRAGMENT.

THE Almighty Author of all beings,* in his various providences, whereby he conducts the lives of men from the
cradle to the tomb, exercises no less wisdom and goodness
than he manifests power and greatness, in their creation; but
such is the stupidity of blind mortals, that instead of employ-
ing their studies in these admirable books of providence,
wherein God daily exhibits to us glorious characters of his
love, kindness, wisdom, and justice, they ungratefully regard
them not, and call the most wonderful operations of the great
God the common accidents of human life, especially if they
be such as are usual, and exercised towards them in ages

---

* That noble turn of thought which led Mrs. Hutchinson to open her
work with thanks to her Maker, instead of apologies to the readers, besides
the claim it has to their respect instead of their indulgence, will probably
by its originality recommend itself, and prevent the distaste which the air
of religion it wears might give to many, in times when it is so little in
fashion.   It should be borne in mind that the usage of the times in which
it was written was so very different from the present, that those who wish
to read with pleasure the works then written, will do well to set their taste
according to that standard.

Through the whole of both these works, moral and religious reflections
will be seen to abound, but so as neither to confuse nor fetter, but rather
elevate the mind.

B

wherein they are not very capable of observation, and wh
on they seldom employ any reflection; for in things great and
extraordinary, some, perhaps, will take notice of God's working, who either forget or believe not that he takes as well a
care and account of their smallest concernments, even the
hairs of their heads.

Finding myself in some kind guilty of this general neglect,
I thought it might be a means to stir up my thankfulness for
things past, and to encourage my faith for the future, if I
recollected as much as I have heard or can remember of the
passages of my youth, and the general and particular providences exercised to me, both in the entrance and progress of
my life. Herein I meet with so many special indulgences as
require a distinct consideration, they being all of them to be
regarded as talents intrusted to my improvement for God's
glory. The parents by whom I received my life, the places
where I began and continued it, the time when I was brought
forth to be a witness of God's wonderful workings in the
earth, the rank that was given me in my generation, and the
advantages I received in my person, each of them carries
along with it many mercies which are above my utterance,
and as they give me infinite cause of glorifying God's goodness, so I cannot reflect on them without deep humiliation
for the small improvement I have made of so rich a stock;
which, that I may yet by God's grace better employ, I shall
recall and seriously ponder: and, first, as far as I have
since learnt, set down the condition of things in the place of
my nativity, at that time when I was sent into the world. It
was on the 29th day of January, in the year of our Lord
1619-20, that in the Tower of London, the principal city of
the English Isle, I was, about four of the clock in the morning, brought forth to behold the ensuing light. My father
was Sir Allen Apsley, lieutenant of the Tower of London;
my mother, his third wife, was Lucy, the youngest daughter

of Sir John St. John, of Lidiard Tregooze, in Wiltshire, by his second wife. My father had then living a son and a daughter by his former wives, and by my mother three sons, I being her eldest daughter. The land was then at peace (it being towards the latter end of the reign of King James), if that quietness may be called a peace, which was rather like the calm and smooth surface of the sea, whose dark womb is already impregnated with a horrid tempest.

Whoever considers England, will find it no small favour of God to have been made one of its natives, both upon spiritual and outward accounts. The happiness of the soil and air contribute all things that are necessary to the use or delight of man's life. The celebrated glory of this isle's inhabitants, ever since they received a mention in history, confers some honour upon every one of her children, and with it an obligation to continue in that magnanimity and virtue, which hath famed this island, and raised her head in glory higher than the great kingdoms of the neighbouring continent. Britain hath been as a garden enclosed, wherein all things that man can wish, to make a pleasant life, are planted and grow in her own soil, and whatsoever foreign countries yield, to increase admiration and delight, are brought in by her fleets. The people, by the plenty of their country, not being forced to toil for bread, have ever addicted themselves to more generous employments, and been reckoned, almost in all ages, as valiant warriors as any part of the world sent forth : insomuch, that the greatest Roman captains thought it not unworthy of their expeditions, and took great glory in triumphs for imperfect conquests. Lucan upbraids Julius Cæsar for returning hence with a repulse, and it was two hundred years before the land could be reduced into a Roman province, which at length was done, and such of the nation, then called Picts, as scorned servitude, were driven into the barren country of Scotland, where they have ever since remained

a perpetual trouble to the successive inhabitants of this place.
The Britons, that thought it better to work for their conquerors in a good land, than to have the freedom to starve in
a cold or barren quarter, were by degrees fetched away, and
wasted in the civil broils of these Roman lords, till the land,
almost depopulated, lay open to the incursions of every
borderer, and were forced to call a stout warlike people, the
Saxons, out of Germany, to their assistance. These willingly
came at their call, but were not so easily sent out again, nor
persuaded to let their hosts inhabit with them, for they drove
the Britons into the mountains of Wales, and seated themselves in those pleasant countries which from the new masters
received a new name, and ever since retained it, being
called England ; and on which the warlike Dane made many
attempts, with various success, but after about two or three
hundred years' vain contest, they were for ever driven out,
with shame and loss, and the Saxon Heptarchy melted into a
monarchy, which continued till the superstitious prince, who
was sainted for his ungodly chastity, left an empty throne to
him that could seize it. He who first set up his standard in
it, could not hold it, but with his life left it again for the Norman usurper, who partly by violence, partly by falsehood,
laid here the foundation of his monarchy, in the people's
blood, in which it hath swam about five hundred years, till
the flood that bore it was ploughed into such deep furrows as
had almost sunk the proud vessel. Of those Saxons that remained subjects to the Norman conqueror, my father's family
descended ; of those Normans that came in with him, my
mother's was derived ; both of them, as all the rest in England, contracting such affinity, by mutual marriages, that the
distinction remained but a short space ; Normans and Saxons
becoming one people, who by their valour grew terrible to all
the neighbouring princes, and have not only bravely acquitted
themselves in their own defence, but have showed abroad

how easily they could subdue the world, if they did not prefer the quiet enjoyment of their own part above the conquest of the whole.

Better laws and a happier constitution of government no nation ever enjoyed, it being a mixture of monarchy, aristocracy, and democracy, with sufficient fences against the pest of every one of those forms—tyranny, faction, and confusion ; yet is it not possible for man to devise such just and excellent bounds, as will keep in wild ambition, when prince's flatterers encourage that beast to break his fence, which it hath often done, with miserable consequences both to the prince and people; but could never in any age so tread down popular liberty, but that it arose again with renewed vigour, till at length it trod on those that trampled it before. And in the just bounds, wherein our kings were so well hedged in, the surrounding princes have with terror seen the reproof of their usurpations over their free brethren, whom they rule rather as slaves than subjects, and are only served for fear, but not for love ; whereas this people have ever been as affectionate to good, as unpliable to bad sovereigns.

Nor is it only valour and generosity that renown this nation ; in arts we have advanced equal to our neighbours, and in those that are most excellent, exceeded them. The world hath not yielded men more famous in navigation, nor ships better built or furnished. Agriculture is as ingeniously practised; the English archers were the terror of Christendom, and their clothes the ornament; but these low things bounded not their great spirits, in all ages it hath yielded men as famous in all kinds of learning, as Greece or Italy can be ast of.

And to complete the crown of all their glory, reflected from the lustre of their ingenuity, valour, wit, learning, justice, wealth, and bounty, their piety and devotion to God, and his worship, hath made them one of the most truly noble

nations in the Christian world. God having as it were enclosed
a people here, out of the waste common of the world, to serve
him with a pure and undefiled worship.   Lucius the British
king was one of the first monarchs of the earth that received
the faith of Christ into his heart and kingdom ; Henry the
Eighth, the first prince that broke the antichristian yoke off
from his own and his subjects' necks.   Here it was that the
first Christian emperor received his crown; here began the
early dawn of Gospel light, by Wickliffe and other faithful
witnesses, whom God raised up after the black and horrid
midnight of antichristianism ; and a more plentiful harvest
of devout confessors, constant martyrs, and holy worshippers
of God, hath not grown in any field of the church, throughout all ages, than those whom God hath here glorified his
name and gospel by.   Yet hath not this wheat been without
its tares ; God in comparison with other countries hath made
this as a paradise, so, to complete the parallel, the serpent
hath in all times been busy to seduce, and not unsuccessful ;
ever stirring up opposers to the infant truths of Christ.

No sooner was the faith of Christ embraced in this nation,
but the neighbouring heathens invaded the innocent Christians, and slaughtered multitudes of them; and when, by the
mercy of God, the conquering Pagans were afterwards converted, and there were none left to oppose the name of
Christ with open hostility, then the subtle serpent put off his
own horrid appearance, and comes out in a Christian dress,
to persecute Christ in his poor prophets, that bore witness
against the corruption of the times.   This intestine quarrel
hath been more successful to the devil, and more afflictive to
the church, than all open wars ; and, I fear, will never happily be decided, till the Prince of Peace come to conclude
the controversy, which at the time of my birth was working
up into that tempest, wherein I have shared many perils,
many fears, and many sorrows ; and many more mercies, con-

ʂolations, and preservations, which I shall have occasion to mention in other places.

From the place of my birth I shall only desire to remember the goodness of the Lord, who hath caused my lot to fall in a good ground ; who hath fed me in a pleasant pasture, where the well-springs of life flow to all that desire to drink of them. And this is no small favour, if I consider how many poor people perish among the heathen, where they never hear the name of Christ ; how many poor Christians spring up in countries enslaved by Turkish and antichristian tyrants, whose souls and bodies languish under miserable slavery. None know what mercy it is to live under a good and wholesome law, that have not considered the sad condition of being subject to the will of an unlimited man ; and surely it is too universal a sin in this nation, that the common mercies of God to the whole land are so slightly regarded, and so inconsiderately passed over ; certainly these are circumstances which much magnify God's loving-kindness and his special favour to all that are of English birth, and call for a greater return of duty from us than from all other people of the world.

Nor is the place only, but the time of my coming into the world, a considerable mercy to me. It was not in the midnight of popery, nor in the dawn of the gospel's restored day, when light and shades were blended and almost undistinguished, but when the Sun of truth was exalted in his progress, and hastening towards a meridian glory. It was, indeed, early in the morning, God being pleased to allow me the privilege of beholding the admirable growth of gospel light in my days : and oh ! that my soul may never forget to bless and praise his name for the wonders of power and goodness, wisdom and truth, which have been manifested in this my time.

The next blessing I have to consider in my nativity is my

parents, both of them pious and virtuous in their own conversation, and careful instructors of my youth, not only by precept but example; which, if I had leisure and ability, I should have transmitted to my posterity, both to give them the honour due from me in such a grateful memorial, and to increase my children's improvement of the patterns they set them; but since I shall detract from those I would celebrate, by my imperfect commemorations, I shall content myself to sum up some few things for my own use, and let the rest alone, which I either knew not, or have forgotten, or cannot worthily express.

My grandfather by the father's side was a gentleman of a competent estate, about £700 or £800 a year, in Sussex. He being descended of a younger house, had his residence at a place called Pulborough; the family out of which he came was an Apsley of Apsley, a town where they had been seated before the conquest, and ever since continued, till of late the last heir male of that eldest house, being the son of Sir Edward Apsley, died without issue, and his estate went with his sister's daughters into other families. Particularities concerning my father's kindred or country I never knew much of, by reason of my youth at the time of his death, and my education in far distant places; only in general I have heard, that my grandfather was a man well reputed and beloved in his country, and that it had been such a continued custom for my ancestors to take wives at home, that there was scarce a family of any note in Sussex to which they were not by intermarriages nearly related; but I was myself a stranger to them all, except my Lord Goring, who living at court, I have seen with my father, and heard of him, because he was appointed one of my father's executors, though he declined the trouble. My grandfather had seven sons, of which my father was the youngest; to the eldest he gave his whole estate, and to the rest, according to the custom of those times, slight annuities. The eldest brother married to a gentlewoman of a good family, and by her had only one son, whose mother dying, my uncle married himself again to one of his own maids, and by her had three more sons, whom, with their mother, my cousin William Apsley, the son of the first wife, held in such contempt, that a great while after, dying without children, he gave his estate of inheritance to my father, and two of my brothers, except about £100 a year to the eldest of his half brothers, and annuities of £30 a piece to the three for their lives. He died before I was born, but I have heard very honourable mention of him in our family. The rest of my father's brothers went into the wars in Ireland and the Low Countries, and there remained none of them, nor their issues, when I was born, but only three daughters who bestowed themselves meanly, and their generations are worn out, except two or three unregarded children. My father, at the death of my grandfather, being but a youth at school, had not patience to stay the perfecting of his studies, but put himself into present action, sold his annuity, bought himself good clothes, put some money in his purse, and came to London ; and by means of a relation at court, got a place in the household of Queen Elizabeth, where he behaved himself so that he won the love of many of the court; but being young, took an affection to gaming, and spent most of the money he had in his purse. About that time, the Earl of Essex was setting forth on a voyage to Cadiz, and my father, that had a mind to quit his idle court life, procured an employment from the victualler of the navy, to go along with that fleet. In which voyage he demeaned himself with so much courage and prudence, that after his return he was honoured with a very noble and profitable employment in Ireland. There a rich widow, that had many children, cast her affections upon him, and he married her; but she not living many years with him, and having no children by him,

after her death he distributed all her estate among her
children, for whom he ever preserved a fatherly kindness,
and some of her grand-children were brought up in his
house after I was born. He, by God's blessing, and his
fidelity and industry, growing in estate and honour, received
a knighthood from king James soon after his coming to the
crown, for some eminent service done to him in Ireland
which, having only heard in my childhood, I cannot perfectly
set down. After that, growing into a familiarity with Sir
George Carew, made now by the king Earl of Totness, a
niece of this earl's, the daughter of Sir Peter Carew, who
lived a young widow in her uncle's house, fell in love with
him, which her uncle perceiving, procured a marriage between
them. She had divers children by my father, but only two
of them, a son and daughter, survived her, who died whilst
my father was absent from her in Ireland. He led, all the
time of his widowhood, a very disconsolate life, careful for
nothing in the world but to educate and advance the son and
daughter, the dear pledges she had left him, for whose sake
he quitted himself of his employments abroad, and procured
himself the office of Victualler of the Navy, a place then
both of credit and great revenue. His friends, considering
his solitude, had procured him a match of a very rich widow,
who was a lady of as much discretion as wealth ; but while
he was upon this design he chanced to see my mother, at the
house of Sir William St. John, who had married her eldest
sister ; and though he went on his journey, yet something in
her person and behaviour, which he carried along with him,
would not let him accomplish it, but brought him back to my
mother. She was of a noble family, being the youngest
daughter of Sir John St. John, of Liddiard Tregooze in the
county of Wilts ; her father and mother died when she was
not above five years of age, and yet at her nurse's, from
whence she was carried to be brought up in the house of the

Lord Grandison, her father's younger brother; an honourable and excellent person, but married to a lady so jealous of him, and so ill-natured in her jealous fits, to anything that was related to him, that her cruelties to my mother exceeded the stories of step-mothers. The rest of my aunts, my mother's sisters, were dispersed to several places, where they grew up till my uncle, Sir John St. John, being married to the daughter of Sir Thomas Laten, they were all again brought home to their brother's house. There were not in those days so many beautiful women found in any family as these, but my mother was by the most judgments preferred before all her elder sisters, who, something envious at it, used her unkindly. Yet all the suitors that came to them still turned their addresses to her, which she in her youthful innocency neglected, till one of greater name, estate, and reputation than the rest, happened to fall deeply in love with her, and to manage it so discreetly, that my mother could not but entertain him. My uncle's wife, who had a mother's kindness for her, persuaded her to remove herself from her sisters' envy, by going along with her to the Isle of Jersey, where her father was governor; which she did, and there went into the town, and boarded in a French minister's house, to learn the language, that minister having been, by the persecution in France, driven to seek his shelter there. Contracting a dear friendship with this holy man and his wife, she was instructed in their Geneva discipline, which she liked so much better than our more superstitious service, that she could have been contented to have lived there, had not a powerful passion in her heart drawn her back. But at her return she met with many afflictions; the gentleman who had professed so much love to her, in her absence had been, by most vile practices and treacheries, drawn out of his senses, and into the marriage of a person, whom, when he recovered his reason he hated. But that served only to aug-

ment his misfortune, and the circumstances of that story not
being necessary to be here inserted, I shall only add that my
mother lived in my uncle's house, secretly discontented at
this accident, but was comforted by the kindness of my
uncle's wife, who had contracted such an intimate friendship
with her, that they seemed to have but one soul.   And in
this kindness she had some time a great solace, till some
malicious persons had wrought some jealousies, which were
very groundless, in my uncle concerning his wife; but his
nature being inclinable to that passion, which was fomented
in him by subtle wicked persons, and my mother endeavouring
to vindicate injured innocence, she was herself not well
treated by my uncle, whereupon she left his house, with a
resolution to withdraw herself into the island, where the
good minister was, and there to wear out her life in the
service of God.   While she was deliberating, and had fixed
upon it in her own thoughts, resolving to impart it to none,
she was with Sir William St. John, who had married my
aunt, when my father accidentally came in there, and fell so
heartily in love with her, that he persuaded her to marry
him, which she did, and her melancholy made her conform
cheerfully to that gravity of habit and conversation, which
was becoming the wife of such a person, who was then forty-
eight years of age, and she not above sixteen.   The first
year of their marriage was crowned with a son, called after
my father's name, and born at East Smithfield, in that house
of the king's which belonged to my father's employment in
the navy.   The next year they removed to the tower of
London, whereof my father was made lieutenant, and there
had two sons more before me, and four daughters, and
two sons after; of all which only three sons and two
daughters survived him at the time of his death, which
was in the sixty-third year of his age, after he had three
years before languished of a consumption, that succeeded

a fever which he got in the unfortunate voyage to the Isle of Rhee.

He died in the month of May, 1630, sadly bewailed by not only all his dependants and relations, but by all that were acquainted with him; for ne never conversed with any to whom he was not at some time or in some way beneficial; and his nature was so delighted in doing good, that it won him the love of all men, even his enemies, whose envy and malice it was his custom to overcome with obligations. He had great natural parts, but was too active in his youth to stay the heightening of them by study of dead writings; but in the living books of men's conversations he soon became so skilful that he was never mistaken, but where his own good would not let him give credit to the evil he discerned in others. He was a most indulgent husband, and no less kind to his children; a most noble master, who thought it not enough to maintain his servants honourably while they were with him, but, for all that deserved it, provided offices or settlements, as for children. He was a father to all his prisoners, sweetening with such compassionate kindness their restraint, that the affliction of a prison was not felt in his days. He had a singular kindness for all persons that were eminent either in learning or arms, and when, through the ingratitude and vice of that age, many of the wives and children of Queen Elizabeth's glorious captains were reduced to poverty, his purse was their common treasury, and they knew not the inconvenience of decayed fortunes till he was dead: many of those valiant seamen he maintained in prison, many he redeemed out of prison, and cherished with an extraordinary bounty. If among his excellencies one outshined the rest, it was the generous liberality of his mind, wherein goodness and greatness were so equally distributed that they mutually embellished each other. Pride and covetousness had not the least place in his breast. As he was in love with true honour, so he contemned vain titles; and though in his youth he accepted an addition to his birth, in his riper years he refused a baronetcy, which the king offered him. He was severe in the regulating of his family, especially would not endure the least immodest behaviour or dress in any woman under his roof. There was nothing he hated more than an insignificant gallant, that could only make his legs and prune himself, and court a lady, but had not brains to employ himself in things more suitable to man's nobler sex. Fidelity in his trust, love and loyalty to his prince, were not the least of his virtues, but those wherein he was not excelled by any of his own or succeeding times. The large estate he reaped by his happy industry, he did many times over as freely resign again to the king's service, till he left the greatest part of it at his death in the king's hands. All his virtues wanted not the crown of all virtue, piety and true devotion to God. As his life was a continued exercise of faith and charity, it concluded with prayers and blessings, which were the only consolations his desolate family could receive in his death. Never did any two better agree in magnanimity and bounty than he and my mother, who seemed to be actuated by the same soul, so little did she grudge any of his liberalities to strangers, or he contradict any of her kindness to all her relations; her house being a common home to all of them, and a nursery to their children. He gave her a noble allowance of £300 a year for her own private expense, and had given her all her own portion to dispose of how she pleased, as soon as she was married; which she suffered to increase in her friend's hands; and what my father allowed her she spent not in vanities, although she had what was rich and requisite upon occasions, but she laid most of it out in pious and charitable uses. Sir Walter Raleigh and Mr. Ruthin being prisoners in the Tower, and addicting themselves to chemistry, she suffered them to make their rare experiments at her cost, partly to comfort and divert the poor prisoners, and partly to gain the knowledge of their experiments, and the medicines to help such poor people as were not able to seek physicians. By these means she acquired a great deal of skill, which was very profitable to many all her life.* She was not only to these, but to all the other prisoners that came into the Tower, as a mother. All the time she dwelt in the Tower, if any were sick she made them broths and restoratives with her own hands, visited and took care of them, and provided them all necessaries; if any were afflicted she comforted them, so that they felt not the inconvenience of a prison who were in that place. She was not less bountiful to many poor widows and orphans, whom officers of higher and lower rank had left behind them as objects of charity. Her own house was filled with distressed families of her relations, whom she supplied and maintained in a noble way. The worship and service of God, both in her soul and her house, and the education of her children, were her principal care. She was a constant frequenter of week-day lectures, and a great lover and encourager of good ministers, and most diligent in her private reading and devotions.

When my father was sick she was not satisfied with the attendance of all that were about him, but made herself his

* This anecdote of Sir Walter Raleigh will no doubt attract the notice of the observant reader : it merits to be borne in mind, as it will account for a passage in the memoirs, where Mrs. Hutchinson is represented as acting the part of a surgeon in the siege of Nottingham Castle; and as the treatment Sir Allen Apsley and his lady gave their prisoners forms a striking contrast with that which it will appear at the end of the history was practised by some of his successors, at a time when mildness seemed most requisite, and was most professed. Perhaps prejudice will render it incredible, that in the Bastile of Paris, which has become a proverbial expression to signify cruel durance, the conduct of the murdered governor resembled that of Sir Allen Apsley; it is nevertheless true.

nurse, and cook, and physician, and, through the blessing of
God, and her indefatigable labours and watching, preserved
him a great while longer than the physicians thought it
possible for his nature to hold out. At length, when the
Lord took him to rest, she showed as much humility and
patience, under that great change, as moderation and bounty
in her more plentiful and prosperous condition, and died in
my house at Owthorpe, in the county of Nottingham, in the
year 1659. The privilege of being born of, and educated by,
such excellent parents, I have often revolved with great
thankfulness for the mercy, and humiliation that I did no
more improve it. After my mother had had three sons, she
was very desirous of a daughter, and when the women at my
birth told her I was one, she received me with a great deal
of joy ; and the nurses fancying, because I had more complexion and favour than is usual in so young children, that I
should not live, my mother became fonder of me, and more
endeavoured to nurse me. As soon as I was weaned a
French woman was taken to be my dry-nurse, and I was
taught to speak French and English together. My mother,
while she was with child of me, dreamed that she was walking in the garden with my father, and that a star came down
into her hand, with other circumstances, which, though I
have often heard, I minded not enough to remember perfectly ; only my father told her, her dream signified she
should have a daughter of some extraordinary eminency;
which thing, like such vain prophecies, wrought as far as it
could its own accomplishment :* for my father and mother

* This is an ingenious way of accounting for the fulfilment of superstitious predictions and expectations, which might frequently with close
attention be traced to their source, as is here done. It is clear that in the
present case it occasioned a peculiar care to be taken of her education; and
this again caused her mind and disposition to take that singular stamp
which attracted the notice of Mr. Hutchinson, and led her to the highest

fancying me then beautiful, and more than ordinarily apprehensive, applied all their cares, and spared no cost to improve me in my education, which procured me the admiration of those that flattered my parents. By the time I was four years old I read English perfectly, and having a great memory, I was carried to sermons ; and while I was very young could remember and repeat them exactly, and being caressed, the love of praise tickled me, and made me attend more heedfully. When I was about seven years of age, I remember I had at one time eight tutors in several qualities, languages, music, dancing, writing, and needlework; but my genius was quite averse from all but my book, and that I was so eager of, that my mother thinking it prejudiced my health, would moderate me in it ; yet this rather animated me than kept me back, and every moment I could steal from my play I would employ in any book I could find, when my own were locked up from me. After dinner and supper I still had an hour allowed me to play, and then I would steal into some hole or other to read. My father would have me learn Latin, and I was so apt that I outstripped my brothers who were at school, although my father's chaplain, that was my tutor, was a pitiful dull fellow. My brothers, who had a great deal of wit, had some emulation at the progress I made in my learning, which very well pleased my father; though my mother would have been contented if I had not so wholly addicted myself to that as to neglect my other qualities. As for music and dancing, I profited very little in them, and would never practise my lute or harpsichords but when my masters were with me ; and for my needle I absolutely hated it. Play among other children I despised, and

situation that she could wish for, that of the lady of a counsellor of state in her beloved, but short-lived, republic. When the reader shall have followed her to the end of her labours, let him judge whether there could be any situation to which she was not adequate.

c

when I was forced to entertain such as came to visit me, I tired them with more grave instructions than their mothers, and plucked all their babies to pieces, and kept the children in such awe, that they were glad when I entertained myself with elder company ; to whom I was very accep*able, and living in the house with many persons that had a great deal of wit, and very profitable serious discourses being frequent at my father's table and in my mother's drawing-room, I was very attentive to all, and gathered up things that I would utter again, to great admiration of many that took my memory and imitation for wit. It pleased God that, through the good instructions of my mother, and the sermons she carried me to, I was convinced that the knowledge of God was the most excellent study, and accordingly applied myself to it, and to practise as I was taught. I used to exhort my mother's maids much, and to turn their idle discourses to good subjects ; but I thought, when I had done this on the Lord's day, and every day performed my due tasks of reading and praying. that then I was free to any thing that was not sin ; for I was not at that time convinced of the vanity of conversation which was not scandalously wicked. I thought it no sin to learn or hear witty songs and amorous sonnets or poems, and twenty things of that kind, wherein I was so apt that I became the confidant in all the loves that were managed among my mother's young women; and there was none of them but had many lovers, and some particular friends beloved above the rest. Among these I have* . . . Five years after me my mother had a daughter that she nursed at her own breast, and was infinitely fond of above all the rest ; and I being of too serious a temper was not so pleasing to my† . . .

* At this place is a great chasm, many leaves being torn out, apparently by the writer herself.

† Here the story of herself abruptly ends.

MRS. HUTCHINSON TO HER CHILDREN

CONCERNING

THEIR FATHER.

"TO MY CHILDREN."

THEY who dote on mortal excellencies, when by the inevitable fate of all things frail, their adored idols are taken from them, may let loose the winds of passion to bring in a flood of sorrow; whose ebbing tides carry away the dear memory of what they have lost; and when comfort is essayed to such mourners, commonly all objects are removed out of their view, which may with their remembrance renew the grief; and in time these remedies succeed, and oblivion's curtain is by degrees drawn over the dead face, and things less lovely are liked, while they are not viewed together with that which was most excellent. But I that am under a command not to grieve at the common rate of desolate women,* while I am

---

* The command of her husband at his death. It will be readily admitted that she does indeed not grieve after any common rate, but with that noble sorrow which raises instead of depressing the soul : it would be an affront to the reader's taste to point out the beauties of this dirge; but it is only a just commendation of our authoress's judgment and modesty to observe, that having shown her ability to ornament and embellish, she confines herself to such occasions as are most suitable, and employs the greatest simplicity in her narrative.

studying which way to moderate my woe, and if it were possible to augment my love, can for the present find out none
more just to your dear father nor consolatory to myself than
the preservation of his memory; which I need not gild with
such flattering commendations as the hired preachers do
equally give to the truly and titularly honourable. A naked
undressed narrative, speaking the simple truth of him, will
deck him with more substantial glory, than all the pane-
gyrics the best pens could ever consecrate to the virtues of
the best men.

Indeed, that resplendent body of light, which the beginning and ending of his life made up, to discover the defor-
mities of this wicked age, and to instruct the erring children
of this generation, will, through my apprehension and expression, shine as under a very thick cloud, which will obscure much of their lustre; but there is need of this medium
to this world's weak eyes, which I fear hath but few people
in it so virtuous as can believe (because they find themselves
so short), that any other could make so large a progress in the
race of piety, honour, and virtue : but I am almost stopped
before I set forth to trace his steps; finding the number of
them, by which he still outwent himself, more than my imperfect arithmetic can count, and the exact figure of them
such as my unskilful pen cannot describe. I fear to injure
that memory which I would honour, and to disgrace his name
with a poor monument ; but when I have beforehand laid
this necessary caution, and ingenuously confessed that through
my inability either to receive or administer much of that
wealthy stock of his glory that I was intrusted with for the
benefit of all, and particularly his own posterity, I must
withhold a great part from them, I hope I shall be pardoned
for drawing an imperfect image of him; especially when even
the rudest draft that endeavours to counterfeit him, will have
much delightful loveliness in it.

Let not excess of love and delight in the stream make us forget the fountain; he and all his excellencies came from God, and flowed back into their own spring: there let us seek them, thither let us hasten after him; there having found him, let us cease to bewail among the dead that which is risen, or rather was immortal. His soul conversed with God so much when he was here, that it rejoices to be now eternally freed from interruption in that blessed exercise; his virtues were recorded in heaven's annals, and can never perish; by them he yet teaches us and all those to whose knowledge they shall arrive. It is only his fetters, his sins, his infirmities, his diseases, that are dead never to revive again, nor would we have them; they were his enemies and ours; by faith in Christ he vanquished them. Our conjunction, if we had any with him, was indissoluble; if we were knit together by one spirit into one body of Christ, we are so still; if we were mutually united in one love of God, good men, and goodness, we are so still. What is it then we wail in his remove? the distance? Faithless fools! sorrow only makes it. Let us but ascend to God in holy joy for the great grace given his poor servant, and he is there with us. He is only removed from the malice of his enemies, for which, in being afflicted, we should not express our love to him we may mourn for ourselves that we come so tardily after him; that we want his guide and assistance in our way; and yet if our tears did not put out our eyes we should see him even in heaven, holding forth his flaming lamp of virtuous examples and precepts, to light us through the dark world. It is time that I let in to your knowledge that splendour which while it cheers and enlightens your heavy senses, should make us remember to give all his and all our glory to God alone, who is the father and fountain of all light and excellence.

Desiring, if my treacherous memory have not lost the dearest treasure that ever I committed to its trust, to relate

to you his holy, virtuous, honourable life, I would put his
picture in the front of his book, but my unskilful hand will
injure him.   Yet to such of you as have not seen him to remember his person, I leave this—

HIS DESCRIPTION.

HE was of a middle stature, of a slender and exactly well-
proportioned shape in all parts, his complexion fair, his hair
of light brown, very thick set in his youth, softer than the
finest silk, and curling into loose great rings at the ends; his
eyes of a lively grey, well-shaped and full of life and vigour,
graced with many becoming motions; his visage thin, his
mouth well made, and his lips very ruddy and graceful, although the nether chap shut over the upper, yet it was in such
a manner as was not unbecoming; his teeth were even and
white as the purest ivory; his chin was something long, and
the mould of his face ; his forehead was not very high ; his
nose was raised and sharp; but withal he had a most amiable
countenance, which carried in it something of magnanimity
and majesty mixed with sweetness, that at the same time
bespoke love and awe in all that saw him ; his skin was
smooth and white, his legs and feet excellently well-
made ; he was quick in his pace and turns, nimble and active
and graceful in all his motions; he was apt for any bodily exercise, and any that he did became him; he could dance admirably well, but neither in youth nor riper years made any
practice of it; he had skill in fencing, such as became a gentleman; he had a great love of music, and often diverted himself with a viol, on which he played masterly; and he had an
exact ear and judgment in other music; he shot excellently in
bows and guns, and much used them for his exercise; he had
great judgment in paintings, graving, sculpture, and all
liberal arts, and had many curiosities of value in all kinds;

he took great delight in perspective glasses, and for his other
rarities was not so much affected with the antiquity as the
merit of the work; he took much pleasure in improvement
of grounds, in planting groves, and walks, and fruit-trees, in
opening springs and making fish-ponds; of country recreations he loved none but hawking, and in that was very eager
and much delighted for the time he used it, but soon left it
off; he was wonderfully neat, cleanly, and genteel in his habit,
and had a very good fancy in it, but he left off very early the
wearing of anything that was costly, yet in his plainest negligent habit appeared very much a gentleman; he had more
address than force of body, yet the courage of his soul so
supplied his members that he never wanted strength when
he found occasion to employ it; his conversation was very
pleasant, for he was naturally cheerful, had a ready wit and
apprehension; he was eager in everything he did, earnest in
dispute, but withal very rational, so that he was seldom overcome; everything that it was necessary for him to do he did
with delight, free and unconstrained; he hated ceremonious
compliment, but yet had a natural civility and complaisance
to all people; he was of a tender constitution, but through
the vivacity of his spirit could undergo labours, watchings,
and journeys, as well as any of stronger compositions; he
was rheumatic, and had a long sickness and distemper occasioned thereby, two or three years after the war ended, but
else, for the latter half of his life, was healthy though tender;
in his youth and childhood he was sickly, much troubled
with weakness and toothaches, but then his spirits carried
him through them; he was very patient under sickness or
pain, or any common accidents, but yet, upon occasions,
though never without just ones, he would be very angry, and
had even in that such a grace as made him to be feared, yet
he was never outrageous in passion; he had a very good
faculty in pursuading, and would speak very well, pertinently,

and effectually without premeditation upon the greatest occasions that could be offered, for indeed, his judgment was
so nice, that he could never frame any speech beforehand
to please himself; but his invention was so ready, and
wisdom so habitual in all his speeches, that he never had
reason to repent himself of speaking at any time without
ranking the words beforehand; he was not talkative, yet
free of discourse; of a very spare diet, not given to sleep, and
an early riser when in health; he never was at any time idle,
and hated to see any one else so; in all his natural and ordinary inclinations and composure, there was something extraordinary and tending to virtue, beyond what I can describe, or
can be gathered from a bare dead description; there was a life
of spirit and power in him that is not to be found in any
copy drawn from him.   To sum up, therefore, all that can be
said of his outward frame and disposition, we must truly
conclude, that it was a very handsome and well furnished
lodging prepared for the reception of that prince, who in
the administration of all excellent virtues reigned there a
while, till he was called back to the palace of the universal
emperor.

HIS VIRTUES.

To number his virtues is to give the epitome of his life, which
was nothing else but a progress from one degree of virtue to
another, till in a short time he arrived to that height which
many longer lives could never reach; and had I but the power
of rightly disposing and relating them, his single example
would be more instructive than all the rules of the best
moralists, for his practice was of a more divine extraction,
drawn from the word of God, and wrought up by the assistance of his Spirit; therefore in the head of all his virtues I
shall set that which was the head and spring of them all, his

Christianity—for this alone is the true royal blood that runs through the whole body of virtue, and every pretender to that glorious family, who hath no tincture of it, is an impostor and a spurious brat. This is that sacred fountain which baptizeth all the gentle virtues that so immortalize the names of Cicero, Plutarch, Seneca, and all the old philosophers, herein they are regenerated, and take a new name and nature. Dug up in the wilderness of nature, and dipped in this living spring, they are planted and flourish in the paradise of God.

By Christianity I intend that universal habit of grace which is wrought in a soul by the regenerating Spirit of God, whereby the whole creature is resigned up into the divine will and love, and all its actions directed to the obedience and glory of its Maker. As soon as he had improved his natural understanding with the acquisition of learning, the first studies in which he exercised himself were the principles of religion, and the first knowledge he laboured for was a knowledge of God, which by a diligent examination of the Scripture, and the several doctrines of great men pretending that ground, he at length obtained. Afterwards, when he had laid a sure and orthodox foundation in the doctrine of the free grace of God given us by Jesus Christ, he began to survey the superstructures, and to discover much of the hay and stubble of men's inventions in God's worship, which his spirit burned up in the day of their trial. His faith being established in the truth, he was full of love to God and all his saints.* He hated persecution for religion, and was always a champion for all religious people against all their great oppressors. He detested all scoffs at any practice of worship, though such a one as he was not persuaded of it.

* Saints. An expression commonly used in that time to signify good and religious people.

Whatever he practised in religion was neither for faction nor advantage, but contrary to it, and purely for conscience' sake. As he hated outsides in religion, so could he worse endure those apostacies and those denials of the Lord and base com. pliances of his adversaries, which timorous men practise under the name of prudent and just condescensions to avoid persecution.   Christianity being in him as the fountain of all his virtues, and diffusing itself in every stream, that of his prudence falls into the next mention.   He from a child was wise, and sought to by many that might have been his fathers for counsel, which he could excellently give to himself and others ; and whatever cross event in any of his affairs may give occasion to fools to overlook the wisdom of the design, yet he had as great a foresight, as strong a judgment, as clear an apprehension of men and things as any man.   He had rather a firm impression than a great memory, yet he was forgetful of nothing but injuries. His own integrity made him credulous of other men's, till reason and experience convinced him; and he was as unapt to believe cautions which could not be received without entertaining ill opinions of men ; yet he had wisdom enough never to commit himself to a traitor, though he was once wickedly betrayed by friends whom necessity and not mistake forced him to trust.*   He was as ready to hear as to give counsel, and never pertinacious in his will when his reason was convinced.   There was no opinion which he was most settled in, either concerning divine or human things, but he would patiently and impartially hear it debated.   In matters of faith his reason always submitted to the Word of God, and what he could not comprehend, he would believe because it was written ; but

* It is not known what peculiar transaction this refers to, though it may be conjectured to refer to the false protestations of Monk and Sir Ashley Cooper at the Restoration; whom he and many others trusted much against their will.

ιn all other things, the greatest names in the world could
never lead nim without reason: he would deliberate when
there was time, but never, by tedious dispute, lost an opportunity of any thing that was to be done.   He would hear as
well as speak, and yet never spoke impertinently or unsea-
sonably.   He very well understood his own advantages, natural parts, gifts, and acquirements, yet so as neither to glory
of them to others, nor overvalue himself for them; for he
had an excellent virtuous modesty, which shut out all vanity
of mind, and yet admitted that true understanding of himself
which was requisite for the best improvement of all his
talents.   He no less understood and was more heedful to
remark his defects, imperfections, and disadvantages, but
that too only to excite his circumspection concerning them,
not to damp his spirit in any noble enterprise.   He had a
noble spirit of government, both in civil, military, and domestic administrations, which forced even from unwilling
subjects a love and reverence of him, and endeared him to the
souls of those who rejoiced to be governed by him.   He had
a native majesty that struck an awe of him into the hearts of
men, and a sweet greatness that commanded love.   He had
a clear discerning of men's spirits, and knew how to give
every one their just weight.   He contemned none that were
not wicked, in whatever low degree of nature or fortune they
were otherwise : wherever he saw wisdom, learning, or other
virtues in men, he honoured them highly, and admired them
to their full rate, but never gave himself blindly up to the
conduct of the greatest master.   Love itself, which was as
powerful in his as in any soul, rather quickened than blinded
the eyes of his judgment in discerning the imperfections of
those that were most dear to him.   His soul ever reigned as
king in the internal throne, and never was captive to his
sense ; religion and reason, its two favoured counsellors, took
order that all the passions kept within their own just bounds,

did him good service there, and furthered the public weal. He found such felicity in that proportion of wisdom that he enjoyed, as he was a great lover of that which advanced it— learning and the arts; which he not only honoured in others, but had by his industry arrived to be himself a far greater scholar than is absolutely requisite for a gentleman. He had many excellent attainments, but he no less evidenced his wisdom in knowing how to rank and use them, than in gaining them. He had wit enough to have been subtle and cunning, but he so abhorred dissimulation that I cannot say he was either. Greatness of courage would not suffer him to put on a vizor, to secure him from any ; to retire into the shadow of privacy and silence was all his prudence could effect in him. It will be as hard to say which was the predominant virtue in him, as which is so in its own nature. He was as excellent in justice as in wisdom; nor could the greatest advantage, or the greatest danger, or the dearest interest or friend in the world, prevail on him to pervert justice even to an enemy. He never professed the thing he intended not, nor promised what he believed out of his own power, nor failed the performance of anything that was in his power to fulfil. Never fearing anything he could suffer for the truth, he never at any time would refrain a true or give a false witness ; he loved truth so much that he hated even sportive lies and gulleries. He was so just to his own honour that he many times forbore things lawful and delightful to him, rather than he would give any one occasion of scandal. Of all lies he most hated hypocrisy in religion; either to comply with changing governments or persons, without a real persuasion of conscience, or to practise holy things to get the applause of men or any advantage. As in religion so in friendship, he never professed love when he had it not, nor disguised hate or aversion, which indeed he never had to any party or person, but to their sins : and he

loved even his bitterest enemies so well, that I am witness
how his soul mourned for them, and how heartily he desired
their conversion.   If he were defective in any part of justice,
it was when it was in his power to punish those who had
injured him; whom I have so often known him to recompense
with favours instead of revenge, that his friends used to tell
him, if they had any occasion to make him favourably partial
to them, they would provoke him by an injury.   He was as
faithful and constant to his friends as merciful to his enemies:
nothing grieved him more than to be obliged where he could
not hope to return it.   He that was a rock to all assaults of
might and violence, was the gentlest, easiest soul to kindness,
of which the least warm spark melted him into anything
that was not sinful.   There never was a man more exactly
just in the performance of duties to all relations and all persons.
Honour, obedience, and love to his father, were so natural and
so lasting in him, that it is impossible to imagine a better son
than he was; and whoever would pray for a blessing in
children to any one, could but wish them such a son as he.*
He never repined at his father's will in anything, how much
soever it were to his prejudice, nor would endure to hear any
one say his father was not so kind to him as he might have
been; but to his dying day preserved his father's memory
with such tender affection and reverence as was admirable,
and had that high regard for his mother-in-law and the
children she brought his father, that he could not have been
more dearly concerned in all their interest if she had been his
own mother—which, all things considered, although they
were deserving persons, was an example of piety and goodness that will not easily be matched.   For conjugal affection
to his wife, it was such in him, as whoscever would draw out

* This we shall find called in question by his mother-in-law, and will be
discussed in the course of the history.

a rule of honour, kindness, and religion, to be practised in
that estate, need no more, but exactly draw out his example;
never man had a greater passion for a woman, nor a more
honourable esteem of a wife; yet he was not uxorious, nor
remitted he that just rule which it was her honour to obey,
but managed the reins of government with such prudence
and affection that she who would not delight in such an
honourable and advantageable subjection, must have wanted
a reasonable soul. He governed by persuasion, which he
never employed but to things honourable and profitable for
herself; he loved her soul and her honour more than her
outside, and yet he had even for her person a constant indulgence, exceeding the common temporary passions of the
most uxorious fools. If he esteemed her at a higher rate
than she in herself could have deserved, he was the author
of that virtue he doated on, while she only reflected his own
glories upon him; all that she was, was *him*, while he was
here, and all that she is now at best is but his pale shade. So
liberal was he to her, and of so generous a temper, that he
hated the mention of severed purses; his estate being so
much at her disposal, that he never would receive an account
of anything she expended; so constant was he in his love,
that when she ceased to be young and lovely, he began to
show most fondness; he loved her at such a kind and generous rate as words cannot express; yet even this, which was
the highest love he or any man could have, was yet bounded
by a superior, he loved her in the Lord as his fellow-creature,
not his idol, but in such a manner as showed that an affection,
bounded in the just rules of duty, far exceeds every way all
the irregular passions in the world. He loved God above
her, and all the other dear pledges of his heart, and at his
command and for his glory cheerfully resigned them. He
was as kind a father, as dear a brother, as good a master, and
as faithful a friend as the world had, yet in all these relations,

the greatest indulgence he could have in the world never
prevailed on him to indulge vice in the dearest person;
but the more dear any were to him, the more was he offended
at anything that might take off the lustre of their glory.   As
he had great severity against errors and follies pertinaciously
pursued, so had he the most merciful, gentle, and compassionate frame of spirit that can be imagined to those who
became sensible of their errors and frailties, although they
had been ever so injurious to himself.

Nor was his soul less shining in honour than in love.
Piety being still the bond of all his other virtues, there was
nothing he durst not do or suffer, but sin against God ; and
therefore, as he never regarded his life in any noble and just
enterprise, so he never staked it in any rash or unwarrantable
hazard.   He was never surprised, amazed, nor confounded
with great difficulties or dangers, which rather served to
animate than distract his spirits ; he had made up his accounts
with life and death, and fixed his purpose to entertain both
honourably, so that no accident ever dismayed him, but he
rather rejoiced in such troublesome conflicts as might signalise his generosity.   A truer or more lively valour there
never was in any man, but in all his actions it ever marched
in the same file with wisdom.   He understood well, and as
well performed when he undertook it, the military art in all
parts of it; he naturally loved the employment, as it suited
with his active temper more than any, conceiving a mutual
delight in leading those men that loved his conduct ; and
when he commanded soldiers, never was man more loved and
reverenced by all that were under him ; for he would never
condescend to them in anything they mutinously sought, nor
suffer them to seek what it was fit for him to provide, but
prevented them by his loving care ; and while he exercised
his authority no way but in keeping them to their just duty,
they joyed as much in his commands as he in their obe-

dience. He was very liberal to them, but ever chose just times and occasions to exercise it. I cannot say whether he were more truly magnanimous or less proud; he never disdained the meanest person, nor flattered the greatest; he had a loving and sweet courtesy to the poorest, and would often employ many spare hours with the commonest soldiers and poorest labourers, but still so ordering his familiarity as it never raised them to a contempt, but entertained still at the same time a reverence with love of him; he ever preserved himself in his own rank, neither being proud of it so as to despise any inferior, nor letting fall that just decorum which his honour obliged him to keep up. He was as far from envy of superiors as from contemning them that were under him; he was above the ambition of vain titles, and so well contented with the even ground of a gentleman, that no invitation could have prevailed upon him to advance one step that way; he loved substantial not airy honour. As he was above seeking or delighting in empty titles for himself, so he neither denied nor envied any man's due precedency, but pitied those that took a glory in that which had no foundation of virtue. As little did he seek after popular applause, or pride himself in it, if at any time it cried up his just deserts; he more delighted to do well than to be praised, and never set vulgar commendations at such a rate, as to act contrary to his own conscience or reason for the obtaining them; nor would he forbear a good action which he was bound to, though all the world disliked it, for he ever looked on things as they were in themselves, not through the dim spectacles of vulgar estimation. As he was far from a vain affectation of popularity, so he never neglected that just care that an honest man ought to have of his reputation, and was as careful to avoid the appearances of evil as evil itself; but if he were evil spoken of for truth or righteousness' sake, he rejoiced in taking up the reproach; which all good men that dare bear their testimony against an evil generation must suffer. Though his zeal for truth and virtue caused the wicked, with the sharp edges of their malicious tongues, to shave off the glories from his head, yet his honour springing from the fast root of virtue, did but grow the thicker and more beautiful for all their endeavours to cut it off.* He was as free from avarice as from ambition and pride. Never had any man a more contented and thankful heart for the estate that God had given, but it was a very narrow compass for the exercise of his great heart. He loved hospitality as much as he hated riot ; he could contentedly be without things beyond his reach, though he took very much pleasure in all those noble delights that exceeded not his faculties. In those things that were of mere pleasure, he loved not to aim at that he could not attain ; he would rather wear clothes absolutely plain, than pretend to gallantry ; and would rather choose to have none than mean jewels or pictures, and such other things as were not of absolute necessity. He would rather give nothing than a base reward or present, and upon that score he lived very much retired, though his nature was very sociable, and delighted in going into and receiving company ; because his fortune would not allow him to do it in such a noble manner as suited with his mind. He was so truly magnanimous, that prosperity could never lift him up in the least, nor give him any tincture of pride or vain-glory, nor diminish a general affability, courtesy, and civility, that he always showed to all persons. When he was most exalted, he was most merciful and compassionate to those that were humbled. At the same time that he vanquished any enemy, he cast away all his ill-will to him, and entertained thoughts of love and kindness as soon as he

* Samson and Delilah,

D

ceased to be in a posture of opposition. He was as far from meanness as from pride, as truly generous as humble, and showed his noble spirit more in adversity than in his prosperous condition; he vanquished all the spite of his enemies by his manly suffering, and all the contempts they could cast at him were their shame not his.

His whole life was the rule of temperance in meat, drink, apparel, pleasure, and all those things that may be lawfully enjoyed; and herein his temperance was more excellent than in others, in whom it is not so much a virtue, but proceeds from want of appetite or gust of pleasure; in him it was a true, wise, and religious government of the desire and delight he took in the things he enjoyed. He had a certain activity of spirit which could never endure idleness either in himself or others, and that made him eager, for the time he indulged it, as well in pleasure as in business; indeed, though in youth he exercised innocent sports a little while, yet afterwards his business was his pleasure. But how intent soever he were in anything, how much soever it delighted him, he could freely and easily cast it away when God called him to something else. He had as much modesty as could consist with a true virtuous assurance, and hated an impudent person. Neither in youth nor riper age could the most fair or enticing women ever draw him into unnecessary familiarity or vain converse or dalliance with them, yet he despised nothing of the female sex but their follies and vanities; wise and virtuous women he loved, and delighted in all pure, holy, and unblameable conversation with them, but so as never to excite scandal or temptation. Scurrilous discourse even among men he abhorred; and though he sometimes took pleasure in wit and mirth, yet that which was mixed with impurity he never would endure. The heat of his youth a little inclined him to the passion of anger, and the goodness of his nature to those of love and grief, but reason was never dethroned by them, but continued governor and moderator in his soul.*

* In this place Mrs. Hutchinson has written, " All this and more is true, but I so much dislike the manner of relating it, that I will make another essay." And accordingly she proceeds to write his character over again, but it has the appearance of being much *more laboured*, and much *less characteristic*, and therefore the former is preferred.

At the same place is written : " This book was written by Lucy, the widow and relict of Col. John Hutchinson, of Owthorp."   J. H.

(Julius Hutchinson, grandfather of the Editor.)

LIFE OF JOHN HUTCHINSON,

He was the eldest surviving son of Sir Thomas Hutchinson, and the Lady Margaret, his first wife, one of the daughters of Sir John Biron, of Newstead, in the same county, two persons so eminently virtuous and pious in their generations, that to descend from them was to set up in the world upon a good stock of honour, which obliged their posterity to improve it, as much as it was their privilege to inherit their parents' glories. Sir Thomas was he that removed his dwelling to Owthorpe; his father, though he was possessor of that lordship, having dwelt at Cropwell, another town, within two miles of which he had an inheritance, which, if I mistake not, was the place where those of the family that began to settle the name in this county, first fixed their habitation. The family for many generations past have been of good repute in Yorkshire, and there is yet a gentleman in that county, descendant of the elder house, that possesses a fair estate and reputation in his father's ancient inheritance.* They have been in Nottinghamshire for generations; wherein I observe that as if there had been an Agrarian law in the family, as soon as they arrived to any considerable fortune beyond his who was first transplanted hither, they began

* At Wykeham Abbey, in the county of York, where it is believed they still reside.

other houses, of which one is soon decayed and worn out in an unworthy branch, (he of Basford,) another began to flourish, and long may it prosper.* It is further observable in their descent that though none of them before Sir Thomas Hutchinson advanced beyond an esquire, yet they successively matched into all the most eminent and noble families in the country; which shows that it was the unambitious genius of the family rather than their want of merit, which made them keep upon so even a ground, after their first achievements had set them on a stage elevated enough from the vulgar, to perform any honourable and virtuous actions. I spoke with one old man who had known five generations of them in these parts, where their hospitality, their love to their country, their plain and honest conversation with all men, their generous and unambitious inclinations, had made the family continue as well beloved and reputed as any of the prouder houses in the country.† Although they changed not their titles, yet every succession increased the real honour of their house. One disadvantage they had, that few of them were so long lived as to prevent their sons from the bondage of wardship, whereby they fell into the hands of wicked guardians, that defaced instead of cultivating their seats, and made every heir a new planter. Sir Thomas Hutchinson, as I have heard, was not above eight years of age when his father died, and his wardship fell into the hands of an unworthy person, Sir Germaine Poole, who did him so many injuries, that he was fain, after he came of age, to have suits with him. This so raised the malice of the wicked man that he watched an opportunity to assassinate

* It stood only two generations ; the last possessor, who was the great grandson of Sir Thomas Hutchinson, directing by his will the estate to be sold, and the produce given to strangers.

† Sir Thomas Hutchinson's son and grandson fell no way short of him in this.

him unawares, and as Sir Thomas was landing out of a boat
at the Temple stairs in London, Poole having on a private
coat, with some wicked assistants, before he was aware, gave
him some cuts on the head and his left hand that was upon
the boat; but he full of courage drew his sword, run at
Poole and broke his weapon, which could not enter his false
armour; whereupon he run in to him, resolved not to be murdered without leaving some mark on the villain, and bit off
his nose; and then, by the assistance God sent him of an
honest waterman, being rescued, he was carried away so
sorely wounded that his life was in some danger: but the
fact being made public, his honorable carriage in it procured
him a great deal of glory, and his adversary carried the
mark of his shame to the grave.*   After this, returning into
the country, he there lived with very much love, honour, and
repute; but having been tossed up and down in his youth,
and interrupted in his studies, he grew into such an excessive
humour for books, that he wholly addicted himself to them;
and deeply engaging in school divinity, spent even his hours
of meat and sleep among his books, with such eagerness,
that though he himself attained a high reputation of learning
thereby, and indeed a great improvement in wisdom and
piety, yet he too much deprived his dear friends and relations

* This is a singular tale, and savours almost two much of the ridiculous
for the gravity of an historian : however Rushworth recites a story of this
same man not a little resembling it, in the appendix to his 2nd vol.
" Sir German Poole vowed revenge against a Mr. Brighthouse, shot two
pistols at him out of a window, set two servants on him with swords, who
ran him through the cloak between the arm and body, but killed him not,
he defending himself effectually till Sir German came on, who wounded
him, and for which he and another were committed to the Fleet, fined
1100l. &c." This does not seem to have cured him ; perhaps the mark
set on him by Sir Thomas H. succeeded better. Did Charles the Second
take the hint from this when he set assassins to slit Mr. Coventry's nose,
which caused the Coventry act to pass !

of his conversation. When he was entered into this studious
life, God took from him his dear wife, who left him only two
weak children; and then being extremely afflicted for so
deplorable a loss, he entertained his melancholy among the
old fathers and schoolmen, instead of diverting it; and having
furnished himself with the choicest library in that part of
England, it drew to him all the learned and religious men
thereabouts, who found better resolutions from him than from
any of his books. Living constantly in the country, he could
not be exempted from administering justice among them,
which he did with such equity and wisdom, and was such a
defender of the country's interest, that, without affecting it
at all, he grew the most popular and most beloved man in
the country, even to the envy of those prouder great ones
that despised the common interest. What others sought, he
could not shun, being still sought by the whole county, to be
their representative, to which he was several times elected,*
and ever faithful to his trust and his country's interest, though
never approving violence and faction. He was a man of a
most moderate and wise spirit, but still so inclined to favour
the oppressed saints and honest people of those times, that,
though he conformed to the government, the licentious and
profane encroachers upon common native rights branded him
with the reproach of the world, though the glory of good
men—Puritanism; yet notwithstanding he continued constant to the best interest, and died at London in the year
1643, a sitting member of that glorious Parliament that so
generously attempted, and had almost effected, England's
perfect liberty. He was a person of great beauty and come-

* He was omitted only in that parliament which was chosen at a time
when he and other patriots were imprisoned to prevent their being re-elected.
See note, page 48.

liness in all ages,* of a bounteous and noble nature, of clear
courage, sweet and affable conversation, of a public spirit, of
great prudence and reputation, a true lover of all pious
learned persons, and no less of honest plain people; of a
most tender conscience, and therefore declaring much for and
endeavouring moderation, if it had been possible in the
beginning of our wars that the greatest wisdom could have
cast on any drops of healing counsel, to have allayed the
furious rage of both parties.   Though never man was a
deeper nor truer mourner than he for his first wife, yet that
long dropping grief did but soften his heart for the impression
of a second love, which he conceived for a very honourable
and beautiful lady, who was Katherine the youngest daughter
of Sir John Stanhope, of Elvaston, a noble family in Derbyshire, by whom he had a son and two daughters surviving
him, not unworthy of their family.

Mr. John Hutchinson, the eldest of his surviving sons, by
his first wife, was born at Nottingham in the month of
September, in the year 1616.   That year there had been a
great drought, by reason of which the country would not
afford his father any provision for his stables, so that he was
forced to remove from Owthorpe to winter in the town of
Nottingham, somewhat before his lady's time of account.
She being in the coach on her way thither, and seeing her
husband in some danger by reason of a mettled horse he rode

---

* His picture remained at Owthorpe, and very well justified this description, and is now in the editor's possession in high preservation. For the
bounty and nobleness of his nature take this instance from Thoroton's
History of Notts. " Henry Sacheverell, Esq. being dissatisfied with his only
daughter for an improper marriage, left the whole estate at Ratcliff upon
Soar to Sir Thomas Hutchinson, his sister's son, who willingly divided it
with the disinherited lady." His moiety came afterwards to Alderman
Ireton, being sacrificed to him through necessity by Col. Hutchinson, as
will hereafter be shown.

upon, took a fright, and was brought to bed the next day, as
they imagined some three weeks before her time, and they
were confirmed in that opinion by the weakness of the child,
which continued all his infancy.   When he was born there
was an elder brother in the family, but he died a child.   Two
years and a half after this Mr. George Hutchinson, his younger
brother, was born at Owthorpe; and half a year after his
birth the two children lost their mother, who died of a cold
she had taken, and was buried at Owthorpe.   She was a lady
of as noble a family as any in the county, of an incomparable
shape and beauty, embellished with the best education those
days afforded; and above all had such a generous virtue
joined with attractive sweetness, that she captivated the
hearts of all that knew her.   She was pious, liberal, courteous,
patient, kind above an ordinary degree, ingenuous to all
things she would apply herself to; and notwithstanding she
had had her education at court, was delighted in her own
country habitation, and managed all her family affairs better
than any of the homespun housewifes, that had been brought
up to nothing else.   She was a most affectionate wife, a great
lover of her father's house, showing that true honour to
parents is the leading virtue, which seldom wants the con-
comitancy of all the rest of honour's train.   She was a wise
and bountiful mistress in her family, a blessing to her tenants
and neighbourhood, and had an indulgent tenderness to her
infants; but death veiled all her mortal glories in the 26th
year of her age.   The stories I have received of her have
been but scanty epitaphs of those things which were worthy of
a large chronicle, and a better recorder than I can be; I shall
therefore draw again the sable curtain before that image
which I have ventured to look at a little, but dare not
undertake to discover to others.   One that was present at her
death told me that she had an admirable voice, and skill to
manage it; and that she went away singing a psalm, which

this maid apprehended she sung with so much more than usual sweetness, as if her soul had already ascended into the celestial choir.

There is a story of her father and mother so memorable that though it be not altogether pertinent to their grandchild's affairs, which I only intend to record, yet I shall here put it in, since the third generation, for whom I make this collection, is not altogether unconcerned in the great grandfather. He the great grandfather) was not the eldest son of his father Sir John Biron, but he had an elder brother who had married a private gentleman's daughter in the country, and so displeased his father in that match, that he intended an equal part of his estate to this Sir John Biron, his younger son, and thereupon married him to a young lady who was one of the daughters of my lord Fitzwilliam, that had been deputy of Ireland in the reign of Queen Elizabeth, and lived as a prince in that country.* This daughter of his having an honourable aspiring to all things excellent, and being assisted by the great education her father gave her, attained to a high degree of learning and language, and to such an excellency in music and poetry, that she made rare compositions in both kinds ; and there was not any of those extraordinary qualities, which are therefore more glorious because more rare in the female sex, but she was excellent in them : and besides all these ornaments of soul, she had a body of as admirable a form and beauty, which justly made her husband so infinitely enamoured of her as never man was more. She could not set too high a

---

* By mistake Mrs. Hutchinson calls him lord. The person here meant was Sir William Fitzwilliam, appointed governor of Ireland seven times with the different titles of Lord Justice and Lord Deputy, by that distinguishing and judicious princess. A sufficient eulogy ! From him descends in a direct line the present Earl Fitzwilliam. *Fortes creantur, fortibus et bonis.* The reader will most likely find this episode too beautiful and affecting to think it needs the apology the writer makes.

vaiue on herself if she compared herself with other women of
those times; yet it was an alloy to her glories that she was a
little grieved that a less woman, the elder brother's wife, was
superior to her in regard of her husband, though inferior in regard of her birth and person; but that grief was soon removed
by a sad accident. That marriage wherein the father had not
been obeyed was fruitless, and the young gentleman himself
being given to youthful vanity, as he was one day to go out a
hunting with his father, had commanded something to be put
under the saddle of a young serving man, that was to go out
with them, to make sport at his affright when his horse should
prove unquiet. The thing succeeded as it was designed, and
made them such sport, that the young gentleman, in the
passion of laughter, died, and turned their mirth into
mourning; leaving a sad caveat by his example, to take heed
of hazarding men's precious lives for a little sport. The
younger brother by this means became the heir of the family,
and was father of a numerous and hopeful issue. But while
the incomparable mother shined in all the human glory she
wished, and had the crown of all outward felicity to the full,
in the enjoyment of the mutual love of her most beloved
husband, God in one moment took it away, and alienated her
most excellent understanding in a difficult child-birth;
wherein she brought forth two daughters which lived to be
married, and one more that died I think as soon or before it
was born.* But after that, all the art of the best physicians
in England could never restore her understanding : yet she
was not frantic, but had such a pretty deliration, that her
ravings were more delightful than other women's most

---

* The twins here mentioned as daughters are said by Thoroton to have
been sons, viz. Sir John, presently herein spoken of as the brother-in-law
of Sir Thomas Hutchinson, and Sir Nicholas, who served Charles the First
with the same zeal as the rest of that family.

rational conversations.   Upon this occasion her husband
gave himself up to live retired with her, as became her
condition, and made haste to marry his son; which he did so
young that I have heard say when the first child was born,
the father, mother, and child, could not make one-and-thirty
years old.   The daughters and the rest of the children as
soon as they grew up were married and dispersed.   I think
I have heard she had some children after that child-birth
which distempered her, and then my lady Hutchinson must
have been one of them, for she was the youngest daughter,
and at nine years old so taking, and of such an amiable conversation, that the lady Arabella* would needs take her from
her parents, along with her to the court; where she minded
nothing but her lady, and grew up so intimate in all her
counsels, that the princess was more delighted in her than in
any of the women about her; but when she (the princess)
was carried away from them to prison, my lady's brother
fetched her home to his house.   There, although his wife,
a most prudent and virtuous lady, laboured to comfort her
with all imaginable kindness, yet so constant was her friendship to the unfortunate princess, that I have heard her servants
say, she would steal many melancholy hours to sit and weep
in remembrance of her, even after her marriage.   Meanwhile her parents were driving on their age, in no less
constancy of love to each other; for even that distemper
which had estranged her mind in all things else, had left her
love and obedience entire to her husband, and he retained the
same fondness and respect for her, after she was distempered,
as when she was the glory of her age.   He had two beds in
one chamber, and she being a little sick, two women watched

* By the lady Arabella is here meant the lady Arabella Stuart, whose
romantic and melancholy story is told by Rapin, vol. ii. p. 161 and 189, in
the reign of James the First.   That mean-souled tyrant shut her up in the
Tower, where she died, not without suspicion of poison.

by her, some time before she died. It was his custom, as
soon as ever he unclosed his eyes, to ask how she did ; but
one night, he being as they thought in a deep sleep, she
quietly departed towards the morning. He was that day to
have gone a hunting, his usual exercise for his health, and it
was his custom to have his chaplain pray with him before he
went out ; and the women, fearful to surprise him with the ill
news, knowing his dear affection to her, had stolen out and
acquainted the chaplain, desiring him to inform him of it.
Sir John waking, did not on that day, as was his custom, ask
for her, but called the chaplain to prayers, and joining with
him, in the midst of the prayer, expired, and both of them
were buried together in the same grave. Whether he perceived her death, and would not take notice, or whether some
strange sympathy in love or nature, tied up their lives in one,
or whether God was pleased to exercise an unusual providence
towards them, preventing them both from that bitter sorrow
which such separations cause, it can be but conjectured ; but
the thing being not ordinary, and having received it from the
relation of one of his daughters and his grandchild, I thought
it not impertinent here to insert it. I shall now proceed to our
own story.

As soon as my lady Hutchinson* was dead, her brother,
Sir John Biron, came over and found the most desolate
afflicted widower that ever was beheld, and one of his sisters,
the lady Ratcliffe, who was the dear sister of the dead lady,
scarce alive for sorrow ; and indeed such a universal lamen-
tation in the house and neighbourhood, that the protraction
of their griefs for such a funeral as was intended her, might
possibly have made them all as she : Sir John therefore the
next morning privately, unknown to her husband, with only
her own family, carried her to the church, which was but the
next door, and interred her without further ceremony. It

* The mother of Col. Hutchinson, see page 41.

booted not Sir Thomas to be angry at her brother's care of
him; who pursued it so far, that the next day he carried away
Sir Thomas, lady Radcliffe, and Mr. John Hutchinson,
towards his own house at Bulwell, leaving Mr. George at his
nurse's. But the horses of the coach being mettled, in the
halfway between Owthorpe and Nottingham they ran away,
overthrew it, and slightly hurt all that were in the coach;
who all got out, one by one, except the maid that had the
child in her arms, and she stayed as long as there was any
hope of preventing the coach from being torn to pieces: but
when she saw no stop could be given to the mad horses, she
lapped him as close as she could in the mantle, and flung him
as far as she could from the coach into the ploughed lands,
whose furrows were at that time very soft; and by the good
providence of God the child, reserved to a more glorious
death, had no apparent hurt. He was taken up and carried
to Bulwell, where his aunt had such a motherly tenderness
for him that he grew and prospered in her care. As the
fresh memory and excessive love they bore the mother,
endeared the young child to all her relations at the first; so
as he grew, he discovered so much growing wisdom, agility,
and pretty sprightfulness, had such a natural gravity without
sullenness, and such sweet innocence, that every child of the
family loved him better than their own brothers and sisters,
and Sir John Biron and my lady were not half so fond of
any of their own. When it was time for them to go to
school, both the brothers were sent to board with Mr.
Theobalds, the master of the free school at Nottingham, who
was an excellent scholar; but having no children, some
wealth, and a little living that kept his house, he first grew
lazy, and afterwards left off his school. Sir Thomas then removed his sons to the free school at Lincoln, where there was a
master very famous for learning and piety, Mr. Clarke; but
he was such a supercilious pedant, and so conceited of his

own pedantic forms, that he gave Mr. Hutchinson a disgust
of him, and he profited very little there. At this place it
was that God began early to exercise him with affliction and
temptation; he was deprived of the attendance and care he
had been used to, and met with many inconveniences unsuitable to his tender and nice constitution; but this was
little, for he had such discretion in his childhood that he
understood what was fit for him to require, and governed
wherever he lived; for he would not be denied what was
reasonable, and he would not ask other things. He was as a
father over his brother, and having some advantage of years,
took upon him to be the guide of his youth, yet with such
love, that never were children more commendable and happy
in mutual affections. But it pleased God to strike his brother
with a sad disease, the falling sickness, wherein Mr. Hutchinson most carefully attended him while he continued at
Lincoln; which his father permitted him to do, for the opportunity of Dr. Pridgeon, one of the best physicians in those
parts. When he had in vain exercised all his art on the
young gentleman, and found no success in it, he advised he
should return to his father's house, and be entertained with
all the sports that could be found to delight his mind or
exercise his body. Accordingly he was carried home, and
had a pack of hounds, huntsmen, and horses kept for him,
and was something recreated, but not cured thereby; till
afterwards it pleased God to effect that cure by a young
practitioner, which the ablest physicians of the country could
not work. This separation from his brother, to whom he
had such an entire affection, considered with the sad occasion
of it, was a great affliction to the elder brother; who remained in a place where he had little to delight him, having
an aversion to his austere, pedantic master, increased by an
opinion that his severity had been the cause of his dear
brother's distemper.

The great encouragement Sir Thomas had to trust his sons in this town was, because at that time a gentleman inhabited it who had married his uncle's widow, and had been his fellow-sufferer in a confinement in Kent, when King Charles the First had broken up a parliament to the disgust of the people, and durst not trust those gentlemen that had been most faithful defenders of their country's interest, to return for some time to their own counties, for which they served.* Of these worthy patriots, Sir Thomas Hutchinson and Sir Thomas Grantham, the gentleman of whom I am speaking, were confined from Nottingham and Lincolnshire to the house of one Sir Adam Newton in Kent; the good father little thinking then, that in that fatal country his son should suffer an imprisonment upon the same account, to the destruction of his life and family. Sir Thomas Grantham was a gentleman of great repute in his country, and kept up all his life the old hospitality of England, having a great retinue and a noble table, and a resort for all the nobility and gentry in those parts. He had only two sons, whereof the eldest was a fine gentleman, bred beyond the seas, according to the best education of those times; the other was a foolish youth, schoolfellow with Mr. Hutchinson, who every Saturday night was fetched from school to Sir Thomas Grantham's, and returned again the Monday morning. Upon the intimate friendship between Sir Thomas Hutchinson and this gentleman, Sir Thomas Hutchinson had a lodging always kept for him at Lincoln, and was very

* This piece of history is mentioned by Rapin; Sir Thomas Grantham is named, but Sir Thomas Hutchinson and many others not named. It appears, in Thoroton's History of Nottingham, edited by Throsby, that this confinement so far answered the purpose of Charles the First, that it caused another to be chosen instead of Sir Thomas Hutchinson, knight of the shire; but as soon as Sir Thomas got free he was again chosen, and continued to represent the county till his death.

often there. My Lady Grantham had with her a very pretty
young gentlewoman, whom she brought with her out of
Kent, the daughter of Sir Adam Newton ; my lady's design was
to begin an early acquaintance, which might afterwards draw
on a marriage between her and Mr. Hutchinson, and it took
such effect that there was a great inclination in the young
gentlewoman to him ; and there was so much good nature on
his side, as amounted to a mutual respect, and to such a friendship as their youth was capable of, which the parents and others
that wished so, interpreted to be a passion of love ; but if it
were so, death quenched the flame, and ravished the young
lady from him in the sweet blooming of her youth. That
night she died, he lay in his father's chamber, and by accident
being very sick, it was imputed to that cause ; but he himself
least perceived he had any more of love for her than gratitude
for her kindness to him, upon which account her death was
an affliction to him, and made that house which had been his
relief from his hated school less pleasant to him ; especially
when he met there continual solicitations to sin by the
travelled gentleman, who, living in all seeming sobriety before
his father, was in his own chamber not only vicious himself,
but full of endeavour to corrupt Mr. Hutchinson, who by the
grace of God resisted, and detested his frequent temptations of
all kinds. An advantage he had at this school, was that there
being very many gentlemen's sons there, an old Low-country
soldier was entertained to train them in arms, and they all
bought themselves weapons ; and, instead of childish sports,
when they were not at their books, they were exercised in all
their military postures, and in assaults and defences ; which
instruction was not useless a few years after, to some of
them. Colonel Thornhagh, who was now trained in this
sportive militia, with Colonel Hutchinson, afterwards was his
fellow soldier in earnest, when the great cause of God's and
England's rights came to be disputed with swords against

E

encroaching princes.   Sir Thomas Grantham dying, Mr.
Hutchinson was removed from Lincoln to the free-school at
Nottingham, where his father married a second wife, and for
a while went up to London with her ; leaving his son at board
in a very religious house, where new superstitions and phari-
saical holiness, straining at gnats and swallowing camels,
gave him a little disgust, and was for a while a stumbling-block
in his way of purer profession, when he saw among professors
such unsuitable miscarriages.   There was now a change in
the condition and contentment of his life ; he was old enough
to be sensible that his father's second love and marriage to a
person of such quality, as required a settlement for her son,
must needs be a lessening to his expectation ; but he was so
affectionate to his father that he received it very contentedly,
and rejoiced in his removal, coming from a supercilious
pedant to a very honest man, who using him with respect,
advanced him more in one month than the other did in a
year.   This tied him to no observation, and restrained him
from no pleasure, and needed not, for he was so moderate
when he was left at his liberty, that he needed no regulation.
The familiar kindness of his master made him now begin to
love that which the other's austerity made him loath ; and in
a year's time he advanced exceedingly in learning, and was
sent to Cambridge.   He was made a fellow-commoner of
Peter House, under the tuition of one Mr. Norwich, an
admirable scholar, who by his civil demeanour to him won so
much upon his good nature, that he loved and reverenced
him as a father, and betook himself with such delight to his
studies that he attained to a great height of learning, performed public exercises in his college with much applause,
and upon their importunity took a degree in the university ;
whereof he was at that time the grace, there not being any
gentleman in the town that lived with such regularity in
himself, and such general love and good esteem of all persons

as he did. He kept not company with any of the vain young
persons, but with the graver men, and those by whose conversation he might gain improvement. He was constant at
their chapel, where he began to take notice of their stretching
superstition to idolatry ; and was courted much into a more
solemn practice of it than he could admit, though as yet he
considered not the emptiness and carnality, to say no more,
of that public service which was then in use. For his exercise he practised tennis, and played admirably well at it ;
for his diversion, he chose music, and got a very good hand,
which afterwards he improved to a great mastery on the viol.
There were masters that taught to dance and vault, whom he
practised with, being very agile and apt for all such becoming
exercises. His father stinted not his expense, which the
bounty of his mind made pretty large, for he was very liberal
to his tutors and servitors, and to the meaner officers of the
house. He was enticed to bow to their great idol, learning,
and had a higher veneration for it a long time than can
strictly be allowed ; yet he then looked upon it as a hand-
maid to devotion, and as the great improver of natural reason.
His tutor and the masters that governed the college while he
was there, were of Arminian principles, and that college was
noted above all for popish superstitious practices; yet through
the grace of God, notwithstanding the mutual kindness the
whole household had for him and he for them, he came away,
after five years' study there, untainted with those principles or
practices, though not yet enlightened to discern the spring of
them in the rites and usages of the English church.

When he came from the university, he was about twenty
years of age, and returned to his father's house, who had
now settled his habitation at Nottingham ; but he there
enjoyed no great delight, another brood of children springing
up in the house, and the servants endeavouring with tales
and flatteries to sow dissension on both sides   Therefore,

having a great reverence for his father, and being not willing
to disturb him with complaints, as soon as he could obtain
his leave he went to London. In the mean time the best
company the town afforded him, was a gentleman of as exquisite breeding and parts as England's court ever enjoyed,
one that was now married, and retired into this town;
one of such admirable power of language and persuasion
as was not any where else to be found; but after all this,
discontents, or the debaucheries of the times, had so infected
him, that he would not only debauch himself, but make a
delight to corrupt others for his sport. Some he would commend into such a vain-glorious humour, that they became
pleasantly ridiculous; some he would teach apish postures,
and make them believe themselves rare men; some he would
encourage to be poets, and laugh at their ridiculous rhymes;
some young preachers he would make stage-players in their
pulpits; and several ways sported himself with the follies of
most of the young men that he conversed with. There was
not any way which he left unpractised upon Mr. Hutchinson;
but when, with all his art and industry he found he could
not prevail, then he turned seriously to give him such excellent advice and instructions for living in the world, as were
not afterwards unuseful to him.* There was besides this
gentleman, a young physician, who was a good scholar and
had a great deal of wit, but withal a professed atheist, and so
proud, insolent, and scurrilous a fellow, daring to abuse all
persons how much soever above him, that he was thrown out
of familiarity with the great people of the country, though
his excellency in his profession made him to be taken in
again. There was also an old man, who had been Mr.
Hutchinson's first schoolmaster, a person once of great

* Who the first gentleman was does not appear. The physician here
meant is Dr. Plumtre, of whom much more will be said in this work.

learning, but afterwards becoming a cynic, yet so pleasantly maintaining that kind of humour, that his conversation was sometimes a good diversion. These were Mr. Hutchinson's companions, yet, through the grace of God, they had not power to infect him, who, like a bee, sucked a great deal of honey from these bitter flowers. At that time there was in the town a young maid, beautiful, and esteemed to be very rich, but of base parentage and penurious education, though else ingenuous enough. She was the grandchild of an old physician, and from her childhood having been acquainted with Mr. Hutchinson, who used to visit her grandmother, she had conceived a kindness for him, which though he civilly resented,* his great heart could never stoop to think of marrying into so mean a stock; yet by reason of some liking he showed for her company, and the melancholy he had, with some discontents at home, she was willing to flatter herself it was love for her, wherein, when she discovered her mistake, it was a great grief. However, she was, without much love on either side, married to an earl's son, and both of them, wanting the ground of happiness in marriage, mutual love, enjoyed but little felicity, either in their great fortunes or in one another.†

In the house with Mr. Hutchinson there was a young gentlewoman of such admirable tempting beauty, and such excellent good nature, as would have thawed a rock of ice,

* Resent, in English, never used but in a bad sense; in French, *ressentir* is used to signify a reciprocal sentiment of kindness as well as unkindness.

† It is written in the margin by Julius Hutchinson, Esq., probably from the information given him by Lady Catharine Hutchinson, that this lady's name was Martin, and the gentleman who married her Mr. Pierrepont. It would not have been thought worth while to inform the reader of these minute particulars in a note, but for the sake of pointing out the accuracy with which Mr. Julius Hutchinson read and remarked upon this history, and the full knowledge he had of all the circumstances of Colonel Hutchinson's life.

yet even she could never get an acquaintance with him.
Wealth and beauty thus in vain tempted him, for it was not
yet his time of love; but it was not far off. He was now
sent to London, and admitted of Lincoln's Inn, where he was
soon coveted into the acquaintance of some gentlemen of the
house; but he found them so frothy and so vain, and could so
ill centre with them in their delights, that the town began to
be tedious to him, who was neither taken with wine, nor gaming,
nor the converse of wicked or vain women; to all which he
wanted not powerful tempters, had not the power of God's
grace in him been above them. He tried a little the study
of the law, but finding it unpleasant and contrary to his
genius, and the plague that spring beginning to drive people
out of the town, he began to think of leaving it, but had no
inclination to return home, finding his father's heart so set
upon his second family, that his presence was but disturbance : yet his father was wonderfully free and noble to
him in allowance, at all places, as large as any of his quality
had made to them ; and it was very well bestowed on him,
who consumed nothing in vain expense, but lived to the
honour of his friends and family. For his diversion he
exercised himself in those qualities he had not had such good
opportunities for in the country, as dancing, fencing, and
music, wherein he had great aptness and address ; and
entertaining the best tutors, was at some expense that way,
and loth to leave them off before he had perfected himself.
However, many things putting him into thoughts of quitting the town, while he was in deliberation how to dispose of himself, and had some reflections upon travel, a
cousin-german of his, a French merchant, came to visit him
one morning, and told him he was immediately going into
France, and understanding Mr. Hutchinson had some such
inclination, had almost persuaded him to go along with him.
The only obstacle in the way, was that his father could not

be acquainted with it time enough to receive his answer
before they went. While he was in this deliberation, his
music-master came in, to whom he communicated his
thoughts; and the man told him it was better to go into
France at the latter end than the beginning of summer, and
that if he pleased, in the mean time, to go to Richmond,
where the Prince's court was, he had a house there, where
he might be accommodated; and there was very good company and recreations, the king's hawks being kept near the
place, and several other conveniences. Mr. Hutchinson considering this, resolved to accept his offer; and that day
telling a gentleman of the house whither he was going, the
gentleman bid him take heed of the place, for it was so fatal
for love, that never any young disengaged person went
thither, who returned again free. Mr. Hutchinson laughed
at him, but he to confirm it told him a very true story
of a gentleman who not long before had come for some time
to lodge there, and found all the people he came in company
with, bewailing the death of a gentlewoman that had lived
there. Hearing her so much deplored, he made inquiry after
her, and grew so in love with the description that no other
discourse could at first please him, nor could he at last
endure any other; he grew desperately melancholy, and
would go to a mount where the print of her foot was cut, and
lie there pining and kissing of it all the day long, till at
length death, in some months' space, concluded his languish-
ment. This story was very true; but Mr. Hutchinson was
neither easy to believe it, nor frighted at the example, thinking himself not likely to make another. He therefore went
to Richmond, where he found a great deal of good young
company, and many ingenuous persons that, by reason of the
court, where the young princes were bred, entertained themselves in that place, and had frequent resort to the house
where Mr. Hutchinson tabled. The man being a skilful

composer in music, the rest of the king's musicians often met
at his house to practise new airs and prepare them for the
king; and divers of the gentlemen and ladies that were
affected with music, came thither to hear; others that were
not, took that pretence to entertain themselves with the company.   Mr. Hutchinson was soon courted into their acquaintance, and invited to their houses, where he was nobly treated,
with all the attractive arts that young women and their
parents use to procure them lovers; but though some of them
were very handsome, others wealthy, witty, and well qualified,
and all of them set out with all the gaiety and bravery that vain
women put on to set themselves off, yet Mr. Hutchinson
could not be entangled in any of their fine snares; but without
any taint of incivility, he in such a way of handsome raillery
reproved their pride and vanity, as made them ashamed of
their glory, and vexed that he alone, of all the young gentlemen that belonged to the court or neighbourhood, should be
insensible of their charms.   In the same house with him
there was a younger daughter of Sir Allen Apsley, late
lieutenant of the Tower, tabled for the practice of her lute,
staying till the return of her mother; who was gone into Wiltshire for the accomplishment of a treaty that had been made
some progress in, about the marriage of her elder daughter with
a gentleman of that country, out of which my lady herself
came, and where her brothers, Sir John St. John and Sir
Edward Hungerford, living in great honour and reputation,
had invited her to visit them.   This gentlewoman, that was
left in the house with Mr. Hutchinson, was a very child, her
elder sister being at that time scarcely passed it; but a child
of such pleasantness and vivacity of spirit, and ingenuity in
the quality she practised, that Mr. Hutchinson took pleasure
in hearing her practise, and would fall in discourse with her.
She having the keys of her mother's house, some half a mile
distant, would sometimes ask Mr. Hutchinson, when she

went over, to walk along with her. One day when he was there, looking upon an odd by-shelf in her sister's closet, he found a few Latin books ; asking whose they were, he was told they were her elder sister's ; whereupon, inquiring more after her, he began first to be sorry she was gone, before he had seen her, and gone upon such an account that he was not likely to see her. Then he grew to love to hear mention of her, and the other gentlewomen who had been her companions used to talk much to him of her, telling him how reserved and studious she was, and other things which they esteemed no advantage. But it so much inflamed Mr. Hutchinson's desire of seeing her, that he began to wonder at himself, that his heart, which had ever entertained so much indifference for the most excellent of womankind, should have such strong impulses towards a stranger he never saw ; and certainly it was of the Lord (though he perceived it not), who had ordained him, through so many various providences, to be yoked with her in whom he found so much satisfaction. There scarcely passed any day but some accident or some discourse still kept alive his desire of seeing this gentlewoman ; although the mention of her, for the most part, was inquiries whether she had yet accomplished the marriage that was in treaty. One day there was a great deal of company at Mr. Coleman's, the gentleman's house where he tabled, to hear the music ; and a certain song was sung, which had been lately set, and gave occasion to some of the company to mention an answer to it, which was in the house, and upon some of their desires, read. A gentleman saying it was believed that a woman in the neighbourhood had made it, it was presently inquired who ; whereupon a gentleman, then present, who had made the first song, said, there were but two women that could be guilty of it, whereof one was a lady then among them, the other Mrs. Apsley. Mr. Hutchinson, fancying something of raticnality in the sonnet beyond the

customary reach of a she-wit, although, to speak truth, it
signified very little, addressed aimself to the gentleman, and
told him he could scarcely believe it was a woman's; whereupon this gentleman, who was a man of good understanding
and expression, and inspired with some passion for her himself, which made him regard all her perfections through a
multiplying-glass, told Mr. Hutchinson, that though, for
civility to the rest, he entitled another lady to the song, yet
he was confident it was Mrs. Apsley's only, for she had sense
above all the rest; and fell into such high praises of her, as
might well have begotten those vehement desires of her
acquaintance, which a strange sympathy in nature had before
produced. Another gentleman, that sat by, seconded this
commendation with such additions of praise as he would not
have given if he had known her. Mr. Hutchinson hearing
all this, said to the first gentleman, " I cannot be at rest till
this lady's return, that I may be acquainted with her." The
gentleman replied, " Sir, you must not expect that, for she is
of a humour she will not be acquainted with any of mankind;
and however this song is stolen forth, she is the nicest creature in the world of suffering her perfections to be known;
she shuns the converse of men as the plague; she only lives
in the enjoyment of herself, and has not the humanity to
communicate that happiness to any of our sex." " Well,"
said Mr. Hutchinson, " but I will be acquainted with her:"
and indeed the information of this reserved humour pleased
him more than all else he had heard, and filled him now with
thoughts how he should attain the sight and knowledge of her.
While he was exercised in this, many days passed not, but a foot-
boy of my lady her mother's came to young Mrs. Apsley* as
they were at dinner, bringing news that her mother and sister

---

* It was the custom at that time to call young ladies Mistress, not Miss.
Shakespeare calls Ann Page, Mrs. Ann.

would in a few days return ; and when they inquired of him, whether Mrs. Apsley was married ; having before been instructed to make them believe it, he smiled, and pulled out some bride laces, which were given at a wedding, in the house where she was, and gave them to the young gentlewoman and the gentleman's daughter of the house, and told them Mrs. Apsley bade him tell no news, but give them those tokens, and carried the matter so, that all the company believed she had been married. Mr. Hutchinson immediately turned pale as ashes, and felt a fainting to seize his spirits in that extraordinary manner, that, finding himself ready to sink at table, he was fain to pretend something had offended his stomach, and to retire from the table into the garden ; where the gentleman of the house going with him, it was not necessary for him to feign sickness, for the distemper of his mind had infected his body with a cold sweat, and such a depression of spirit, that all the courage he could at present collect, was little enough to keep him alive. His host was very troublesome to him, and to be quit of him he went to his chamber, saying he would lie down. Little did any of the company suspect the true cause of his sudden qualm, and they were all so troubled at it, that the boy then passed without further examination, When Mr. Hutchinson was alone he began to recollect his wisdom and his reason, and to wonder at himself, why he should be so concerned in an unknown person ; he then remembered the story that was told him when he came down, and began to believe there was some magic in the place, which enchanted men out of their right senses ; but it booted him not to be angry at himself, nor to set wisdom in her reproving chair, nor reason in her throne of council, the sick heart could not be chid nor advised into health. This anxiety of mind affected him so, that it sent him to his bed that afternoon, which indeed he took to entertain his thoughts alone that night, and having fortified himself

with resolution, he got up the next day ; but yet could not
quit himself of an extravagant perplexity of soul concerning
this unknown gentlewoman, which had not been remarkable in
another light person, but in him, who was from his childhood
so serious and so rational in all his considerations, it was the
effect of a miraculous power of Providence, leading him to
her that was destined to make his future joy.   While she so
ran in his thoughts, meeting the boy again, he found out,
upon a little stricter examination of him, that she was not
married, and pleased himself in the hopes of her speedy
return ; when one day, having been invited by one of the
ladies of that neighbourhood to a noble treatment at Sion
Garden, which a courtier, that was her servant, had made for
her and whom she would bring, Mr. Hutchinson, Mrs. Apsley,
and Mr. Coleman's daughter were of the party, and having
spent the day in several pleasant divertisements, at evening
when they were at supper, a messenger came to tell Mrs
Apsley her mother was come.   She would immediately have
gone, but Mr. Hutchinson, pretending civility to conduct her
home, made her stay till the supper was ended, of which he
ate no more, now only longing for that sight which he had
with such perplexity expected.   This at length he obtained ;
but his heart, being prepossessed with his own fancy, was
not free to discern how little there was in her to answer so
great an expectation.   She was not ugly in a careless riding-
habit, she had a melancholy negligence both of herself and
others, as if she neither affected to please others, nor took
notice of anything before her ; yet, in spite of all her indifference, she was surprised with some unusual liking in her
soul when she saw this gentleman, who had hair, eyes, shape,
and countenance enough to beget love in any one at the first,
and these set off with a graceful and generous mien, which
promised an extraordinary person.   He was at that time, and
indeed always very neatly habited, for he wore good and

rich clothes, and had a variety of them, and had them well
suited and every way answerable; in that little thing, showing
both good judgment and great generosity, he equally becoming them and they him, which he wore with such equal
unaffectedness and such neatness as we do not often meet in
one. Although he had but an evening sight of her he had so
long desired, and that at disadvantage enough for her; yet the
prevailing sympathy of his soul made him think all his pains
well paid, and this first did whet his desire to a second sight,
which he had by accident the next day, and to his joy
found that she was wholly disengaged from that treaty,
which he so much feared had been accomplished; he found
withal, that though she was modest, she was accostable, and
willing to entertain his acquaintance. This soon passed into
a mutual friendship between them, and though she innocently
thought nothing of love, yet was she glad to have acquired
such a friend, who had wisdom and virtue enough to be
trusted with her councils, for she was then much perplexed
in mind. Her mother and friends had a great desire she
should marry, and were displeased that she refused many
offers which they thought advantageous enough; she was
obedient, loth to displease them, but more herself, in marrying such as she could find no inclination to. The troublesome pretensions of some of the courtiers, had made her
willing to try whether she could bring her heart to her
mother's desire; but being, by a secret working which she
then understood not, averted, she was troubled to return, lest
some might believe it was a secret liking for them which had
caused her dislike for others; and being a little disturbed with
these things and melancholy, Mr. Hutchinson, appearing, as
he was, a person of virtue and honour, who might be safely
and advantageously conversed with, she thought God had
sent her a happy relief. Mr. Hutchinson, on the other side,
having been told, and seeing how she shunned all other men,

and how civilly she entertained him, believed that a secret
power had wrought a mutual inclination between them; and he
daily frequented her mother's house, and had the opportunity
of conversing with her in those pleasant walks, which, at
that sweet season of the spring, invited all the neighbouring
inhabitants to seek their joys; where, though they were
never alone, yet they had every day opportunity for converse
with each other, which the rest shared not in, while every
one minded their own delights.

They had not six weeks enjoyed this peace, but the young
men and women, who saw them allow each other that kindness which they did not afford commonly to others, first began
to grow jealous and envious at it, and afterwards to use all
the malicious practices they could invent to break the friendship.   Among the rest, that gentleman who at the first had
so highly commended her to Mr. Hutchinson, now began to
caution him against her, and to disparage her, with such
subtle insinuations, as would have ruined any love less constant and honourable than his.   The women, with witty spite,
represented all her faults to him, which chiefly terminated in
the negligence of her dress and habit, and all womanish
ornaments, giving herself wholly up to study and writing.
Mr. Hutchinson, who had a very sharp and pleasant wit,
retorted all their malice with such just reproofs of their idleness and vanity, as made them hate her, who, without affection
it, had so engaged such a person in her protection, as they
with all their arts could not catch.   He, in the meanwhile,
prosecuted his love with so much discretion, duty, and
honour, that at the length, through many difficulties, he accomplished his design.   I shall pass by all the little amorous
relations, which, if I would take the pains to relate, would
make a true history of a more handsome management of love
than the best romances describe; but these are to be forgotten
as the vanities of youth, not worthy of mention among the

greater transactions of his life. There is this only to be
recorded, that never was there a passion more ardent and less
idolatrous ; he loved her better than his life, with inexpress-
ible tenderness and kindness, had a most high obliging
esteem of her, yet still considered honour, religion, and duty
above her, nor ever suffered the intrusion of such a dotage as
should blind him from marking her imperfections ; these he
looked upon with such an indulgent eye as did not abate his
love and esteem of her, while it augmented his care to blot
out all those spots which might make her appear less worthy
of that respect he paid her ; and thus indeed he soon made
her more equal to him than he found her; for she was a
very faithful mirror, reflecting truly, though but dimly, his
own glories upon him, so long as he was present; but she,
that was nothing before his inspection gave her a fair figure,
when he was removed, was only filled with a dark mist, and
never could again take in any delightful object, nor return
any shining representation. The greatest excellency she had
was the power of apprehending and the virtue of loving his ;
so as his shadow she waited on him everywhere, till he was
taken into that region of light which admits of none, and then
she vanished into nothing. It was not her face he loved,
her honour and her virtue were his mistresses ; and these
(like Pygmalion's) images of his own making, for he polished
and gave form to what he found with all the roughness of
the quarry about it ; but meeting with a compliant subject
for his own wise government, he found as much satisfaction
as he gave, and never had occasion to number his marriage
among his infelicities. That day that the friends on both
sides met to conclude the marriage, she fell sick of the
small pox, which was in many ways a great trial upon him.
First, her life was almost in desperate hazard, and then the
disease, for the present, made her the most deformed person
that could be seen, for a great while after she recovered ; yet

he was nothing troubled at it, but married her as soon as she
was able to quit the chamber, when the priest and all that
saw her were affrighted to look on her; but God recom-
pensed his justice and constancy by restoring her, though she
was longer than ordinary before she recovered to be as well
as before.   One thing is very observable, and worthy imitation in him : although he had as strong and violent affections for her, as ever any man had, yet he declared it not to her
till he had acquainted first his father ; and afterwards he never
would make any engagement but what his love and honour
bound him in ; wherein he was more firm and just than all the
promissory oaths and ties in the world could have made him,
notwithstanding many powerful temptations of wealth and
beauty, and other interests, that were laid before him.   For
his father had concluded another treaty, before he knew his
son's inclinations were this way fixed, with a party in many
things much more advantageous for his family, and more
worthy of his liking ; but his father was no less honourably
indulgent to his son's affection, than the son was strict in the
observance of his duty ; and at length, to the full content of
all, the thing was accomplished, and on the third day of July,
in the year 1638, he was married to Mrs. Lucy Apsley, the
second daughter of Sir Allen Apsley, late lieutenant of the
Tower of London, at St. Andrew's church in Holborn.   He
lived some time in this neighbourhood with her mother, but
four months were scarcely past after their marriage before
he was in great danger of losing her, when she lost two
children she had conceived by him.   Soon after conceiving
again she grew so sickly, that her indulgent mother and
husband, for the advantage of her health, removed their
dwelling out of the city, to a house they took in Enfield
Chace, called the Blue House, where, upon the third of September, 1639, she was brought to bed of two sons, whereof the
elder he named after his own father, Thomas, the younger was

called Edward, who both survived him. September, 1641,
she brought him another son, called by his own name, John,
who lived scarce six years, and was a very hopeful child, full
of his father's vigour and spirit, but death soon nipped that
blossom.

Mr. Hutchinson, after about fourteen months' various exercise of his mind, in the pursuit of his love, being now at
rest in the enjoyment of his wife, his next design was to draw
her into his own country; but he would not set upon it too
roughly, and therefore let her rest a while, when he had
drawn her ten miles nearer it, out of the city where she had
her birth and education, and where all her relations were
most conversant, and which she could not suddenly resolve
to quit altogether, to betake herself to the north, which
was a formidable name among the London ladies. While
she was weaning from the friends and places she had so long
conversed in, Mr. Hutchinson employed his time in making
an entrance upon the study of school divinity, wherein his
father was the most eminent scholar of any gentleman in
England, and had a most choice library,* valued at a thousand pounds; which Mr. Hutchinson, mistakingly expecting
to be part of his inheritance, thought it would be very inglorious for him not to understand how to make use of his father's books. Having therefore gotten into the house with
him an excellent scholar in that kind of learning, he for two
years made it the whole employment of his time. The gentleman that assisted him he converted to a right belief in that

* This is spoken of in the preface, and did in fact remain at Owthorpe,
but probably was placed there by Charles, the son of Sir Thomas Hutch
inson by his second wife : it was of excessively small value when taken
possession of in the year 1776.

It is apparent, from Sir Thomas Hutchinson being upon all the committees for religion, as may be seen in Rushworth's collection, that he was in
repute for this kind of knowledge.

great point of predestination, he having been before of the
Arminian judgment, till, upon the serious examination of both
principles, and comparing them with the Scriptures, Mr.
Hutchinson convinced him of the truth, and he grew so well
instructed in this principle, that he was able to maintain it
against any man. At that time, this great doctrine grew
much out of fashion with the prelates, but was generally embraced by all religious and holy persons in the land. Mr.
Hutchinson being desirous to inform himself thoroughly of it,
when he was able to manage the question, offered it to his
father; but Sir Thomas would not declare himself on the point
to him, nor indeed in any other, as we conceived, lest a
father's authority should sway against his children's light,
who he thought ought to discern things with their own eyes,
and not with his. Mr. Hutchinson, taking delight in the
study of divinity, presently left off all foolish nice points, that
tended to nothing but vain brangling, and employed his whole
study in laying a foundation of sound and necessary principles, among which he gave the first place to this of God's absolute decrees. This was so far from producing a carelessness of life in him, a thing generally objected against this
faith,* that, on the other side, it excited him to a more strict

* Mrs. Hutchinson, in exculpating her husband, goes no part of the way
towards showing that the natural tendency of this principle differs from that
which is objected against it, but merely that he resisted this bias from another
consideration. This is certainly not a suitable place to discuss such a subject;
and it is therefore dismissed with this remark, that the partisans of the two
opposite, or supposed opposite, principles of predestination and free will,
while they endeavour to implicate each other in absurdity and irreligion,
agree in practice, and, guiding their actions by the best discretion they are
masters of, end with referring the event to Providence, and praying to God
for a blessing on their endeavours—much more rational in so doing than
farther exposing the weakness of human understanding by disquisitions far
too refined for its reach. The conduct of modern times is in this respec
more commendable than that of the past.

and holy walking in thankfulness to God, who had been
pleased to choose him out of the corrupted mass of lost mankind, to fix his love upon him, and give him the knowledge
of himself by his ever-blessed Son. This principle of love
and life in God, which had been given him when he discerned
not what it was in himself, had from a child preserved him
from wallowing in the mire of sin and wickedness,wherein most
of the gentry of those times were miserably plunged, except a
few, that were therefore the scorn of mankind; and there were
but few of those few, that had not natural and superstitious
follies, that were in some kind justly ridiculous and contemptible. It was a remarkable providence of God in his
life, that must not be passed over without special notice, that
he gave him these two years' leisure, and a heart so to employ it, before the noise of war and tumult came upon him.
Yet about the year 1639, the thunder was heard afar off
rattling in the troubled air, and even the most obscured woods
were penetrated with some flashes, the forerunners of the
dreadful storm which the next year was more apparent; but
Mr. Hutchinson was not yet awakened till it pleased God to
deliver him from a danger into which he had run himself,
had not mercy prevented him. His wife having already two
sons, and being again with child, considered that it would be
necessary to seek an augmentation of revenue, or retire into
a cheaper country; and more inclining to the first, than to leave
at once her mother, and all the rest of her dear relations, she
had propounded to him to buy an office, which he was not of
himself very inclinable to; but, to give her and her mother satisfaction, he hearkened to a motion that was made him in that
kind. Sir William Pennyman, who had married his cousin-
german, a very worthy gentleman, who had great respect
both for and from his father, had purchased the chief office in
the Star-chamber; the gentleman who held the next to him
was careless and debauched, and thereby a great hindrance

of Sir William's profits, who apprehended that if he could get an honest man into that place, they might mutually much advantage each other; whereupon he persuaded Mr. Hutchinson to buy the place, and offered him any terms, to go any share with him, or any way he could desire. Mr. Hutchinson treated with the gentleman, came to a conclusion, went down into the country, provided the money, and came up again, thinking presently to enter into the office; but the gentleman that should have sold it, being of an uncertain humour, thought to make the benefit of another term before he sold his place; and it pleased God, in the mean time, that arbitrary court was, by the parliament then sitting, taken away. Mr. Hutchinson was very sensible of a peculiar providence to him herein, and resolved to adventure no more such hazards; but to retire to that place whither God seemed to have called him by giving him so good an interest there, and to study how he was to improve that talent. His wife, convinced by this kind check which God had given to her desires, that she ought to follow her husband where the Lord seemed to call him, went along with him, and about October 1641, they came to their house at Owthorpe. Here Mr. George Hutchinson (Sir Thomas being then chosen knight for Nottinghamshire, and sitting in the parliament at London,) came and gave a glad entertainment of his brother and sister into the country, by his good company; and they were, for a few months' peaceful and happy in their own house, till the kingdom began to blaze out with the long-conceived flame of civil war. But here I must make a short digression from our particular actions, to sum up the state of the kingdom at that time, which though I cannot do exactly, yet I can truly relate what I was then able to take notice of; and if any one have a desire of more particular information, there were so many books then written, as will sufficiently give it them. And although those of our enemies are all fraught with abo-

minable lies, yet if all ours were suppressed, even their
own writings, impartially considered, would be a sufficient
chronicle of their injustice and oppression; but I shall only
mention what is necessary to be remembered, for the better
carrying on of my purpose.*

When the dawn of the gospel began to break upon this
isle, after the dark midnight of papacy, the morning was
more cloudy here than in other places by reason of the state-
interest, which was mixing and working itself into the
interest of religion, and which in the end quite wrought it
out. King Henry the Eighth, who, by his royal authority
cast out the pope, did not intend the people of the land
should have any ease of oppression; but only changed their
foreign yoke for home-bred fetters, dividing the pope's spoils
between himself and his bishops, who cared not for their
father at Rome, so long as they enjoyed their patrimony and
their honours here under another head: so that I cannot
subscribe to those who entitle that king to the honour of the
reformation. But even then there wanted not many who
discerned the corruptions that were retained in the church
and eagerly applied their endeavours to obtain a purer reformation; against whom, those who saw no need of further reformation, either through excess of joy for that which was already

* In a small book, entitled, a Parallel of Clarendon and Whitelock,
this is set in the clearest light possible, and in a variety of instances the
unfaithfulness of Clarendon's testimony made evident by the production of
palpable self-contradictions. Most of those who read the summary account
Mrs. Hutchinson gives of the public transactions, will extremely regret that
she was not much more full in it, seeing the candour and perspicuity with
which she writes: short as it is, however, it will be found to throw light
upon many obscure points; and, from being so much concentrated, will
be useful and acceptable to many, as serving to fix a general and just
idea of the public mind. as well as transactions, in the times of which she
treats.

brought forth, or else through a secret love of superstition
rooted in their hearts thought this too much,—were bitterly
incensed, and, hating that light which reproved their darkness,
everywhere stirred up spirits of envy and persecution against
them. Upon the great revolution which took place at the
accession of Queen Elizabeth to the crown, the nation became
divided into three great factions, the papists, the state protestants, and the more religious zealots, who afterwards were
branded with the name of Puritans. In vain it was for
these to address the queen and the parliament; for the
bishops, under the specious pretences of uniformity and obedience, procured severe punishments to be inflicted on such
as durst gainsay their determinations in all things concerning
worship, whereupon some even in those godly days lost their
lives.

The papists had a most inveterate hatred to all the protestants, but especially to those who were godly;* and they again
many of them suffered their zeal to run out into bitter personal hate. Between these two extremes, the common protestants were in the middle, though I cannot reckon them as a
virtuous medium; for of them the more profane and ignorant
only left popery because it grew out of fashion, but in their
hearts inclined that way; those who were peaceable, conscientious, or moral persons, inclined to the puritans, of whom
there were many that unwillingly bore the burden of the
ceremonies, for quietness' sake, and through false doctrine of
their unfaithful teachers, as well as some that discerned the
base and carnal minds of those seducers, and would not be
persuaded by them to defile their consciences. The former
sort of these, in zeal to reduce the whole land from their

* Godly. The name always given by the puritans to those of their
own party, and not unfrequently so used by different sectaries at the present day.

idolatrous practices, procured laws and invented oaths to suppress popery, which they little thought, but we now sadly find, are the bitterest engines to batter down the pure worship and destroy the pure worshippers of God; which I have often looked upon as an evidence that God is not pleased with the conversions that are enforced by men's laws. We have spiritual weapons given us for spiritual combats, and those who go about to conquer subjects for Christ with swords of steel, shall find the base metal break to shivers when it is used, and hurtfully fly in their own faces.

About the time of the reformation, there was a great change in the civil interest of all that part of the world which had long lain under the bondage of the Roman prelate and his tyrannical clergy. These had by degrees so encroached upon all the secular princes, that they were nothing but vassals and hangmen to the proud insolent priest. Obtaining his empire by fraud, false doctrine, lies, and hypocrisy, he maintained it by blood and rapine, till it pleased God to cause that light to break forth about Luther's time, which hath ever since been increasing; and, notwithstanding all the attempts of Satan and his ministers, it will in the end grow up to a glorious flame and quite devour that bloody city. When the wrath of princes and priests was in vain at first blown up against the professors of the gospel, and their blood and ashes became fruitful seed in God's field, then the old fox comes into the fold as a lamb, and seduces some of them that saw the approach of Christ's kingdom, to set it up irregularly; and, indeed (though I know not whether they perceived their own delusion), to set up themselves in Christ's throne, casting down the thrones of all other magistrates, and destroying the properties of men, and ruling by their own arbitrary lust, which they brought forth in the name of God's law.* This

* A description of the principles of the most extravagant of those whom in history they call Fifth Monarchy Men, from their affecting to set up the

example was so threatening to all mankind, that the gospel
itself, from the adversaries thereof, suffered much reproach
upon this miscarriage; whereupon the protestants, in all
places, to clear themselves from the just aspersions which
the Munster anabaptists and others had occasioned, fell into
an error on the other hand, not much less hurtful in the consequence; for to flatter the princes of the world, whether
popish or protestant, they invested them with God's prerogative, and preached to them and the people such doctrines as only changed the idol, but left the idolatry still
in practice.*

The popes of Rome had for many ages challenged and
practised a power to dethrone princes, to give away their
realms, to interdict whole kingdoms and provinces, and
devote them to slaughter, to loose subjects from all bonds
and oaths of allegiance to their sovereigns, and to stir up
both princes and people to the mutual murder of each
other; which abominable courses, had been justly cast upon them as reproach, they pretending to do all these

empire of Christ as the fifth; the Assyrian, Persian, Grecian, and Roman,
being the first four.

* This could hardly be carried further any where than in England,
where in all cases passive, in most cases active, obedience was indiscriminately inculcated; where two divines stating in their discourses, one, "that
it was the king's duty to make laws, and the subject's to obey them;" another, that " the king is not bound to observe the laws of the realm, but
that his royal will and command in imposing taxes and loans without consent of parliament, doth oblige the subject's conscience, upon pain of eternal
damnation." For refusing to license the publication of the first sermon,
the good Archbishop Abbot was banished, and confined to a bad and unhealthy country-house. For the latter, the preacher, though sentenced by
the lords to be fined and imprisoned, was by the king pardoned, and promoted to a bishoprick. After this, let it be decided whether Charles reverenced episcopacy as a divine institution, or valued it as an engine of state !
and in what light he caused his subjects to view it ?

things for the propagation of the true worship and the advance of God's glory. This reproach they retorted when some protestants, upon the same pretence, did maintain that idolatrous princes were to be removed, and such magistrates set up as feared God, who were guardians of both tables, and were bound to compel all their people to the right religion. This confusion was there among the sons of darkness at the first appearance of gospel light.

About this time in the kingdom of Scotland there was a wicked queen, daughter of a mother that came out of the bloody house of Guise,* and brought up in the popish religion, which she zealously persevered in, as most suitable to her bloody lustful temper; she being guilty of murders and adulteries, and hateful for them to the honestest of the people, was deposed, imprisoned, and forced to fly for her life; but her son was received upon the throne, and educated after the strictest way of the protestant religion according to Calvin's form. Those who were chiefly active and instrumental in the justice executed on this wicked queen, were the reformers of religion in Scotland, which made the neighbouring idolatrous princes fear them of the same faith. About the same time likewise, the provinces of the Netherlands united themselves in a resistance against the king of Spain, and cast off that yoke wherewith he had most barbarously galled them. The king of France, persecuting his protestant subjects with much inhuman violence, forced them to defend themselves against his unsanctified league. and much blood was shed in those civil wars; till at length those who had had so much experience of God's providence in delivering them from their cruel princes, were persuaded to make up an alliance with the enemies of God and religion, and by the treacherous foe drawn into his snares,

---

* Mary Queen of Scots.

where they were most wickedly and barbarously massacred.[*]
Now, although religion was the main ground of those bloody
quarrels, yet there were, in all these countries, many disputes of civil right, which for the most part were borne on
the face of the wars, whereat I have only hinted, in this
survey of the condition of other states, and their interests
in those days and since; which is something necessary to
be known for the better understanding of our own, with
which I shall now proceed.

The civil government of England, from the time called
the Conquest, had been adminstered by a King, Lords, and
Commons, in a way of Parliaments; the parliament entrusted
with the legislative, and the king with the executive power;
but several of the kings, not satisfied with their bounded
monarchy, made attempts to convert it into an absolute
sovereignty, attempts fatal both to themselves and their
people, and ever unsuccessful. For the generous people of
England, as they were the most free and obsequious subjects
in the world to those princes that managed them with a
kind and tender hand, commanding them as freemen, not as
slaves, so were they the most untameable, invincible people,
in defence of their freedoms against all those usurping lords
that scorned to allow them liberty.   The nobility of the
realm having at first the great balance of the lands, and
retaining some of that free honourable virtue, for which they
were exalted above the vulgar, ever stood up in the people's
defence and curbed the wild ambition of the tyrants, whom they
sometimes reduced to moderation, and sometimes deposed
for their misgovernments; till, at length the kings, eager to
break this yoke, had insensibly worn out the interest of the
nobility, by drawing them to their courts, where luxuries
melted away the great estates of some, others were destroyed

* The famous massacre on St. Bartholomew's day at Paris.

by confiscations in divers civil wars, and others otherwise mouldered with time. While the kings were glad to see the abatement of that power, which had been such a check to their exorbitancies, they perceived not the growing of another more dangerous to them; and that when the nobility shrunk into empty names, the throne lost its supporters, and had no more but a little puff of wind to bear it up, when the full body of the people came rolling in upon it.* The interest of the people, which had been many years growing, made an extraordinary progress in the days of King Henry the Eighth, who returning the vast revenues of the church into the body of the people, cast the balance clear on their side, and left them now only to expect† an opportunity to resume their power into their own hands; and had not differences in religion divided them among themselves, and thereby prolonged the last gasps of expiring monarchy, they had long since exercised it in a free commonwealth.

England was not an idle spectator of the great contest between the papist and protestant, in which all Christendom

* It is wonderful that the experience of so many ages and so many other states had not been sufficient to warn the princes of the house of Bourbon of this fatal error! From the moment of Cardinal Richelieu's coming into power under Louis XIII. to Neckar's return to power after his rustication under Louis XVI. the plan of lowering the power of the noblesse of France had been systematically pursued. The last stroke was given to it when this delusive and deluded minister advised that unfortunate monarch to give to the commons a double number of representatives in the states general, and to blend the noblesse with them. It was in vain that the Prince of Conti gave him a short note of admonition, written on the spur of the occasion upon his hat :—" Sire, the moment you sign this arret your throne is overturned." He rejected the advice, and betrayed the author.

† Expect, a Latinism ; expectare, to wait for ; or, Italian, aspettare, id.

seemed to be engaged. During the reign of Queen Elizabeth, the protestant interest, being her peculiar interest, that
princess became not only glorious in the defence of her own
realm, but in the protection she gave to the whole protestant
cause in all the neighbouring kingdoms; wherefore, as if it
had been devolved upon her person, the pope shot all his
arrows at her head, and set on many desperate assassinations
against her, which, by the good providence of God, were all
frustrated, and she, not only miraculously delivered from those
wretches, but renowned at home and abroad for successes
against her rebellious subjects in England and Ireland, and
for the assistance of her distressed neighbours; but, above
all, for the mercy which it pleased God to afford her and this
realm in the year 1588, when the invading Spaniard had
devoured us in his proud hopes, and by the mighty hand of
God was scattered as a mist before the morning beams.
That which kept alive the hopes of the papists, most part of
her reign, was the expectation of the Queen of Scots, who,
entering into confederacy with them, lost her head for the
forfeit, wherein the duke of Norfolk suffered also for her
the loss of his. The Queen of England was very loath to
execute this necessary justice; but the true-hearted protestants of her council, foreseeing the sad effects that might
be expected if ever she arrived to the crown, urged it on;*
and after the death of Queen Elizabeth, the wiser of them
much opposed the admission of her son. But he, dissembling
the resentment of his mother's death, by bribes and greater

* The signing and expediting the warrant for the execution of Mary
Queen of Scots is an enigma which has employed the wits of many to
solve—perhaps this may be the true solution of it; it is at least clear,
that it thus appeared to well-informed persons, living in times when the
thing was recent, and accounts for it more naturally than the mean jealousy
attributed to Queen Elizabeth, which would in fact have been a better
reason for putting her to death many years sooner.

promises, managed a faction in the court of the declining queen, which prevailed on her dotage to destroy the Earl of Essex, the only person who would have had the courage to keep out him they thought it dangerous to let in.* So subtlely brought they their purpose about, that wise counsel was in vain to a blinded and betrayed people. The anti-prelatical party hoping that, with a king bred up among the Calvinists, they should now be freed from the episcopal yoke, were greedy of entertaining him, but soon cured of their mistake ; when, immediately after his entry into the kingdom, himself being moderator at a dispute between both parties, the nonconformists were cast out of doors, and the offensive ceremonies, instead of being removed, were more strictly imposed; the penalties against papists were relaxed, and many of them taken into favour; whilst those families who suffered for his mother were graced and restored as far as the times would bear, and those who consented any way to the justice done upon her, disfavoured. A progress was made suitable to this beginning, the protestant interest abroad was deserted and betrayed, the prelates at home daily exalted in pride and pomp, and declining in virtue and godliness. Arminianism† crept in to the corruption of sound doctrine, till at length they had the impudence to forbid the preaching of those great and necessary truths concerning the decrees of God ; secret treaties were entertained with the court of Rome ;‡ and, notwithstanding that hellish powder plot, the

---

* In Heylin's History of the Presbyterians, it is said that the Earl of Essex was much courted by the puritans, and in return caressed them; that a title to the crown was drawn out for him, and he began to look up to it; that he encouraged an opinion, that inferior magistrates might curb and control their sovereign ; that he was outwitted and brought to the scaffold by Cecil and Raleigh, very opportunely for king James, whose entrance might have been opposed and his title questioned.

† James, however, professed himself a great enemy to it.

‡ The first volume of Clarendon's State Papers is half filled with them.

papists lost not their credit at court, where they now wrought
no longer by open and direct ways, but humouring the king and
queen in their lusts and excesses, they found the most ready
way to destroy the doctrine of the gospel was to debauch
the professors. The court of this king was a nursery of lust
and intemperance; he had brought in with him a company
of poor Scots, who, coming into this plentiful kingdom, were
surfeited with riot and debaucheries, and got all the riches of
the land only to cast away. The honour, wealth, and glory
of the nation, wherein Queen Elizabeth left it, were soon pro-
digally wasted by this thriftless heir; and the nobility of the
land was utterly debased by setting honours to public sale, and
conferring them on persons that had neither blood nor merit
fit to wear, nor estates to bear up their titles, but were fain
to invent projects to pill* the people, and pick their purses
for the maintenance of vice and lewdness. The generality of
the gentry of the land soon learned the court fashion, and
every great house in the country became a sty of uncleanness.
To keep the people in their deplorable security, till vengeance
overtook them, they were entertained with masks, stage plays,
and various sorts of ruder sports. Then began murder, incest,
adultery, drunkenness, swearing, fornication, and all sort of
ribaldry, to be no concealed but countenanced vices, because
they held such conformity with the court example. Next to
this, a great cause of these abominations was the mixed
marriages of papist and protestant families, which, no
question, was a design of the popish party to compass and
procure; and so successful, that I have observed that there
was not one house in ten, where such a marriage was made,
but the better party was corrupted, the children's souls were
sacrificed to devils, the worship of God was laid aside in that
family, for fear of distasting the idolater; the kindred,

* Pill—pillage, plunder.

tenants, and neighbours, either quite turned from it, or cooled in their zeal for religion.   As the fire is most fervent in a frosty season, so the general apostacy from holiness, if I may so call it, and defection to lewdness, stirred up sorrow, indignation, and fear, in all that retained any love of God in the land, whether ministers or people ; the ministers warned the people of the approaching judgments of God, which could not be expected but to follow such high provocations ; God in his mercy sent his prophets into all corners of the land, to preach repentance, and cry out against the ingratitude of England, who thus requited so many rich mercies that no nation could ever boast of more ; and by these a few were every where converted and established in faith and holiness ; but at court they were hated, disgraced, and reviled, and in scorn had the name of Puritan* fixed upon them.   And now the ready way to preferment there, was to declare an opposition to the power of godliness, under that name ; so that their pulpits might justly be called the scorner's chair, those

* This artifice of affixing a name of reproach on those of an opposite party, in order indiscriminately to subject them to hatred or ridicule, could hardly be better exposed than it is here.   That Mrs. Hutchinson is guilty of no exaggeration, may well be conjectured from some speeches in parliament preserved by Rushworth, peculiarly one of Sir Benjamin Rudyard, at least a moderate man, if not a favourer of the king, complaining of the very same thing,   Rushworth, vol. ii. 1355, " It is the artifice of the favourers of the catholic and of the prelatical party to call all who are sticklers for the constitution in church or state, or would square their actions by any rule, human or divine, Puritans."   In the petition and remonstrance this is stated nearly in the same manner.   It was no way inconsistent with the other injustices of the French revolutionists to invent the term of Aristocrat, and mark out by it every one whom the populace or their demagogues designed to plunder or destroy; it would not be so excusable if in this country we should suffer cant terms or nicknames to pass for reasoning or proof.   For the rest, the name of Puritan should have no bad meaning.

sermons only pleasing that flattered them in their vices, and
told the poor king that he was Solomon, and that his sloth
and cowardice, by which he betrayed the cause of God and
honour of the nation, was gospel meekness and peaceableness;
for which they raised him up above the heavens, while he lay
wallowing like a swine in the mire of his lust. He had a
little learning, and this they called the spirit of wisdom, and
so magnified him, so falsely flattered him, that he could not
endure the words of truth and soundness, but rewarded these
base, wicked, unfaithful fawners with rich preferments, attended with pomps and titles, which heaped them up above
a human height.   With their pride, their envy swelled
against the people of God, whom they began to project how
they might root out of the land ; and when they had once
given them a name, whatever was odious or dreadful to the
king, they fixed upon the puritan, who, according to their
character, was nothing but a factious hypocrite.

The king had upon his heart the dealings both of England
and Scotland with his mother, and harboured a secret desire
of revenge upon the godly in both nations, yet had not
courage enough to assert his resentment like a prince, but
employed a wicked cunning he was master of, and called
king-craft, to undermine what he durst not openly oppose,—
the true religion ; this was fenced with the liberty of the
people, and so linked together, that it was impossible to make
them slaves, till they were brought to be idolaters of royalty
and glorious lust ; and as impossible to make them adore
these gods, while they continued loyal to the government of
Jesus Christ.   The payment of civil obedience to the king
and the laws of the land satisfied not ; if any durst dispute
his impositions in the worship of God, he was presently
reckoned among the seditious and disturbers of the public
peace, and accordingly persecuted ; if any were grieved at
the dishonour of the kingdom, or the griping of the poor, or

the unjust oppressions of the subject, by a thousand ways,
invented to maintain the riots of the courtiers, and the swarms
of needy Scots the king had brought in to devour like locusts
the plenty of this land, he was a puritan; if any, out of mere
morality and civil honesty, discountenanced the abominations
of those days, he was a puritan, however he conformed to
their superstitious worship; if any showed favour to any
godly honest persons, kept them company, relieved them in
want, or protected them against violent or unjust oppression,
he was a puritan; if any gentleman in his country maintained the good laws of the land, or stood up for any public
interest, for good order or government, he was a puritan: in
short, all that crossed the views of the needy courtiers, the
proud encroaching priests, the thievish projectors, the lewd
nobility and gentry—whoever was zealous for God's glory or
worship, could not endure blasphemous oaths, ribald conversation, profane scoffs, sabbath breaking, derision of the word
of God, and the like—whoever could endure a sermon,
modest habit or conversation, or anything good,—all these
were puritans; and if puritans, then enemies to the king and
his government, seditious, factious hypocrites, ambitious disturbers of the public peace, and finally, the pest of the
kingdom. Such false logic did the children of darkness use
to argue with against the hated children of light, whom they
branded besides as an illiterate, morose, melancholy, discontented, crazed sort of men, not fit for human conversation;* as such they made them not only the sport of the

---

* Such is the idea entertained of them in general even at this day;
whoever shall read these memoirs will be well convinced that not one of
these qualities needs or does by any natural consequence accompany the
character. It is a great misfortune that many of the zealous professors
of piety should give it so austere an aspect, and this can never be better
contrasted than by the cheerful and amiable one this professed puritan
gives it.

pulpit, which was become but a more solemn sort of stage,
but every stage, and every table, and every puppet-play,
belched forth profane scoffs upon them, the drunkards made
them their songs, and all fiddlers and mimics learned to abuse
them, as finding it the most gameful way of fooling. Thus
the two factions in those days grew up to great heights and
enmities one against the other; while the papist wanted not
industry and subtlety to blow the coals between them, and
was so successful that, unless the mercy of God confound
them by their own imaginations, we may justly fear they will
at last obtain their full wish.

But to deal impartially, we must, with sadness enough,
confess, that the wolf came into the fold in a sheep's
clothing, and wrought more slaughter that way among the
lambs than he could have done in his own skin; for it is true
that many of wit and parts, discontented when they could
not obtain the preferments their ambition gaped at, would
declare themselves of the puritan party. And such were
either bought off, or, if the adversary would not give their
price, seduced their devout hearers sometimes into indiscreet
opposition to work out their own revenge; others, that had
neither learning, nor friends, nor opportunities to arrive to
any preferments, would put on a form of godliness, finding
devout people that way so liberal to them, that they could
not hope to enrich themselves so much in any other way.
Some that had greater art and parts, finding there was no
inconsiderable gain to be made of the simple devotion of
men and women, applied their wits to it, and collected great
sums for the advancement of the religious interest, of which
they converted much to their own private uses. Such as
these tempted the people of God to endeavour to shelter
themselves in human policies, and found out ways, by bribes
and other not less indirect courses, to procure patrons at
court, and to set up against the prelates with countermines

and other engines, which, being of man's framing, were all at last broken.

The puritan party being weak and oppressed, had not faith enough to disown all that adhered to them for worldly interests, and indeed it required more than human wisdom to discern at the least all of them ; wherefore they, in their low condition, gladly accepted any that would come over to them, or incline towards them; and their enemies, through envy at them, augmented much their party, while, with injuries and reproaches, they drove many, that never intended it, to take that party ; which in the end got nothing but confusion by those additions.   While these parties were thus counter-working, the treasure of the kingdom being wasted by court-caterpillars, the parliaments were called to re-supply the royal coffers, and therein there wanted not some, that retained so much of the English spirit as to represent the public grievances, and desire to call the corrupt ministers of state to an account. But the king, grudging that his people should dare to gainsay his pleasure, and correct his misgovernment in his favourites, broke up parliaments, violated their privileges, imprisoned their members for things spoken in the house, and grew disaffected to them, and entertained projects of supply by other grievances of the people.   The prelates, in the mean time, finding they lost ground, meditated reunion with the popish faction, who began to be at a pretty agreement with them ;* and now there was no more endeavour in their public sermons to confute the errors of that church, but to reduce our doctrines and theirs to an accommodation.   The king, to bring it about, was deluded† into the treaty of a match for his son with the Infanta of Spain ; and the prince,

* The first volume of Clarendon's State Papers abounds with instances

† It is very rare to see a delusion so long and successfully carried on as this appears to have been, at the expense of this modern Solomon, in the State Papers just mentioned.

with the Duke of Buckingham, was privately sent into Spain, from whence he came back with difficulty, but to the great rejoicing of the whole people in general, who were much afflicted at his going thither.   During this treaty the papists got many advantages of the king, to the prejudice of the protestant interest at home and abroad, and the hearts of all but the papists were very much saddened; and the people loath to lay the miscarriages of things at the king's own door, began to entertain a universal hatred of the Duke of Buckingham, raised from a knight's fourth son to that pitch of glory, and enjoying great possessions, acquired by the favour of the king, upon no merit but that of his beauty and his prostitution.   The parliament had drawn up a charge against him, and though the king seemed to protect him, yet knowing the fearfulness of his nature, and doubting his constancy, it was believed he added some help to an ague that killed that king; however the king died, and the duke continued as high in the favour of the next succeeding as of the deceased prince ; whereupon one, not unaptly, says of him, " he seemed as an unhappy exhalation, drawn up from the earth, not only to cloud the setting, but the rising sun."*

The face of the court was much changed in the change of the king, for King Charles was temperate, chaste, and serious; so that the fools and bawds, mimics and catamites, of the former court, grew out of fashion ; and the nobility and courtiers, who did not quite abandon their debaucheries, yet so reverenced the king as to retire into corners to practise them.   Men of learning and ingenuity in all arts were in esteem, and received encouragement from the king, who was a most excellent judge and a great lover of paintings, carvings, gravings, and many other ingenuities, less offensive than the

* The justice of the character here given of James, as well as the candour of that about to be given to Charles will, it is hoped, be recognised by every reader.

bawdry and profane abusive wit which was the only exercise
of the other court. But, as in the primitive times, it is observed
that the best emperors were some of them stirred up by Satan
to be the bitterest persecutors of the church, so this king was
a worse encroacher upon the civil and spiritual liberties of his
people by far than his father.   He married a papist, a French
lady, of a haughty spirit, and a great wit and beauty, to whom
he became a most uxorious husband.   By this means the court
was replenished with papists, and many who hoped to advance
themselves by the change, turned to that religion.   All the
papists in the kingdom were favoured, and, by the king's
example, matched into the best families ; the puritans were
more than ever discountenanced and persecuted, insomuch that
many of them chose to abandon their native country, and
leave their dearest relations, to retire into any foreign soil or
plantation, where they might, amidst all outward inconveniences, enjoy the free exercise of God's worship.   Such
as could not flee were tormented in the bishops' courts, fined,
whipped, pilloried, imprisoned, and suffered to enjoy no rest, so
that death was better than life to them ; and notwithstanding
their patient sufferance of all these things, yet was not the
king satisfied till the whole land was reduced to perfect
slavery.   The example of the French king was propounded
to him, and he thought himself no monarch so long as his
will was confined to the bounds of any law ; but knowing
that the people of England were not pliable to an arbitrary
rule, he plotted to subdue them to his yoke by a foreign
force, and till he could effect it, made no conscience of grant-
ing anything to the people, which he resolved should not
oblige him longer than it served his turn ; for he was a
prince that had nothing of faith or truth, justice or generosity,
in him.   He was the most obstinate person in his self-will
that ever was, and so bent upon being an absolute, uncon-
trollable sovereign, that he was resolved either to be such a

king or none. His firm adherence to prelacy was not for conscience of one religion more than another, for it was his principle that an honest man might be saved in any profession; but he had a mistaken principle that kingly government in the state could not stand without episcopal government in the church; and, therefore, as the bishops flattered him with preaching up his sovereign prerogative, and inveighing against the puritans as factious and disloyal, so he protected them in their pomp and pride, and insolent practises against all the godly and sober people of the land.* In the first parliament after he came to the crown, the Duke of Buckingham was impeached concerning the death of King James. and other misdemeanors; but the present king, who had received him into the same degree of favour that he was with the former, would not endure the question of his favourite, and, to deliver him from it, broke up the parliament, which gave too just a suspicion that he favoured the practice; for it is true that the duke's mother, without the consent of the physicians, had made an application to the wrists of the king for his ague, after which he died in his next fit. Some other parliaments there were, but still abruptly broken up when

* In note, page 72, it has been shown that their political, not their religious principles, were the criterion whereby the king judged the prelates of the church of England. That the same served for the church of Rome is shown pretty clearly in the first volume of Clarendon's State Papers, where Mr. Courtenay having refused some compliances against conscience, and giving as his reason that "the king was not the law-maker, but the king and parliament, and that the king has not a dispensing power;" and father Scudamore, alias Leander, asserting that he has, Courtenay is committed to prison, held there, and a trial refused him; Leander protected, encouraged, and rewarded; and it is stated that "Laud was at the helm of the king's counsel in these matters." This opinion of the king's candour, or even indifference, as to the mode of religion, is stated in nearly the same manner in Rushworth, but it is not said on what authority. The Stuarts sported with and ruined all religions, and in turn were ruined by them.

they put forth any endeavour to redress grievances. The protestants abroad were all looked upon as puritans, and their interests, instead of being protected, sadly betrayed ; ships were let out to the French king to serve against them ; and all the flower of the English gentry were lost in an ill-managed expedition to the Isle of Rhee, under pretence of helping them, but so ordered that it proved the loss of Rochelle, the strong fort and best defence of all the protestants in France. Those in Germany were no less neglected in all treaties, although his own sister and her children were so highly concerned. The whole people were sadly grieved at these misgovernments, and, loath to impute them to the king, cast all the odium upon the Duke of Buckingham, whom at length a discontented person stabbed, believing he did God and his country good service by it. All the kingdom, except the duke's own dependents and kindred, rejoiced in the death of this duke ; but they found little cause, for after it the king still persisted in his design of enslaving them, and found other ministers ready to serve his self-willed ambition, such as were Noy, his attorney-general, who set on foot that hateful tax of ship-money, and many more illegal exactions ; and ten of the judges, who perverted judgment in the cause of those who refused the illegal imposition ; although there were, even in that time, found two honest judges, who durst judge rightly against the king, although he had changed the words usual in their commissions, which were *Quamdiù bene se gesserint,** into another form, *Durante bene placito.* Besides these, and a great rascally company of flatterers and projectors, there were all the corrupted, tottering bishops, and others of the proud, profane clergy of the land, who, by their insolencies, grown odious to the people, bent their strong

* "Quamdiù bene se gesserint," during good behaviour, as long as .hey act right. "Durante bene placito," during the king's good pleasure.

endeavours to disaffect the prince to his honest, godly subjects, and to get a pretence of power from him, to afflict those
who would not submit to their insolent dominion.   But there
were two above all the rest, who led the van of the king's
evil counsellors, and these were Laud, archbishop of Canterbury, a fellow of mean extraction and arrogant pride, and the
Earl of Strafford, who as much outstripped all the rest in
favour as he did in abilities, being a man of deep policy,
stern resolution, and ambitious zeal to keep up the glory of
his own greatness.   In the beginning of this king's reign,
this man had been a strong asserter of the liberties of the
people, among whom he had gained himself an honourable
reputation, and was dreadful to the court party ; who, thereupon strewed snares in his way, and when they found a
breach at his ambition, his soul was that way entered and
captivated.   He was advanced first to be lord president of the
council in the north, to be a baron, afterwards an earl, and then
deputy of Ireland ; he was the nearest to a favourite of any man
since the death of the Duke of Buckingham, who was raised
by his first master, and kept up by the second, upon no
account of personal worth or any deserving abilities in him,
but only from the violent and private inclinations of the princes.
But the Earl of Strafford wanted not any accomplishment
that could be desired in the most serviceable minister of
state : besides, he having made himsel odious to the people
by his revolt from their interest to that of the oppressive
court, he was now obliged to keep up his own interest with
his new party, by all the malicious practices that pride and
revenge could inspire him with.*   But above all these the
king had another instigator of his own violent purpose, more
powerful than all the rest, and that was the queen, who,
grown out of her childhood, began to turn her mind from

* Called by Lord Digby the grand apostate of the Commonwealth.

those vain extravagancies she lived in at first, to that which did less become her, and was more fatal to the kingdom; which is never in any place happy where the hands which were made only for distaffs affect the management of sceptres.—If any one object the fresh example of Queen Elizabeth, let them remember that the felicity of her reign was the effect of her submission to her masculine and wise counsellors; but wherever male princes are so effeminate as to suffer women of foreign birth and different religions to intermeddle with the affairs of state, it is always found to produce sad desolations; and it hath been observed that a French queen never brought any happiness to England. Some kind of fatality, too, the English imagined to be in her name of Marie, which, it is said, the king rather chose to have her called by than her other, Henrietta, because the land should find a blessing in that name, which had been more unfortunate; but it was not in his power, though a great prince, to control destiny. This lady being by her priests affected with the meritoriousness of advancing her own religion, whose principle it is to subvert all other, applied that way her great wit and parts, and the power her haughty spirit kept over her husband, who was enslaved in his affection only to her, though she had no more passion for him than what served to promote her designs. Those brought her into a very good correspondence with the archbishop and his prelatical crew, both joining in the cruel design of rooting the godly out of the land. The foolish protestants were meditating reconciliations with the church of Rome, who embraced them as far as they would go, carrying them in hand, as if there had been a possibility of bringing such a thing to pass; meanwhile they carried on their design by them, and had so ripened it, that nothing but the mercy of God prevented the utter subversion of protestantism in the three kingdoms.—But how much soever their designs were framed in the dark, God revealed them to his servants, and most miraculously ordered providences for their preservation.   About the year 1639, the Scots, having the English service-book obtruded upon them violently, refused it, and took a national covenant against it, and entered England with a great army, to bring their complaints to the king, which his unfaithful ministers did, as they supposed, much misreport.   The king himself levied an army against them, wherein he was assisted by the nobility and gentry, but most of all by the prelates, insomuch that the war got the name of *bellum episcopale*, or "bishops' war;" but the commonalty of the nation, being themselves under grievous bondage, were loath to oppose a people that came only to claim their just liberties.   When the king was at York, the chief of the Scotch covenanters came, under a pretence of treating with the king, but their principal intent was to disabuse the nobility of England, and to take off their edge against them, by remonstrating upon those grievances and oppressions of the prelatical innovators, which had forced them thus to defend their religion and liberties.   This they did so effectually, that the hearts of the English were much moved towards them, and the king perceiving it, by their mediations, consented to a dissembled peace for that time, and returned home.   But the Scots, unsatisfied in the performance of their articles, made preparation for a second return into England; whereupon the king, in his anger and necessity, was forced to have recourse to the long neglected remedy of parliaments, and assembled one at Westminster the 13th of April, 1640, which he suffered to sit but twenty-one days, and broke it up again, apprehending that if he had suffered them to sit a day longer, they would have voted against the war with Scotland, which he was violently bent to prosecute.

The bishops at that time devised as an anti-covenant, in their convocation house, that execrable oath known by the name

of the *et cætera*, wherein all ministers were required to swear
to uphold the government of the church of England by
archbishops, deans, archdeacons, &c. After this the Scots
enter England, the king makes a second expedition into the
north against them, and sends part of his army to keep the
passes upon the river Tyne; but the soldiers being raw and
heartless in this war, and the commanders themselves inex-
perienced, they were vanquished, and the Scots forced their
way, after they had been refused to pass quietly by, with
their petitions in their hands, and thus possessed themselves of Newcastle and Durham. At that time the Scots
had put forth a declaration, wherein they had affirmed their
intentions not to lay down arms till the reformed religion
was settled in both nations upon sure grounds, and the
causers of these present troubles brought to public justice, and that in a parliament. This was so plausible to the
English, that the king, finding both the hearts and hands of
his people fail him on this occasion, was induced to grant the
petition of twelve noble lords, who at that time interposed ;
and, calling together all his lords at York, agreed upon a
parliament to be convened at London on the third of November following. In the mean time, a treaty was condescended
to, by sixteen lords of each side, Scotch and English, who
agreed upon a cessation between both armies for the present,
in order to a peace, to be concluded at London with the parliament, who met, as appointed, in November.

They began with throwing down monopolies, and then
impeached the Earl of Strafford of high treason, who, after a
solemn trial and hot disputes on both sides, was at length
attainted of treason, and the king, against his own mind, to
serve his ends, gave him up to death.* The archbis op of

* Whoever has read the propositions delivered to his majesty by the
Earl of Strafford, for bridling parliaments and increasing his revenue,
whic. is preserved in the third volume of Ludlow's Memoirs, p. 322, in-

Canterbury was also made prisoner upon an accusation of
high treason, for which he afterwards suffered;* Wren, bishop
of Norwich, was likewise committed to the Tower; several
other prelatical preachers were questioned for popish and
treasonable doctrines; the Star Chamber, an unjust and ar
bitrary court, was taken away, and also the High Commission
Court; an act was procured for a triennial parliament, and
another for the continuation of this, that it should not be
broken up without their own consent. There were great necessities for money by reason of the two armies that were then
maintained in England, and the people would give the king
no money without some ease of grievances, which force l

genious, bold, and dangerous beyond example, will think him richly to
have deserved his fate, but not at the hand of Charles, who herein acted
so treacherously to his friends, that their very adversaries are shocked at
it, and fixed on his reputation a deep and indelible stain; accordingly he
seems all his life long to have borne in mind an incessant regret of this
crime. As it was a thing thought of but little consequence at the time,
perhaps it will ere long be forgotten that Louis the Sixteenth suffered sentence of death to be executed on a Mr. De Favras for planning to assist
him, or his brother, or both to escape, but when he did really effect his
escape in part, there appeared great earnestness and zeal in stopping him!
Did he not merit this !

May says, that the cause of Lord Strafford's condemnation was a note
produced by Sir H. Vane, proving that as a privy counsellor he had proposed to the king to bring his army from Ireland to reduce this kingdom to
obedience; but Ludlow's seems the stronger reason.

* It may well be doubted whether it was justifiable to change the proceedings against Laud from impeachment to attainder, in order to vote his
death, which the law would not have condemned him to; but certainly
deposition and banishment at least were due to the man who brought ruin
and disgrace upon that pure and moderate system of religion of which he
was the unworthy head: that to his conduct its ruin was principally attri-
butable may be clearly seen by the speeches preserved by Rushworth, ir
his fourth volume, of Lord Digby, Falkland, Fiennes, and especially Grim
ston. At this day there is perhaps hardly to be found a son of the church
who would condescend to meddle in such base projects as this archbishop
assiduously employed himself in.

him, against his inclination, to grant those bills, with which, after he had granted, he found he had bound up his own* hands, and therefore privately encouraged plots that were in those times contrived against the parliament. One of them was to have rescued the Earl of Strafford out of prison, and put him at the head of eight thousand Irish, which the king would not consent to disband, when the parliament had some time before moved him to it: then the English army in the north was to have been brought up and engaged against the parliament itself upon a pretence of maintaining the king's prerogative, episcopacy, and some other such things. This plot was managed by Percy, Germyn, Goring, Wilmot, Ashburnham, Pollard, Suckling, O'Neale, and others, of whom some confessed and impeached their fellows, others fled, others were put in prison. While this parliament was sitting, the king would needs, contrary to their desires, take a journey to Scotland, and passed by the two disbanding armies in his journey, where some report that he secretly attempted to urge the Scotch army against the parliament, which then succeeded not. The houses had adjourned for some time, and left a standing committee of fifty to prepare business. About that time a plot was discovered to them from Scotland, against the lives of some of the greatest peers of that kingdom; the committee, fearing the like attempts from the same spring, placed strong guards in divers parts of the city of London. The king's design in going to

* This act for perpetuating the parliament was, in fact, that which gave them a clear ascendancy over the king. The proposing this, as it showed the ingenuity and judgment of Mr. Pierrepont, to whom Mrs. Hutchinson attributes it, so does it the weakness of the king and his counsellors, who having granted this, had no longer any power of refusal left. For extraordinary evils extraordinary remedies are often sought; but this, as it soon proved too strong for the king, so was it at last thought too strong for the people. The omnipotence of parliament would be indeed dreadful alike to both, if, instead of being immovable, it was permanent.

Scotland was variously conjectured; but this was a certain effect of it, that it retarded all the affairs of the government of England, which the king had put into such disorder that it was not an easy task to reform what was amiss, and redress the real grievances of the people; but yet the parliament showed such a wonderful respect to the king, that they never mentioned him, as he was the sole author of all those miscarriages, but imputed them to evil counsellors, and gave him all the submissive language that could have been used to a good prince, fixing all the guilt upon his evil counsellors and ministers of state, which flattery I fear they have to answer for: I am sure they have thereby exposed themselves to much scandal.* While the king was in Scotland, that cursed rebellion in Ireland broke out, wherein above 200,000 were massacred in two months' space, being surprised, and many of them most inhumanly butchered and tormented; and besides the slain, abundance of poor families stripped and sent naked away out of all their possessions; and, had not the providence of God miraculously prevented the surprise of Dublin Castle the night it should have been seized, there had not been any remnant of the protestant name left in that country.   As soon as this sad news came to the parliament, they vigorously set themselves to the work of relieving them; but then the king returned from Scotland, and being sumptuously welcomed home by the city, took courage thereby against the parliament, and obstructed all its proceedings for the effectual relief of Ireland. Long was he before he could be drawn to proclaim these murderers rebels, and when he did, by special command, there were but forty proclamations

* This is an oversight of Mrs. Hutchinson's, of which she is seldom guilty. Good policy required then, as it does now, that the king should be held incapable of wrong, and the criminality fixed on ministers, who are amenable to the law. If the patriots of that day were the inventors of this maxim, we are highly obliged to them.

printed, and care was taken that they should not be much dispersed; which courses afflicted all the good protestants in England, and confirmed them that the rebellion in Ireland received
countenance from the king and queen of England.* The
parliament, beset with so many difficulties, were forced for
their own vindication to present the king with a petition and
a remonstrance on the state of the kingdom, wherein they
spared him as much as truth would bear, and complained
only of his ill counsellors and ministers; but this, instead of
admonishing, exasperated him, and was answered with another declaration of his; and upon several occasions the parliament being enforced to justify their proceedings publicly,
and the king setting forth replies, these open debates were
but the prologue to the ensuing tragedy. The city, declaring
their good affections to the parliament by a petition, gave the
king distrust, and he was observed to entertain an extraordinary guard of cavaliers, who killed and wounded some of
the poor unarmed men that passed by his house at Whitehall; and the parliament, conceiving themselves not safe,
desired a guard might be allowed them under the command
of the Earl of Essex; but he refused it, with an assurance
that he would command such a guard to wait upon them

---

* It would be difficult to draw a distinction so nice as would discrimi-
nate between the countenance shown to the rebels both before and after
the rebellion breaking out, and the encouraging the rebellion itself: now
that passion and prejudice have subsided there are probably many more
that condemn than acquit the king and queen; but whilst the blood of
the massacred protestants yet reeked, and indignation glowed, it was
neither to be wondered at nor blamed that persons the most tolerant, as the
independents professed to be, and Mrs. Hutchinson especially, should speak
with enmity of the queen and catholics, and attribute to them those principles of intolerance and antipathy to protestants which, whether they
professed or not, they practised. It will hereafter been seen that, when
they ceased to be dangerous, Mr. Hutchinson did not persecute, but protect them.

as he would be responsible to Almighty God for, and that the safety of all and every one of them was as dear to him as that of his own person and children. Yet the very next day after this false message, he came to the House of Commons, attended with his extraordinary guard, of about four hundred gentlemen and soldiers, armed with swords and pistols, and there demanded five of their members, whom not finding there (for a great lady at court had before informed one of them of his coming, and the house ordered them to retire,) he returned, leaving the house under a high sense of this breach of their privilege.* At this time the people began in great numbers to bring petitions to the king and parliament, to beg a more cheerful concurrence between them for the relief of Ireland, and to encourage the parliament in their honourable

* The force of opinion being the only real force of any prince, and the notion of inviolability his best protection, it was a strange infatuation in him to overthrow them both.

> Turno tempus erit magno cùm optaverit emptum
> Intactum Pallanta, et cum spolia ista diemque
> Oderit   VIRG. Æn. 10.

> *The time shall come when Turnus, but in vain,*
> *Shall wish untouched the trophies of the slain,*
> *And curse the dire remembrance of that day.*
>   DRYDEN.

An English gentleman, who was resident in France at the time that Louis the Sixteenth sent his guards to the parliament of Paris to seize some the members (one of whom was the famous Duval Despresmenil), and sent out decrees and manifestoes, as has been here just before related, made this remark, " He has entered upon the career of Charles the First, and he will follow it to the end." *Il est entré dans la carriere de Charles I. et il la suivra jusqu'au bout.* When he saw again in England, as emigrants, the same French gentlemen before whom he had made this remark, they reminded him of it ; saying how little probable this had seemed to them at the period of its being spoken, a year before the holding of the states general.

endeavours for the relief of both kingdoms.   The king was
offended at this, and retired first to Hampton Court, then
went with the queen to Canterbury, whom he sent from
thence into Holland with her daughter, lately married to the
Prince of Orange, under pretence of conducting her to her
own court, but really to manage his business abroad, and
procure arms to be employed against the parliament, by the
sale of the crown jewels, which she carried over with her.
After her departure, the king, taking the prince and the Duke
of York with him, went to Theobalds, whither the parliament sent a petition to him to return to his parliament and
abide near London, and that he would not carry the prince
away with him, and that he would grant the militia of the
kingdom to be put into such hands as the parliament should
recommend, and might confide in; all which he denied, and
went immediately to Newmarket, and from thence to York;
all this while, by many false pretences, really obstructing the
relief of bleeding Ireland, and seducing many of the poor
people of England into blood and ruin.

In conducting the state of England, in those days, wherein
he, whose actions I am tracing, began to enter into his part
in this great tragedy, I have been too long for that I intended,
and too short to give a clear understanding of the righteousness of the parliament's cause;* which I shall desire you to
inform yourselves better of by their own printed papers, and
Mr. May's history, which I find to be impartially true, so far as
he hath carried it on, saving some little mistakes in his own
judgment, and misinformations which some vain people gave

* Probably few people will think Mrs. Hutchinson has been too prolix,
many will think that she has been too concise. Mr. May's history comes down
only to September, 1643, which is much to be regretted, as he may justly
be called an impartial and clear historian, but is little read, probably
because his history finishes before that period which was the most
interesting.

of the state, and more indulgence to the king's guilt than can justly be allowed.

To take up my discourse of Mr. Hutchinson where I left it: he was now come to his own house at Owthorpe, about the time when the Irish massacre was acted, and finding humours begin to be very stirring, he applied himself to understand the things then in dispute, and read all the public papers that came forth between the king and parliament, besides many other private treatises, both concerning the present and foregoing times. Hereby he became abundantly informed in his understanding, and convinced in conscience of the righteousness of the parliament's cause in point of civil right; and though he was satisfied of the endeavours to reduce* popery and subvert the true protestant religion, which indeed was apparent to every one that impartially considered it, yet he did not think that so clear a ground for the war as the defence of the just English liberties; and although he was clearly swayed by his own judgment and reason to the parliament, he, thinking he had no warrantable call at that time, to do anything more, contented himself with praying for peace. At that time Mr. Henry Ireton was in the country, and being a kinsman of Mr. Hutchinson's, and one that had received so much advantage to himself and his family in the country by Sir Thomas Hutchinson's countenance and protection, that he seemed a kind of dependent upon him, and being besides a very grave, serious, religious, person, there was a great league of kindness and good-will between them.† Mr. Ireton being very active in promoting he parliament, and the godly interest in the country, found

---

* Reduce, Latin *reducere*, to bring back, restore, revive.

† As it will be seen in the sequel that Mr. Hutchinson reposed a very great confidence in Ireton, and even allowed to the information he received from him such weight in forming his judgment as he did to that of no one

great opposition from some projectors, and others of corrupt
interest that were in the commission of the peace; whereupon,
making complaint at the parliament, he procured some of
them to be put out of the commission, and others, better
affected, to be put in their rooms, of which Mr. Hutchinson
was one; but he then forbore to take his oath, as not willing
to launch out rashly into public employments, while such a

else, it may be well to examine how far the one was deserving, and the other
discerning, in this.

The question will be probably decided to general satisfaction upon the
testimony of Whitelock and Ludlow, men of very different dispositions, but
both of great good sense and knowledge of their subject. Whitelock, in
speaking of some reforms proposed in the election and composition of the
House of Commons, says, " Ireton was chiefly employed in them, having
learned some grounds of law, and having a laborious and working brain and
fancy." When he comes to speak of the reforms of the law which Ireton
likewise meditated, he says, " he was a man full of invention and industry,
who had a little knowledge of the law, which led him into the more errors."
But when by his death the jealousy lest he should bring about those reforms which Whitelock, and most of the lawyers, were averse to, had ceased,
he says of him, page 516, "this gentleman was a person very active,
industrious, and stiff in his ways and purposes; he was of good abilities for
council as well as action, made much use of his pen, and was very forward
to reform the proceedings in law, wherein his having been bred a lawyer
was a great help to him. He was stout in the field, and wary and prudent
in councils; exceedingly forward as to the business of a commonwealth.
Cromwell had a great opinion of him, and no man could prevail so much,
nor order him so far, as Ireton could." But Ludlow, who viewed him
more constantly and closely in a post of great power and temptation, that
of deputy of Ireland, being himself next in command to him, gives the
following account of his conduct in one instance, which will render all
others superfluous. " The parliament also ordered an act to be brought in
for settling two thousand per annum on the lord-deputy Ireton, the news
of which being brought over was so unacceptable to him, that he said, they
had many just debts, which he desired they would pay before they made
any such presents; that he had no need of their land, and would not have
it; and that he should be more contented to see them doing the service
of the nation, than so liberal in disposing of the public treasure."

storm hung threatening over head. Yet his good affections
to godliness and the interest of his country, being a glory
that could not be concealed, many of his honest neighbours made applications to him, and endeavoured to learn his
conduct, which he at first in modesty and prudence would not
too hastily rush into.* The parliament had made orders to
deface the images in all churches. Within two miles of his
house there was a church, where Christ upon the cross, the
virgin, and John, had been fairly set up in a window over the
altar, and sundry other superstitious paintings, of the priest's
own ordering, were drawn upon the walls. When the order
for rasing out those relics of superstition came, the priest
only took down the heads of the images, and laid them carefully up in his closet, and would have had the church officers to have certified that the thing was done according to
order; whereupon they came to Mr. Hutchinson, and desired
him that he would take the pains to come and view their
church, which he did, and upon discourse with the parson,
persuaded him to blot out all the superstitious paintings, and
break the images in the glass; which he consented to, but
being ill-affected, was one of those who began to brand Mr.
Hutchinson with the name of Puritan.

At that time most of the gentry of the country were disaffected to the parliament; most of the middle sort, the able
substantial freeholders, and the other commons, who had not
their dependence upon the malignant nobility and gentry,
adhered to the parliament. These, when the king was at
York, made a petition to him to return to the parliament,
which, upon their earnest entreaty, Mr. Hutchinson went,

* Mr. Hutchinson being born in the latter end of the year 1616, was
only about three and twenty years old at this period; when some may think
this modesty became nim. It was not the fashion of those times to arrive
at the perfection of wisdom and judgment so early as in our days!

with some others, and presented at York ;* where, meeting
his cousins the Byrons, they were extremely troubled to see
him there on that account. After his return, Sir John Byron
being likewise come to his house at Newstead, Mr. Hutchinson went to visit them there, and not finding him, returned
to Nottingham, five miles short of his own house. There
going to the mayor to hear some news, he met with such as
he expected not, for as soon as he came in, the mayor's wife
told him, that the sheriff of the county was come to fetch
away the magazine that belonged to the trained bands of the
county, which was left in her husband's trust; and that her
husband had sent for the country to acquaint them, but she

* Persons of the description which now bears the name of yeomanry,
seem to have been passed over by Charles and his advisers as of little consequence, and perhaps this was the real ground of the grand error they
were in of supposing they had all or most of the strength of the nation
with them, because they had most of the nobility and richer gentry; whereas it was found, when a general movement took place, that the great bulk
of the people was against them, and, like an overwhelming tide, bore down
all before it. Yet he and they had abundant warnings by this and such
like petitions, and by associations which began very early to be entered
into; or still earlier in the expedition against the Scots, wherein the averseness of the common soldiers to the war was so evident, that it compelled
the patching up a peace. " And, astonishing as it might be (says May, p.
64), it was seen that the common people were sensible of public interest
and religion, when lords and gentlemen seemed not to be." It is true that
the mass of the people, having little time for contemplation, are content to
let those to whom affluence gives leisure think for them; but when they
do think for themselves, and strongly adopt a sentiment, he is a bold man,
and ought to have astonishing resources, who contravenes it. That will be
generally, if not always, found the wiser government which informs itself
well as to the real bent of the public mind; and if it is misled by a faction,
takes the way of candour and frankness to dispel the mist of error or prejudice, but avoids to do violence to the general opinion. The editor of this
work is proud of being the first person who, two years before its adoption,
suggested an appeal to the sense and spirit of the nation by the association
of armed volunteers.

feared it would be gone before they could come in. Where-upon Mr. Hutchinson, taking his brother from his lodgings along with him, presently went to the town-hall, and going up to my Lord Newark,* lord lieutenant, told him, that

* Eldest son of the Earl of Kingston, and brother of two Mr. Pierre-ponts mentioned in this work; this nobleman was afterwards created Mar-quis of Dorchester, and will be spoken of under that title in the sequel. In the diary mentioned in the second page of the preface, the dialogue be-tween Lord Newton and Mr. Hutchinson, is set down at full length, and as it may be an object of curiosity to some of our readers, it is here inserted in smaller type.

Mr. Hutchinson asking who were above, was told that the lord lieu-tenant, my Lord Newark, was there, to whom he sent his name and desired to speak with him ; and being come up, found in the room, where the powder was weighing, my Lord Newark, the sheriff Sir John Digby, and two or three captains : Mr. Hutchinson, addressing himself to my lord only, spoke to him:—

H. My lord, hearing that there were some question concerning the coun-ty's powder, I am come to kiss your lordship's hands, and to beseech you that I may know what your desires and intents are concerning it ?

N. Cousin, the king desires to borrow it of the country, to supply his great necessities.

H. I beseech your lordship, what commission have you to demand this ?

N. Upon my honour, I have a commission from his majesty, but it is left behind me ; but I will engage my honour it shall be repaid the country.

H. Your lordship's honour as an engagement, would be accepted for more than I am worth; but in such an occasion as this, the greatest man's engagement in the kingdom, cannot be a satisfaction to the country.

N. The king's intents are only to borrow it, and if the country will not lend it, he will pay for it.

H. My lord, it is not the value of the powder we endeavour to preserve, but in times of danger, as these are, those things which serve for our defence, are not valuable at any price, should you give as many barrels of gold as you take barrels of powder.

N. Upon my faith and honour, cousin, it shall be restored in ten days.

hearing some dispute concerning the country's powder, he was come to wait on his lordship, to know his desires and intents

H. My lord, such is the danger of the times, that for aught we know, we may in less than four days be ruined for want of it; and I beseech your lordship to consider how sad a thing it is in these times of war, to leave a poor country and the people in it, naked and open to the injury of every passenger; for if you take our powder, you may as well take our arms, without which we are unable to make use of them, and I hope your lordship will not disarm the country.

N Why, who should the country fear? I am their lord-lieutenant, and engaged with my life and honour to defend them! What danger are they in?

H. Danger! yes, my lord, great danger; there is a troop of horse now in the town, and it hath often happened so that they have committed great outrages and insolencies, calling divers honest men puritans and rogues, with divers other provoking terms and carriages. I myself was abused by some of them, as I passed on the road. I chanced to meet some of these gentlemen, who, as soon as I was past, inquired my name, and being told it, gave me another, saying among themselves, that I was a puritan and a traitor; as two or three honest men that came behind told me. Besides, your lordship may be far off, and we ruined before you can come to us, being unarmed, and not able to defend ourselves from any body, and this country being a road through which, under the name of soldiers, rude people daily pass from the north to south, and terrify the country; which if they knew to be naked and unarmed, they would thereby be encouraged to greater insolencies and mischiefs.

N. The king's occasions are such, and so urgent, as I cannot dispense with it for any reasons, but must needs have it.

H. I hope your lordship will not deny that the country hath a right, interest, and property in it.

N. I do not deny it.

H. Then, my lord, I hope his majesty will not command it from them

N. No, he doth but desire to borrow it.

H. Then, I hope, if he do but desire to borrow it, his majesty hath signified his request to those that have interest in it, under his hand.

N. Upon my honour he hath, but I left it behind me.

H. I beseech your lordship, then, that you would not take it away till you have acquainted the country with it, who only have power to lend it; and if your lordship be pleased to do this, I will engage myself that by

concerning it.   My lord answered him, that the king, having
great necessities, desired to borrow it of the country.   Mr.

to-morrow at twelve of the clock, that part of the country who have interest
in the powder shall all wait on your lordship, and give you their resolutions.

N. The king's occasions cannot admit of that delay.

H. I beseech of your lordship, yet be pleased to consider the dangerous
consequence of taking it without the country's consent, and be pleased but
to stay till they can come in.

N. That time is more than his majesty's necessities can dispense withal.

With that Mr. Hutchinson went down stairs, where by that time a good
company of the country were gathered together, to whom Mr. Hutchinson
told what my lord had said to him, and they desired him that he would
but stand to them, and they would part with every drop of blood out of
their bodies before he should have it; and said besides, that they would go
up and break my lord's neck and the sheriff's out of the windows; but
Mr. Hutchinson desired them to stay below, till he had once more spoken
to my lord, and then, taking only one or two more with him, went up and
spoke to my lord.

H. My lord, I am again, at the request of the country, that are below,
come to your lordship, and do once more humbly beseech you to consider
the business you are about, before you proceed further in it, for it may
prove of dangerous consequence if you go on.

N. Cousin, I am confident it cannot, for the country will not deny this
to the king.

H. It's very probable they will not, if your lordship please to have
patience till they can be called in, that they may be acquainted with his
majesty's desire .

N. His majesty is very well assured of the willingness and cheerfulness
of the greater part of the country to it.

H. My lord, I do not know what assurance his majesty hath of it, but if
you please to look out of this window (pointing to the countrymen below
in the streets), you will see no inconsiderable number gathered, who, I fear,
will not be willing to part with it.

N. Those are but some few factious men, not to be considered.

H. My lord, we have been happy yet, in these unhappy differences, to
have had no blood shed, and I am confident your lordship is so noble and
tender of your country, that it would very much trouble you to have a
hand in the first man's blood that should be spent in this quarrel.

N. Cousin, it cannot come to that, fear it not (this was spoken very

Hutchinson asked my lord what commission he had from his majesty. My lord told him he had one, but he had left it slightly and contemptuously), his majesty's occasions are urgent, and must be served.

(With that, the country came very fast up, which when the cavalier captains saw, they slunk down.)

H. Why then, my lord, I must plainly tell you, not one here but will lose every drop of blood in his body, before he will part with one corn of it, without your lordship can show either a command or a request for it under his majesty's hand and seal, or that the country be called together to give their free consent to it, for we have all property and interest in it, being members of this county, and it being bought with our money, for the particular defence and safety of the same.

My lord desired to borrow part of it, but that being denied, he turned to Sir John Digby and took him to the window, where, after he had whispered with him a while, Sir John Digby laid down his pen, ink, and paper, with which he had been taking an account of the powder, match, and bullet. The countrymen desired my lord aloud, that he would not take away their powder out of the country ; upon which, turning to them, he thus spoke :—

" Gentlemen,—His majesty was assured by some of the cheerfulness of this country's affections to him, which I am very sorry to see them so much failing in, and that the country should come so much short of this town, which hath cheerfully lent his majesty one barrel of powder, but it seems he can have none from you; I pray God you do not repent this carriage of yours towards his majesty, which he must be acquainted withal."

A countryman, standing forth, asked his lordship this question, " Whether, if he were to take a journey into a place where probably he might be set upon by thieves and robbers, and having a charge about him, if any friend should ask him to lend his sword, he would part with it and go himself without ?" My lord, the case is ours; our wives, children, and estates, all depend upon this country's safety; and how can it be safe in these dangerous times, when so many troops and companies pass through and commit outrages and abuses among us, if we have not arms and powder wherewith to defend us !

My lord made no reply, but bade the men whom he had employed to weigh up the powder desist; and so went down the stairs. Mr. Hutchinson followed him, and as he went, an ancient gentleman, who was with my lord, whose face and name were both unknown to him, came to him and

behind. Mr. Hutchinson replied, that my lord's affirmation was satisfactory to him, but the country would not be willing

said these words : " Stand to it; I'll warrant you, gentlemen, it is well done." And as they passed through a low room, my lord took Mr. Hutchinson aside, and said,—

N. Cousin, I must acquaint the king with this !

H. My lord, it is very likely you must, being employed upon his majesty's service, give him an account.

N. Nay, cousin (smiling), I mean not so; but I must acquaint him, and I am sorry I must, that you are the head and ringleader of a faction, whereby you hinder his majesty's service.

H. My lord, I do not conceive how this can be a faction, I speaking only, out of the noble respect and honour I bear your lordship, in private to you, to prevent a mischief, the sense of these men, who I perceived were come to know by what authority, and why, their powder, which is their proper goods, and only means of safety in these times of danger, should be taken from them; and if it were a faction, I am not the head of it; I, accidentally coming to town from Sir John Byron's last night, and neither knowing nor imagining any of this business, was this morning importuned to wait on your lordship, at the town's hall, by many countrymen, who informed me you were taking away their powder out of the country.

N. Cousin, if you can answer it I shall be glad of it ; but I will assure you I must let his majesty know.

H. If his majesty must know it, I am very happy I spoke to none but your lordship; who, I am confident, is so noble, that you will neither add nor diminish anything to my prejudice; and then I am confident the justness and reasonableness of what I have said, with my own innocency in speaking it, will bear me out.

N. I, cousin, but your name is up already.

H. It may be so, my lord; and I believe those that set it up had no good wishes to me; and as it rose, so, in the name of God let it fall; for I know my own clearness and innocency in anything that can be objected against me.

N. Well, cousin, well; I am glad of your good resolution.

And so my lord left him. The gentlemen of the country that were there, upon consideration, what they should do with their powder, determined to return my lord thanks for sparing it, and to lock it up with two locks, whereof the sheriff should have one key, and the mayor another; which accordingly was done; but Mr Hutchinson came no more to my lord.

to part with their powder in so dangerous a time, without an absolute command. My lord urged that he would restore it in ten days. Mr. Hutchinson replied, they might have use for it sooner, and he hoped my lord would not disarm his country in such a time of danger. My lord contemned the mention of danger, and asked what they could fear while he was their lord-lieutenant, and ready to serve them with his life. Mr. Hutchinson told him they had some grounds to apprehend danger by reason of the daily passing of armed men through the country, whereof there was now one troop in the town, and that before they could repair to my lord, they might be destroyed in his absence, and withal urged to him examples of their insolence; but my lord replied to all, the urgency of the king's occasions for it, which were such that he could not dispense with it. It was in vain to argue with him the property the country had in it, being bought with their money, and therefore not to be taken without their consent; my lord declared himself positively resolved to take it, whereupon Mr. Hutchinson left him. There were in the room with him Sir John Digby, the high sheriff of the county, who was setting down the weight of the powder and match, and two or three captains and others, that were busy weighing the powder. By the time Mr. Hutchinson came down, a good company of the country was gathered together; whom Mr. Hutchinson acquainted with what had passed between him and my lord, and they told him that if he would but please to stand by them, they would part with all their blood before he should have a corn of it; and said, moreover, they would go up and tumble my lord and the sheriff out of the windows. Mr. Hutchinson, seeing them so resolved, desired them to stay below while he went up yet once again to my lord, which they did; and he told my lord some of the country were come in, at whose request he was again come to beseech his lordship to desist from his design, which if pursued might be of dangerous consequence. My lord replied, it could not be, for the king was very well assured of the cheerful compliance of the greatest part of the country with his service. Mr. Hutchinson told him, whatever assurance his majesty might have, if his lordship pleased to look out, he might see no inconsiderable number below that would not willingly part with it. My lord replied, they were but a few factious men; whereupon Mr. Hutchinson told him, since it was yet the happiness of these unhappy times that no blood had been spilt, he should be sorry the first should be shed upon my lord's occasion, in his own country. My lord scornfully replied, Fear it not, it cannot come to that, the king's occasions are urgent and must be served. Whereupon Mr. Hutchinson, looking out at the countrymen, they came very fast up the stairs; and Mr. Hutchinson told him, however he slighted it, not one was there but would part with every drop of his blood before they would part with it, except he could show a command or request for it under the king's hand, or would stay till the country were called in to give their consent; for it was their property, and all had interest in it, as bought with their money for the particular defence of the country. Then my lord fell to entreaties to borrow part of it, but that being also denied, he took the sheriff aside, and, after a little conference, they put up their books and left the powder; when my lord, turning to the people, said to them, " Gentlemen, his majesty was by some assured of the cheerfulness of this country's affections to him, whereof I am sorry to see so much failing, and that the county should fall so much short of the town, who have cheerfully lent his majesty one barrel of powder, but it seems he can have none from you; I pray God you do not repent this carriage of yours towards his majesty, which he must be acquainted withal." A bold countryman then stepping forth, by way of reply, asked my lord, whether, if he were to take a journey

with a charge into a place where probably he should be set
upon by thieves, if any friend should ask to borrow a sword
he would part with it: my lord, said he, the case is ours;
our lives, wives, children, and estates, all depend upon this
country's safety; and how can it be safe in these dangerous
times, when so many rude armed people pass daily through
it, if we be altogether disarmed? My lord made no reply,
but bade the men who were weighing the powder desist, and
went down. Mr. Hutchinson followed him down the stairs,
when an ancient gentleman, that was sitting with my lord,
came and whispering him, commended his and the country's
zeal, and bade them stand to it, and they would not be foiled.
As they passed through a long room below, my lord told
Mr. Hutchinson he was sorry to find him at the head of a
faction. Mr. Hutchinson replied, he could not tell how his
lordship could call that a faction which arose from the accident of his being at that time in the town; where, hearing
what was in hand, and out of respect to his lordship, he only
came to prevent mischief and danger, which he saw likely to
ensue. My lord replied, he must inform the king, and told
him his name was already up; to which Mr. Hutchinson answered, that he was glad, if the king must receive an information of him, that it must be from so honourable a person;
and for his name, as it rose, so in the name of God let it
fall; and so took his leave and went home. The rest of the
country that were there, determined to give my lord thanks
for sparing their ammunition, and locked it up with two
locks, whereof the key of the one was entrusted with the
mayor of Nottingham, the other with the sheriff of the
county, which accordingly was done.*

* How my lord may have reported this matter to the king signifies
little; but he probably remembered as a kindness Mr. Hutchinson's interposition between him and the more rough arguments of the countrymen;

In the mean time, at York, the king had sent the parliament a message, that he intended to go in person to Ireland, and to raise a guard for his own person, about West Chester, which he would arm out of his magazine at Hull. But the parliament, having before intercepted a letter of the Lord Digby's, sent to the queen from Middleburgh in Zealand, wherein he intimated, that, if the king would retire to some safe place, and declare himself, he should be able to wait upon him from thence, &c. Upon this letter, and other presumptions, they suspected that the chief end of the king's going northward was to seize the magazine at Hull, and arm himself from thence against them ; wherefore they sent a petition, for leave to remove that magazine to the tower of London, and accordingly had sent Sir John Hotham thither to do it. Sir John prevented the Earl of Newcastle, whom the king had sent for the same purpose, to seize the magazine, and kept him out; at which the king was much incensed, and on the 23d of April, 1642, went himself to Hull, attended with some noblemen, gentlemen, and soldiers, and demanded entrance ; but the gates were shut ; and Hotham, kneeling upon the wall, entreated the king not to command that which, without breach of trust, he could not obey.

In conclusion, the king not getting entrance, proclaimed Hotham a traitor, and sent a complaint of the affront to the parliament. The parliament justified Hotham. Many declarations about it were published on both sides, and many cross-commands ; the parliament authorizing Hotham to issue out warrants to constables and other officers, to come in armed to the defence of Hull, and the king forbidding it. The king meanwhile in the north, summoned divers of the nobility and gentry to attend him, and made speeches to them to desire a guard for his person, pretending danger from

for there appears to have existed, on all suitable occasions, an intercourse of friendship during the remainder of their lives.

the parliament. He then began to entertain soldiers, and was much encouraged by the defection of divers lords and many of the Commons' house, who forsook their trust and came to him at York; whereupon he called those who remained only a faction, a pretended parliament, and such names; but they continued still petitioning to him, and the well-affected and godly, in all countries, did the like, that he would return to his parliament. The papists all over England were high partakers with him and promoters of his designs, and all the debauched nobility and gentry, and their dependents, and the lewder rout of people; yet even of these there were some that had English hearts, who came in to the parliament; but finding afterwards that the advance of liberty and righteousness could not consist with riot and ungodliness, they forsook their party, and were content to be the king's slaves rather than divorce themselves from those lusts, which found countenance from both priests and princes on one side, and on the other were preached down by the ministers, and punished by the magistrates.*

Towards the end of May, the parliament sent the king word, that if he would not disband his forces, and rely upon the laws and affections of his people for his security, as all good princes before him had done, they held themselves bound in duty to God and the people's trust reposed in them, and by the fundamental laws, to employ their utmost care and power for securing the parliament and preserving the

* Whatever may be said at this day of the hypocrisy of the religionists of those times, the most that can possibly be allowed is, that their professions might somewhat outgo their practice; but this must in some degree befall every Christian. No one can deny that, instead of captivating vulgar minds by breaking the bonds of morality, as modern demagogues have done, the forefathers of our liberties set the pattern of a religious and decent conduct, and caused the same to be observed in their armies with an exactness that surprises us, and of which rigour many striking examples are to be found in Whitelock's Memorials.

kingdom's peace.   Whereupon they voted, "That it seems that
the king, seduced by wicked counsel, intends a war against
the parliament, &c.

" That whensoever the king makes war upon the parliament, it is a breach of the trust reposed in him by the people,
contrary to his oath, and tending to the dissolution of this
government.

" That whosoever shall assist him in such wars are traitors,
by the fundamental laws of this kingdom, and have been so
adjudged in two acts of parliament, 11 Richard II. and
1 Henry IV. ; and that such persons ought to suffer as
traitors."

Hereupon nine of the lords, that first went to the king,
were summoned to return ; who, sending a letter of denial,
were, by the whole house of peers, sentenced to be incapable
of ever sitting again as members of that house, or of benefi
or privilege of parliament, and to suffer imprisonment during
pleasure.   Then the lord keeper, who had appeared firm to
the parliament, and voted with them, for settling the militia
by ordinance of parliament, ran away to the king, after he
had delivered up his seal, the day before, to one the king sen
for it.   The king, having this, issued out many proclamations,
and among the rest, one that no man should obey the parliament's warrants about settling the militia.   The parliament,
on the other side, made ordinances forbidding all men to
raise arms, by warrant from the king, without authority of
parliament.   And now they began to settle the kingdom's
militia, both by land and sea, and made the Earl of Warwick
admiral ; which place the king had conferred upon Sir John
Pennington, in the room of the Earl of Northumberland, and
commanded my lord of Warwick to resign ; but he chose
to obey the parliament, and got the fleet at length wholly
into his hands, and took a ship with ammunition coming to
the king out of Holland.   The parliament now, despairing

of the king's return, made an ordinance for money and plate
to be brought in, and for raising arms for the cause; which
came in, in great abundance, upon public faith, and likewise
horses and arms for the service. The king, who had received
money, arms, and ammunition, which the queen had procured
in Holland, by pawning the crown jewels, sent out commissions of array, to arm the people in all counties; and
mocked the parliament, using their own words, wherein
they invited men to arm for the defence of the protestant
religion, the king's person, dignity, and authority, the laws
of the land, the peace of the kingdom, and privilege of
parliament; and thus he deceived many people, and got
contributions of plate, money, and arms in the country.
While these things were in transaction, the king made a
solemn protestation before the lords, as in the presence of
God, declaring that he would not engage them in any war
against the parliament, but only for his necessary defence;
that his desire was to maintain the protestant religion, the
liberties of the subject, and privilege of parliament. But
the next day he did some action, so contrary to this protestation, that two of the lords durst not stay with him, but returned to the parliament; and one of them, coming back
through Nottinghamshire, acquainted Mr. Hutchinson with
the sad sense he had in discovering that falsehood in the
king.

Now had the king raised an army of three thousand foot
and one thousand horse, with which he went to Beverley, in
order to besiege Hull. When he was within two hours'
march of the place, Sir John Hotham floated the country
about it, and Sir John Meldrum, sallying out of the town,
with five hundred townsmen, made the king's party retreat to
Beverley. But, however, they beleaguered the town, into
which the parliament sent a relief of five hundred men, by
water, with whom Meldrum made another sally, routed the

leaguer-soldiers, killed some, made others prisoners, took the
magazine of arms and ammunition, which was in a barn, with
their fire-balls, and fired the barn. Hereupon the king's
council of war broke up the siege, from whence the king
went back to York, and about the middle of August came to
Nottingham, where he set up his standard royal ; and hither
his two nephews, Prince Rupert and Prince Maurice, came
to him, and were put into commands. The king, marching
through Nottingham, Derby, and Leicestershire, called together
the trained bands, to attend him, disarmed those counties,
and marched to Shrewsbury, and there set up a mint, and
coined the plate that had been brought in to him. Here a
great many men came in to him, with whom, marching into
Warwickshire, he there fought his first battle at a village
called Keynton ;* it not being yet agreed who gained the
victory that day.

   As the king, on his part, made this progress, so the parliament, on theirs, upon the twelfth of July, voted an army to
be raised, and the Earl of Essex to be general of it. Divers
of the lords, and several members of the House of Commons,
took commissions, and raised regiments and companies under
his command, who marched with his army of about fourteen
thousand horse and foot to his rendezvous at Northampton,
whither the parliament sent a petition to him, to be delivered
to the king, in a safe and honourable way ; the sum of which
was, to beseech him to forsake those wicked people with
whom he was, and not to mix his danger with theirs, but to
return to his parliament, &c. The king, intending to make
Worcester a garrison, sent Prince Rupert thither ; the Earl
of Essex, to prevent him, sent other forces, between whom

   * Commonly called Edge-hill fight. Both king and parliament claimed
the victory, but our authoress shows rather more candour than either. The
king's main design of marching to London was however frustrated, and
therefore the parliament might be most properly termed gainers.

there was some skirmish, but the prince left the town at their approach. My lord of Essex left a garrison in Northampton, put others into Coventry and Warwick, and went to Worcester. Here he made some stay, till the king, marching from Shrewsbury, occasioned some apprehension of his going up to London; for which cause my lord left part of his artillery behind him, and followed the king's motions, which the king perceiving, took an opportunity, before his artillery and the foot left with it were come up to him, and resolved to give him battle, which was not declined on the other side, but fought with doubtful success, the circumstances whereof may be read at large in the stories of those things. The king's general was slain, and his standard was taken though not kept; but on the other side also there were many brave men slain and prisoners. My lord of Essex marched to Coventry; the king took up his winter quarters at Oxford, from whence Prince Rupert flew about the country with his body of horse, plundered and did many barbarous things; insomuch that London, growing into apprehensions of the king's army, the parliament called back the Earl of Essex to quarter about London; and he being returned thither, the king was advanced as far as Colebrooke, where he was presented with a petition from the parliament for accommodation, to which he answered, with a protestation to God, how much he was grieved for his subjects' sufferings, and, in order to peace, was willing to reside near London, to receive their propositions, and to treat with them. As soon as ever the commissioners were gone, the king advanced, with his horse and artillery, towards London, and, taking the advantage of a great mist, fell upon a broken regiment of Colonel Hollis's, quartered at Brentford, and killed many of them, and had destroyed them all, but that Brooke's and Hampden's regiments, by Providence, came seasonably to their rescue; and then so many forces flocked with the general, out of London,

I 2

that the king was enclosed, and the war had been ended, but that, I know not how, three thousand of the parliament's forces were called away by their procurement who designed the continuance of the war; and so the king had a way of retreat left open, by which he got back to Oxford, and the parliament's general was sent out again* with their army; whose proceedings I shall take up again in their due places, so far as is necessary to be remembered, for the story I most particularly intend.

Before the flame of the war broke out in the top of the chimneys, the smoke ascended in every country; the king had sent forth commissions of array, and the parliament had given out commissions for their militia, and sent off their members into all counties to put them in execution. Between these, in many places, there were fierce contests and disputes, almost to blood, even at the first; for in the progress every county had the civil war, more or less, within itself. Some counties were in the beginning so wholly for the parliament, that the king's interest appeared not in them; some so wholly for the king, that the godly, for those generally were the parliament's friends, were forced to forsake their habitations, and seek other shelters: of this sort was Nottinghamshire. All the nobility and gentry, and their dependents, were generally for the king; the chief of whose names I shall sum up here, because I shall often have occasion to mention them. The greatest family was the Earl of Newcastle's,† a lord once

* The account Mrs. Hutchinson gives of the affair of Brentford is much more clear and probable than that given by Rapin, vol. ii. p. 465. Indeed, he himself seems dissatisfied with those varying accounts he could collect of that business from Clarendon and others; but Ludlow, who was a military man and an eye-witness, gives a clear account, agreeing with that of Mrs. Hutchinson.

† This title was at that time in the family of Cavendish, of which this line ceased with the nobleman here mentioned.

so much beloved in his country, that when the first expedition was against the Scots, the gentlemen of the country set him forth two troops, one all of gentlemen, the other of their men, who waited on him into the north at their own charges. He had, indeed, through his great estate, his liberal hospitality, and constant residence in his country, so endeared them to him, that no man was a greater prince in all that northern quarter; till a foolish ambition of glorious slavery carried him to court, where he ran himself much into debt, to purchase neglects of the king and queen, and scorns of the proud courtiers. Next him was the Earl of Kingston, a man of vast estate, and no less covetous, who divided his sons between both parties, and concealed himself; till at length his fate drew him to declare himself absolutely on the king's side, wherein he behaved himself honourably, and died remarkably. His eldest son* was lord-lieutenant of the county, and at that time no nobleman had a greater reputation in the court for learning and generosity than he; but he was so high in the king's party, that the parliament was very much incensed against him. Lord Chesterfield, and all his family, were high in the royal party; so was the Lord Chaworth. The Earl of Clare was very often of both parties, and, I think, never advantaged either. All the popish gentry were wholly for the king, whereof one Mr. Golding, next neighbour to Mr. Hutchinson, had been a private collector of the catholics' contributions to the Irish Rebellion, and for that was, by the queen's procurement, made a knight and baronet. Sir John Byron, afterwards Lord Byron, and all his brothers, bred up in arms, and valiant men in their own persons, were all passionately the king's. Sir John Savill, a man of vast estate, was the like: so were Sir Gervas Eyre, Sir John Digby, Sir

* Lord Newark, before spoken of. In Collins's Peerage, under the title of Duke of Kingston, there are cited singular proofs of this nobleman's learning.

Matthew Palmer, Sir Thomas Williamson, Sir Roger Cowper, Sir W. Hickman, Sir Hugh Cartwright, Sir T. Willoughby, Sir Thomas Smith, Sir Thomas Blackwell, Markham, Perkins, Tevery, Pearce, Palme, Wood, Sanderson, Moore, Mellish, Butler, with divers others. Of the parliament men, Mr. Sutton, afterwards Lord Lexington, and Sir Gervas Clifton, forsook the parliament, went to the king, and executed his commission of array. Mr. William Stanhope left the parliament, and came home disaffected to them; whose eldest son was afterwards slain in the king's service. Mr. William Pierrepont,* second son of the Earl of Kingston, was of the parliament, though he served not for his own country, to which notwithstanding he was an ornament, being one of the wisest counsellors and most excellent speakers in the house, and by him was that bill promoted and carried on which passed for the continuation of this parliament. He had a younger brother living at Nottingham, who coldly owned the parliament. Sir Thomas Hutchinson continued with the parlia-

---

* From this gentleman the late Duke of Kingston and the present Earl Manvers are lineally descended. His wisdom as a politician is sufficiently evinced by this masterly stroke, which decided the fate of the king and the parliament. Of his moderation Whitelock speaks repeatedly. Of his eloquence there are preserved by Rushworth some specimens, from one of which is extracted this as a singular trait of candour and delicacy:—" It is pleasing to the nature of man that others should obey his will, and well-framed dispositions of princes may easily be persuaded their power is unlimited, when they are also put in mind that they have therefore more cause to do well, and for doing well are more renowned. For the most oppressive designs we have suffered under, the pretences to his majesty have been the good of his subjects : his is the sin, who is to judge by the laws, who knows the laws are to the contrary, yet puts and confirms such thoughts in his prince. He that incites another to arbitrary government usually doth it for self-ends, and when they are compassed, hates him for taking that power he himself persuaded him unto." This will be found an elegant solution of the paradox which appears in the character given by Mrs. Hutchinson of Charles the First, "that so good a man should make so bad a prince."

ment, was firm to their cause, but infinitely desirous that the
difference might rather have been composed by accommodation, than ended by conquest; and therefore did not improve
his interest to engage the country in the quarrel, which, if he
could have prevented, he would not have had come to a war.
He was, however, clearly on the parliament's side, and never
discouraged his two sons, who thought this prudential tardi-
ness in their father was the declension of that vigour which
they derived from him, and which better became their youth.
It is true, they were the foremost in point of time and in
degree, except a piece of a nobleman that was afterwards
drawn in, who owned the parliament's interest in their country.
Mr. Henry Ireton, their cousin, was older than they, and
having had an education in the strictest way of godliness, and
being a very grave and solid person, a man of good learning,
great understanding, and other abilities, to which was joined
a willing and zealous heart in the cause and his country, he
was the chief promoter of the parliament's interest in the
county; but finding it generally disaffected, all he could do,
when the king approached it, was to gather a troop of those
godly people which the cavaliers drove out, and with them
to go into the army of my lord of Essex; which he, being
a single person, could better do.   Mr. Hutchinson was not
willing so soon to quit his house, to which he was so lately
come, if he could have been suffered to live quietly in it;
but his affections to the parliament being taken notice of, he
became an object of envy to the other party.

   Sir Thomas Hutchinson, a little before the standard was
set up, had come to Nottingham, where his house was, to
see his children and refresh himself; when, hearing of the
king's intentions to come to the town, he, some days before
his coming, went over to Owthorpe, his son's house, to remain
there till he could fit himself to return to the parliament.
One day, as Mr. Hutchinson was at dinner, the mayor of

Nottingham sent him word that the high-sheriff had broken open the lock of the country's ammunition, which was left in his trust, and was about to take it away.   Mr. Hutchinson immediately went in all haste to prevent it, but before he came to the town it was gone, and some of the king's soldiers were already come to town, and were plundering all the honest men of their arms.   As one of them had taken a musket, seeing Mr. Hutchinson go by, he said he wished it loaded for his sake, and hoped the day would shortly come when all such roundheads would be fair marks for them. This name of roundhead coming so opportunely in, I shall make a little digression to tell how it came up.   When puritanism grew into a faction, the zealots distinguished themselves, both men and women, by several affectations of habit, looks, and words, which, had it been a real forsaking of vanity, and an embracing of sobriety in all those things, would have been most commendable ; but their quick forsaking of those things, when they had arrived at their object, showed that they either never took them up for conscience, or were corrupted by their prosperity to take up those vain things they durst not practice under persecution.   Among other affected habits, few of the puritans, what degree soever they were of, wore their hair long enough to cover their ears, and the ministers and many others cut it close round their heads, with so many lit*le peaks, as was something ridiculous to behold ; whereupon Cleaveland, in his Hue and Cry after them, begins,

" With hayre in Characters and Luggs in Text," &c.

From this custom of wearing their hair, that name of round-head became the scornful term given to the whole parliament party, whose army indeed marched out as if they had been only sent out till their hair was grown.   Two or three years

after, any stranger that had seen them, would have inquired
the reason of that name. It was very ill applied to Mr.
Hutchinson, who, having naturally a very fine thickset head
of hair, kept it clean and handsome, so that it was a great
ornament to him; although the godly of those days, when he
embraced their party, would not allow him to be religious
because his hair was not in their cut, nor his words in their
phrase, nor such little formalities altogether fitted to their
humour; who were, many of them, so weak as to esteem such
insignificant circumstances, rather than solid wisdom, piety,
and courage, which brought real aid and honour to their
party. But as Mr. Hutchinson chose not them, but the God
they served, and the truth and righteousness they defended,
so did not their weaknesses, censures, ingratitude, or dis-
couraging behaviour, with which he was abundantly exercised
all his life, make him forsake them in any thing wherein they
adhered to just and honourable principles or practices; but
when they apostatised from these, none cast them off with
greater indignation, how shining soever the profession was
that gilt, not a temple of living grace, but a tomb, which
only held the carcase of religion. Instead of digressing, I
shall ramble into an inextricable wilderness, if I pursue this
sad remembrance: to return therefore to his actions at that
time.

When he found the powder gone, and saw the soldiers
taking up quarters in the town, and heard their threats and
revilings, he went to his father's house in the town, where
he had not been long before an uncivil fellow stepped into the
house, with a carabine in his hand. Mr. Hutchinson asked
what he would have; the man replied, he came to take possession of the house; Mr. Hutchinson told him, he had the
possession of it, and would know on what right it was
demanded from him; the man said, he came to quarter the
general there; Mr. Hutchinson told him, except his father

and mother, and their children, were turned out of doors,
there was no room. The quarter-master, upon this, growing
insolent, Mr. Hutchinson thrust him out of the house, and
shut the doors upon him. Immediately my lord of Lindsey
came himself, in a great chafe, and asked who it was that
denied him quarter? Mr. Hutchinson told him, he that
came to take it up for him deserved the usage he had, for his
uncivil demeanour; and those who had quartered his lordship
there had much abused him, the house being no ways fit to
receive a person of his quality, which, if he pleased to take a
view of it, he would soon perceive. Whereupon my lord,
having seen the rooms, was very angry they had made no
better provision for him, and would not have lain in the
house, but they told him the town was so full that it was
impossible to get him room any where else. Hereupon he
told Mr. Hutchinson, if they would only allow him one room,
he would have no more; and when he came upon terms of
civility, Mr. Hutchinson was as civil to him, and my lord only
employed one room, staying there, with all civility to those
that were in the house. As soon as my lord was gone, Mr.
Hutchinson was informed by a friend, that the man he had
turned out of doors was the quarter-master general, who,
upon his complaint, had procured a warrant to seize his
person; whereupon Mr. Hutchinson, with his brother, went
immediately home to his own house at Owthorpe. About
four or five days after, a troop of cavaliers, under the command
of Sir Lewis Dives, came to Stanton, near Owthorpe, and
searched Mr. Needham's house, who was a noted puritan in
those days, and a colonel in the parliament's service, and
governor of Leicester: they found not him, for he hid himself in the gorse, and so escaped them. His house being
lightly plundered, they went to Hickling, and plundered
another puritan house there, and were coming to Owthorpe,
of which Mr. Hutchinson having notice, went away to

Leicestershire; but they, though they had orders to seize Mr. Hutchinson, came not at that time because the nigh grew on. But some days after he was gone, another company came and searched for him and for arms and plate, of which finding none, they took nothing else.

Two days after Mr. Hutchinson was in Leicestershire, he sent for his wife, who was then big with child, to come thither to him; where she had not been a day, but a letter was brought him from Nottingham, to give him notice that there was a warrant sent to the sheriff of Leicestershire to seize his person. Upon this he determined to go the next day into Northamptonshire, but at five of the clock that evening, the sound of their trumpets told him a troop was coming into the town. He stayed not to see them, but went out at the other end as they came in; who, by a good providence for his wife (somewhat afflicted to be so left alone in a strange place), proved to be commanded by her own brother, Sir Allen Apsley, who quartered in the next house to that where she was, till about two or three days before all the king's horse that were thereabouts marched away, being commanded upon some service to go before the rest.

Mr. Hutchinson, in the mean time, was carried by a servant that waited on him, to the house of a substantial honest yeoman, who was bailiff to the lord of the town * of Kelmarsh, in Northamptonshire. This man and his wife, being godly, gave Mr. Hutchinson very kind entertainment, and prevailed upon him to be acquainted with their master, who had just then made plate and horses ready to go in to the king, that had now set up his standard at Nottingham; but Mr. Hutchinson diverted him, and persuaded him and another gentle-man of quality, to carry in those aids they had provided for the king, to my lord general Essex, who was then at North-

* It is customary, in Nottinghamshire, to call every village of any size a town.

ampᵗon, where Mr. Hutchinson visited him, and would gladly at that time have engaged with him, but that he did not then find a clear call from the Lord; and therefore, intelligence being brought of the king's removal, he was now returning to his wife, when unawares he came into a town, where one of Prince Rupert's troops was; which he narrowly escaped, and returning to his former honest host, sent a letter to his wife, to acquaint her what hazard he was in by attempting to come to her, but that as soon as the horse was marched away, he would be with her. This letter was intercepted at Prince Rupert's quarters, and opened and sent her. There was with Prince Rupert, at that time, one Captain Welch, who having used to come to Captain Apsley, and seen Mrs. Hutchinson with him, made a pretence of civility to visit her that day that all the prince's horse marched away. They marched by the door of the house where she was, and all the household having gone out to see them, had left her alone in the house, with Mr. George Hutchinson, who was in her chamber when Captain Welch came in, and she went down into the parlour to receive him. He, taking occasion to tell her of her husband's letter, by way of compliment, said it was a pity she should have a husband so unworthy of her, as to enter into any faction which should make him not dare to be seen with her; whereat she being piqued, and thinking they were all marched away, told him he was mistaken, she had not a husband that would at any time hide himself from him, or that durst not show his face where any honest man durst appear; and to confirm you, said she, he shall now come to you. With that she called down her brother, who, upon a private hint, owned the name of husband, which she gave him, and received a compliment from Welch, that in any other place he had been obliged to make him a prisoner, but here he was in sanctuary; and so, after some little discourse, went away   When the gentleman of the house and the rest of the family, that had been seeing the march, were returned, and while they sat laughing together, at those that went to see the prince, telling how some of the neighbouring ladies were gone along with him, and Mrs. Hutchinson telling how she had abused the captain, with Mr. Hutchinson instead of her husband, the captain came back, bringing another gentleman with him; and he told Mr. Hutchinson, that his horse having lost a shoe, he must be his prisoner till the smith released him. But they had not sat long, ere a boy came in with two pistols, and whispered the captain, who desiring Mr. Hutchinson and the gentleman of the house to walk into the next room, seized Mr. George, in the name of Mr. John Hutchinson. It booted not for them both to endeavour to undeceive him, by telling him Mr. John was still at Northampton, for he would not, at least would seem not, to believe them, and carried him away, to be revenged of Mrs. Hutchinson, at whom he was vexed for having deluded him. So, full of wicked joy, to have found an innocent gentleman, whom he knew the bloodhounds were after, he went and informed the prince, and made it of such moment, as if they had taken a much more considerable person. The prince had sent back a troop of dragoons to guard him to them, which troop had beset the house and town, before Welch came in to them the second time; and, notwithstanding all informations of his error, he carried away Mr. Hutchinson, and put his sister into affright and distemper with it; which, when the women about her saw, they railed at him for his treachery and baseness, but to no purpose. As soon as he overtook the body of horse with his prisoner, there was a shout from one end to the other of the soldiers. Mr. Hutchinson, being brought to the prince, told him he was the younger brother, and not the person he sent for, which three or four of the Byrons, his cousin-germans, acknowledged to be so; yet Welch outswore them all that it was Mr. John

Hutchinson. The Lord Viscount Grandison, a cousin-german of Mrs. Hutchinson's, was then in the king's army, to whom she immediately despatched a messenger, to entreat him to oblige her by the procurement of her brother's liberty, who, upon her imprudence, had been brought into that trouble. My lord sent her word, that, for the present, he could not obtain it, but he would endeavour it afterwards; and in the meantime he gave her notice that it was not safe for her husband to return, there being forty men left to lie close in the country, and watch his coming to her. So Mr. George Hutchinson was carried to Derby, and there, with some difficulty, his liberty was obtained by the interposition of my Lord Grandison and the Byrons. They would have had him give them an engagement, that he would not take arms with the parliament; but he refused, telling them that he lived peaceably at home, and should make no engagement to do anything but what his conscience led him to; that if they pleased, they might detain him, but it would be no advantage to them, nor loss to the other side; upon which considerations they were persuaded to let him go. Immediately after his release, he went to London to his father, where his elder brother was before him; for as soon as he understood from his wife what his brother suffered in his name, he took post to London to procure his release; and there they both stayed till they received assurance that the king's forces were quite withdrawn from the country, and then they together returned to Leicestershire, where Mrs. Hutchinson, within a few days after her brother was taken, was brought to bed of her eldest daughter; which, by reason of the mother's and the nurse's griefs and frights, in those troublesome times, was so weak a child that it lived not four years, dying afterwards in Nottingham Castle. When Mr. Hutchinson came to his wife, he carried her and her children, and his brother, back again to his house, about the time that the battle was fought at Edge Hill. After this the two brothers, going to Nottingham, met there most of the godly people, who had been driven away by the rudeness of the king's army, and plundered on account of their godliness, who now returned to their families, and were desirous to live in peace; but having, by experience, found they could not do so, unless the parliament interest was maintained, they were consulting how to raise some recruits for the Earl of Essex, to assist in which, Mr. Hutchinson had provided his plate and horses ready to send in.

About this time Sir John Gell, a Derbyshire gentleman, who had been sheriff of the county, at that time when the illegal tax of ship-money was exacted, and was so violent in the prosecution of it, that he starved Sir John Stanhope's cattle in the pound, and would not suffer any one to relieve them there, because that worthy gentleman stood out against that unjust payment; and he had by many aggravating circumstances, not only concerning his prosecution of Sir John Stanhope, but others, so highly misdemeaned himself that he looked for punishment from the parliament; to prevent it, he very early put himself into their service, and after the king was gone out of these countries, he prevented the cavalier gentry from seizing the town of Derby, and fortified it, and raised a regiment of foot. These were good, stout, fighting men, but the most licentious, ungovernable wretches, that belonged to the parliament. As regards himself, no man knew for what reason he chose that side; for he had not understanding enough to judge the equity of the cause, nor piety or holiness; being a foul adulterer all the time he served the parliament, and so unjust, that without any remorse, he suffered his men indifferently to plunder both honest men and cavaliers; so revengeful, that he pursued his malice to Sir John Stanhope, upon the forementioned account, with such barbarism after his death, that he, pretending to search for arms and plate, came into the church and defaced his monument that cost six hundred pounds, breaking off the nose and other parts of it. He dug up a garden of flowers, the only delight of his widow, upon the same pretence; and then wooed that widow, who was by all the world believed to be the most prudent and affectionate of womankind, till, being deluded by his hypocrisies, she consented to marry him, and found that was the utmost point to which he could carry his revenge, his future carriage making it apparent he sought her for nothing else but to destroy the glory of her husband and his house. This man kept the journalists* in pension, so that whatever was done in the neighbouring counties, against the enemy, was attributed to him; and thus he hath indirectly purchased himself a name in story, which he never merited. He was a very bad man, to sum up all in that word, yet an instrument of service to the parliament in those parts. I thought it necessary to insert this little account of him here, because there will be often occasion to mention him in my following discourse; and because, although there never was any personal acquaintance between him and Mr. Hutchinson, yet that natural antipathy which is between good and evil, rendered him a very bad neigh-

* Sir John Gell succeeded so far as to get some of his puffing intelligence introduced even into his Memorials by Whitelock; who, p. 186, talks of an expedition where he killed five of the enemy! He likewise gives him the honour of taking Shelford Manor, at least two years before it was really taken by Colonel Hutchinson. It is very much to be wondered at, that Mrs. Hutchinson nowhere speaks of this trial and condemnation for misprison of treason, which Whitelock notes in the year 1650, during the time of Mr. Hutchinson's being in the second council of state. He is said to have been convicted on the full evidence of Bernard and Titus. Colonel Andrews, who was condemned along with him, gave an attestation on his behalf a little before his death. Whitelock does not say what this treason consisted in, but he was pardoned by the third council, just before Cromwell's usurpation; and was among those members of parliament who opposed him boldly.

bour to Mr. Hutchinson's garrison, and one that, under the
name of a friend and assistant, spoiled our country, as much
as our enemies. He indeed gave his men leave to commit
all insolences without any restraint; whereas Mr. Hutchinson took up arms to defend the country as much as was
possible from being a prey to rude soldiers, and did oftentimes preserve it both from his and other rude troops,*
which stirred up in him envy, hate, and ill-will against
his neighbour. He was not wise in ordering the scouts
and spies he kept out, and so had the worst intelligence
in the world. Mr. Hutchinson, on the other side, employed ingenuous persons, and was better informed of
the true state of things, so that oftentimes he communicated
those informations to the chief commanders, which proved
the falsehood of his; and that was another cause of envy.
Some that knew him well, said he was not valiant, though
his men once held him up, among a stand of pikes, while
they obtained a glorious victory, when the Earl of Northampton was slain; certain it is he was never by his good
will in a fight, but either by chance or necessity ; and
that which made his courage the more questioned was, the
care he took, and the expense he was at, to get it weekly
mentioned in the journals, so that when they had nothing
else to renown him for, they once put in that the troops of
that valiant commander, Sir John Gell, took a dragoon with
a plush doublet. Mr. Hutchinson, on the other side, that
did well for virtue's sake, and not for the vainglory of it,
never would give anything to buy the flatteries of those
scribblers; and when one of them had once, while he was in
town, made mention of something done at Nottingham, with

* To the interposition of such men as Colonel Hutchinson we must
attribute the proportionably small quantity of mischief that was suffered
by this nation, in so long and sharp a civil war : as this was.

falsehood, and had given Gell the glory of an action wherein
he was not concerned, Mr. Hutchinson rebuked him for it,
whereupon the man begged his pardon, and told him he
would write as much for him the next week; but Mr. Hutchinson told him he scorned his mercenary pen, warning
him not to dare to lie in any of his concernments, whereupon the fellow was awed, and he had no more abuse of
that kind.

But to turn out of this digression into another, not altogether impertinent to the story which I would carry on. In
Nottinghamshire, upon the edge of Derbyshire, there dwelt
a man, who was of mean birth and low fortunes, yet had
kept company with the underling gentry of his neighbourhood. This man had the most factious, ambitious, vainglori-
ous, envious, and malicious nature imaginable; but he was
the greatest dissembler, flatterer, traitor, and hypocrite that
ever was, and herein had a kind of wicked policy; knowing himself to be inferior to all gentlemen, he put on a vizard
of godliness and humility, and courted the common people
with all the plausibility and flattery that could be practised.
All this while he was addicted to many lusts, especially to
that of women, but practised them so secretly, that they
were not vulgarly taken notice of, though God, to shame
him, gave him up to marry a wench out of one of the ale-
houses he frequented; but to keep up a fame of godliness,
he gave large contributions to puritan preachers, who had
the art to stop the people's mouths from speaking ill of their
benefactors. By a thousand arts this fellow became popular,
and so insinuated himself into all the gentlemen that owned
the parliament's party, that till he was discovered some
years after, they believed him a most true-hearted, faithful,
vigilant, active man for the godly interest; but he could never
climb higher than a presbyterian persecutor, and in the end,
fell quite off to a declared cavalier. In Sir George Booth's

business, thinking he could sway the scales of the country, he raised a troop, brought them into Derby, and published a declaration of his own for the king; then ran away to Nottingham, and lost all his troop in the route there, and hid himself till the king* came in, when he was rewarded for his revolt with an office, which he enjoyed not many months, his wife and he, and some of his children, dying altogether in a few days of a fever little less than a plague. This man, called Charles White, at the beginning of the civil war, got a troop of dragoons, who armed and mounted themselves out of devotion to the parliament's cause, and being of his neighbourhood, marched forth in his conduct, he having procured a commission to be their captain; but they, having stocks and families, were not willing to march as far as the army, but joined themselves to those who were already in arms at Derby.

After the battle at Edge-hill, Sir John Digby, the high sheriff of Nottinghamshire, returned from the king, and had a design of securing the county against the parliament; whereupon he sent out summons to all the gentlemen resident in the country to meet him at Newark. Mr. Hutchinson was at the house of Mr. Francis Pierrepont, the Earl of Kingston's third son, when the letter was delivered to him, and another of the same to Mr. Pierrepont; and while they were reading them, and considering what might be the meaning of this summons, an honest man, of the sheriff's neighbourhood, came and gave them notice, that the sheriff had some design in agitation; for he had assembled and armed about fourscore of his neighbours, to go out with him to Newark, and, as they heard, from thence to Southwell, and from thence to Nottingham, through which town many armed men marched day and

* By the king is here meant Charles the Second; the Rebellion under Sir George Booth having taken place in 1659, after the death of Cromwell.

night, to their great terroi   Mr. Hutchinson, upon this intimation, went home, and, instead of going to meet the sheriff, sent an excuse by an intelligent person, well acquainted with all the country, who had orders to find out their design ; which he did so well, that he assured Mr. Hutchinson if he and some others had gone in, they would have been made prisoners; for the sheriff came into Newark with a troop of eighty men, with whom he was gone to Southwell, and was to go the next day to Nottingham, to secure those places for the king.   Mr. Hutchinson immediately went with his brother and acquainted them at Nottingham with his intelligence, which they had likewise received from other hands.   Although the town was generally more malignant than well affected, yet they cared not much to have cavalier soldiers quarter with them, and therefore agreed to defend themselves against any force which should come against them ; and being called hastily together, as the exigence required, about seven hundred listed themselves, and chose Mr. George Hutchinson for their captain, who having lived among them, was very much loved and esteemed by them.   The sheriff hearing this, came not to Nottingham, but those who were now there thus became engaged to prosecute the defence of themselves, the town, and country, as far as they could.   They were but few, and those not very considerable, and some of them not very hearty; but it pleased God here, as in other places, to carry on his work by weak and unworthy instruments.   There were seven aldermen in the town, and of these only Alderman James, then mayor, owned the parliament.   He was a very honest, bold man, but had no more than a burgher's discretion ; he was yet very well assisted by his wife, a woman of great zeal and courage, and with more understanding than women of her rank usually have.   All the devout people of the town were very vigorous and ready to offer their lives and families, but there was

not a quarter of the town that consisted of these; the ordinary civil sort of people coldly adhered to the better, but
all the debauched, and such as had lived upon the bishops'
persecuting courts, and had been the lackeys of projectors and
monopolizers and the like, they were all bitterly malignant;
yet God awed them, that they could not at that time hinder
his people, and he overruled some of their greatest enemies
to assist them, such as were Chadwick and Plumptre,
who, at the first, put themselves most forward in the
business.   Plumptre was a doctor of physic, an inhabitant
of Nottingham, who had learning, natural parts, and understanding enough to discern between natural civil righteousness and injustice; but he was a horrible atheist, and had
such an intolerable pride that he brooked no superiors, and
naving some wit, took the boldness to exercise it in the
abuse of all gentlemen wherever he came.*   Sir Thomas
Hutchinson first brought him into credit and practice in
the country, it having pleased God to make him instrumental in the cure of Mr. George Hutchinson, who had in
vain tried the skill of the best doctors in England against an
epileptic disease, under which he laboured for some years
Upon this occasion, Sir Thomas and both his sons paid him
much respect, and this cure gave him reputation, and introduced him into practice in all the gentlemen's houses in the
country; which he soon lost again by his most abusive
tongue and other ill carriages, and was even got out of favour
with Sir Thomas Hutchinson himself, for some abusive scoffs

---

* It said of him, in Thoroton's History of Notts, "He was a person
eminent in his profession, of great note for wit and learning, as he had
formerly been for poetry, when he printed a book of epigrams :" a species
of composition which the more it pleases the reader, the less it renders the
author beloved.   This inclination to sport with the feelings of others was
not at all likely to recommend him to Mr. Hutchinson, nor make him a
good associate in weighty and serious business.

given out against his lady. But Mr. Hutchinson and his brother, in pity to him, and in remembrance of what God had done through him, still owned him, and protected him a little against the bitter zealots, though it was impossible for his darkness and their light long to continue mixed. This man had seen enough to approve the parliament's cause, in point of civil right, and pride enough to desire to break the bonds of slavery, whereby the king endeavoured to chain up a free people ; and upon these scores, appearing high for the parliament's interest, he was admitted into the consultations of those who were then putting the country into a posture of defence.* Chadwick was a fellow of a most pragmatical temper, and, to say truth, had strangely wrought himself into a station

* Doubtless many adhered to the parliament's side merely on a civil and political account, and these would naturally unite with the independents, as having no inclination to support the pretensions of the presbyterians. It is said by Clarendon, that many deists took part with the independents; and it is not improbable that Dr. Plumptre might have an inclination at least to scepticism, as sarcasm was his talent, and for this he was termed an atheist by Mrs. Hutchinson, who was a rigorist.

After the deaths of Colonel Hutchinson and Dr. Plumptre, there began a great friendship between their families, which lasted many generations. Charles, the half-brother of Colonel Hutchinson, and his successor in his estate at Owthorpe and in the borough of Nottingham, was guardian of Dr. Plumptre's son, and is represented by Thoroton to have executed his trust with great fidelity.

The Editor has in his possession several pieces, in verse and prose, written by the late Dr. Charles Hutchinson, in favour of the last Mr. Plumptre, who represented the town of Nottingham, and in vindication of him against a party headed by Langford Collin, Esq., a lineal descendant of Colonel Hutchinson's master gunner, who will be spoken of hereafter; they are all in a jocose or satirical style; but one of them, a short advertisement, which too well described Mr. Collin, was deemed libellous, and cost Dr. Hutchinson £500, which was well repaid by Mr. Plumptre's obtaining for him a king's living of £350 per annum. At this time Mr. Plumptre and Mr. Hutchinson's families were of the Whig or Hanover party, Mr. Collin of the Tory or Jacobite.

unfit for him. He was at first a boy that scraped trenchers
in the house of one of the poorest justices in the county, but
yet such a one as had a great deal of formality and understanding of the statute law, from whom this boy picked such
ends of law, that he became first the justice's, then a lawyer's
clerk. He then, I know not how, got to be a parcel-judge in
Ireland, and came over to his own country swelled with the
reputation of it, and set on foot a base, obsolete, arbitrary
court there, which the Conqueror of old had given to one
Peverel, his bastard, which this man entitling my lord Goring
unto, executed the office under him, to the great abuse of
the country. At the beginning of the parliament they would
have prosecuted him for it, but my lord Goring begged of
Sir Thomas Hutchinson to spare him, and promised to lay it
down for ever; so from the beginning of the parliament he
executed not that office, but having an insinuating wit and
tongue, procured himself to be deputy recorder of Nottingham, my lord of Clare being chief. When the king was in
town a little before, this man so insinuated himself into the
court, that, coming to kiss the king's hand, the king told him
he was a very honest man; yet by flatteries and dissimulations he kept up his credit with the godly, cutting his hair,
and taking up a form of godliness, the better to deceive. In
some of the corrupt times he had purchased the honour of a
barrister, though he had neither law nor learning, but he had
a voluble tongue, and was crafty; and it is almost incredible
that one of his mean education and poverty should arrive to
such things as he reached. He was very poor, although he
got abundance of money by a thousand cheats and other
base ways, wherein he exercised all his life; but he was as
great a prodigal in spending as knave in getting. Among
other villanies which he secretly practised, he was a libidinous
goat, for which his wife, they say, paid him with making
him a cuckold; yet were there not two persons to be found

that pretended more sanctity than these two, she having a
tongue no less glavering and false than his. Such baseness
ne had, that all the just reproaches in the world could not
move him, but he would fawn upon any man that told him
of his villanies to his face, even at the very time. Never
was a truer Judas, since Iscariot's time, than he, for he would
kiss the man he had in his heart to kill; he naturally delighting in mischief and treachery, and was so exquisite a
villain, that he destroyed those designs he might have thriven
by, with overlaying them with fresh knaveries. I have been
a little tedious in these descriptions, yet have spoken very
little in comparison of what the truth would bear; indeed,
such assistants as these were enough to disgrace the best
cause by their owning of it; but the truth of God being
above the testimony of men, could neither receive credit from
the good, nor discredit from the worst men; but they were
not all such, who first offered themselves to carry on the Lord's
work with him of whom we chiefly treat. There was then
dwelling at Nottingham a third son of the Earl of Kingston,
a man of good natural parts, but not of education according
to his quality, who was in the main well affected to honest
men and to righteous liberty; a man of a very excellent
good nature, and full of love to all men; but his goodness
received a little allay by a vain-glorious pride, which could
not well brook that any other should outstrip him in virtue
and estimation.* Mr. Francis Thornhagh, the eldest son of
Sir Francis Thornhagh, was a man of the most upright
faithful heart to God and his people, and to his country's
true interest, comprehended in the parliament's cause; a man
ot greater valour or more noble daring, fought not for them,

---

* Mr. Francis Pierrepont, who will frequently be mentioned again in
the course of the story, when t will be clearly seen that Mrs. Hutchinson
here speaks with candour, or rather favour of him, though he was her
husoand's opponent.

nor indeed ever drew sword in any cause; he was of a most excellent good nature to all men, and zealous for his friend; he wanted counsel and deliberation, and was sometimes too facile to flatterers, but had judgment enough to discern his errors when they were represented to him, and worth enough not to persist in an injurious mistake because he had once entertained it.* Mr. Pigott was a very religious, serious, wise gentleman, true-hearted to God and his country, of a generous and liberal nature, and who thought nothing too dear to expose, nor too difficult to undertake, for his friend; one that delighted not in the ruin of his neighbours, but could endure it, rather than the destruction of religion, law, and liberty; one that wanted not courage, yet chose rather to venture himself as a single person than as a leader in arms, and to serve his country in counsel rather than in action; no man in his nature, and his whole deportment, showed himself more of a gentleman than he.† There was one Mr. Widmer-

* Colonel Thornhagh is often mentioned by other writers, and always with praise in his military capacity, in which only he was known to the public. Mrs. Hutchinson here delineates with a masterly hand a frank, open, unsuspecting, amiable soldier. The family of Colonel Thornhagh continued to flourish in the county of Nottingham so late as the year 1750, at which time one of them represented the county; they are believed to be now extinct in the male line, and their possessions to have centered in a female who was the lady of Francis Ferrand Foljambe, Esq.

† Mr. Pigott survived Colonel Hutchinson about five years. He was summoned to parliament by Cromwell, but it is very uncertain whether he condescended to sit or not to sit. Thoroton, in his History of Nottinghamshire, says of him that " he was a person of great parts, natural and acquired; he was sheriff of the county in 1669, and died presently after the summer assizes ; at which time, being in mourning for his daughter Mary wife of Robert, eldest son of Sir Francis Burdett, of Formark, he gave his attendants black liveries with silver trimmings, which served for his own funeral. His sobriety, ingenuity, generosity, piety, and other virtues, few of his rank will ever exceed, if any equal."

It is thought necessary to take more particular notice of what may ap-

poole, a man of good extraction, but reduced to a small fortune, in whom had declined all the splendour of an old house, and who had sunk into the condition of the middle men of the country, yet had a perfect honest heart to God, his country, and his friend; he had a good discretion, and though older than all the rest, was so humble as to be content to come in the rear of them all; having through the declining of his family, the slenderness of his estate, and the parsimony of his nature, less interest in the country.* To yoke with him, there was a very honest man, who could not be reckoned among the gentry, though he was called by the name of *Mr.* Lomax; he was in the strength and perfection of his age, a stout and an understanding man, plain and blunt, but withal godly, faithful to his country, and honest to all men. There lived at Nottingham, a man called Mr. Salisbury, who had very good abilities with his pen, upon which he was taken in to be their secretary; but he proved ambitious and froward, and being poor, when he was afterwards made treasurer, he fell into some temptation; but carried at first a fair colour of religion and honesty. These were they with whom Mr. Hutchinson was first mated, whose character it was necessary thus far to hint at, for the better carrying on of his story.

Sir John Digby having notice that they had prevented him, by getting arms in their hands before, came not to Nottingham; where they, having now taken up the sword, saw it was not safe to lay it down again, and hold a naked throat to their enemy's whetted knives. Wherefore, upon

pertain to Ireton, Colonel Thornhagh, and Mr. Pigott, because they are the three persons who enjoyed the greatest share in the friendship and esteem of Colonel Hutchinson, and made him a due return.

* The pedigree of the family of Widmerpoole, in Thoroton, shows him to have been of very ancient and good descent; his ancestor represented the town of Nottingham in the reign of Edward the Third.

the parliament's commission for settling the militia sometime before, there having been three colonels nominated, viz. Sir Francis Thornhagh, Sir Francis Molineux, and Mr. Francis Pierrepont, they propounded to them to raise their regiments. Sir Francis Molineux altogether declined; Sir Francis Thornhagh appointed his son for his lieutenant-colonel, and began to raise a regiment of horse, with whom many of the honest men that first enlisted themselves with Mr. George Hutchinson, became troopers. Mr. John Hutchinson and his brother were persuaded to be lieutenant-colonel and major to Colonel Pierrepont's regiment of foot; and accordingly Mr. George Hutchinson had immediately a very good standing company of foot, formed out of those townsmen who first came in to enlist under him. Mr. John Hutchinson had a full company of very honest, godly men, who came for love of him and the cause, out of the country. It was six weeks before the colonel could be persuaded to put on a sword, or to enlist any men, which at length he did, of substantial honest townsmen; and Mr. Poulton, a nephew of Sir Thomas Hutchinson, a stout young gentleman, who had seen some service abroad, was his captain-lieutenant. There were two companies more raised, one under Captain Lomax, and another under one Captain Scrimpshire. The first thing these gentlemen did was to call home Captain White with his dragoons, raised in Nottinghamshire, to the service of his own country; for Sir John Gell, at Derby, had received from Hull a regiment of grey coats, who were at first sent down from London, for the assistance of that place, when the king attempted it. They also sent to the Earl of Essex, to desire that Captain Ireton, with a troop of horse, which he had carried out of the country into his excellency's army, might be commanded back, for the present service of his country, till it was put into a posture of defence; which accordingly he was, and was major of the horse regiment. They sent also to the parliament, and received from them a commission, with instructions, whereby they were empowered to levy forces and to raise contributions for maintaining them ; with all authority for seizing delinquents, sequestrating, and the like.   The committee appointed were the parliament-men that served for the county, Mr. Francis Pierrepont, Mr. John Hutchinson, Mr. Francis Thornhagh, Mr. Gervas Pigott, Mr. Henry Ireton, Mr. George Hutchinson, Mr. Joseph Widmerpoole, Mr. Gervas Lomax, Dr. Plumptre, the mayor of Nottingham, Mr. James Chadwick, and Mr. Thomas Salisbury. Then did neighbouring counties everywhere associate for the mutual assistance of each other ; and the parliament commissioned major-generals, who commanded in chief, and gave out commissions to the several commanders o ' t e regiments. Nottinghamshire was put into the association with Leicestershire and other counties, whereof Lord Crey of Grooby, eldest son of the Earl of Stamford, was commander-in-chief, and from him the gentlemen of Nottingham took their first commissions.

The high sheriff and the malignant gentry, finding an opposition they expected not, wrote a letter to Mr. Francis Pierrepont and Mr. John Hutchinson, excusing the sheriff's force, that he brought with him, and desiring a meeting with them, to consult for the peace of the country, security of their estates, and such like fair pretences ; which letter was civilly answered them again, and the treaty kept on foot some fourteen days, by letters signed by the Lord Chaworth, Sir Thomas Williamson, Mr. Sutton, Sir Gervas Eyre, Sir John Digby, Sir Roger Cooper Mr. Palmer, Mr. John Millington. At length a meeting was appointed at a village in the country, on the forest side, where Mr. Sutton should have met Mr. John Hutchinson. Mr. Hutchinson came to the place, but found not Mr. Sutton there, only the Lord Chaworth came in and called for sack, and treated Mr. Hut-

chinson very kindly; when Mr. Hutchinson, telling my lord
he was come according to appointment, to conclude the treaty
which had been between Nottingham and Newark, my lord
told him he knew nothing of it.   Whereupon, Mr. Hutchinson being informed that some of my Lord Newcastle's
forces were to be in that town that night, and that Mr. Sutton
was gone to meet them, and conduct them into the country,
returned to Nottingham, where he received a kind of lame
excuse from Mr. Sutton for his disappointing of him, and for
their bringing strange soldiers into Newark, which they
pretended was to save the town from the plunder of some
Lincolnshire forces.   But Mr. Hutchinson, seeing all their
treaties were but a snare for him, would no longer amuse
himself about them; but being certainly informed that
Henderson, who commanded the soldiers at Newark, if he
were not himself a papist, had many Irish papists in his
troops, he, with the rest of the gentlemen, sent notice to all
the towns about Nottingham, desiring the well-affected to
come in to their assistance; which the ministers pressing
them to do, upon Christmas-day, 1642, many came to them,
and stayed with them till they had put themselves into some
posture of defence.

As soon as these strange soldiers were come into Newark,
they presently began to block up and fortify the town, as on
the other side, they at Nottingham began works about that
town; but neither of them being yet strong enough to
assault each other, they contented themselves to stand upon
their own defence.   The Earl of Chesterfield had raised some
horse for the king, and was in the vale of Belvoir with them,
where he had plundered some houses near Mr. Hutchinson's;
whereupon Mr. Hutchinson sent a troop of horse in the
night, for they were not strong enough to march in the day,
and fetched away his wife and children to Nottingham.

The preservation of this town was a special service to the

parliament, it being a considerable pass into the north, which, if the enemy had first possessed themselves of, the parliament would have been cut off from all intercourse between the north and south; especially in the winter time, when the river Trent is not fordable, and only to be passed over by the bridges of Nottingham and Newark, and higher up at a place called Wilden Ferry, where the enemy also had a garrison.* The attempting to preserve this place, in the midst of so many potent enemies, was a work of no small difficulty; and nothing but an invincible courage, and a passionate zeal for the interest of God and his country, could have engaged Mr. Hutchinson, who did not, through youthful inconsideration and improvidence, want a foresight of those dangers and travails he then undertook. He knew well enough that the town was more than half disaffected to the parliament; that had they been all otherwise, they were not half enough to defend it against any unequal force; that they were far from the parliament and their armies, and could not expect any timely relief or assistance from them; that he himself was the forlorn hope of those who were engaged with him, and had then the best stake among them; that the gentlemen who were on horseback, when they could no longer defend their country, might at least save their lives by a handsome retreat to the army; but that he must stand victorious, or fall, tying himself to an indefensible town. Although his colonel (Pierrepont) might seem to be in the same hazard, yet he was wise enough to content himself with the name, and leave Mr. Hutchinson to act in all things, the

* In the place of Wilden Ferry has been substituted in modern days a very beautiful bridge, called Cavendish Bridge, with a good and firm road of considerable length at each end to approach it; it is about midway on the high road between Loughborough and Derby. There is near to it a place called Sawley Ferry, little used, and hardly at all practicable in winter.

glory of which, if they succeeded, he hoped to assume ; if they failed, he thought he had a retreat. But Mr. Hutchinson, though he knew all this, yet was he so well persuaded in his conscience of the cause, and of God's calling him to undertake the defence of it, that he cast by all other considerations, and cheerfully resigned up his life, and all other particular interests, to God's disposal, though in all human probability he was more likely to lose than to save them.

He and his brother were so suddenly called into this work, that they had not time beforehand to consult their father; but they sent to him to buy their armour and useful swords, which he did, giving them no discouragement, but promoting all their desires to the parliament very effectually.*

By reason of the coldness of the colonel, the affairs of the war at Nottingham went on more tardily than otherwise they would have done; but the gentlemen there, thinking it would be easier to prevent Newark from being made a fortified garrison, than to take it when it was so, sent over to Lincoln and Derby, to propound the business to them. At length, about Candlemas, it was agreed and appointed that the forces of Nottingham and Derby should come on their side of the town, and those of Lincoln on the other. All the disaffected gentry of both those countries, were at that time gone into Newark, and one Ballard, a gentleman who, decayed in his family, and owing his education to many of them, had been bred up in the wars abroad, was commander-in-chief for the parliament in Lincolnshire. Much

* The reader is desired to bear this in mind, as it tends much to invalidate the credibility of an assertion made by the stepmother of these gentlemen, which will be noticed in its proper place. It is said, in a note by Julius Hutchinson, Esq., that Sir Thomas Hutchinson bought his two sons armour, though he knew not of their accepting commissions against the king. What was the armour for ! Was it to serve the king aga'nst the parliament !

ado had the gentlemen of that county to engage him in the design against Newark; but when he could not divert them, he was resolved to cast them away rather than ruin his old benefactors. He had appointed the forces of Nottingham and Derby to come to a rendezvous within a mile of Newark, upon Saturday, upon which day, all the persuasion the Lincolnshire gentlemen could use, could not prevail with him to march out, according to appointment; which those at Newark had notice of, and had prepared an ambuscade to have cut off all those forces if they had then come to the place; but by providence of an extraordinary stormy season, they marched not till the next day, and so were preserved from that danger, which no doubt was treacherously contrived. As soon as they came, being about a thousand horse, foot, and dragoons, the Lincolnshire commanders informed ours of the sloth and untoward carriage of Ballard, and told them how that day he had played his ordinance at a mile's distance from the town; and how, when the Newark horse came out to face them, upon the Beacon Hill, he would not suffer a man of the Lincolnshire troops to fall upon them, though the Lincoln horse were many more in number than they, and in all probability might have beaten them. The next day, notwithstanding Mr. Hutchinson went to him, to give him an account of the forces they had brought, and to receive orders, he could have none, but a careless answer 'o stand at such a side of the town and fall on as they saw occasion. Accordingly they did, and beat the enemy from their works, with the loss of only four or five men, and entrenched themselves; the night coming on upon them, they provided straw to have lodged in their trenches all the night. On the other side of the town, Captain King, of Lincolnshire, had taken a street, cut up a chain, and placed a drake* in a house; whereupon the Newark gentlemen

* Drake, a piece of cannon so called.

were almost resolved to yield up the town, and some of them began to fly out of it, but Ballard would not suffer the horse to pursue them; only one captain went out without his leave and took fifty horses, and turned back Mr. Sutton and many others that were flying out of the town. At length, when he could no other way preserve his old patrons, but by betraying his friends, he ordered Captain King to retreat; whereupon the whole force of Newark fell upon the forces of Nottingham and Derby, in their trenches, where they fought very resolutely, till a Lincolnshire trooper came and bade them fly for their lives, or else they were all lost men. At this, two hundred Lincolnshire men, whom Ballard with much entreaty had sent to relieve them, first ran away, and then Sir John Gell's grey coats made their retreat after them. Major Hutchinson and Captain White all this while kept their trenches, and commanded their Nottingham men not to stir, who accordingly shot there, till all their powder was spent. The lieutenant-colonel in vain importuned Ballard to send them ammunition and relief, but could obtain neither, and so they were forced, unwillingly, to retreat, which they did in such good order, the men first, and then their captains, that they lost not a man in coming off. The town was sallying upon them, but they discharged a drake and beat them back. The next day all the captains importuned Ballard that they might fall on again, but he would neither consent nor give any reason for his denial; so that the Nottingham forces returned with great dissatisfaction, though Ballard, to stop their mouths, gave them two pieces of ordnance.

It being necessary to carry on the main story, for the better understanding the motion of those lesser wheels that moved within the great orb, I shall now name in what posture things were abroad in the kingdom, while these affairs I relate were transacted at Nottingham. After the retreat from Brainford fight, a treaty was ineffectually carried on between the king and

parliament from the 31st of January, 1642, to the 17th of
April, 1643; after which my Lord of Essex marched to Reading, where the king had a garrison, and besieged it. The king's
horse came to relieve it, and had an encounter with my lord's
army, wherein many gentlemen of quality fell on the king's
side, the king himself being in a place where he saw them.
A few days after, Reading was yielded upon composition
to the Earl of Essex, whose soldiers having been promised
their pay and a gratuity to spare the plunder of the town,
fell into a mutiny upon the failing of the performance, and
many of them disbanded. Among those who remained there
was a great mortality, occasioned by the infected air in the
town of Reading; insomuch that my lord was forced to
return and quarter his sick and weak army about Kingston
and those towns near London. And now were all the countries in England no longer idle spectators, but several stages,
whereon the tragedy of the civil war was acted; except the
eastern association, where Mr. Oliver Cromwell, by his diligence, prevented the designs of the royal party; these were
so successful the first year in all other places, and the parliament's condition appeared so desperate, that many of the
members of both houses, ran away to Oxford to the king,
and others sat among them conspiring against them. One
plot, conducted by Mr. Waller, and carried on among many
disaffected persons in the city, was near taking effect, to the
utter subversion of the parliament and people; but that God,
by his providence, brought it timely to light, and the authors
were condemned, and some of them executed; but Waller, for
being more a knave than the rest, and impeaching his accom-
plices, was permitted to buy his life for ten thousand pounds.
This summer all the west was reduced by the king, the Earl
of Stamford yielding up Exeter, and Colonel Fiennes Bristol. Sir William Waller had lost all his army, which
had been victorious in many encounters. The king was
master of all or most part of Wales, and the parliament

had no army left in the field, so that had he taken the opportunity to have gone immediately to London that summer, he had accomplished his design; but being denied the town of Gloucester, and taking it in disdain, that that town, in the heart of the land, should make a resistance when the greater cities were yielded to him, he stopped his course to take in that place, where he stayed to turn the tide of his good fortune, as his general, my Lord of Newcastle did at the siege of Hull.* My Lord Newcastle was general of the north, and master of all the strong places to the very borders of Scotland, and formidable to all the neighbouring counties. Only the Lord Fairfax, with his son Sir Thomas, headed all the religious, honest Englishmen they could raise in those parts, and with a far inferior force, kept him in

* The impolicy of this measure is more fully noticed and explained, and the cause of it set down by Sir Philip Warwick, in his Memoirs, p. 260. " One or the like counsel in both quarters, north and west, soon blasted the prosperity in each place, for the king pitched upon that fatal resolution, recommended to him by Lord Culpeper, of besieging Gloucester, thinking it a good policy not to leave a strong town behind him : but the counsel proved fatal, for had the king at that time resolved in himself to have struck at the proud head of London, and had had authority enough at that time to have required the Earl of Newcastle to have joined with him, humanly speaking, he had raised such confusion among the two houses and the Londoners, that they had either sent him his own terms, or if they had fought him, most probably he had been victorious. But the king fixes on Gloucester and the Earl of Newcastle upon Hull, upon the advice of his Lieutenant-General King, who was suspected."

A few pages further, he reckons among the king's misfortunes the Earl of Newcastle's too much affecting independency, which may serve to account for some other matters which will occur; but it is here natural to observe, that the king having, by separating himself from his parliament, lost his acknowledged and unquestionable authority, he retained only a very precarious one over the different chiefs of his party : which, on many occasions, turned to the disadvantage of his cause. After all, it is in no way certain that his march to London would have been so effectual and so little opposed, as it is here taken for granted it would have been.

play, and in several skirmishes came off conquerors.* But
as the fortune of the parliament declined in other places, so
those who had not principle strong enough to hold them
fast to a just, though falling cause, sought early to secure
their lives by treasons which destroyed them. The Earl of
Newcastle's army was judged to be about eight thousand,
horse and foot; my Lord Fairfax had not above two thousand one hundred foot, and seven troops of horse. After
this there was a great accession of strength to my Lord
Newcastle, by the coming, first of the Lord Goring, with
many old commanders; then of General King, with six
thousand arms, from beyond the seas; then of the queen
herself, who, in February 1642,† landed near Sunderland,
coming out of Holland, with large provisions of arms, ammunition, and commanders of note, with which she was convoyed, by the Earl of Newcastle, to York. Thither came to
her the Earl of Montrose, out of Scotland, with a hundred
and twenty horse: then Sir Hugh Cholmly, governor of
Scarborough, revolted from the parliament, whereof he was
a member, and came to the queen, with three hundred men.
Browne Bushell also, who was left in charge of the town,
yielded it up. Then had the queen's practices wrought so
upon the two Hothams, that their treason was not altogether
undiscerned; but my Lord Fairfax, having only strong
presumptions, and no power to secure them, while they had
the strong town of Hull in their hands, all he could do
was to be vigilant and silent, till God should give opportunity to secure that great danger. My Lord of Newcastle had

* In fact, the resistance so long maintained, and frequently with such
success, by Lord Fairfax and his sons, against so superior a force, has
been always thought next to miraculous, and marked out Sir Thomas as
the fittest man in the kingdom to command the forces and fix the fortunes
of the parliament.

† Clarendon says February, 1643,

given the papists in the north commissions to arm in the king's defence,* and now the queen was preparing to march up with the assistance she had gotten to the king. Those countries through which she was to pass, could not but be sensible of their danger, especially the gentlemen at Nottingham, who were but a few young men, environed with garrisons of the enemy, and scarcely firm among themselves, and hopeless of relief from above, where the parliament, struggling for life, had not leisure to bind up a cut finger. But God was with them in these difficulties, and gave an unexpected issue.

The Earl of Kingston a few months stood neuter, and would not declare himself for either party, and being a man of great wealth and dependencies, many people hung in suspense, by his example; whereupon the gentlemen of Nottingham often spoke to his son, to persuade his father to declare himself; but he told them, he knew his father's affections were firm to the parliament, that he had encouraged him to join with them, and promised him money to carry it on, and such like things, which he continually assured them; till the colonel's cold behaviour, and some other passages, made them at length, those at least who were firm to the cause, jealous both of the father and the son. Hereupon, when the danger grew more imminent, and my lord lay out a brave prey to the enemy, they sent Captain Lomax, one of the committee, to understand his affections from himself, and to press him to declare for the parliament, in that so needful a season. My lord,

* The king pretended never to do this himself; but the Earl of Newcastle did it, as most people would in his place, and avowed it as it became him. Sir Philip Warwick recites a witticism of his on the occasion of his going to see him at the siege of Hull, where his men being very badly entrenched, he said to Sir Philip, who remarked it, " You hear us often called the popish army, but you see we trust not in our *good works.*"

professing himself to him as rather desirous of peace, and
fully resolved not to act on either side, made a serious imprecation on himself in these words : " When," said he, "I take
arms with the king against the parliament, or with the parliament against the king, let a cannon-bullet divide me between
them ;" which God was pleased to bring to pass a few months
after ; for he, going to Gainsborough, and there taking up
arms for the king, was surprised by my Lord Willoughby,
and, after a handsome defence of himself, yielded, and was
put prisoner into a pinnace, and sent down the river to Hull;
when my Lord Newcastle's army marching along the shore,
shot at the pinnace, and being in danger, the Earl of Kingston went up on the deck to show himself and to prevail
with them to forbear shooting ;* but as soon as he appeared,
a cannon-bullet flew from the king's army, and divided him
in the middle, and thus, being then in the parliament's pinnace, he perished according to his own unhappy imprecation.
His declaring himself for the king, as it enforced the royal,
so it weakened the other party.

Sir Richard Byron was come to be governor of Newark.
A house of my Lord Chaworth's in the vale was fortified, and
some horse put into it, and another house of the Earl of
Chesterfield's, both of them within a few miles of Nottingham.†
Ashby de la Zouch, within eighteen miles of Nottingham, on
the other side, was kept by Mr. Hastings.   On the forest side
of the country, the Earl of Newcastle's house had a garrison,
and another castle of his, within a mile, was garrisoned.   Sir
Roger Cooper's house, at Thurgaton, was also kept ; so that
Nottingham, thus beleaguered with enemies, seemed very

---

* This is a most singular story, and no doubt peculiarly gratifying to a
fatalist to recite; it is however assuredly true, being mentioned by several
historians, with only the difference of his being said to be under, instead of
on, the deck; the latter of which is by far the most probable.

† Wiverton-house and Shelford manor.

unlike.y to be able either to resist the enemy or suppo·t itself.* Therefore the gentlemen, upon the news of my Lord Newcastle's intended approach that way, sent up Mr. John Hutchinson to acquaint the parliament with their condition; who so negotiated their business that he procured an order for Colonel Cromwell, Colonel Hubbard, my Lord Grey, and Sir John Gell, to unite their forces, and rendezvous at Nottingham, to prevent the queen from joining with the king, and to guard those parts against the cavaliers. Accordingly, in the Whitsun holidays, 1643, they all came, and the younger Hotham also brought some more rude troops out of Yorkshire, and joined himself to them. The forces now united at Nottingham were about five or six thousand, my Lord Grey being their commander-in-chief. Upon the urgency of the gentlemen at Nottingham, he drew them out against Wiverton-house in the vale, but, upon a groundless apprehension, quitted it, when they might in all probability have taken it, and retreated to Nottingham, where, two or three days after, the enemy's horse faced them; but they would not be prevailed upon to go out, though they were not inferior to them. Young Hotham, at that time, carried on a private treaty with the queen, and every day received and sent trumpets, of which he would give no account. Then was Nottingham more sadly distressed by their friends than by their enemies; for Hotham's and Gell's men not only lay upon free quarter, as all the rest did, but made such a havoc and plunder of friend and foe, that it was a sad thing for any one that had a generous heart to behold it. When the committee offered Hotham to assign him quarters for his men, because they were better acquainted with the country, he would tell them he was no stranger in any English ground. He had a great deal of wicked wit, and would make

* In a letter to the king, the queen writes from Newark that "all the force the parliament had in those parts was only one thousand men in Nottingham."

sport with the miseries of the poor country; and, having treason
in his heart, licensed his soldiers, which were the scum of
mankind, to all the villanies in the country that might make
their party odious.   Mr. Hutchinson was much vexed to see
the country wasted, and that little part of it, which they could
only hope to have contribution from, eaten up by a company of men who, instead of relieving, devoured them; and
Hotham's soldiers, having taken away goods from some honest
men, he went to him to desire restitution of them, and that
he would restrain his soldiers from plunder; whereupon
Hotham replied, " he fought for liberty, and expected it in all
things."   Replies followed, and they grew to high language;
Hotham bidding him, if he found himself grieved, to complain
to the parliament.   Mr. Hutchinson was passionately concerned, and this being in the open field, Colonel Cromwell,
who had likewise had great provocations from him, began to
show himself affected with the country's injuries, and the idle
waste of such a considerable force, through the inexperience
of the chief commander, and the disobedience and irregulari-
ties of the others.   So they, at that time, being equally zealous
for the public service, advised together to seek a remedy, and
despatched away a post to London, who had no greater joy
in the world than such employments as tended to the dis-
placing of great persons, whether they deserved it or not;
him they sent away immediately from the place, to inform
the parliament of Hotham's carriages, and the strong presumptions they had of his treachery, and the ill management
of their forces.   This they two did, without the privity of any
of the other gentlemen or commanders; some of whom were
little less suspected themselves, and others, as my Lord Grey,
through credulous good nature, were too great favourers of Hotham.   The messenger was very diligent in his charge, and returned, as soon as it was possible, with a commitment of Hotham; who accordingly was then made prisoner in Nottingham

Castle, and Sir John Meldrum was sent down to be commander-in-chief of all those united forces. When they
marched away, a troop of my Lord Grey's, having the charge
of guarding Hotham towards London, suffered him to escape,
and thereby put the town of Hull into a great hazard ; but
that the father and son were there unexpectedly surprised,
sent up prisoners to London, and after some time executed.
Those who knew the opinion Cromwell afterwards had of Mr.
Hutchinson, believed he registered this business in his mind
as long as he lived, and made it is care to prevent him from
being in any power or capacity to pursue him to the same
punishment, when he himself deserved it ; but from that time,
growing into more intimate acquaintance with him, he always
used to profess the most hearty affections for him, and the
greatest delight in his plainness and open-heartedness imaginable.*

* Those who consider and represent Cromwell as a prodigy not only of
treachery, design, ambition, and artifice, but likewise of sagacity and fore-
knowledge, will deem this a proof of his having thus early conceived his
scheme of aggrandizement; but to those who are better satisfied with the
probable than the marvellous it will seem to prove no such thing; they
must well know that if he had so soon any great views, they must have
been very distant and indistinct; they will find here only the first of a long
series of instances, wherein will be seen the quick and clear discernment,
the strong and well-poised judgment, the promptitude and firmness of
decision, which enabled him to seize and convert to his advantage every
opportunity that presented itself, and even the actions, thoughts, and inclinations, of other men; and they will see united to these such a command
over his own thoughts and passions as permitted exactly so much, and no
more of them than was convenient, to appear : these qualities, though less
astonishing than the prescience and almost the power of creating events,
which is attributed to him, would and did equally well answer the purpose
of his progression; which he effected in such a manner as to fill with the
greatest propriety all the intermediate situations through which he passed,
to take as it were a firm footing at each gradation, and to arrive at the
pinnacle of power without having once run any considerable risk of an

As soon as Sir John Meldrum came down to his charge at Nottingham, the queen's forces came and faced the town; whereupon the cannon discharging upon them, the Duke of Vendome's son and some few others were slain. The parliament horse drew out of Nottingham to receive the queen's, but they came not on, after this execution of the cannon, for in the meantime the queen was passing by, and although the parliament horse pursued them, yet they would not engage, for it was not their business; so when they saw they had lost their design, the horse returned again to Nottingham, where the foot had stayed all the while they were out. When the Earl of Kingston declared himself for the king, he raised what forces he could, and went into Gainsborough, a town in Lincolnshire, situated upon the river Trent. There, before he was fortified, my Lord Willoughby, of Parham, surprised the town and all his soldiers, who disputed it as long as they could, but being conquered, were forced to yield; and the earl himself retreated into the strongest house, which he kept till it was all on flame round him, and then giving himself up only to my Lord Willoughby, he was immediately sent prisoner to Hull, and shot according to his own imprecation. Immediately part of my Lord Newcastle's army, with all that Newark could make, besieged my Lord Willoughby in Gainsborough; and General Essex sent a command to Sir John Meldrum to draw all the horse and foot he could out of Nottingham, to relieve my lord, leaving only a garrison in the castle of Nottingham. Sir John Meldrum called the

overthrow in his career. Such rational observers will likewise see here, what will in the sequel still more strikingly appear, that if he must be called a traitor, he was not of that paltry treachery which sacrifices a man's party to self; he was steadily bent on procuring the triumph of his own party over their opponents, but too covetous of commanding his party himself. It may be thought there wanted but little, perhaps only the survivance of Ireton, to have made Cromwell intrinsically as well as splendidly great.

committee of Nottingham together, to consult what was to be
done for the settlement of the place, which upon deliberation
he had judged it not fit to leave in the hands it was, nor in
Colonel Pierrepont's, who, with some appearance, lay under
suspicion at that time; and therefore conceiving Mr. Hutchinson the most able to manage, and the most responsible
for it, both Sir John and the whole committee ordered him to
take the castle into his charge; which, though there were
many causes why he should decline, yet believing that God
hereby called him to the defence of his country, and would
protect him in all the dangers and difficulties he led him into,
he accepted it, and on the 29th June, 1643, received an order
for that government from Sir John Meldrum and the whole
committee. Whereunto Col. Pierrepont subscribed, though
with a secret discontent in his heart; not from any ill opinion
or ill affection he had to Mr. Hutchinson's person, but because
he resented it as a great affront that himself should be passed
by. It is true that this discontent produced some envious and
malicious practices, secretly in him, against Mr. Hutchinson,
who however in the end overcame him, with so many good
offices, in requital of his bad ones, that he lived and died full
of love, and acknowledgment of kindness to him.

The castle was built upon a rock, and nature had made it
capable of very strong fortification, but the buildings were
very ruinous and uninhabitable, neither affording room to
lodge soldiers nor provisions. The castle stands at one end
of the town, upon such an eminence as commands the chief
streets of the town. There had been enlargements made to
this castle after the first building of it. There was a strong
tower, which they called the old tower, built upon the top of
all the rock, and this was that place where Queen Isabel, the
mother of King Edward the Third, was surprised with her
paramour Mortimer, who, by secret windings and hollows in
the rock, came up into her chamber from the meadows lying

low under it, through which there ran a little rivulet, called
the Line, almost under the castle rock.   At the entrance of
this rock there was a spring, which was called Mortimer's
Well, and the cavern Mortimer's Hole.   The ascent to the
top is very high, and it is not without some wonder that at
the top of all the rock there should be a spring of water.   In
the midway to the top of this tower there is a little piece of
the rock, on which a dove-coat had been built, but the
governor took down the roof of it, and made it a platform for
two or three pieces of ordnance, which commanded some
streets and all the meadows better than the higher tower.
Under that tower, which was the old castle, there was a larger
castle, where there had been several towers and many noble
rooms, but the most of them were down ; the yard of that
was pretty large, and without the gate there was a very large
yard that had been walled, but the walls were all down, only
it was situated upon an ascent of the rock, and so stood a
pretty height above the streets ; and there were the ruins of
an old pair of gates, with turrets on each side.

Before the castle, the town was on one side of a close,
which commanded the fields approaching the town ; which
close the governor afterwards made a platform.   Behind it
was a place called the Park, that belonged to the castle, but
then had neither deer nor trees in it, except one tree, growing
under the castle, which was almost a prodigy, for from the
root to the top, there was not a straight twig or branch in
it ; some said it was planted by King Richard the Third, and
resembled him that set it.   On the other side the castle, was
the little river of Line, and beyond that, large flat meadows,
bounded by the river Trent.   In the whole rock there were
many large caverns, where a great magazine and many hundred
soldiers might have been disposed, if they had been cleansed
and prepared for it ; and they might have been kept secure
from any danger of firing the magazines by any mortar-pieces

shot against the castle. In one of these places, it is reported,
that one David, a Scotch king, was kept in cruel durance, and
with his nails, had scratched on the wall the story of Christ
and his twelve apostles. The castle was not defended by
lateral fortifications, and there were no works about it, when
Mr. Hutchinson undertook it, but only a little breastwork,
before the outermost gate. It was as ill provided as fortified,
there being but ten barrels of powder, eleven hundred and
fifty pounds of butter, and as much cheese, eleven quarters of
bread corn, seven beeves, two hundred and fourteen flitches
of bacon, five hundred and sixty fishes, and fifteen hogsheads
of beer. As soon as the governor received his charge, he
made proclamation in the town, that whatsoever honest persons
desired to secure themselves or their goods in the castle,
should have reception there, if they would repair their quarters ; which divers well-affected men accepting, it was presently made capable of receiving 400 men commodiously.

In the beginning of July, 1643, Sir John Meldrum, with
all the force that was quartered in Nottingham, marched forth
to the relief of Gainsborough, leaving the town to be guarded
by few more than the very townsmen. There had been large
works made about it, which would have required at least three
thousand men to man and defend well, and upon these works
there were about fourteen guns, which the governor, when
the forces were marching away, before they went, drew up to
the castle ; whereupon the townsmen, especially those that
were ill-affected to the parliament, made a great mutiny,
threatening they would pull the castle down, but they would
have their ordnance again upon their works, and wishing it on
fire, and not one stone upon another. Hereupon the governor
sent Alderman Drury, with fourteen more, who were heads of
this mutiny, prisoners to Derby, whither Major Ireton convoyed
them with his troop. The reasons which made the governor
carry the ordnance from the town-works up into the castle

were, 1st. That the town, being so ill affected, the ordnance
remaining in it, would but be an invitation to the enemy to
come to take them away, and a booty for them if they should.
2ndly. He had often visited the guards, and found them
much exposed by their carelessness, wherefore he thought it
his duty to preserve them, by soldiers more under his command.   3rdly. Intelligence was brought to the committee, by
a friend, then with the Earl of Newcastle, that Mr. Francis
Pierrepont kept intelligence with his mother, the Countess of
Kingston, carrying on a design for betraying the town to
the earl; and that letters were carried between them by a
woman, who often came to town to the colonel; and that two
aldermen and a chief officer, employed about the ordnance,
were confederates in the plot; whereupon a suspected cannonier was secured, who, as soon as he obtained his liberty,
ran away to Newark.   4thly. When the town was full of
troops, there had been several attempts to poison and betray
them, which, if it should be again attempted, after the
most of the forces were gone, might prove effectual.   5thly.
The main reason was, that if the town should be surprised or
betrayed (which was then most to be feared), the ordnance
would be useless; if any considerable force came against the
town, it was impossible then to keep the works against them,
with so few men, and it would be difficult, at such a time, to
draw off the artillery; if any force they were able to deal
with came, it would then be time enough, after the alarm
was given, to draw them to the works, unless they were
surprised.

It was not only the town malignants that murmured at the
drawing up of the ordnance, but Dr. Plumptre, hearing that
the forces were to march away, was raging at it; whereupon
being answered, that it was more for the public interest of the
cause, in great passion he replied, " What is the cause to me
if my goods be lost?"   The governor told him, he might

prevent that hazard and secure them in the castle.   He replied,
" It pitied him to soil them, and he had rather the enemy
had them, than they should be spoiled in removing."   While
this was boiling upon his spirit, he met the governor, with
some other gentlemen, in the street, and began to rail at him
for countenancing the godly townsmen, whom he called a
company of puritanical prick-eared rascals, and said, that the
worst of the malignants the governor had sent out of the
town, were honester men than the best of those he favoured;
and in spite of his teeth he would have three of the most
eminent of them turned out of the castle.   The governor telling
him, he would maintain them as the most faithful friends to
the cause, Plumptre replied he was as honest to the cause as
the governor.   "No," said the governor (who was not ignorant
of his atheism), " that you cannot be, for you go not upon the
same principles."   The doctor told him, it was false, with
such uncivil insolence, that the governor struck him, at which
he departed quietly home ; and after two or three days, retired
with his wife and children to the house of Mr. Parkyns of
Bunney, who was at that time in arms against the parliament,
where he stayed till the parliament-forces were routed, and
Nottingham castle summoned and preparing for a siege; and
then he sent a ridiculous challenge to the governor, with all
the foolish circumstances imaginable, which the governor, at
that present, only answered with contempt.   The pretence he
made was a distress, wherein the committee had employed
some of the governor's soldiers, for the levying of an assessment, which his brother would not pay, and this distress he
called the governor's affront to his family.   Though these
passages may seem too impertinent here, yet as they have
been grounds and beginnings of injurious prosecutions, wherewith the governor was afterwards much exercised. it was not
altogether unnecessary to insert them ; since even these little

things were links in the chain of providences which measured out his life.*

All the horse that had been raised in Nottinghamshire, marched away with Sir John Meldrum, namely, the troops of Colonel Thornhagh, Major Ireton, Captain White, and Captain Farmer; which, together with Captain Lomax and Captain Schrimpshire's foot companies, joining with Colonel Cromwell's men, marched to Gainsborough, and engaged those that besieged it, and were victorious, killing their general, Sir Charles Cavendish, with many more commanders, and some hundreds of soldiers; and this was opportunely done, as my Lord Newcastle was hastening to come over the water and join them, and who, by a bridge of boats, passed all his army over, and came near Gainsborough, just in a season to behold the rout of all his men. The parliament's forces expected he would have fallen upon them, and drew up in a body and faced him, but he advanced not; so they contented themselves by relieving Gainsborough, and made a very honourable retreat to Lincoln; but Gainsborough not being fortified, nor provided, this relief did not much advantage them, for my Lord Newcastle again besieged it, which was rendered to him, after eight days, upon conditions honourable for the defendants, though they were not performed by the besiegers; for all my Lord Willoughby's men were disarmed contrary to to articles,† and with them, some of the Nottingham soldiers that had gone into the town to refresh themselves, and so were shut up with them, when my lord laid siege to it; the rest had gone to Lincoln. They had behaved themselves

* To some readers the recital of these bickerings and intrigues may seem little interesting, to others highly so; certain it is, that whoever refuses to read them, refuses to acquaint himself with the temper of those times, which they characterise in the most peculiar manner.

† Particularly noticed by Whitelock.

very well in the fight, when Captain White received a wound
in his hand in the forlorn hope; Colonel Thornhagh, who
had fought very gallantly, was taken prisoner, and after he
was stripped of his arms and coat, a major of the enemy's,
whom the colonel had slightly wounded in the fervour of the
fight, came and basely wounded the colonel, being disarmed,
so that he left him for dead. But by the good providence of
God, that wound, by which the enemy intended to give him
death, gave him liberty; for coming to himself a little after
his hurt, he crept into one of his own tenant's houses, and
there had his wounds bound up, and found means to get to
Lincoln, from whence all the forces that went from Nottingham dispersed into different services. Major Ireton quite left
Colonel Thornhagh's regiment, and began an inseparable
league with Colonel Cromwell, whose son-in-law he afterwards
was. None of them could return to Nottingham, by reason
of my Lord Newcastle's army, which lay between them and
their home.

And now it was time for them at Nottingham to expect
my Lord Newcastle, which the governor made provision for
with all the diligence that it was possible under so many
difficulties and obstacles, which would to any one else have
been discouragements; but he had so high a resolution that
nothing conquered it. The townsmen, through discontent
at the drawing out of the forces, whereby their houses,
families, and estates were exposed, began to envy, then to
hate the castle, as grieved that anything should be preserved
when all could not; and indeed those who were more concerned in private interests than in the cause itself, had some
reason, because the neighbourhood of the castle, when it
was too weak to defend them, would endanger them. In this
hate and discontent, all the soldiers being townsmen, except
some of the governor's own company, they resolved they
would not go into the castle to behold the ruin of their

M

houses ; little considering that when the governor first came into Nottingham to defend them, at their earnest desire, he left a house and a considerable estate to the mercy of the enemy, rather desiring to advance the cause than to secure his own stake ; but their mean and half-affected hearts were not capable of such things. The governor, perceiving this defection, set some of the most zealous honest men to find out how many there were in the town who, neglecting all private interests, would cheerfully and freely come in and venture all with him ; intending, if he could not have found enough to defend the place, that he would have sent to other neighbouring garrisons to have borrowed some. Upon this inquiry, it was found that many of Colonel Pierrepont's own company were desirous to come in, but first wished to know their colonel's resolution as to how he would dispose of them; whereupon a hall was called, and the danger of the place declared to the whole town, that they might have time to provide for their goods and persons before the enemy came upon them. The colonel being present, his company asked him what he would advise them to do ; to whom his answer was, " You have but three ways to choose, either leave the town and secure yourselves in some other parliament-garrisons, or list into the castle,* or stand on the works and have your throats cut." Two or three days after this he went to his mother's, and carried his children with part of his goods, and sent his wife to Sir Gervas Clifton's house. Notwithstanding this public resolution in the hall to his company, he told them, and many others in private, that ne preferred the interest of the town above that of his life, and

* The particular account which has before been spoken of, has in this place a little difference of expression, which yet perhaps signifies much. There Colonel Pierrepont says, " List into the castle with *John,* for so in a jesting way he used to call Colonel Hutchinson," alluding no doubt to his frank and downright mode of speaking and acting.

would expose his life for the good of it, and stand on the
works of the town as long as they could be defended, and
when they could no longer be kept, he would retire to some
other parliament-garrison. Others he told, he scorned that his
colours should serve in the castle; that if his company went
up thither he would get him a new one, which should follow
him wherever he went, and many more such things in private;
but he openly, both to the governor and others, approved and
encouraged their going into the castle. According to his
advice, the townsmen, as they were diversely affected, disposed of themselves; the malignants all laid down their arms
and stayed in the town, but some honest and well-affected,
not bold enough to stand the hazard, went to other parliament-garrisons and served there; others secured themselves, their goods, and families in the country; some enlisted
into the castle; one Alderman Nix, captain of two hundred,
gave up his commission, and disbanded all his men except
about forty, who came into the castle and filled up the broken
companies there. At length, out of all the four companies
and the whole town, about 300 men enlisted into the castle.

The governor had procured forty barrels of powder, and
two thousand weight of match from London, and had increased the store of provision as much as the present poverty
of their condition would permit him. Then the committee
of Nottingham, so many of them as were remaining in the
town, and all the ministers of the parliament's party there,
came up to the castle, and, with the officers of the garrison,
ate at the governor's, to his very great charge; considering
that he was so far from receiving pay at that time, that all
the money he could procure of his own credit, or take up
with others, he was forced to expend for the several necessities of the soldiers and garrison; yet were the soldiers then,
and a long time after, kept together as long as they could

live, without any pay, and afterwards paid part in victuals, and the rest run on in arrears.*

The townsmen who came into the castle disposed their families into several villages in the country ; and at length a trumpet was sent, for a safe conduct for a gentleman, from my Lord Newcastle ; and having it, Major Cartwright came from him, with a summons for the delivery of the town and castle, to which the committee for the town, and the governor for the castle, returned a civil defiance in writing, about the 10th day of August.   Cartwright, having received it, and being treated with wine by the governor and the rest of the officers, grew bold in the exercise of an abusive wit he had, and told both the Mr. Hutchinsons that they were sprightly young men, but when my lord should come with his army, he would find them in other terms, beseeching my lord to spare them, as misled young men, and to suffer them to march away with a cudgel, and " then," said he, " shall I stand behind my lord's chair and laugh."   At which the governor, being angry, told him he was much mistaken, for he scorned ever to yield on any terms, to a papistical army led by an atheistical general.†   Mr. George Hutchinson told

* In all the histories of those times we read so much of the soldiers' complaints of want of pay, and of auditing their officers' accounts, which being no way reconcilable with modern practice, makes one suppose the officers fraudulent, and the soldiers mutinous; but this opinion will be corrected by observing what is here recited.   Hence we shall likewise conceive a high idea of the virtue of those men, who started forth out of every rank of life to devote themselves to the service of God and their country, and persevered through such privations and difficulties; and consider their interference in the settling the constitution of their country, for which they had fought, in a far different light from the tumult and mutiny of mercenary soldiers.

† Charles the First, when accused of retaining papists, denied having any in his army, and tried to have it believed that those which the Earl of

him, "If my lord would have that poor castle he must wade
to it in blood." Which words they say he told his general.
After these summonses were received, the governor drew all
his soldiers into the castle, and committed the guard of the
town to the aldermen, who were to set guards of fifty in a
night, according to their wards. Then calling together his
soldiers, he once again represented to them their condition,
and told them, that being religious and honest men, he could
be assured no extremity would make them fail in what they
found themselves strong enough to undertake ; and therefore
he should not fear to let them freely understand their danger,
which yet they had power to shun, and therefore whatever
misery might be the issue of their undertaking, they could
not justly impute it to him, it being their own election. For
after this summons they must expect the enemy, and to be
reduced to the utmost extremity by them that thought could
reach. It must not move them to see their houses flaming,
and, if need were, themselves firing them for the public
advantage, or to see the pieces of their families cruelly
abused and consumed before them ; they must resolve upon
hard duty, fierce assaults, poor and sparing diet, perhaps
famine, and the want of all comfortable accommodations. Nor
was there very apparent hope of relief at last, but more than
common hazard of losing their lives, either in defence of their
fort or of the place ; which, for want of good fortifications,
and through disadvantage of a neighbouring mount and
building, was not, in human probability, tenable against such
an army as threatened it. All which, for his own part, he

Newcastle had enlisted were unknown to him, although there is ample proof
that it was done by his order; that nobleman acted in a much more ingenuous manner, and, as is before related in a quotation from Sir P. Warwick's
Memoirs, turned the imputation into a jest; probably his indifference about
the religion of his soldiers caused the epithet of *atheistical* to be applied
to him, certainly without sufficient reason.

was resolved on; and if any of them found their courage
failing, he only desired they would provide for their safety in
time elsewhere, and not prejudice him and the public interest
so highly, as they would do, to take upon them the defence
of the castle, except they could be content to lay down their
lives and all their interests in it.   The soldiers were none of
them terrified at the dangers which threatened their undertaking; but at the latter end of August took, upon the
solemn fast-day, the national covenant, and besides it, a particular mutual covenant between them and the governor, to
be faithful to each other, and to hold out the place to the
death, without entertaining any parley, or accepting any
terms from the enemy.   This the governor was forced to do
to confirm them, for he had his experience not only of the
ungodly and ill-affected, but even of the godly themselves,
who thought it scarcely possible for any one to continue a
gentleman, and firm to a godly interest, and therefore repaid
all his vigilancy and labours for them with a very unjust
jealousy.*   The governor of Newark was his cousin-german,
to whom he was forced, against his nature, to be more uncivil than to any others that were governors in that place.
Whether it was that the dissension of brethren is always
most spitefully pursued, or that Sir Richard Byron, as it was
reported, suffered under the same suspicions on his side, it is
true they were to each other the most uncivil enemies that
can be imagined.   After this summons, my Lord Newcastle
came not, according to their bravadoes, but diverted his army
to Hull, to besiege my Lord Fairfax there; they of Newark

* It passes for a saying of Charles the Second, that the presbyterian
might be a very good religion, but it was not the religion of a gentleman;
these good folks seem to have been of the same mind.   The French have
taken care not to fall short in imitating this malicious prejudice, but
stamp with the hated name of Aristocrat every person at all elevated
above the vulgar, though ever so generous a friend of liberty.

having gotten him to send this summons upon confidence, knowing the condition of the place, that it would have been yielded to a piece of paper. The governor immediately set upon the fortification of his castle, made a work behind it, another on the Line side, turned the dovecote into a platform, and made a court of guard in Mortimer's Hole.

At this time Sir Thomas Hutchinson died in London,* and gave all his personal estate, and all that was unsettled at Mr. Hutchinson's marriage, to his second wife and her children; at which his two sons had not the least repining thought, but out of tender love, were very much afflicted for his loss, and procured a pass from Newark for Mr. George Hutchinson, to go to London, to visit his mother and fetch mournings, which accordingly he did; and upon a letter the committee sent up by him, he brought down an order of parliament to allow a table to the governor and committee, whom Mr. Hutchinson had till that time entertained at his own cost, with all the officers of the garrison and the ministers, which was no small charge to him; but he had a noble heart, and could not basely evade the expense, which that place necessarily drew upon him, not only by the constant entertainment of the committee, officers, and ministers, and all parliament officers, that came and went through the garrison, but by relieving the poor soldiers, who had such short pay, that they were, for the most part, thirty weeks and more behind; and when they marched out at any time, the governor would not suffer them to take a cup of drink, unpaid for, in the country, but always, wherever

---

* August 18, 1643, as appeared by his tombstone, under the communion table in St. Paul's, Covent Garden, London, and that he was 55 when he died. J. H.

A marginal note, written by Julius Hutchinson, grandfather of the editor.

they took any refreshment in their marches, paid it himself.
He gave them besides much from his own house, especially when any of them were sick or wounded, and lent
money to those who were most necessitous. All this run
him into a great private debt, besides many thousands of
pounds, which he engaged himself in with other gentlemen, and took up for the supply of the garrison and carrying on of the public service. Although the allowance for his
table was much envied by those mean fellows, that never
knew what the expense of a table was, and although it was
to him some ease, yet it did not defray the third part of his
expense in the service, being but ten pounds a week allowed
by the state; and his expenses all that time, in the public
service only, and not at all in any particular of his own
family, being, as it was kept upon account, above fifteen
hundred pounds a year. As soon as his father was dead,
and rents became due to him, the enemies, in the midst of
whom his estate lay, fetched in his tenants and imprisoned
them, and took his rents; his estate was begged and promised
by the king; those who lived not upon the place, flung up his
grounds, and they lay unoccupied, while the enemy prevailed in
the country. He was not so cruel as others were to their tenants, who made them pay over again those rents with which
the enemy forced them to redeem themselves out of prison,
but lost the most part of his rents, all the while the country was
under the adverse power. He had some small stock of his own
plundered, and his house, by the perpetual haunting of the
enemy, defaced, and for want of inhabitation, rendered almost
uninhabitable. For these things he had some subscriptions,* but never received one penny of recompense; and

---

* By subscriptions are here meant acknowledgments or certificates given
by the committees, which parliament professed to make good, but many
times did not. But Col. Hutchinson's disinterestedness and devotion to the

his arrears of pay, which he received after all the war was done, did not half pay the debts of those services contracted. But when he undertook this engagement, it was for the defence of his country's and God's cause, and he offered himself and all he had a willing sacrifice in the service; and rather praised God for what was saved, than repined at what was spent, it being above his expectation, that deliverance which God gave him out of his enemies' hands. He might have made many advantages by the spoil of his enemies, which was often brought in, and by other encroachments upon the country, which almost all the governors, on both sides, exacted everywhere else, but his heart abhorred it: the soldiers had all the prizes, and he never shared with them; all the malignants' goods the committee disposed off; and it ever grieved his heart to see the spoil of his neighbours, how justly soever they deserved it; but he chose all loss, rather than to make up himself* by violence and rapine. If in a judicial way, he was forced at any time, in discharge of his trust, to sign any harsh orders against any of the gentlemen of the country, it was with grief that they should deserve that severity; but this testimony is a truth of him, that in

cause did not suffice to exempt him from calumny, for in Walker's History of Independency, p. 166, *et seq* a list is given of members of parliament, who were unduly returned, who held commands contrary to the self-denying ordinance, or had moneys or offices given them. And Colonel Hutchinson is accused of all *three ;* how absurdly and unjustly every one must perceive. He was regularly elected to parliament in place of his father deceased : he had a regiment which he raised, and in a great degree subsisted himself ; he had a government, which at the time of his undertaking it, was a charge others feared to accept, and which for a long time was a loss and a detriment to him, and at the end of all he fell far short of receiving as much as he had expended. In the same place, Mr. William Pierrepont is most invidiously accused of getting £40,000.—*but how ? it was the personal estate of his own father !*

* Make himself up, make himself whole, reimburse himself.

his whole actings in this cause, he never prosecuted any private lust, either of revenge, ambition, avarice, or vain glory, under a public vizard, but was most truly public-spirited. Conscience to God, and truth and righteousness, according to the best information he could get, engaged him in that party he took ; that which engaged him, carried him through all along, though he encountered no less difficulties and contradictions from those of his own party, that were not of the same spirit he was, than he did from his enemies.

The death of Sir Thomas Hutchinson made every way a great reverse in the affairs of his eldest son, who had before been looked upon as his father's heir, and reverenced as much, or rather more, upon his father's score, than his own, so that no man durst attempt to injure him, whom they looked upon as under such a powerful protection. Sir Thomas and his fathers before him had ever deserved very well of their country, and, as lovers of their country, their neighbours had an implicit faith in all their dictates and actions, insomuch that Sir Thomas Hutchinson's single authority swayed with many, more than all the greater names of the country. But he at his death having divided, all things considered, his estate between the children of his two wives, though it be true the latter deserved more than they had, yet it is as true the first deserved not to be so much lessened as they were : and Mr. Hutchinson having been known to be the most pious and obedient son, from his childhood, that ever any father was blessed with, when it came to be known that his father had given away all that was in his power to give from him, those that had a great reverence and esteem for Sir Thomas would not believe him to be so defective in justice as to do this without some secret cause ; and therefore it was given out that he was displeased with his son's engagement, and for that cause disposed away so much of his estate

from them. But that was not so; indeed, at the time of his
death the parliament's interest was so low, that he might well
look upon them as lost persons, and so what he gave away
to the unengaged infant he might well look upon as all that
could be preserved. Mr. Hutchinson had only an allowance
from his father, while he lived, which was duly paid him;
but as soon as he died all his estate was seized by the enemy,
who had so much desire not to injure publicly a person so
popular, that they disturbed not Sir Thomas's tenants while
he lived, though he continued with the parliament, and faithful to their interest; because he was moderate, and one that
applied all his endeavours to peace, which he did not out of
policy, but out of conscience to his country, and by a wise
foresight of the sad consequences of a conquest by either side;
for he had often expressed, that accommodation was far
more desirable than war, and he dreaded that the spirits of
those men would become most insolent after conquest, who
were so violently bent to prosecute a war; that some of them
whom we have since known to be vile apostates, then professed that they abhorred accommodation. This report of Sir
Thomas's dislike of his son's engagement was raised and
dispersed by those who themselves were ill-affected to it;
but, however, it abated all the respect men had for him, upon
every account but his own. Those who had entertained a
secret envy of him, now feared not to manifest it, and began to work secret mines, to blow him up on all sides; but
God was with him, and disappointed all his enemies, and
made his virtues more illustrious by the oppositions they
encountered, and by the removal of all those props of
wealth and power which are necessary to hold up weaker
fabrics.*

* Here is in the original a marginal note in the following words: "The division of Sir Thomas Hutchinson's estate. Sir Thomas Hutchinson being

Soon after the death of his father, one Mr. Ayscough, a
gentleman of the country, allied to Sir Richard, since Lord
Byron, then governor of Newark, came to the governor of
Nottingham, and told him that Sir Richard Byron, out of
that tender, natural affection which he ever had for him, and
still preserved, desired him now to consider his wife and

mightily beloved in the country, and a moderate man, using all his endeavours for peace, his estate was never plundered in his lifetime ; and
though it is here falsely insinuated that he approved of his son's conduct
in taking arms against the king, it is most true that he was extremely
afflicted at it, being altogether for peace, and condemned such rash counsels as arms on both sides ; and the miseries he saw his king and country
involved in were certainly the occasion of his death : and though Sir
Thomas Hutchinson sat longer in the house than many honest men, it was
only in hopes by his moderate counsels to effect a happy peace between
his king and country. All this I have heard attested by his lady and
relict, my grandmother. Teste J. Hutchinson." This is that testimony
of Lady Katharine Hutchinson which was spoken of in the preface, and
which, in attempting to impeach the veracity of the author in a single
point, contributes largely to corroborate it in all. In the very instance before us there seems much more reason for the opinion of Mrs. Hutchinson
than of Lady Katharine : Sir Thomas Hutchinson had before been imprisoned for his opposition to the court ; was in this parliament on all com
mittees for the reform of religion ; sat with the parliament after the war
was deeply engaged in ; sent his sons arms, and promoted their desires to
the parliament : it is incredible that he should have any great objection to
the part they took, other than the general one of regretting that arms
were taken on either side. The most probable thing is that this lady, being
of the same party and opinion as her brother and family, and jealous of
Sir Thomas Hutchinson's children by his former wife, influenced him to
their disadvantage in the making of his will, and set up these reasons to
countenance it after his death. The other estates of Sir T. Hutchinson in
Nottinghamshire were fully equal, if not superior, in value to that of
Owthorpe. This being the only instance wherein the truth of the narrative is called in question, and this certainly invidiously, if not unjustly,
we may safely say we have the testimony of an adversary in our favour to
all the rest.

children, and the loss of his whole estate, which was inevitable, if he persisted in the engagement he was in; that some had already been suing to the Earl of Newcastle for it; but if he would return to his obedience to the king, he might not only preserve his estate, but have what reward he pleased to propound for so doing. To which the governor telling him this was a thing he ought to scorn, Mr. Ayscough told him that Sir Richard had, only out of love and tender compassion to him, given him this employment, with many protestations how much Sir Richard desired to employ all his interest to save him, if it were possible, and therefore begged of him that if he would still persist in this party, that he would yet quit himself of this garrison, and go into my Lord of Essex's army; for there, he said, Sir Richard would find pretence to save his rents for him for the present, and his estate for the future; for, said he, he can plead, " you were an inconsiderate young man, rashly engaged, and dares assure himself of your pardon; but to keep a castle against your king is a rebellion of so high a nature, that there will be no colour left to ask favour for you." The governor told him he should deliver the same propositions, and receive his answer, before some witnesses; whereupon he carried the gentleman to two of the committee, before whom he repeated his message, and the governor bade him return Sir Richard this answer, "That except he found his own heart prone to such treachery, he might consider there was, if nothing else, so much of a Byron's blood in him, that he should very much scorn to betray or quit a trust he had undertaken; but the grounds he went on were such, that he very much despised such a thought as to sell his faith for base rewards or fears, and therefore could not consider the loss of his estate, which his wife was as willing to part with as himself in this cause, wherein he was resolved to persist, in the same place in which it had pleased God to call him* to the defence of it."

About this time a woman was taken, whereof the committee had before been informed that she carried intelligence between Colonel Pierrepont and his mother, the countess of Kingston. The woman was now going through Nottingham, with letters from the old countess to her daughter-in-law, the colonel's wife, who was then at Clifton, Sir Gervas Clifton's house. In this packet there was a letter drawn, which the countess advised her daughter to sign, to be sent to Colonel Stanton, one of the king's colonels, to entreat back from him some goods of her husband's, which he had plundered; wherein there were these expressions : " That though her husband was unfortunately engaged in the unhappy rebellion, she hoped ere long he would approve himself a loyal subject to his majesty." The committee having read these letters, sealed them up again, and inclosed them in another to the colonel, then at Derby, telling him, that having intercepted such letters, and not knowing whether his wife might follow her mother's advice, which if she should would prove very dishonourable to him, they had chosen rather to send the letters to him than to her. The colonel was vexed that they had opened them, but for the present took no notice of it. All the horse having been drawn out of Nottingham to the relief of Gainsborough, and the Newarkers, knowing that the garrison was utterly destitute, plundered all the country even to the walls of Nottingham ; upon which some godly

---

* Notice is taken by Whitelocke of several attempts to prevail on Colonel Hutchinson to betray his trust, and of his steady adherence to it : there will be seen other instances more remarkable than this ; but here are two things extremely well worth notice ; this elegant and forcible apostrophe to Sir Richard Byron ; and the patriotic and disinterested devotion of Mrs. Hutchinson to the cause, at least a rare example in her sex.

men offered themselves to bring in their horses, and form a troop for the defence of the country, and one Mr. Palmer, a minister, had a commission to be their captain.* This man had a bold, ready, earnest way of preaching, and lived holily and regularly as to outward conversation, whereby he got a great reputation among the godly ; and this reputation swelled his spirit, which was very vain-glorious, covetous, contentious, and ambitious. He had so insinuated himself as to make these godly men desire him for their captain, which he had more vehement longing after than they, yet would have it believed that it was rather pressed upon him, than he pressed into it ; and therefore being at that time in the castle with his family, and feeding at the governor's table, who gave him room in his own lodgings, and all imaginable respect, he came to the governor and his wife, telling them that these honest people pressed him very much to be their captain, and desiring their friendly and Christian advice whether he should accept or refuse it. They freely told him, that having entered into a charge of another kind, they thought it not fit for him to engage in this ; and that he might as much advance the public service, and satisfy the men, in marching with them in the nature of a chaplain as in that of a captain. He, that asked not counsel to take any contrary to his first resolve, went away confused when he found he was not advised as he would have been, and said he would endeavour to persuade them to be content ; and afterwards said, they would not be otherwise satisfied, and so he was forced t⟩ accept the commission. The governor, having only declared his own judgment when he was asked, as a Christian ought to do according to his conscience, left the captain to act according to his own, and censured him not, but entertained him with the same freedom and kindness he had done befcre ;

* This, f not unique, is at least a singular trait.

but the man, being guilty of the avarice and ambition of his own heart, never afterwards looked upon the governor with a clear eye, but sought to blow up all factions against him whenever he found opportunity, and in the meantime dissembled it as well as he could. And now, before his troop was well raised, Colonel Thornhagh being recovered, brought back his troop from Lincoln, and both the troops quartered in the town ; which being a bait to invite the enemy, the governor gave charge to all that belonged to the castle, being about three hundred men, that they should not upon any pretence whatever be out of their quarters ; but they having, many of them, wives and better accommodations in the town, by stealth disobeyed his commands, and seldom left any more in the castle than what were upon the guard.

The townsmen were every night out upon the guard of the town, according to the wards of the aldermen ; but the most of them being disaffected, the governor, fearing treachery, had determined to quarter the horse in those lanes which were next to the castle, and to block up the lanes for the better securing them. Just the night before these lanes should have been blocked up, Alderman Toplady, a great malignant, having the watch, the enemy was, by treachery, let into the town, and no alarm given to the castle. Though there were two muskets at the gate where they entered, both of them were surrendered without one shot to give notice ; and all the horse, and about two parts of the castle soldiers, were betrayed, surprised, and seized on in their beds, but there were not above fourscore of the castle foot taken ; the rest hid themselves, and privately stole away, some into the country, some by night came up to the castle and got in, in disguises, by the river side ; but the cavaliers were possessed of the town, and no notice at all given to the castle. When, at the beating of reveille, some of the soldiers, that had been on the watch all night, were going down into the town to

refresh themselves, they were no sooner out of the castle
gates but some of the enemy's musketeers discharged upon
them, and they hasting back, got in with such care that the
enemy was prevented of their design of falling in with them.
They brought a strong alarm into the castle, when the
governor coming forth, was exceedingly vexed to find that
his men were, so many of them, contrary to his command,
wanting in their quarters; but it was no time to be angry,
but to apply himself to do what was possible to preserve the
place; wherefore he immediately despatched messengers by a
private sally-port, to Leicester and Derby, to desire their
assistance, either to come and help to beat the enemy out of
the town, or to lend him some foot to help keep the castle, in
which there were but fourscore men, and never a lieutenant
nor any head officer but his brother, nor so much as a surgeon
among them. As soon as the governor had despatched his
messengers he went up to the towers, and from thence played
his ordnance into the town, which seldom failed of execution
upon the enemy; but there was an old church, called St.
Nicholas Church, whose steeple so commanded the platform
that the men could not play the ordnance without woolpacks
before them. From this church the bullets played so thick
into the outward castle-yard, that they could not pass from
one gate to the other, nor relieve the guards, but with very
great hazard; and one weak old man was shot the first day,
who, for want of a surgeon, bled to death before they could
carry him up to the governor's wife, who at that time supplied that want as well as she could; but at night the governor and his men dug a trench between the two gates,
through which they afterwards better secured their passage.
In the meantime the cavaliers that came from Newark, being
about six hundred, fell to ransack and plunder all the honest
men's houses in the town, and the cavaliers of the town, who
had called them in, helped them in this work. Their pri-

soners they at first put into the sheep-pens in the market-place,* whereupon an honest townsman, seeing four or five commanders go into his own house, procured a cunning boy that came with him, while the enemy regarded more their plunder than their prisoners, to run privately up to the castle and give them notice, who presently sent a cannon bullet into the house. The cavaliers called in all the country as soon as they were in the town, and made a fort at the Trent bridges, and thither they carried down all their considerable plunder and prisoners. The next day after Sir Richard Byron had surprised the town, Mr. Hastings, since made lord of Loughborough, then governor of Ashby-de-la-Zouch, came with a body of about four hundred men ; but being displeased that the plunder was begun before he came, he returned again and left the Newark gentlemen to themselves ; who, as they made a fort at the bridges, threw down the half moons and bulwarks that had been raised about the town. They stayed five days, but very unquietly, for the cannon and muskets from the castle failed not of execution daily upon many of them, and they durst not in all that time go to bed. The third day Major Cartwright sent a letter, desiring the governor or his brother to come and meet him in St. Nicholas church, and promised them safe passage and return ; but the governor read the letter to his soldiers, and commanded a red flag to be set upon the tower to bid them defiance, and shot three pieces of cannon at the steeple in answer to his desired parley.

Five days the enemy stayed in the town, and all that time the governor and his soldiers, were none of them off from the guard, but if they slept, which they never did in the night, it was by the side of them that watched. At length, on Saturday, September 23d, in the afternoon, the governor saw a great

* It appears, by Deering's account of Nottingham, that these once occupied a considerable portion of the market-place.

many goods and persons going over the Line bridge, and not knowing what it meant, sent some cannon bullets after them ; when on the other side of the town he discerned a body of men, whom he knew not at first, whether to be friends or foes, but having at that time about eightscore men in the castle, for in that five days' space fourscore were come in by stealth, he caused them all to be drawn out in the castle-yard, and perceiving that those he last saw were friends, he sent out his brother, Major Hutchinson, with all the musketeers that could be spared, to help drive the enemy out of the town. They having effected what they came for, in fortifying the bridges, had nothing more to do but to get safe off, which they endeavoured with more haste and disorder than became good and stout soldiers. When Major Hutchinson came into the town with his men, they, greedy of knowing what was become of their wives and houses, dropped so fast from behind him to make the inquiry, that they had left him at the head of only sixteen men, when Sir Richard Byron, with Captain Hacker, followed by a whole troop of horse and a company of foot, came upon him. The major commanded his men to charge them, which they did, but shot over ; yet falling in with them pell-mell, they had gotten Sir Richard Byron down, and they had his hat, but he escaped, though his horse was so wounded that it fell dead in the next street.

These men that came to the governor's relief were Captain White with his troop, who were quartered at Leicester, on his return from Lincolnshire, from whence he was coming back to Nottingham ; and at Leicester he met the messenger the governor had sent for assistance, which he prosecuted so well, that from the two garrisons of Leicester and Derby, with his own troop, he brought about four hundred men. As soon as they were come into the town, Sir John Gell's men, seeing the cavaliers had a mind to be gone, interrupted them not, but being as dexterous at plunder as at fight, they

presently went to Toplady's house, who had betrayed the
town, and plundered it and some others, while the governor's
soldiers were busy in clearing the town of the enemy. When
they had done this, the governor did what he could to restrain the plunder; but the truth is, Gell's men were nimble
youths at that work, yet there was not very much mischief
done by them. Toplady's house fared the worst, but his
neighbours saved much of his goods; he himself, with
several other townsmen and countrymen, who had been very
active against the well-affected, at this time were brought up
prisoners to the castle. There were not above five-and-
twenty of the Newark soldiers taken; how many were slain
at their going off, and during the time of their stay, we
could not certainly tell, because they had means of carrying
them off by the bridge, where they left Captain Hacker
governor* of their new fort with fourscore men. Their prisoners and plunder they sent away in boats to Newark;
many of the townsmen went with them, carrying away not
only their own but their neighbours' goods; and much more
had been carried away, but that the unexpected sally from the
castle prevented them. Dr. Plumptre, one of the committee
of Nottingham, whom they found prisoner at the marshal's
house in the town, and released, went out of the town with
them. This man, when he had provoked the governor to
strike him, for his malicious and uncivil railings against him
for the respect he showed to the godly men of the town, had
retired to the house of a malignant gentleman in arms against

---

* The brother of Colonel Hacker, who was tried, condemned, and executed for attending the execution of Charles the First. This brother, who
served the king during the whole war with great zeal, could not obtain the
pardon of Colonel Hacker, nor prevent the confiscation of his family
estate, which was granted to the Duke of York, the king's brother, from
whom he was obliged to ransom it at a high rate. It lay at Colston Basset,
oining to Owthorpe.

the parliament; had received a protection from the governor of Newark, and had divers meetings with the Newark officers; yet after all this had the impudence to come into the town of Nottingham: and in all the taverns and ale-houses he came into, he belched out abominable scoffs and taunts against the governor and the committee-men, before Colonel Thornhagh's face, who commanded him out of the room for it; and upon information of these things to the governor and the committee, he was sent for by some mus-keteers, and the enemy's protection for himself and his goods being found about him, he was committed prisoner, but there being no good accommodation for him in the castle, the governor, in more civility than he deserved, suffered him to be in the town, whence he went with them, and afterwards retired to Derby. At the same time, the cavaliers having taken some prisoners upon the parliament's score who lived quietly in the country, the committee had fetched in some gentlemen's sons of their party, who were left at their fathers' houses; whereof one was remaining at the marshal's house when the cavaliers came into the town, whom the governor suffered to be there upon his parole, there being no good accommodation for him in the castle. Him the cavaliers would have had to have gone away with them, but he would not; which handsome behaviour so pleased the governor, that he freely gave him his liberty without exchange.*

As soon as the enemy was driven out of the town, the governor brought down two pieces of ordnance to the market-place, and entreated the soldiers that were come from Leicester and Derby to march with him immediately, to assault them in their fort at the bridges, before they had time to put them-selves in order, and re-collect their confused souls, after their

---

* This story resembles some of those recited in the early and virtuous times of the Roman republic. Such anecdotes serve to relieve the mind, fatigued with reading of the crimes and follies of mankind.

chase; but the mayor of Derby, an old dull-headed Dutchman, said ten thousand men could not do it, and could by no means be entreated to go on, nor to stay one day longer, but to stand by, while the governor made the attempt, with his own men. He, when he saw he could not prevail, thought it not convenient, at that time, to urge his men beyond their power, after they had had a week of such sore labour, and so, much discontented that he could not effect his desire, he drew back his ordnance into the castle.   Here his women, while the men were all otherwise employed, had provided him as large a supper as the time and present condition would permit, at which he entertained all the strangers, and his own officers and gentlemen.

There was a large room, which was the chapel, in the castle : this they had filled full of prisoners, besides a very bad prison, which was no better than a dungeon, called the Lion's Den; and the new Captain Palmer, and another minister, having nothing else to do, walked up and down the castle-yard, insulting and beating the poor prisoners as they were brought up.   In the encounter, one of the Derby captains was slain, and five of our men hurt, who for want of another surgeon, were brought to the governor's wife, and she having some excellent balsams and plasters in her closet, with the assistance of a gentleman that had some skill, dressed all their wounds, whereof some were dangerous, being all shots, with such good success, that they were all well cured in convenient time.*   After our wounded men were dressed, as she stood

* The reader will remember that the mother of Mrs. Hutchinson had patronized and assisted Sir Walter Raleigh, when prisoner in the Tower, in his chemical experiments, and had acquired a little knowledge of medicine; whether her daughter had obtained instructions from her mother, or the mother herself was here (for she passed the latter part of her life with her daughter, and died in her house at Owthorpe), is uncertain.   Mrs. Hutchinson was certainly an extraordinary woman, and this is not one of the least singular, nor least amiable instances of it.

at her chamber-door, seeing three of the prisoners sorely cut, and carried down bleeding into the Lion's Den, she desired the marshal to bring them in to her, and bound up and dressed their wounds also : which while she was doing, Captain Palmer came in and told her his soul abhorred to see this favour to the enemies of God ; she replied, she had done nothing but what she thought was her duty, in humanity to them, as fellow-creatures, not as enemies.   But he was very ill satisfied with her, and with the governor presently after, when he came into a very large room where a very great supper was prepared, and more room and meat than guests ; to fill up which the governor had sent for one Mr. Mason, one of the prisoners, a man of good fashion, who had married a relation of his, and was brought up more in fury, than for any proof of guilt in him, and I know not whether two or three others, the governor had not called to meat with them ; for which Captain Palmer bellowed loudly against him, as a favourer of malignants and cavaliers.*   Who could have thought this godly, zealous man, who could scarce eat his supper for grief to see the enemies of God thus favoured, should have after-wards entered into a conspiracy, against the governor, with those very same persons, who now so much provoked his zeal ?   But the governor took no notice of it, though he set the very soldiers a muttering against himself and his wife, for these poor humanities.

The next day the neighbouring forces returned home. Colonel Thornhagh having lost most of his troop, went to London to get another.   Captain White -stayed at Nottingham with his, where intelligence being given that the cavaliers intended to possess themselves of Broxtowe and Woollerton (two gentlemen's houses each within two miles of Nottingham), Captain Palmer was sent, with the remainder of his men to keep Broxtowe-house, and the governor's

---

* Behold a presbyterian and a sectary, a Levite and a Samaritan !

captain-lieutenant, with his company, to Woollerton. The
governor, at Nottingham, broke up the Line Bridge to prevent
the cavaliers coming suddenly by that way into the town;
then he blocked up the lanes next the castle, and cut up all
the hedges, that were dangerous to make approaches to the
castle; and having the experience of the mischief of it,
pulled down St. Nicholas's church by the advice of the committee. *

Presently after the cavaliers were gone out of town, some
naughty people, set on by them, fired the town, but it was
quenched without burning above two or three houses; yet for
a fortnight together it was perpetually attempted, fire being
laid to hay-barns and other combustible places, insomuch that
the women were forced to walk nightly by fifties to prevent
the burning;† which the committee perceiving to be attempted
by the instigation of the Newark gentlemen, they wrote them
word, that if they forbade not their instruments, if so much
as one house were fired, they would fire all the cavaliers'
houses near them. The gentlemen returned them a scornful
letter, full of taunts and disdain, but after that no more houses
were attempted with fire.

---

* It is said, in Deering's History of Nottingham, that this church was
pulled down by Colonel Hutchinson, and the bells carried to Owthorpe;
which last was at that time impossible, the enemy being in possession of the
Vale of Belvoir and the ways to it. And moreover, the church at Owthorpe
was, as Deering in another place observes, too small to contain them. In
Throsby's edition of Thoroton, he remarks that neither Deering nor Thoroton were properly acquainted with the circumstances of that affair, and
mentions, that in digging near the foundation of the present tower (for the
church has been rebuilt), a bell was found, evidently broken to pieces at
the demolition of the church; probably by the cannon-shot which was sert
in answer to Major Cartwright's message. The situation of this church was
both very near to the castle, and on a parallel height.

† This is a curious fact, and points out a way of turning to use and profit
the timorousness and watcfulness of her sex.

The Derby soldiers, when they returned home, being asked why they left the cavaliers at the bridges unassaulted, made answer, they would have beaten them out, but the governor would not lend them a piece of ordnance out of his castle; which false report, when the governor heard, piqued him heartily, being so notorious a lie; for he drew down two pieces of ordnance, and could not entreat them to do more than stand by, while he attempted it with his own men; but their Major Molanus, being an old soldier, discouraged our soldiers, and told them it was a vain and impossible attempt. For this cause, the governor resolved he would set upon it alone, whenever it was seasonable; and watching an opportunity, he soon took it, at a time when intelligence was brought him that all the forces Newark could send forth, were gone upon a design into Lincolnshire. Then, on the Lord's day, under colour of hearing a sermon at the great church in the town, he went thither, and after sermon, from the steeple, took a view of the fort at the bridges; no one perceiving his design, but his engineer, who was with him, and took a full survey of Hacker's works. Then, after supper, he called the committee together, and communicated his intentions to them, which they approved of. So all that night he spent in preparations against the next morning; he sent away orders to the horse and foot that lay at Broxtowe to come to him in the morning by eight o'clock, with all the pioneers they could gather up in the country; he sent into the town, and caused all the pioneers there to be brought up, under pretence of making a breastwork before the castle-gates, and pretending to set them upon the platforms, caused all the cannon-baskets to be filled, which he intended for rolling trenches. All things, betimes in the morning, being gotten into perfect readiness, and so discreetly ordered, that the enemy had no notice from any of their friends in town, nor knew anything of the design, till it was ready; the governor,

about eleven o'clock on Monday morning, marched out,
although the weather at that time, being very tempestuous
and rainy, seemed to have combined with his enemies to
withstand the attempt; but the soldiers were rather animated
than discouraged, thinking that difficulties, after they were
vanquished, would increase their glory.   So when the ugly
storm had, for three or four hours, wasted itself in its fury on
them, it fell at their feet, and no more envious clouds obscured
the cheerful face of heaven, so long as they continued in the
field.   The governor's own company marched through the
meadows, and gave the alarm to the enemy's foot, while Mr.
George Hutchinson's company went through the lanes, to
gain a nook, which was very advantageous for the approaches
of our men, and of which they easily possessed themselves,
and then advancing, planted their colours within musket-shot
of the fort.   Although they planted so many colours, the
governor had but eightscore foot, and a hundred horse, in all
that went with him out of the castle, but he set the pioneers
fairly among them to make the better show.

When the colours were thus planted, the pioneers were set
at work to cast up a breastwork ; and being left in a safe
posture with the inferior officers, the governor and his brother
went up to the castle, to order the drawing down of the
ordnance.   Meanwhile the cavaliers sallied out of their fort
to gain the colours, at whose approach all the pioneers ran
away from their works ; but the soldiers kept their ground
and their colours, and beat back the enemy into their own
fort, killing some of them, whereof two were left dead before
our men, whom they thought it not safe to carry off.   Our
horse meeting the flying pioneers, brought them back again
to their works, which they continued all that day, and the
cavaliers attempted no more sallies.   At evening the ordnance were brought down and planted within musket-shot
of the fort, and then the governor despatched a messenger to

Derby to tell Sir John Gell, if he pleased to send any of his men, they might come and see the fort taken. Accordingly, on Tuesday the Dutch major came, with about sixscore foot and dragoons. Hard by the fort at the bridges, and at that side which our men approached, there were two houses full of coals, into which, if the cavaliers had put any men, they might have done much mischief to the assailants; wherefore the governor sent two or three soldiers, who very boldly went almost under their works and fired them both, by the light of which, they burning all night, the governor's men wrought all that night in their trenches, and cut a trench in the meadows, some of them calling to the cavaliers in the fort, and keeping them in abusive replies, one upon another, while the pioneers carried on their works. The governor and his brother, and all the other officers, continuing all night in the trenches with them, they behaved themselves so cheerfully, that the governor gave them the next morning twenty pounds; and they had very good drink and provisions brought them out of the garrison, which much encouraged them, but the governor's presence and alacrity among them much more. When the Derby men came on Tuesday, the Dutch major came down to the trenches, and told the governor that he wondered he would attempt the fort, for it was impregnable, and therefore much dissuaded him from going on, and said that he and his men would return. The governor told him that he and the soldiers with him were resolved to leave their lives rather than their attempt; and if they failed for want of seconding by that force which was sent with him to their assistance, let the blame lie on him. When the Derby officers saw him so resolute to persist, they, after much dissuasion and dispute, determined to stay, and the officers went up with the governor to supper in the castle, and the soldiers to quarters provided for them in the town: but after supper, the governor went down again, and stayed all night in the trenches

with his men, and left them not as long as they stayed there,
but only to fetch down what was necessary for them. He,
his brother, and all the officers, were every night with them,
and made them continue their custom of railing at each other
in the dark, while they carried on their approaches. There
was in the Trent, a little piece of ground of which, by damming
up the water, the cavaliers had made an island; and while
some of the soldiers held them in talk, others on Wednesday
night cut the sluice, and by break of day on Thursday morning had pitched two colours in the island, within carbine-shot
of the fort, and the governor's company had as much advanced
their approach on the other side. When they in the fort
saw, in the morning, how the assailants had advanced, while
they were kept secure in talk all the night, they were extremely
mad, and swore like devils, which made the governor and his
men great sport: and then it was believed they in the fort
began to think of flight; which the besiegers not expecting,
still continued their approaches, and that day got forty yards
nearer to the island and also to the other side. Although Sir
John Gell's men came but on Tuesday, on Thursday the second
messenger came from him, to call them back. The governor
entreated them to stay that night and keep the trenches,
while his men refreshed themselves: which they did, but his
men would not go out of their trenches, but slept there to fit
themselves for the assault, which the governor had resolved on
for the morning, and for that purpose, after he had left them
with all things provided in their trenches, he went to the
castle to see the fire-balls and other necessaries for the assault
brought down, and at three in the morning came to them,
when the soldiers told him the cavaliers in the fort had for
two hours left off shooting. He sent some soldiers then to
the work sides to discover what this meant; but they, perceiving the place empty, went in and found that all the garrison
had stolen away, and had left behind them fourscore sheep,

a hundred loads of coals, twenty quarters of oats, much hay, a great deal of plundered lead, and a fort so strong, that if they had had such courage as became men of their profession, they would never have quitted it. They left all their works standing, and only broke up two arches of the Trent bridges, to hinder the governor's men from following them. Their flight was by that means secured, the river being so out that the horse could not ford over. Mr. George Hutchinson and his company were appointed to possess and keep the fort at the bridges, which he did; and the next week the garrison kept a day of solemn thanksgiving to God, for this success and the mercy in it, whereby all their men were preserved, notwithstanding their very bold adventures, so that not one of them was slain, and but four of them wounded, whereof three were so slightly hurt, that they returned again next day into the field. To increase their thanks to God, news was brought them that the same week the forces that went out from Newark, joined with Henderson's, had received a great overthrow by Cromwell; and that my Lord Newcastle had been forced to raise his siege of Hull with great loss and dishonour. Some time after the bridge was recovered, the horse went forth and brought in some oxen of Mr. John Wood's, a justice of the county, disaffected to the parliament, but not in action against them. He, following his oxen, came to the governor, and, after he had despatched his business, told him how Mr. Sutton would have once employed him on a message, to offer the governor any terms he would ask the king, to come over to his side and deliver up the castle to his use. Mr. Wood told him (Sutton), that such a message would not obtain credit, unless he had some propositions in writing; whereupon Sutton called for pen and ink, and wrote that he should offer the governor, if he would resign his castle, not only to be received into favour, but to have what reward of honour, money, or command, he himself would propound; which paper when Mr. Wood had received, Sir Richard Byron came in, and Mr. Sutton told him the business; to which Sir Richard answered, he believed it would not take effect, for he himself had made the like offers to him, and been rejected :* which Mr. Wood hearing, would not undertake the employment, but the governor made him declare the story to two of the gentlemen of the committee.

The governor not growing secure by his successes, was but stirred up to more active preparations for the defence of the place he had undertaken; and having a very ingenious person, Mr. Hooper, who was his engineer, and one that understood all kind of operations, in almost all things imaginable, they procured some saltpetre men and other necessary labourers, and set up the making of powder and match in the castle, both of which they made very good; they also cast mortar pieces in the town, and finished many other inventions for the defence of the place. The governor also caused a mount near the castle to be bulwarked, and made a platform for ordnance, and raised a new work before the castle-gates, to keep off approaches, and made a new in-work in the fort at the bridges.

Sir Thomas Fairfax, being overmastered in the north, by the Earl of Newcastle's great army, after his father was retired into Hull, came with those horse that were left him, into the Vale of Belvoir, and so visited Nottingham Castle; where he and the commanders that were with him, considering of what advantage it was to the parliament to keep that place, by reason of the commodious situation of it, and the pass which might be there maintained, between the north and south, and the happy retreat it might afford to their northern forces, very much pressed the governor and the committee

* This is the second instance of attempting Colonel Hutchinson's fidelity, but the most remarkable one will be found in the sequel.

to raise all the force they could, offering arms and commissions for them: especially he pressed the governor to complete a regiment for himself, which at that time he would not accept, because Colonel Pierrepont had not yet declared what he would do with his regiment. The colonel was then at Derby, whither some of his officers going to him, to know what they should do, he dismissed them; yet coming to the town, he gave out strange envious whispers, and behaved himself so disingenuously to the governor, that he had just cause to have no more regard for him; and being again importuned by Sir Thomas Fairfax, he received a commission to raise a regiment of twelve hundred. He presently recruited his own companies, and began to raise more: Mr. George Hutchinson was his lieutenant-colonel, and one Mr. Widmerpoole his major; there was a company raised by one Captain Wright; there remained a broken piece of Colonel Pierrepont's company, and Captain Poulton, who had been their captain-lieutenant, being dismissed by the colonel, had a new commission under the governor for a company; and those soldiers of Colonel Pierrepont's not knowing what to do, it was determined at a council of war of strangers, whereof Sir William Fairfax was president, that they should enlist under Captain Poulton. Sir William and Sir Thomas Fairfax, both of them, when the governor made scruple of passing by Colonel Pierrepont, assured him that they had intelligence given them in the north of his intentions to deliver over Nottingham to the king.

About this time Chadwick, the deputy recorder of Nottingham, and one of the committee, came to Nottingham, from whence he had gone, when the soldiers were all drawn out, and all that were fearful went to other places to secure themselves. This fellow being sent on a message to the Lord Fairfax, general of the north, had received letters of credence from the committee; but instead of prosecuting their business,

which was to have procured some force from my lord to help
keep the place, when my Lord Newcastle was daily expected
to come against it, he procured himself a commission for a
regiment, and a joint commission for himself and Colonel
Pierrepont to be governors of the town and castle.   The last
he kept very private; the first he bragged of as a thing,
which, my lord considering his great abilities, would needs
enforce upon him.   In execution of this, he raised seven
men, who were his menial servants, went into Staffordshire,
possessed a papist's fine house, and fired it to run away
by the light, when the enemy was thirty miles off from it;
and he also cheated the country of pay for I know not how
many hundred men: for which, if he had not stolen away
in the night, he had been stoned; and as his wife passed
through the towns, she was in danger of her life, the women
flinging scalding water after her.   But before this, he came
to Nottingham at the time the governor raised his regiment,
and coming up to the castle, behaving himself somewhat insolently, and casting out mysterious words of his authority;
the governor set on a person to find out his meaning, to
whom he showed a commission he had privately obtained
some four months before, for himself and Colonel Pierrepont
to be joint governors of the county, town, and castle; but
neither did he now declare this to any of the committee, but
only made some private brags in the town, that he would
shortly come and take order for the safety of the place, and
so went out of town again.   The governor acquainted the
committee with this, who seemed to have great indignation
at it, and wrote immediately to Mr. Millington, burgess of the
town of Nottingham, to have the government of the castle
confirmed to Colonel Hutchinson by authority of parliament.
Mr. Salisbury, their secretary had also put in " the government of the town," but Colonel Hutchinson caused him to
put it out; and the governor, being informed that Colonel

Pierrepont, at London, was labouring to obtain a regiment, and to be sent down as governor of the town, he for the more speedy despatch, sent his own chaplain with the committee's letters to London, and sent other letters of his own to Sir Thomas Fairfax, to acquaint him how Chadwick had abused my lord, his father, in the surreptitious procurement of this dormant commission; which, during all the time of danger, had lain asleep in his pocket, and now was mentioned, as a thing, whereby he might, when he would, take that place out of Colonel Hutchinson's hands, which he had with so many labours and dangers preserved, by God's blessing, for the parliament's service; he therefore desired a commission for the castle only.

As soon as Mr. Allsop came to London, he was immediately despatched again to Nottingham, with an order of parliament, dated November 20, 1643, for Colonel Hutchinson to be governor both of the town and castle of Nottingham, with an acknowledgment of the good service he had done in preserving the place; and Mr. Millington said he should likewise have a commission from the Earl of Essex. At Leicester, Mr. Allsop met letters, directed to the governor, from Sir Thomas Fairfax, wherein was a commission enclosed from his father, then general of all the north, for the government of both the town and castle. These coming both together, although the general and the parliament had added the government of the town to that of the castle, as more honour to him, Colonel Hutchinson was for many reasons much troubled at it, among which these were some of his considerations. First, they were almost all malignants, there being scarcely a man left who was to be confided in, except those who had already enlisted into the castle. Secondly, they were not so much open, professed enemies, as close, hypocritical, false-hearted people; amongst whom were some leading eminent men, so subtle in their malignity, that though

o

their actions were most prejudicial to the public service, yet did they cast such cunning, specious pretences over them of public good, that even the most upright men of the garrison were often seduced by their fair colours. Thirdly, the most religious and the best people were so pragmatical, that no act, nor scarcely word, could pass without being strictly arraigned and judged at the bar of every common soldier's discretion, and thereafter censured and exclaimed at. Fourthly, the townsmen, being such as had lived free and plentifully by themselves, could not subject themselves to government; but were so saucy, so negligent, and so mutinous, that the most honourable person in the world, could expect nothing but scandal, reproach, and ingratitude, for the payment of his greatest merit; and this the worthy governor found sufficiently from them. Lastly, the few good men were so easily blown up into causeless suspicions and jealousies, and there were so many malignant whispers daily spread abroad of every one in office, that it was impossible for any man so worthily to demean himself, but that a jealous misconstruction of some inconsiderable trifle, was enough to blast the esteem of all his actions, though never so pious and deserving; and of all things in the world, nothing was so contrary to the governor's clear and generous heart, as a base and causeless jealousy of him.* But notwithstanding these and many other reasons, such as the unprofitable expense of his time, estate, and labours, where he should reap neither glory nor advantage to himself, he considered, that since he had rather declined than sought the enlargement of his power and command, and that the parliament and generals had, at such a distance been moved to put it, unsought, upon him, it was a work which God called him to, and that the

---

* In effect it will be seen that this gave him more uneasiness than his enemies, in the plenitude of power, were ever able to do.

Lord, who set him. into the employment. would conquer all the difficulties. For the unjust thoughts or reports of men or their ungrateful returns, he was as much above the grief of that, as the vain-glory of mutable popular applause. It was in all things his endeavour to do and deserve well; and then he never regarded the praise or dispraise of men, for he knew that it was impossible to keep on a constant career of virtue and justice, and to please all. It sufficed him, for his inward peace, that he did not thrust himself into this and other employments, for any popular, ambitious, or advantageous interest of his own ; but that he was called of God, to the carrying on of the interests of truth, righteousness, and holiness, and to the defence of his country, wherein he was faithful, and found the Lord's protection and glorious presence, not only in all he did, but in all he suffered for him and from him.

As soon as the governor had received his commission, he thought it his duty to put it into execution, and to arm and fortify the town ; but my Lord Newcastle coming with all his forces into Nottingham and Derbyshire, the governor, by the advice of the committee, forbore to publish his new commissions, lest the enemy, perceiving an intent to enlarge the garrison, should utterly destroy the town, before they were able to defend it. At the reading of his commission in the committee chamber, Colonel Thornhagh showed much discontent and was melancholy after it; whereupon the governor told him, that as he had not sought that enlargement of command, so if any of them thought themselves abridged by it, or of any other inconvenience to the public service, he would resign it, ar d never make use of his commission. The colonel answere l with much kindness, that he only wondered how the town came to be added, when they wrote for the castle; but he was well satisfied with it, and forced himself to a seeming conte it, though the truth is he had some emulation

but not malice, towards the governor ; and being of a nature
a little jealous and easy to be wrought upon, the wicked
enemies of the cause endeavoured, all they could, by insinuations to work disaffection and division between these two
gentlemen, who were the most faithful, unbiassed, and zealous champions of the public interest, in their country.   But
after Colonel Thornhagh had been wrought up to declare his
discontent, there were many odd passages, by which others
also of the comm'ttee, who durst not before reveal their
envious hearts, showed themselves displeased.   Whereupon,
when they were all together, the governor, who hated secret
heart-boilings, spoke to them, and told them that their carriages since the commission came to him, did manifest their
dissatisfaction in it; and if they would deal ingenuously with
him and let him know it, as he had not sought the additional government of the town, so he would never undertake it, if they had any suspicion that, unknown to them, he
had procured it for himself, and closely sought after the enlargement of his own power, by the abridgment of theirs ;
he assured them he was much misunderstood, and that
neither to Mr. Millington, nor to Sir Thomas Fairfax, had he
mentioned anything more than the government of the castle.
For that of the town he rejoiced not in it, but looked upon
it as a great burden ; yet since it was conferred as an honour
upon him, he should not decline serving them who had
thought him worthy of it, except it gave distaste to any of
those present ; which if it did, he would esteem it an obligation, if they would but declare it before he published his
commission.   They all unanimously replied, they were not
only contented, but exceedingly well pleased in it.   Then the
governor told them, if they were real,* as they professed,
he should expect their ready and free concurrence with him,
in all affairs tending to the public service, and in those

* Real—*Fr.* Vrais—sincere.

courses he should apply himself to, or the good of the garrison : and agair earnestly desired them, if they had any dis-
likes, either of himself personally, or of the alteration of the
town out of the hands it had been in the last year, that they
would now freely declare it: for as he should take it exceedingly kindly of them, to do so at this time; so if, after he had
undertaken the charge, there should be any thwarting or
crossing of powers and commands between them, he should
not bear it; for as he should not stand upon all punctual
niceties in his command, so he would not be abridged of the
just and lawful power due to him in his place. They all
unanimously answered, it was very fit and just he should have
it, and they would rather endeavour to uphold him in it than
in any way to retrench it.

Now was my Lord Newcastle's army come into Derbyshire, and having taken some places there, nothing was expected at Derby and Nottingham but a siege; whereupon
Captain Palmer's troop was called away from Broxtowe, and
all the rest of the horse was sent away into Leicestershire,
except a few left for scouts; and as soon as they were gone,
my Lord Newcastle's forces came and quartered almost at
the town side, and in all the near towns, and Hastings took
this opportunity to make a garrison at Wilden Ferry.* By
the mercy of God the enemy was restrained from com-

* Wilden Ferry was said before to be in the possession of the king's
forces; but whether that was an anachronism, or that the thing now meant
was an increase of the fortifications, and the placing a larger number of
men there, it is clear that the garrison of this place did after this period
become a greater annoyance to the parliament, and Lord Grey, of Groby,
who commanded in chief the associated forces of Leicester, Nottingham,
&c. attacked and took it, assisted, as Whitelocke says, p. 96, by Sir John
Gell, who contrived to get the thanks of the parliament for his services
herein, and for taking Winkfield manor and Shelford manor; although
some time after, we find him besieging " inkfield manor in conjunc-

ing up to the town, though it lay so open that they might have come in at their pleasure ; and they not only miserably wasted and plundered the country all about, but one of them told a malignant, where he quartered, that it was their design in coming to those parts, to devour the country. The regiments that were quartered the nearest to Nottingham were Sir Marmaduke Langdale's and Colonel Dacre's, who had been a familiar acquaintance of Lieutenant-colonel Hutchinson's when he was in the north, and they loved each other as well as if they had been brothers. Colonel Dacre sent a trumpet to desire Lieutenant-colonel Hutchinson to send him a safe convoy, that he might come and see him, which he acquainted the committee with, and would have refused, but that the committee, thinking some good use might be made of it, persuaded him to suffer him to come; accordingly he sent him a ticket under his hand, promising him to come and go safely ; so upon Thursday morning he came, with about eight more, to the top of the hill at Nottingham, and from thence sent his trumpet to the governor, as if not willing to trust himself without his leave, to know whether he would permit him and his two servants to come into his garrison to visit the lieutenant-colonel. The governor sent him a ticket for them to come in ; and though usually they kept no sentinels in the town, yet he sent down some officers and soldiers to show him a guard at his entrance. When the lieutenant-colonel came to him, he made many endearing expressions to him ; how much he rejoiced when his regiment was designed for that place where he was, and how kind an affection he retained for him, notwithstanding their contrary engagements. Falling

tion with Lord Denbigh, and that Shelford manor was not taken till more than two years after by Colonel Hutchinson, acting under the command of Poyntz.

into further discourse of this kind, he said that if he could but be convinced that the king first entertained papists into his army, and that the parliament had none in theirs, he would never fight more on his side. The lieutenant-colonel told him he should easily be able to do that. " Well," said Dacre, " you and I must have some discourse in private,* and I shall be glad if you can satisfy me in that." Then the colonel desired some drink might be sent out to two or three gentlemen, that stayed for him upon the top of the hill; which the lieutenant-colonel hearing, sent some of his own officers and soldiers on horseback to fetch them down, who coming in all together with them, the town rose in an uproar, and came to the governor with a high complaint, that I know not how many cavaliers were come into the town, and rode up and down armed, threatening the people to their great terror. This the governor thinking to be true, was vexed at it, and sent down an angry letter to his brother, requiring him to send up the men that came last into the town. Col. Dacre hearing this, desired the lieutenant-colonel that the gentlemen might pass as they came, and offered to go up himself and answer for the offence they had given. But the lieutenant-colonel presently carried them all out of the town, and came himself up to the castle, taking it something unkindly that his brother should write such a letter to him, and worse, that others should have suspicions of him ; so that though he had made a promise to dine the Saturday following at Dacre's quarters, yet, to take away all offence and suspicions,

* Though this may appear somewhat improbable at a time when religious opinions have so little effect upon political ones, it was otherwise considered at that time; for nearly at this same juncture it is to be seen, in Whitelocke, page 81, tnat Sir E. Deering did on this very account of there being so many papists and Irish rebels entertained in the king's army, quit him and come into the parliament, who admitted him to composition, being the first.

he resolved he would have no more meetings with him, and
to that end wrote him a very civil letter to excuse his not
coming; and the governor wrote another to excuse the mistake, whereupon the gentlemen were sent for to the castle.
Dacre returned complimentary answers to them both, and
wrote another to Captain Poulton, intreating very earnestly
the lieutenant-colonel and Captain Poulton to come and dine
with him on Wednesday, and desiring the governor he might
have the honour to see him.   These letters being communicated to the committee, they would fain have had the lieutenant-colonel to have gone, but he held firm to his resolution and would not; so with their privity Captain Poulton
only went to excuse it, and two of White's officers were sent
along with him, with charge, if they could, to find out how
the enemy lay.   When Captain Poulton came, the colonel
entertained him very kindly, and expressed a great deal of
trouble that the lieutenant-colonel was not come, and took
him aside and told him that the governor of Nottingham and
his brother had now an opportunity whereby they might,
much advantage themselves, and do the king excellent service.
Captain Poulton asking him how, he said, if the governor
would deliver up the castle he should be received into favour,
have the castle confirmed to him and his heirs, have ten
thousand pounds in money, and be made the best lord in the
country.   If the lieutenant-colonel would deliver up the
bridges he should have three thousand pounds, and what
command he would ask in the army; and offered Captain
Poulton two thousand pounds to effect this.   The captain
told him, for his own part, nothing should buy him to such a
villainy, and he believed the same of the governor and his
brother, and made no question but they had before been
attempted.   The colonel told him he did not this without
authority, and thereupon pulled a paper out of his pocket
wherein were words to this effect: " These are to authorize

Colonel Dacre to treat with Colonel Hutchinson and Lieutenant-colonel Hutchinson for the delivery of Nottingham Castle and the bridges, and to make them large promises, which shall be performed by W. Newcastle." Having shown him this warrant, the colonel was very importunate with the captain to acquaint the governor and his brother, and return their answer to him upon the Friday after, when he offered to meet him, if they would, at a place called St. Ann's Well. Captain Poulton told the governor and his brother, and they told the committee, and showed them what very disdainful refusals they all had written to the colonel, and sent him by a drum; who was not long gone out of the garrison but another came from Colonel Dacre with a letter to Captain Poulton, excusing himself that he could not stay in his quarters for him, according to appointment, but assuring him that what he had promised should be really performed. The governor's drum, in the absence of Colonel Dacre, delivered the three letters to Langdale, who wrote them back a good civil letter, saying that he believed my Lord Newcastle and Dacre, out of familiarity and acquaintance with them, might have made these offers in kindness to them, but for his part he should otherwise pursue the king's service.*

After this, the weather being pretty fair, and the moon shining at that time, the governor sent out a foot company to beat up their quarters, and gave them a fierce alarm throughout, and took twelve horses out of one of their

---

* This proposal for betraying the castle, together with the refusal, is mentioned by Whitelocke, p. 79. Mr. Noble, who is mentioned in the preface as having published the lives of one hundred and thirty-six regicides, makes this remark, " that Colonel Hutchinson hereby lost a fine opportunity of aggrandizing himself and his family, which doubtless they must regret." That very discerning gentleman is here informed, that the Editor of this work, who is the only representative of Colonel Hutchinson in these kingdoms, is much more proud of counting amongst his ancestors so firm and faithful a patriot than the most illustrious of traitors.

stables, which they sent home.   On their return, meeting a
great body of horse, they all at once discharged upon them,
and killed some eight of them, as we were told in the
morning.   After this charge the horse immediately retreated
and would not stand another, and the next day removed
their quarters further from the garrison.   Then the governor
and committee sent for the Nottingham horse back from
Leicester, and appointed them to bring five hundred muskets
which were come to Leicester for the governor.   They came,
but left the arms behind them.   Besides this, the colonel
and all his regiment fell into disputes, that the governors of
the parliament garrisons had no command of the horse that
were quartered in their towns; and hereupon the governor
was often prevented of many opportunities advantageable to the public service, and much discouraged to find
such obstructions from the envious pride and humour of
those who should have been his assistants ; but he bore with
it as long as himself only suffered by it, and was willing for
quietness' sake to pass by many injuries offered himself, till
the public service came to be infinitely prejudiced by it.   In
the meantime he went on, as well as he could, through all
difficulties, in the faithful and active discharge of his trust.
He called a committee and council of war, where it was put
to the question and voted that the town should be fortified.
Then he applied himself to the thing, and called a full Hall
of all the town, who declared sufficiently their disaffection to
the parliament, but in such a subtle way as would have entrapped a less prudent person.   But the governor overlooked
many things that he saw, and made use of all the advantages they gave him ; and did not manifest his resentment at
anything which they could cloak under a specious pretence, how
disadvantageously soever it might have been designed against
the parliament interest.   The whole town unanimously voted
that the place should be fortified, except Alderman Drury, and

two or three that followed him. Then the governor gave
them encouraging promises of his protection and care over
them, and his endeavours to preserve them with his regiment, if they wo 'ld assist in their own defence. The town
being well satisfied, or at least seeming so (for he treated
them with that dexterity that they could not for shame openly
oppose him, though he was not ignorant that the cavalier
party cursed him in their hearts, as the only obstacle in their
greater desire of having declared themselves on the other
side), with general outward cheerfulness, in Christmas week
the works were begun. About this time Sir Thomas Fairfax
having to march into Staffordshire, sent for some arms he had
left in Nottingham castle; and by the same convoy that
went with them the governor got his five hundred muskets
brought home from Leicester. Sir Thomas sent orders to
the governor to send him all the horse in the garrison; but
when the governor acquainted them with it, they would none
of them obey him and go, though Sir Thomas sent twice
very earnestly for them, but they stayed in Nottingham, where
they would obey no order of the governor's; and by doing
things that concerned the garrison without and against his
orders, they made a sad confusion and thwarting of powers,
which the governor bore with in respect to Col. Thornhagh,
who did things not so much out of malice in himself, as
out of a little emulation, which did not destroy his kindness
to the governor, and by the subtle instigation of Capt. White,
who wrought upon his facility to do those things which his
malice and factious ambition prompted him to wish, but he
durst not himself attempt. Although the horse would not
obey Sir Thomas Fairfax, it was not out of cowardice, for the
men were very stout and cheerful in the service, but only had
the general fault of all the parliament party, that they were
not very obedient to commands, except they knew and approved their employment. They had no sooner refused Sir

Thomas, but my Lord Grey, sending for two troops, they went to him to Melton, which he had begun to fortify. The governor, notwithstanding these obstacles from secret enemies and refractory friends, carried on his business with good success, and brought about many events according to his endeavours. Among the rest, his men encountering a party where Colonel Frecheville and Sir Henry Humlack were in person, fought them, killed many of their men, and took Frecheville prisoner; but his captain-lieutenant Jammot came to his rescue and freed him, though he himself was taken in his stead and brought to Nottingham. Here, after he had been some time kept, he corrupted a soldier, who disguised and led him out, and went away with him. The man being a Frenchman and a proper black man, some would needs report him to be Prince Rupert, and thereupon raised a great clamour at the governor.

But before his escape, upon the 15th of January, intelligence was brought that all the forces in Newark were marching on a design upon Sleaford in Lincolnshire. The governor, not trusting that pretence, commanded all the soldiers and townsmen to sit up that night and expect them; and the next morning, being Tuesday, two of his intelligencers came and brought him word very early that the design was against Nottingham. After them the horse scouts came in with the news of their approach, the enemy's scouts and they having fired upon each other. Hereupon a strong alarm was given throughout the garrison, and a foot company sent down from the castle to the works, and the horse were there set with them, to dispute the enemy's entrance into the town; but the horse perceiving the enemy's body to be a great one, retreated to the castle, and the foot seeing them gone, and none of the townsmen come forth to their assistance, made also an orderly retreat back to the castle, in which there was not a man lost nor wounded. The works being imperfect

and quitted, were easily entered, though the cannon that
played upon them from the castle took off wholly the second
file of musketeers that entered the gates.   The first was led
up by Lieutenant-colonel Cartwright, who two days before
had sent to the governor for a protection to come in and lay
down his arms.   The enemy being entered, possessed themselves of St. Peter's church and certain houses near the castle,
from whence they shot into the castle-yard and wounded one
man and killed another, which was all the hurt that was done
our men that day.

The governor was very angry with the horse for coming
up so suddenly, and stirred them up to such a generous
shame, that they dismounted, and all took muskets to serve
as foot, with which they did such *ery good service, that
they exceedingly well regained their reputations.   Having
taken foot arms, the governor sent one of his own companies
with part of them, and they beat the cavaliers out of the
nearest lanes and houses, which they had possessed, and so
made a safe way for the rest to sally out and retreat, as there
should be occasion.

When this was done, which was about noon, the governor
sent out all the rest of the horse and foot, to beat the enemy
out of the town.   Sir Charles Lucas, who was the chief
commander of all the forces there, had prepared a letter to
send up to the governor to demand of him the castle; or if
he would not deliver it, that then he should send down the
mayor and aldermen, threatening, that if they came not immediately, he would sack and burn the town.   There were,
at that time, above a thousand cavaliers in the town,
and as many in a body without the town, to have beaten
off the Derby and Leicester forces, if they should have
made any attempt to come in, to the assistance of their
friends in Nottingham.   On the other side the Trent, were
all the forces Mr. Hastings could bring out, from his own
garrison and Belvoir and Wiverton, to force the bridges.

All the cavalier forces that were about the town, were about three thousand. When Sir Charles Lucas had written his letter, he could find none that would undertake to carry it to the castle, whereupon they took the mayor's wife, and with threats, compelled her to undertake it; but just as she went out of the house from them, she heard an outcry, that " the roundheads were sallying forth," whereupon she flung down their letter and ran away ; and they ran as fast, from four hundred soldiers, who came furiously upon them out of the castle, and surprised them; while they were secure the castle would not have made so bold an attempt. But the governor's men chased them from street to street, till they had cleared the town of them, who ran away confusedly : the first that went out shot their pistols into the thatched houses to have fired them, but by the mercy of God neither that, nor other endeavours they showed to have fired the town, as they were commanded, took effect. Between thirty and forty of them were killed in the streets, fourscore were taken prisoners, and abundance of arms were gathered up, which the men flung away in haste, as they ran ; but they put some fire into a hay barn and hay mows, and all other cumbustible things they could discern in their haste, but by God's mercy, the town, notwithstanding, was preserved from burning. While their foot marched away, their horse faced the town in a valley where their reserve stood, till towards evening, and then they all drew off. Many of them died on their return, and were found dead in the woods and in the towns they passed through. Many of them, discouraged by this service, ran away, and many of their horses were quite spoiled : for two miles they left a great track of blood, which froze as it fell upon the snow, for it was such bitter weather that the foot had waded almost to the middle in snow as they came, and were so numbed with cold when they came into the town, that they were fain to be rubbed to get life into them, and in that condition were more eager for fires and

warm meat than for plunder; which, together with their feeling of security, saved many men's goods; as they did not
believe that an enemy, who had unhandsomely, to speak
truth, suffered them to enter the town without any dispute,
would have dared, at such great odds, to have set upon
driving them out.   Indeed, no one can believe, but those
that saw that day, what a strange ebb and flow of courage
and cowardice there was in both parties on that day.   The
cavaliers marched in with such terror to the garrison, and
such gallantry, that they startled not when one of their leading files fell before them all at once, but marched boldly
over the dead bodies of their friends, under their enemies' cannon, and carried such valiant dreadfulness about them, as
made very courageous stout men recoil.   Our horse, who ran
away frighted at the sight of their foes, when they had breast-
works before them, and the advantage of freshness to beat
back assailants already vanquished with the sharpness of the
cold and a killing march, within three or four hours, as men
that thought nothing too great for them, returned fiercely
upon the same men, after their refreshment, when they were
entered into defensible houses.   If it were a romance, one
should say, after the success, that the heroes did it out of
excess of gallantry, that they might the better signalize their
valour upon a foe who was not vanquished to their hands by
the inclemency of the season: but we are relating wonders
of Providence, and must record this as one not to be conceived
of, but by those who saw and shared in it.   It was indeed a
great instruction, that the best and highest courages are
but the beams of the Almighty;   and when he withholds
his influence, the brave turn cowards, fear unnerves the most
mighty, makes the most generous base, and great men to do
those things they blush to think on; when God again in-
spires, the fearful and the feeble see no dangers, believe no
difficulties, and carry on attempts whose very thoughts would,
at another time, shiver their joints like agues.   The events

of this day humbled the pride of many of our stout men, and made them afterwards more carefully seek God, as well to inspire as prosper their valour; and the governor's handsome reproaches of their faults, with showing them the way to repair them, retrieved their straggling spirits, and animated them to very wonderful and commendable actions.

The governor would not let his men pursue the rear, but thought they might, in the night, have completed their day's work, if they had fallen upon the enemy's quarters, which he gave orders to the horse to do; but Colonel Thornhagh would not obey them, because they came from him, and so lost a great opportunity, and contented himself with praising God for the great deliverance of the day, wherein there was not one townsman that came in to the assistance of the soldiers.

The next day, the governor called the town together, and represented to them the mercy of God and the malice of their enemies, who, without regard of any friends they had among them, came purposely to fire the town, which God alone preserved; and, having showed them their danger, he required they should be no longer slothful in their own defence, but should take arms to preserve their families and houses. He propounded to them, that if they would so do, they should choose their own captains. They, considering the just reasons and motives with which he urged them, at length resolved to join in their own defence, and chose four captains; but the captains refusing, the soldiers that day went home unenlisted, yet by the governor's dexterity in managing them, he at last brought four hundred, whereof more than half were high malignants, to enlist themselves under one Mr. Coates, a minister, an honest, godly man, * and Mr.

* It appears from this that Mr. Palmer, mentioned before, and who will be mentioned more than once in the sequel, was not quite singular in taking up arms notwithstanding his function. The famous preacher, Hugh Peters,

Mason,* an attorney. a great cavalier, but a reserved, silent man, who, for an austere knit of his brow, and a grave, severe countenance, had the reputation of a wise man, but was known to be disaffected to the parliament, though cunning enough not to do anything that might expose him to seques-tration.   Into these men's hands he put arms, and so ordered them, that at the last they grew fiercer in the service than those who were uprightly honest.

The next month the Lord Chaworth sent a letter to the governor, acquainting him that he was sick, and desired a protection to come and remain at his own house, in order to make his peace with the parliament ; which protection the governor gave him.

The governor had acquainted the parliament with the late successes, whereupon they ordered a thousand pounds to be sent to the garrison out of the sequestrations of London, and the excise of the town to go to the payment of the garrison ; but through Mr. Millington's negligent prosecution, the thou-sand pounds never came.†

The governor went on again successfully in his employ-ment, and began to endear himself to all the town as well as to the soldiery; which awakening White's sleeping envy, he cast new plots to disturb him ; and first made a motion to send to London for two hundred soldiers : to which the gover-nor answered—If they were honest, there were men enough to keep the garrison ; if they were not, to call in other forces was but to bait their treachery with a greater prize; and that to send for more force, while they had such slender

acted as an officer of horse.   It was in those days common to quote the expression, that the saints should have the praises of God in their mouths, and a two-edged sword in their hands !

* The same whom, when put into confinement at the castle, the gover-nor invited to his table.

† Mentioned by Whitelocke as *given.*

main'enance for these, was to increase trouble without any benefit.

The same afternoon the committee sent the governor a warrant to be signed, which was before subscribed by four of them, White in the front. The warrant was to this effect :—

> " *To* Mr. Hooper, *Engineer of the Garrison of Nottingham.*
>
> " You are hereby required to make your present appearance to this committee, there to give an account of what you have done about the works of the town, and how far you have proceeded in them; how, and in what manner, and by what time you intend to finish them; and what materials are needful for the finishing of them, there being imminent danger to the garrison."

As soon as the governor received the warrant, he took the engineer with him, and went to the committee, to whom, said he, " Gentlemen, I received just now such a strange warrant from you, that I can impute it to nothing but a picked occasion for quarrel. If you desire to question anything in the fortifying of the town, I have not only brought the engineer, but am here myself to answer it: if there be money in his hands, let him give you an account of it; but concerning the fortifications, I conceive he is only to be accountable to me; therefore why this warrant should be made, I cannot tell, unless purposely to affront me; as for that imminent danger you pretend, it is utterly unknown to me, and if there be any, I ought to have been made acquainted with it, and desire now to understand it." They answered, " Were they not in daily peril ?" He replied, " That was certain, but at this time none more imminent than usual that he knew of; and further desired them, if he had been negligent in those things which conduced to the safety of the town, that they would article against him, whatever they could accuse him of; if he had done nothing worthy of blame, he took it exceedingly ill, to be thus thwarted and affronted in his just and lawful command." Upon replies and debate, White said, " If Hooper did not render them an account of his works, they would clap him by the heels." Whereupon the governor, addressing him only, told him, " That from the first opening of his commission, he had manifested his discontent, and that he had taken notice of his secret endeavours to oppose him, and was glad the humour was now so ripe as to vent itself; that for the time to come, since he saw his condescensions did but encourage them to wrest all things from him, and to question all his dues, he would now expect that full observance from them all, that was due from the officers of a garrison to the governor; that he expected the horse should receive orders from him, and that he would no more put up with such affronts and neglects as he had that very day received, when, calling for a muster, of the horse to have been sent out upon a very advantageous design, a whole troop, unknown to him, was by the committee sent out for hay, whereby that opportunity was lost." He told them further, " that protections charging officers and soldiers to forbear plunder, ought to be given only by him upon their certificate, and not by them; and," said he, " Gentlemen, I received that affront from you lately, which no governor in the world, but myself, would have put up with; when at a public council of war, among all the officers, enough to have caused a mutiny, it was propounded how far my command extended, and questioned whether I could command horse in the garrison? And all of you, at a council of war, ordered that the booty taken should be at the disposal of the chief officer that went out; so that if a corporal went out, he must dispose of the booty, which in all garrisons is the governor's right to do."

While they were in this dispute, the lieutenant-colonel came in, and seconded his brother; and after some smart disputes on both sides, they parted for that night.

The next morning the committee sent for the governor, who coming to them, one of them drew a paper out of his pocket, and offered some propositions to the governor; which were, first, that the dispute between them might be silenced and kept private; next, that he would join with them, in a letter to Mr. Millington, to desire him to get the question decided by the close committee, What were the several powers of a governor and a committee? And, lastly, that he would draw up what he conceived his power to be. To this the governor replied, that for silencing the thing, he was very willing to do it; for sending to the close committee, he very well understood his own power, and if they questioned it, they might send whither they pleased, to satisfy themselves; but for setting down the particulars wherein he conceived his power to consist, when he did anything, which they thought belonged not to him, let them call him to question where they pleased, and he should be ready to give an account of his actions, but he would not make himself so ridiculous as to send for satisfaction in unquestionable things; yet for their information he would go along with them, if any of them pleased, either to my Lord of Essex or my Lord Fairfax, to have the power of a governor decided. They told him the generals understood not the power of a committee so well as the parliament, and therefore wrote a letter to Mr. Millington with extraordinary commendations of the governor, yet desiring to know the extent of his power, and showed it to him. He told them, if they believed those things they wrote of him, he wondered whence all this discontent had arisen, for he appealed to them all, whether, ever since he undertook the government, he had usurped any command over them, or done so much as the most inconsiderable act without acquainting them, and receiving their approbation; and what should ail them, he could not imagine, unless they were discontented at his being made governor; which if they were, they might thank themselves, who put it upon him, when he received nothing but trouble, expense, and danger in it. They all acknowledged his appeal true, and said they had desired his establishment in the government of the castle, as the man they esteemed most worthy of it and most fit for it. He told them, if the addition of the town grieved them, that was to be transferred to the parliament, who without his seeking had added that to him. One of them replied, they had so worthy an opinion of him, that they wished the assessing of the country too might be put into his power only. He said he should have been obliged to them had this proceeded from anything but discontent, and that if without his own seeking he should be honoured with that trust, as he was with this, he should endeavour to discharge it faithfully; but he rather desired it might continue in the hands it was, and if he were negligent to fetch in those assessments, which were given him, then let the blame lie on him; but for rating and assessing the towns, those who were acquainted with the country were fittest for it; and thus for the present it rested.

The design they prevented by sending out the troop unknown to him, was, the saving the town of Southwell from being made a garrison for the king; which, the town being unwilling to, sent word to the governor, that if he would come and assist them, they would join with him to beat out some soldiers that intended to fortify themselves there; but the horse, by reason of their employment, failing on those two days, and extraordinary ill weather coming after, that opportunity was lost: this was about the middle of February. Captain White still continued afterwards to prevent all designs

whose events might in any way have conduced to the governor's honour, not weighing what hindrance it was to the
public service, which was a great vexation to the governor;
but his courage was above their malice, and his zeal to the
service carried him vigorously on, in all things which he could
accomplish by his own officers and soldiers, who were more
obedient to him; and, although this exercised his patience,
yet was it also a spur to his diligence, and made his fidelity
more illustrious, and kept him more in waiting upon God, and
more strict in his watch over all his actions, because he knew
how all his enemies watched for his fall.

Upon the eleventh of February, Cornet Palmer, who had
been prisoner at Newark, came home and told the governor
that he had discovered in his prison a design intended about
this time to surprise the bridge by Hacker's soldiers, who were
to come in the habit of market people on the next Saturday.
This intelligence was seconded, whereupon the governor sent
his officers to command all the bridge soldiers to keep in their
quarters that day : he commanded also all the horse in the
town to be ready to go out upon the first sound of the trumpet,
and gave orders for all the drums in the garrison to beat betimes in the morning; the lieutenant-colonel set a guard
beyond the bridge, with charge strictly to examine all passen-
gers. About eleven o'clock on Saturday, the 17th of February,
they took twelve of them* upon the bridge, disguised like
market men and women, with pistols, long knives, hatchets,
daggers, and great pieces of iron about them; whereupon they
sent and acquainted the governor, who being himself on
horseback at the works, went immediately down to the bridge,
and commanded all the horse to come away and pursue them;
but the horse commanders, being always slow in obeying his
commands, came not till the enemy's foot beyond the bridge,

---

* Hacker's soldiers.

perceiving their fellows were taken upon the bridge, retired and got safe off; only nine, who were to have assassinated those at the bridge, and had advanced forwarder than the rest for that purpose, were overtaken, and with their captain leaped into the Trent to have saved themselves, of whom our men plucked four out of the water, five were drowned, and the captain swam to shore on the other side. The governor was in doubt whether these men, taken in disguises, were to be released as prisoners of war, or executed as spies and assassins by martial law; but though he would not have cared if the bridge-soldiers had turned them into the Trent when they took them, he afterwards released them all upon exchange, except one Slater, a soldier of his own that had run away to the enemy, and this day was taken coming into the town, with a montero* pulled close about his face, but denied that he was of the design; yet after, upon trial at a court-martial, he was condemned and executed. The governor had sent out some horse and foot, to drive the grounds at the enemy's garrison at Shelford, which they did, and from under the very works from which the enemy shot at them, brought away many beasts and horses, that belonged to the garrison, and brought them up into the castle-yard. The governor being then in the committee-chamber, told them it was fit the soldiers should have a reward, whereupon it was ordered to give them six pounds, and the governor told the soldiers the committee had assigned them a reward. But when they came to receive it, Salisbury, the treasurer, tithed it out, and gave the soldiers a groat a piece, and sixpence a piece to the officers, which in all came but to forty shillings and odd money; at which the soldiers, being mad, flung back his money, and desired a council of war to do them right; which the governor assented to, and the next day the business being

* A kind of cap so called.

heard at a full council of all the officers of the garrison, it was determined by the unanimous vote of all but Mr. Salisbury, that as the enemy shot at them, when they took the booty, it did of right belong to the soldiers that fought for it. and so they had it. Whereupon Salisbury flung himself away from the board in a great huff and muttering. for which the governor rebuked him, and told him such carriage ought not to be suffered in him, who, as an officer, ought to have more respect for the place and those that sat there.   After this, about eighteen of the lieutenant-colonel's men went out and met twenty-five men in arms; between them there was a brook, the bridge-men called to them, and asked of what side they were, and perceiving they were cavaliers, told them, after some little defies between them, that though the number was unequal, they would fight with them; and passing over the brook, charged them, put them to flight, killed two of them, took eight prisoners, and twelve of their horses. Upon examination they were found to be northern gentlemen, who having enlisted themselves in the prince's own troop, after the death of Sir Thomas Byron that commanded under the prince, were assigned to my Lord Wentworth, at which being discontented, they were now returning into their own country, being almost all of them gentlemen.   Sir Richard Byron, for his brother's memory, exchanged them for prisoners of Nottingham, taken when the town was first surprised.

At the end of this month, on the fast-day, the national covenant was taken, with a great solemnity, both by the soldiers and inhabitants, men and women,* of the garrison. This day, unexpectedly, came Sir Edward Hartup, with a thousand horse from Leicester and Derby, to which the governor added between five and six hundred; Sir Edward being appointed to command the party, should have gone with

* **Nota bene.**

them to take Muscam Bridges, at Newark, before which place
Sir John Meldrum was now come, with about seven thousand
men, and had laid siege to it. The horse of Newark, as soon
the parliament's forces came, made an escape over Muscam
Bridge, which Sir Edward Hartup, having more mind to drink
than to fight, lingering a day at Nottingham, and then marching to no purpose against it, lost his opportunity of taking; yet
God, by a providence, gave it up with 200 men that kept it
to the parliament's forces, who, had they then pursued their
success, might have carried the town too, but it was not
God's time then to deliver the country of that pernicious
enemy. The horse that were escaped out of Newark, went
into all their garrisons in the Vale and Derbyshire, and
gathered up all the force they could make, to about the number of two thousand, and with these they came and quartered
near Nottingham; themselves and the country giving out
that they were about four thousand.

There was a fast kept at Nottingham, to seek God for
his presence with our armies; and before the first sermon
was ended the enemy's horse came to the town side and gave
a strong alarm, and continued facing the town till night, at
which time they returned to their quarters, and those horse
that were in the garrison following their rear, gleaned up
two lieutenants and two or three other officers. The next
day the body marched just by the town side, and so passed
over the river at Wilden Ferry. After they were gone from
about Nottingham, the governor went down to the Leaguer,
at Newark, where Sir John Meldrum had made all things
ready for a general assault on the town; but at a council of
war that was called in the field, it was determined that it
should not then be, whereupon the governor of Nottingham
returned to his garrison; who, coming to take his leave of
Sir John Meldrum, Sir John intreated him that he would
return again and be among them as much as he could, making

a sad complaint of the envyings, heart-burnings, and dissensions that were among the several commanders, so that
he had much ado to hold them together, and had great need
of men of moderation and prudence to assist him, and to
help to mediate among them.   The forces that Sir John
Meldrum commanded before this town, were gathered out of
several associated counties, and the commanders were so
emulous of one another, and so refractory to commands, and
so piquing in all punctilios of superiority, that it galled the
poor old gentleman to the heart; who, having commanded
abroad, and been used to deal with officers that understood
the discipline of war, was confounded among those who
knew not how to obey any orders, but disputed all his commands, and lost their time and honour in a fruitless expedition, through their own vain contentions; whereas, had they
joined in the assault when he then would have made it, they
might probably have carried the town, but missing that opportunity, they came off at last with loss and dishonour.
While the governor was at the Leaguer, Sir John Meldrum
told him, that Colonel Pierrepont had been with him, to get
his hand to a paper, which should have testified, that the
government of Nottingham did of right belong to him;
but Sir John answered he could not testify any such thing,
for it was his own act to confer that government where now
it was; with which Colonel Pierrepont seemed very well
satisfied at that time.   When he could not prevail in this,
he desired Sir John to set his hand to another paper, which
should have certified, that in all things he had approved
himself most firm and faithful to the service of the parliament.
Sir John said he would not injure him so much as to make
any such certificate of a thing not called into question; but
if there should be any doubt of it, he should be ready to
do him all right.   Colonel Pierrepont, moreover, went to the
governor's soldiers, that had formerly been of his regiment,

and giving them twenty shillings to drink, told them he was to be governor of the town, and would shortly come among them.

Sir Edward Hartup was sent with the party of horse he before had at Muscam bridge, to pursue those that were gone out of Newark, and fight with them, and hinder their joining with Prince Rupert, who was expected to come to raise the siege ; and when Sir Edward came into Leicestershire the whole country rose with him, and the governor of Leicester brought out foot and cannon to assist him. His forlorn hope being of the Nottingham horse, charged the enemy's forlorn hope and routed them, and then fell into their body of foot, which they had drained out of their little garrisons, and routed them also, and if Sir Edward Hartup would have come on with his body, they had all been cut off; but the knight would not stir, but commanded the forlorn hope to retreat, who had slain and taken many prisoners of the enemy, and among them Jammot, who had lately made his escape out of Nottingham Castle. The enemy perceiving Sir Edward would not hurt them, rallied again and joined with Prince Rupert ; of which, as soon as Sir Edward had intelligence, he went back to Newark with such shameful haste, that he quitted Melton with all the prisoners the forlorn hope had lately taken.   The Leicester forces, discouraged at this carriage, returned to their garrisons and marched no more with him.*

The governor of Nottingham kept out spies upon the

* In Whitelocke's Memoirs, p. 85, there is an account of this relief, or raising the siege of Newark, agreeing with Mrs. Hutchinson's, except that it is not quite so particular, and omits the account of what befell Colonel Thornhagh. Whitelocke attributes to the misconduct of Sir E. Hartup and Colonel Bingley Prince Rupert's coming with his forces entire to the place, and informs us that a court-martial was directed to decide upon their conduct, but does not state what their decision was.

enemy's motions, and sent word to the Leaguer, but the
gentlemen there were so over-confident, they would not
believe any force could come to raise their siege. At length,
the governor of Nottingham being there himself, word was
brought that Prince Rupert was come to Ashby; wherefore
he, fearing some attempt upon his garrison, to divert the
forces at the siege, returned home with his brother to look
to their charge. It was late upon Wednesday night when
the governor came home, and was certainly informed that
Prince Rupert had, that afternoon, marched by to raise the
siege with about six thousand men. Immediately the governor sent two men, excellently well mounted upon his own
horses, to carry the alarm to Sir John Meldrum, who by two
o'clock on Thursday morning delivered him their letters,
and he presently prepared to fight with the prince, who came
about nine or ten o'clock. Sir John had drawn all his ordnance within the walls of a ruined house, called the spittle,
and the horse were the first to charge the enemy. Colonel
Thornhagh and Major Rossiter gave them a very brave
charge, routed those whom they first encountered, and took
prisoners Major-general Gerrard and others, and had they
been seconded by the rest of the horse, had utterly defeated
the prince's army; but the Lincolnshire troops fled away
before ever they charged, and left Colonel Thornhagh engaged, with only his own horse, with the prince's whole body,
where, they say, he charged the prince himself, and made his
way and passed very gallantly through the whole army, with
a great deal of honour, and two desperate wounds, one in
the arm, the other in the belly. After the Lincolnshire
horse were run away, Sir John Meldrum sent the Derby
horse and the Nottingham foot, with two companies of Col.
King's, to keep Muscam bridge, and Molanus, the Derbyshire major, to be their commander. Colonel Thornhagh
was sent home in a wagon to Nottingham. Sir John himself,

with the few horse and dragoons that were left from Nottingham and Derby, being about five hundred, went into the
spittle to his foot. The prince lost more than Sir John in
the skirmish, but as soon as ever Sir John had betaken
himself to the spittle, the prince sent horse and foot between
him and Muscam bridge.* The horse that were left there to
guard the foot ran every man away, so that they had not a
horse left to fetch them any provision. The major that commanded them told them that he would go to the next town to
buy them some bread, and with that pretence came away and
never saw them more. The enemy was endeavouring to
make a passage over the river, to come on the other side of
them and encompass them, which when they saw and considered that they had no order what to do, nor bread for one
meal, nor bullet more than their muskets were loaded withal,
and that it was impossible for them to come off if they stayed
till the enemy enclosed them ; and further discovering that
their friends in the spittle were in parley, they conceived it
their best way to come home, which they plotted so to do
that the enemy might not perceive it till they were out of
their reach ; so leaving lighted matches and squibs laid at
certain distances, to deceive the enemy, they came safe home.
But within less than half an hour after they were gone the
enemy came on the other side, and not missing them till
morning, by reason of the squibs, they pursued them not, by
which means they came safe to Nottingham ; which was a

* Rapin gives a different account of this matter, but to those who know
or observe the situation of the places, Mrs. Hutchinson's will appear to be
the true one.   Besides Muscam bridge there was a bridge of boats, which
enabled the prince's forces to surround the guard left at Muscam bridge.
This guard, instead of *deserting*, as Rapin says of it, was deserted and
sacrificed for want of support ; the road still lay open to Lincoln, but probably Prince Rupert was too strong and too active to let the besiegers
escape any way, unless they had acted with better accord amongst themselves.

very seasonable mercy, for had they stayed the choicest arms
in the garrison had been lost, and the best and most con-
fiding soldiers disarmed. For Sir John had agreed upon
articles with the prince, to deliver up the spittle wherein he
lay, with all the muskets, ordnance, and ammunition in it;
the foot soldiers to march away with colours flying, swords
and pikes, the horsemen with their horses and swords, and all
the commanders with their pistols; but the prince broke all
these conditions, and pillaged them to their shirts, and sent
many captains quite naked away.

The committee of Nottingham now began again to mutter
at the governor, but he would not take notice of it, but applied himself to take care for the securing of his town, where
the enemy now daily threatened to come. So he floated the
meadows on the Line side, where there was no fortification,
and raised a fort in the midst of the meadows to preserve
the float, and fortified the Trent bridges more strongly; and,
expecting the enemy every hour, was forced to let the work
go on during the Lord's day. When, calling the captains together to consult on the best way of preparing for their defence,
Mason, the new town captain, took this time to revive the
old mutiny, and said the townsmen would not stand to their
works except the ordnance were drawn down from the castle
to the town works; the governor rebuked him for this un-
seasonable insolence, as he and his men were, all the time of
this great exigency, so backward that they were rather an
obstruction than assistance, and there was much ado to get
them either to the works or to the guards. Indeed such a blow
was given to the parliament interest, in all these parts, that it
might well encourage the ill-affected, when even the most
zealous were cast down and gave up all for lost; but the
governor, who on no occasion ever let his courage fall, but,
when things were at the lowest, re-collected all his force,
that his own despondency might not contribute anything to

his malicious fortune, at this time animated all the honest
men, and expressed such vigour and cheerfulness, and such
stedfast resolution, as disappointed all the malignants of their
hopes.   The wives, children, and servants of such as were
in the enemy's garrisons and armies, he thought it not safe to
suffer any longer to be in the town in such a time of danger,
and therefore commanded them all to depart, not sparing
even some of his own relations ; but though this was done by
the concurrence of the whole committee, yet some of them,
who were loath the town should lose any that wished ill to
the governor and his undertakings, privately, without his
consent or knowledge, brought back several persons that
were very dangerous to the place.

And now, upon the twenty-fifth day of March, a letter was
brought to the governor from all the commissioners at Newark, telling him that the parliament's forces had quitted
Gainsborough, Lincoln, and Sleeforth ; and that the prince
intended to advance against Nottingham, and to fire the town,
if he did not immediately throw down the works, which if he
should not do, the world would then take notice of him as the
only ruin of his native country.   To which the governor returned them answer, that as he never engaged himself in this
service, with respect to the success or actions of other places,
so though the whole kingdom were quitted except this town,
he would yet maintain it as long as he was able, and he trusted
that God would preserve it in his hands ; but if it perished,
he was resolved to bury himself in the ruins of it, being confident that God would afterwards vindicate him to have been
a defender, and not a destroyer of his country.   A copy of
the letter which the Newark commissioners sent to the
governor, was sent to one Francis Cooke, a malignant inhabitant of the town, subscribed with all the commissioners'
hands, and desiring him to communicate it to the whole town.
The governor, having taken what care he could at home, sent

immediately to the parliament and to the Earl of Essex, acquainting them with the desperate condition of the place; and desiring that they would send him seasonable relief, if the prince should besiege him, promising to employ his utmost endeavour to hold it for them, or to lose himself with it. My lord general returned a very civil encouraging letter, and now the prince, two days after the letter, was advanced within three miles of Nottingham; when it pleased God to divert him from coming against the town by letters which were brought him from Oxford, which occasioned his hasty return into the south, without any attempt upon the place, which, by God's mercy, was thus delivered from this threatening danger. However, their enemies at Newark, by the late success, were very much exalted, and by the quitting of so many parliament garrisons about them, increased in power, and were left at leisure to turn all their designs against Nottingham, which being so infirm within itself, the governor had a very difficult task to preserve; while the disaffected, who were subtle, did not clearly declare themselves, but watched all opportunities to work the governor's disturbance, by fomenting the ill-humours of the factious committee-men and priests; for they now took occasion to fall in with them, upon the governor's release of his chief cannoniers out of prison, into which he had put them, by the instigation of the ministers and of the godly people, who had animated them almost to mutiny for separating from the public worship, and keeping little conventicles in their own chambers. It was with some reluctance he had committed them, for the men, though of different judgments in matter of worship, were otherwise honest, peaceable, and very zealous and faithful to the cause; but the ministers were so unable to suffer their separation and spreading of their opinions, that the governor was forced to commit them; yet during this great danger, he thought it not prudent to keep them discontented and then employ them,

and therefore set them at liberty, for which there was a great
outcry against him as a favourer of separatists.*

* This being the first time that a disunion in religion among those of the
parliament's party has been plainly named, it is proper here to state, that
in the outset, all those sects, which have since taken so many various names,
joined their forces to repel the encroachments of the *prelates*,—it would
not be fair to say of the *Church of England*, whose characteristic is
moderation itself,—but when they had almost crushed the episcopalians, the
presbyterian ministers began to rise pre-eminent in power, and to show that
though they had changed the name, they by no means intended to diminish
the dominion of the hierarchy.   There are preserved in Whitelocke two
speeches, one of his own and one of Selden's, on this subject.   To resist
this usurpation there arose a very powerful party or faction, under the name
of independents, under whose banner enlisted all who desired liberty of
conscience, of whatever particular persuasion they might be; and, amongst
others, most naturally all such as wished to see the Church of England
restored to her purity, and redeemed from her servility and subserviency to
the usurpations of the crown; but whose hopes would have been totally
destroyed if presbytery had obtained a full and firm establishment.   It is
extraordinary that almost all the historians put the cause for the effect, and
suggest that many members of the parliament, and at the head of them
Cromwell, raised this faction to obtain their own exaltation; whereas in-
tolerancy raised it in the nation at large, and especially in the army, and
Cromwell availed himself of it when raised.—In a scarce book, called
Anglia Rediviva, or the Success of the Army under Fairfax, written by
Joshua Sprigge, he says, " the army was, what by example and justice, kept
in good order both respectively to itself and the country : there were many
of them differing in opinion, yet not in action nor business; they all agreed
to preserve the kingdom; they prospered in their unity more than in uniformity, and whatever their opinions were, they plundered none with them,
they betrayed none with them, nor disobeyed the state with them, and they
were more visibly pious and peaceable in their opinions than many we call
orthodox."   Let the blame of all the misfortunes that flowed from it rest
with those who gave disturbance to such men, not to those who screened
them from persecution.

The chief of these cannoniers was that Langford Collin mentioned in a
former note, page 134.   He continued at Nottingham after all the wars
were over, but being persecuted on account of his religion, applied to
Cromwell for protection, and was effectually screened by him from his

I. will not be amiss, in this place, to carry on the parliament story, that we may the better judge of things at home,

persecutors; he lived to more than ninety years; his descendants rose to
opulence, and one of them founded a very handsome hospital. This
family united themselves to that of Langford, and both being molested on
the score of nonconformity, were peculiarly protected by James the Second,
and stood stedfastly by him at the revolution, at which time he got many
sectaries to join the catholics, and make common cause against the
church of England. By this turn of events and opinions, Langford Collin,
Esq. before mentioned, came to be the head of the country, Jacobite, or
anti-revolutionist party, while the Plumptres and Hutchinsons embraced
the Hanover or Whig party, as mentioned in the note, p. 134, just
spoken of.

Since the publication of the first edition, there has appeared a very
candid critique of this work in the Annual Register for 1807, containing
the following remark : " It may be mentioned as an additional proof of
Mr. Hutchinson's rectitude, that when George Fox, the founder of the
Quakers, was imprisoned at Nottingham, he protected him; thus proving
that, unlike the greater number of those who were engaged in the same
cause, he allowed that liberty of conscience to others which he claimed
for himself."

The Editor thought it his duty, upon this suggestion, to make further
inquiry, and has in pursuance of it been furnished by a respectable friend,
Mr. Barker, surgeon, at Colchester, with the two following extracts, together
with some others, which will appear in their proper places.—G. Fox's
Journal, fol. ed. p. 27. " I went to the Steeple House at Nottingham,
during the time of divine worship, addressed the people, and was committed to prison. When the assizes came on, there was one moved to
come and offer himself up for me, body for body, yea, life also; but when
I should have been brought before the judge, the sheriff's man being
somewhat long in fetching me to the sessions-house, the judge was risen
before I came, at which I understood he was somewhat offended. So I
was returned to prison, and put into the common gaol ; and the Lord's
power was great among friends, but the people began to be very rude,
*wherefore the governor of the castle sent down soldiers and dispersed
them, and after that they were quiet.*" Sewell's Hist. of Quakers, fol. ed.
p. 22. " Now though the people began to be very rude, *yet the governor
of the castle was so very moder te, that he sent down soldiers to disperse
them.*'

when we know the condition of affairs abroad. The queen, being suffered to pass through Nottinghamshire by those forces which were sent down thither to have prevented her, joined with Prince Rupert and came to the king; and was by the parliament voted traitor for many actions, as pawning the crown-jewels in Holland, encouraging the rebellion in Ireland, heading a papistical army in England, &c.

The Earl of Essex's army lay sick about London for recruits; Sir William Waller, after many victories in the west, was at length totally routed, and returned to London, Prince Maurice and Sir Ralph Hopton having recovered and possessed almost the whole west of England for the king. The north my Lord Newcastle's army commanded so fully, that they were advanced into Nottingham and Lincolnshire, and the adjacent counties. The parliament, being in this low condition, had agreed with Scotland, and entered into a solemn national league and covenant, which was taken throughout both kingdoms; and the king had made a cessation of arms with the Irish rebels, and brought over the English army, that had been honoured with so many successes against them, to serve him here. But God never blessed his affairs after they came to him,* though indeed before their arrival God had begun to

* The parliament and the king seem to have been equally injudicious in seeking resources from without. Rapin says, " the presbyterians seized the occasion which was offered them of establishing their system of uniformity, and that it increased the number of the king's friends ;" had he not, through partiality to his sect, withheld a part of the truth, he would have said that, in pursuit of their system of intolerance, they divided the parliament and the friends of liberty, exasperated the army, and having forced them to try their strength against them, caused the subjugation of themselves, and the ruin of their whole cause and party. So much for the league and covenant.

The king, by seeking the assistance of the Irish in a manner so injurious to the true interests of England, blemished his own fame, hurt his cause, ruined his partisans in both countries, and, indeed the Irish nation in gene-

turn the scale; for the city of Gloucester stopping, by its
faithful and valiant resistance, the career of the king's victories, after Bristol and Exeter and all the west was lost, the
king, disdaining to leave it behind him unvanquished, sat
down before it, which employed him and his whole army, till
the Earl of Essex and his recruited army, assisted with the
London auxiliaries, came and relieved it, and pursued the
king's army to an engagement at Newbury; where the parliament obtained a great and bloody victory, and the king for
ever lost that opportunity he lately had of marching up to
London, and in probability of subduing the parliament.   My
Lord Newcastle, by a like error, about the same time, setting
down before Hull, missed the opportunity of wholly gaining
all those neighbouring counties, and much wasted his great
and victorious army, being forced to rise with loss and dishonour from the unyielding town.   After the fight at Newbury, Sir William Waller, having gotten a new army, had
divers successes with it, and at length totally routed all
Hopton's army, about the time that Prince Rupert raised the
siege at Newark, and was the occasion that called the prince
so hastily out of those counties.

The Earl of Essex pursuing the war, had a design to block
up Oxford, where the king was, and accordingly attempted it,
he on one side, and Waller on the other; but the king, with
a few light horse, escaped out of the town, and went to join
with his greater armies; which being done, Essex marched
further into the west, and in Cornwall was besieged where he

ral, which has never recovered from the depopulation which took place in
consequence of those convulsions.

This last fact has been controverted by one reviewer, the Critical; but it
would be easy to establish it by various arguments, one only is here adduced.
The custom of emigrating and entering into the service of foreign powers,
which the Irish began to do at that period, and have continued almost to
the present day.

lost all his foot, ammunition, and ordnance, and came dis-
honourably home to London.   Waller unsuccessfully followed
the king, and the parliament's affairs, all that summer, were
very unprosperous in the west, south, and midland counties,
but contrary in the north, where the Scotch army, under
General Leven, advanced, took some towns and forts, and
wasted the Earl of Newcastle's army more by their patient
sufferance of the ill weather and martial toil, which the
English could not so well abide, than by fighting.   Sir Thomas Fairfax, having again taken the field with his father,
after a miraculous victory they had gained over the Irish
army* which the king had brought over, joined the Scots;
and the Earl of Manchester, having raised a force in the
associated counties, with which he made an expedition to
Lincoln, having Colonel Cromwell for his lieutenant-general,
marched into Yorkshire, and uniting with the other two
armies, they all besieged the Earl of Newcastle in York.   To
raise this siege, Prince Rupert came with a great army out of
the south; the besiegers rose to fight with the prince, and
Newcastle drew all his force out of York to join with him,
when both armies, on a great plain called Marston Moor, had
a bloody encounter, and the Scots and Lord Fairfax had been
wholly routed, and the battle lost, but that Cromwell, with
five thousand men which he commanded, routed Prince Rupert, restored the other routed parliamentarians, and gained
the most complete victory that had been obtained in the
whole war.†   The victors possessed all the prince's ordnance,

* Commanded by Sir John Byron, or Lord Byron, near Nantwich in
Cheshire.

† There are very various and discordant accounts given of this battle, so
that Rapin says he could neither satisfy himself nor his readers with them;
that given by Whitelocke is however pretty clear, and agrees with this of
Mrs. Hutchinson, in ascribing the success principally to Cromwell; and as
Mrs. Hutchinson was by no means partial to Cromwell, nor does Whitelocke

carriages, and baggage; whereupon the prince fled, with as many as he could save, back into the south; the Earl of Newcastle, with some of his choice friends, went into Germany, and left Sir Thomas Glenham governor of York, which he soon after surrendered, and then the three generals parted; Leven went back into the north, and took the town of Newcastle, Fairfax remained in Yorkshire, and Manchester returned into the south, taking in many small garrisons by the way as he passed through the counties.

The queen went that summer into France, to solicit foreign aid for her husband, but ineffectually; meanwhile new treaties were carried on between the king and parliament, but to no purpose; for the king's false dealing and disingenuity therein was so apparent that they came to nothing, but a further discovery of the king's falsehood, and favour to the Irish rebels, with whom he had now employed Ormond to treat and conclude a peace. This treaty was that at Uxbridge, where commissioners met on both sides, but effected nothing; for the parliament itself began to grow into two apparent factions of presbyterians and independents, and the king had hope, by their divisions, to obtain the accomplishment of his own ends.*

It was too apparent how much the whole parliament cause had been often hazarded, how many opportunities of finishing the war had been overslipped by the Earl of Essex's army; and it was believed that he himself, with his commanders, rather endeavoured to become arbiters of war and peace,

upon the whole seem so, we may better believe them than Hollis, who writes a philippic rather than a history.

* Whoever will take the pains to read the king's letters in Clarendon's State Papers, will see that this is a true representation of his sentiments; but Heylin pretends the failure of the treaty arose from the extreme pertinacity of the rigid presbyterians : we may very well allow both their share.

than conquerors for the parliament; for it was known that
he had given out such expressions. Wherefore those in the
parliament, who were grieved at the prejudice of the public
interest, and loath to bring those men to public shame, who
had once well merited it of them, devised to new-model the
army; and an ordinance was made, called the self-denying
ordinance, whereby all members of parliament, of both houses,
were discharged of their commands in the army. Cromwell
had a particular exception, when Essex, Manchester, and
Denbigh, surrendered their commissions; and Sir Thomas
Fairfax was made general of the new-modelled army, Cromwell lieutenant-general, and Skippon major-general. The
army was reduced to twenty-one thousand, who prosecuted
the war not with design of gain and making it their trade,
but to obtain a righteous peace and settlement for the
distracted kingdom, and accordingly it succeeded in their
hands.*

* It is suggested by Rapin and others that this new-model and self-
denying ordinance arose not from the motives here set down, but merely
from intrigue ; yet Whitelocke, who even spoke against it, p. 123, shows
the indispensable necessity for such a new model. " Some members of the
house were sent to their generals to complain of their remissness. The
Earl of Manchester was under a kind of accusation, the lord-general in
discontent, Waller not much otherwise, the forces not carefully ordered,
and the parliament business in an unsettled condition, so that it was high
time for some other course to be taken by them." Mr. Sprigge demon-
strates this more fully. He says, " Cromwell was absent in the west when
the exemption was voted ; that he had come to Windsor over-night to kiss
the general's hand, and take his leave on quitting the service, but the following morning, ere he came from his chamber, those commands, than
which he thought of nothing less in all the world, came to him from the
committee of both kingdoms, in obedience to which he immediately
marched away." And further, " that the house did this for their own
happiness, and that of their general Fairfax."

Mrs. Hutchinson was sufficiently observant of Cromwell's artifices to
have accused him of it on this occasion, if he had deserved it.

To return to Nottingham: after the prince had marched away out of the country, the enemy without was still designing against the garrison, and the governor's enemies within were still perplexing all his affairs. Upon the eleventh of May, a letter was found by a wench in the night-time, dropped in the shoemakers' booths; which letter was directed to Sir Richard Byron, informing him that "the business between them went on with good success, and that the time drawing on, it behoved him to be very diligent, and desiring him to burn the letter;" which was subscribed, "Your careful servant, A. C.;" and a postscript written, "Fail nothing by any means, and there shall be no neglect in me." The governor took all courses that could be imagined to discover this person, but could never find him out. About this time some troopers going by a house, where one Henry Wandall, a debauched malignant apothecary had lived (but the house was now empty, and he had the key of it), they perceived a smoke to come out of it, and went in and found some kindled sticks, laid in a potsherd, just by a rotten post, under the stair-case, with hurdles and other combustible things about it, which it was evident were put there to fire the house, but for what reason, or by whom, was not discovered.

The governor hearing of some troops of the enemy in the Vale, had a design to go thither, and acquainted the committee with it; telling them he would take out all the horse, and himself march with the body, and leave a foot company and thirty horse behind him at the bridges, so that by the time he was marched by Wiverton, which would give Shelford the alarm, the thirty horse, which were more than Shelford had to send out, should face the house on that side next Nottingham, and the foot should march a private way through the closings;* so that if Shelford's horse or foot

* Closings, closes, fields, vulg. Notts. *closen.*

should come forth against those thirty horse, the foot might
get between them and home, or take any advantage that was
offered.   All this the committee very well approved, and so
it was resolved to put it into execution the next night after,
because it would take some time to provide horses for the
musketeers.   The governor coming out of the committee,
met Captain White upon the parade in the castle-yard, and
acquainted him with the design, who with a dejected countenance and a faint voice, pretended to approve it, but desired
the thirty horse who were to stay some hours behind, might
be of his troop ; to which the governor assented to gratify
his desire, though he told him, he was very loath to spare
any of that troop, who were old soldiers and well acquainted
with the country ; but he desired him the rest might not fail
to be ready.   The captain promised they should, and so departed.   When the governor had made ready all the horse
and dragoons, and was himself just ready to march out with
them, being at Colonel Thornhagh's house, White came in ;
the governor, not doubting of his intention to go, asked him
if his troop were ready?   He replied, " They are out upon
service; thirty," said he, " are gone by your consent, and
the rest went to fetch in a malignant at Ekering; some few
odd ones remain, which you may have if you will."   The
governor desired him to go himself and assist him; the
captain desired to be excused, for " to what purpose should
he go when his troop was not there?"   The governor went
from thence to his own lodgings, and meeting the committee,
acquainted them how White had served him, who seemed
to resent it very ill at that time ; and while they were discoursing of it, White's officer came up with warrants to be
signed for hay for the quarters, which being offered the
governor, he tore, and said he would sign no warrants for
such a disorderly troop, as would do no service but what
they list, whose officers knew neither how to give nor obey
commands.

Notwithstanding this discouragement, to lose eighty of his best men, the governor went out with the rest, and when he had drawn them into the Trent Lanes, one of his spies came in with intelligence that at a town in the Vale, called Sierston, and at another next it, called Elston, there were two hundred horse quartered, who having come in weary and secure, might easily be surprised that night. The governor, calling the captains together, imparted the intelligence, and they were all forward to go on in the design, except Captain Pendock, who persuaded him much against it; but while they were discoursing another intelligencer came in, to second the former; whereupon the governor told the captains, that if they would go, he was resolved to do something that night, and because Captain Pendock was best acquainted with that side of the country, he appointed him to lead on the forlorn hope, which accordingly he did, but with such sloth and muttering, that in two or three miles riding, the governor was forced to send up some officers to him, to hasten him on. Yet this was not from cowardice, but only humour and faction, for the man was stout enough when he had a mind to it, but now he rode along, muttering that it was to no purpose, and when he came to Saxondale Gorse, purposely lost himself and his forlorn hope; which the governor missing, was much troubled, fearing that by some misadventure they might have been enclosed and cut off between the enemies' garrisons; but when they came to Saxondale Lane, Pendock and his forlorn hope were found safe in the rear of the body. The governor perceiving Pendock's backwardness, had sent out some parties, one troop under Captain-lieutenant Palmer, and another party with Cornet Peirson, to some near towns, to execute some of the committee's warrants, in fetching in delinquents; when the cornet came back with an alarm that two or three hundred horse were quartered at Elston and Sierston, which he must either fight with or retreat. Captain

Pendock was again wonderfully unwilling to go on, and said it would be day before they should come there; but the governor bade those that would, follow him, for he would go; and accordingly he went, and when he came to the town, drew up his men at the town's end in a body, from which he sent in some parties, to fall into the town, himself staying with the body between them and Newark, to defend them from any of the enemies that might have come upon them:* so they brought out two captain-lieutenants, some cornets, and other gentlemen of quality, thirty troopers, and many more horses and arms; Captain Thimbleby, absolutely refusing quarter, was killed. The governor sent into the town to command all his men immediately away; but a lieutenant and cornet not making haste to obey, while they stayed for some drink, were surprised by a party that came from Newark, before the corporal, whom the governor had sent to fetch them off, was well out of the town; but with those he had taken, and all the booty, and many horses and beasts fetched from malignants in the enemies' quarters, the governor came safe home, to the great discontent of Captain White, who was something out of countenance at it. This may serve, instead of many more, to show how hard a task he had to carry on the service, with such refractory, malicious persons under him.

About this time it happened, that the engineer being by, Captain Pendock took occasion to rail at the town-works, and Hooper making answers which drew on replies, Pendock struck him, whereupon the man, angry, laid his hand upon

* Whoever looks upon the map, and observes the vicinity of these places to Newark, and their great distance from Nottingham, will see it to have been a service of great delicacy and danger   It is mentioned cursorily by Whitlocke, page 89 ; had Sir John Gell been the commander, we should have had it better displayed.

his sword and half drew it out, but thrust it in again. The
maid ran affrighted into the kitchen, where was one Henry
Wandall, who presently called some musketeers, disarmed
Mr. Hooper, and sent him prisoner to the governor; who,
asking him upon what account he came so, he told him he
had no reason to accuse himself; if those that sent him had
anything against him he was ready to answer it. After the
governor had waited till about midnight and nothing came,
he sent for Wandall, and inquiring why and by whose authority he committed Mr. Hooper prisoner? He answered,
" for drawing his sword, he, as an officer of the garrison,
had sent him up." The governor asked who made him an
officer? and taking it upon him, why he did not send up both
parties, but only one in a quarrel? and he being able to give
no answer, but such as showed it was done out of malice,
the governor committed him for his insolency, who being but
a common soldier, presumed to make an officer prisoner,
without rendering an account to the governor, and to let the
other engaged in the quarrel go free. The next day after
this, Plumptre came to the Trent bridges, where, being
stopped, he sent up a pass which he had procured from my
lord general, to come and stay in the town during his own
pleasure; which, when the governor saw he sent him word,
that in regard of my lord general's pass he might stay at his
own house, but bade him take heed, as he would answer it,
that he meddled not to make any mutiny or commotion in
the garrison; to which he sent an insolent reply, that he
was glad the governor was taught manners; he was come
to town for some business, and when he had occasion he
would repair to the committee. The committee, hearing this,
were very sensible of his insolent carriage, and drew up
articles against him, which were signed by six of their
hands, and were sent up to Mr. Millington to be preferred
against him in the parliament, and to be showed to my lord

general, as the lieutenant-colonel should see occasion; **whom**
the governor sent immediately to the general, **to acquaint**
him with the reason why Dr. Plumptre had been forced to procure his pass for his protection.   The governor took this
occasion to send to the general about his cannoniers, whom
some days before he had been forced to confine as prisoners
to their chamber till the general's pleasure could be known
concerning them; for, at the instigation of Captain Palmer,
all the ministers in town, and, to make the cry the louder,
certain loose malignant priests, which they had gotten to
join with them, had most violently urged, in a petition to the
committee, that these men might be turned out of the town
for being separatists; so that the governor was forced, against
his will, to confine them to prevent mutiny, though they
were otherwise honest, obedient, and peaceful.   After the
lieutenant-colonel was gone, with letters concerning these
matters, to the general, Plumptre behaved himself most insolently and mutinously, and he and Mason entering into a
confederacy, had contrived some articles against the governor
for committing Wandall; but when they tried and found
they could do no good with them, Mason came to the governor and was most saucily importunate for his release,
which, by reason of the insolent manner of his seeking it,
the governor would not grant.

The general, upon the governor's letters, sent down a letter
to Plumptre, to discharge him from the garrison, and another to
the governor to release the cannoniers; which he accordingly
did, to the satisfaction of his own conscience, which was not
satisfied in keeping men prisoners for their consciences, so
long as they lived honestly and inoffensively.   But it caused
a great mutiny in the priests against him, and they blew up
as many of their people as they could, to join in faction
against the governor, not caring now what men they entered
into confederacy with, nor how disaffected to the cause, so that

they were but bitter enough against the separatists ; which the cunning malignants perceiving, they now all became zealots, and laughed in secret to see how they brought these men to ruin their own cause and champions.

Plumptre not taking notice of the general's letters, the governor sent him word he expected he should obey them and depart. Plumptre replied, his business was done, and he would go ; but in spite of his teeth he would have a guard. The lieutenant-colonel would have put in the articles into the parliament, which the committee had sent up against Plumptre, but Mr. Millington pretending all kindness and service to the governor, would needs undertake it, and desired the lieutenant-colonel to trouble none of the governor's friends in any business he had to do, but to leave it in his hands, who would employ all his powers, and serve him with all vigilance and faithfulness, against all persons whatsoever ; and whereas he heard the governor had some thoughts of coming to London, he wished him not to trouble himself, but to charge him with any thing he had to do. Notwithstanding all this, the governor went to London, having some occasions thither. A little before his going, he and the rest of the committee had required Mr. Salisbury, their treasurer, to give in his accounts, which he being either unwilling or unable to do, he bent his utmost endeavours to raise a high mutiny and faction against the governor; and Captain White never being backward in any mischief, these, with Plumptre and Mason, made a close confederacy, and called home Chadwick to their assistance, having engaged the persecuting priests and all their idolaters, upon an insinuation of the governor's favour to separatists. During Colonel Thornhagh's sickness, the governor undertook the command of his horse regiment, while it was quartered in the garrison ; and made the men live orderly, and march out upon designs more frequently than they used to do when their colonel was well,

upon whose easiness they prevailed to do what they list;
and some of them, who were great plunderers, were connived at, which the governor would by no means suffer.
Wherefore these men were, by the insinuations of their
officers and the wicked part of the committee, drawn into the
faction, which was working in secret awhile, and at last
broke into open prosecutions.   They had determined that as
soon as the governor was gone, White, the devil's exquisite
solicitor, should also follow to London, but knew not what to
do for a pretence to send him upon the public purse; when
wickedness, which never long wants the opportunity it waits
for, soon found one out, for the committee of both kingdoms
had sent a command for all the horse in Nottingham to
repair to Sir John Meldrum in Lancashire; the town was put
upon a hasty petition that their horse might not go, and
Captain White must carry it, who pretended to have known
nothing of it half an hour before, yet he was ready, and
Dr. Plumptre, too, prepared to make good his brags, and go
with his convoy.   Presently after he was gone, Col. Chadwick,
the engine of mischief, comes to town, whom Mr. Salisbury receives with great joy and exultance, boasting, to use
his own words, that they would now mump the governor.
At the mayor of the town's house he was entertained with
much wine, whereof Mr. Ayscough, a committee man, having
taken a pretty large proportion, coming that night to supper
to the castle, told the lieutenant-colonel and the governor's
wife, that he would advise them to acquaint the governor
there was mischief hatching against him, and that Chadwick
was come to town on purpose to effect it, which, though the
fellow discovered it in his drink, was true enough, and he
himself was one of the conspiring wicked ones.

   To fortify their party, in all haste they endeavoured to
raise a new troop of dragoons, under one Will Hall, a debauched malignant fellow, and therefore one of the governor's

mortal enemies; but some of the honester townsmen perceiving the design, and not yet being seduced, would not
raise him any horse, so at that season the troop was not
formed.

And now Captain White having come home, it was observed that after his return he would not allow the governor
that name, but called him only Colonel Hutchinson, and
when any one else termed him governor, would decline the
acknowledgment of that name; then cajoling his fellow
horse-officers and the troopers, they, through his insinuations,
everywhere began to detract from the governor, and to magnify Captain White, and not only to derogate from the
governor, but from all persons that were well-affected to him.
At this time there was a petition drawn up to be presented
to the committee of both kingdoms, desiring that Mr. Millington might be sent down to compose the differences which
were in the garrison. The lieutenant-colonel and some others
refusing to sign it, Captain White told them it was a pretence, which Mr. Millington desired the favour that they
would make, to obtain leave for him to come down and visit
his wife and children, whom he had a longing desire to see,
and knew not any other way to bring it about. The gentlemen, to gratify Mr. Millington, signed it; and he himself at
London, with the same pretext, obtained the governor's hand
to it, while the governor, deceived by his high and fair professions of service and kindness to him, never entertained
any suspicion of his integrity; and this was the greatest of the
governor's defects, that through the candidness and sincerity
of his own nature he was more unsuspicious of others, and
more credulous of fair pretenders, than suited with the great
prudence he testified in every thing else.   Nothing
awakened jealousy in him but gross flattery, which, when he
saw any one so servile as to make, he believed the soul that
could descend to that baseness might be capable of false-

hood ; but those who were cunning attempted him not that way, but put on a face of fair, honest, plain friendship, with which he was a few times, but not often in his life, betrayed. At Mr. Millington's entreaty the governor released Wandall, but would have prosecuted the committee's petition against Plumptre, which Mr. Millington most earnestly persuaded him not to do, but desired that he would permit him to come and live quietly in his own house, upon engagement that he should not raise nor foment any mutiny nor faction in the garrison, or intermeddle with any of the affairs thereof. The governor was easily wrought to assent to this also, but Plumptre refused to enter into such an engagement for quiet behaviour, and so for that time came not to town.   There was again discovered a new design by the enemy against the garrison, and a spy taken, who owned that a soldier in the major's company had enlisted himself on purpose to effect his mischief; but through careless custody the spy escaped the day that the garrison were celebrating their joy for the great victory at York.   Meanwhile the governor, supposing Mr. Millington to be, as he professed himself, highly his friend and his protector, complained to him of the mutinous carriage of the horse, and his disturbance and discouragement in the public service thereby, and desired him to get a resolution in the thing, whereby his power and their duty might be defined, that he might know wherein he was to command them in his garrison, and they to obey him. Mr. Millington advised him to write a letter to him concerning this, setting down his own apprehensions, what he was to exact from them, and they to render him ; which accordingly the governor did, and left it with Millington, and returned to his garrison.   Mr. Millington told him, that he had showed the letter to the committee of both kingdoms, who had given their opinion of it, that he required no more of them than he ought to have.   Soon after the go-

R

vernor, Mr. Millington came down to Nottingham, with
instructions from the committee of both kingdoms, to hear
and, if he could, compose the differences at Nottingham; if
not, to report them to the committee of both kingdoms.   Mr.
Millington, coming down with these, brought Plumptre as far
as Leicester with him, and begged of the governor to permit
him to return to his house, engaging himself that he should
not meddle with anything belonging to the garrison, nor come
near the castle nor any of the forts: which engagement the
governor received, and suffered the man to come home; and
Millington, lest the governor should suspect his great concern for Dr. Plumptre, made strong professions to him, that
he desired his re-admission into the town for nothing but to
be a snare to him: for he knew the turbulency and pride of
his spirit such, that he would never be quiet; but if, after
this indulgence, he should, as he believed he would, return
to his former courses, he would be inexcusable in the eyes of
all men.   Then Mr. Millington desired the governor to draw
up some heads, wherein he conceived his power to consist,
which he did, reducing almost the words of his commission
into eight propositions; which, when he showed first to Mr.
Millington, before the committee saw them, Mr. Millington
seemed very well to approve of them, and protested again to
the governor, the faithfulness of his heart to him, excusing
his intimacy with his enemies, upon a zeal he had to do him
service, by discovering their designs against him, and called
himself therein, Sir Politic Wouldbe: but the governor dis-
liking this double dealing, though it had been with his enemies,
desired him rather to declare himself ingenuously as his conscience led him, though it should be against him, and told him
freely he liked not this fair carriage to both.   When the
governor put in his propositions to the committee, they desired
each of them might have a copy of them, and all a week's
time to consider them; at the end of which, when the governor

pressed their answer, whether they assented to them, or could object any thing against them; they said, with false flattering apologies to the governor, that if such command were due to any man, they should rather the governor should employ it than any person whatsoever, by reason of his unquestioned merits; but they conceived that such a power given to a governor, would not consist with that which belonged to a committee, whereupon they produced a tedious, impertinent paper, in answer to the governor's propositions, which, when the governor read over, he flung by, saying it was a ridiculous senseless piece of stuff. Some of them taking exceptions, that he should so contemn the committee's paper; he replied, he knew not yet whose it was, not being signed by any one; if any of them would own it, he desired them to subscribe it, and then he should know what to say. Thereupon, the next day, it was again brought out, signed by Mr. Millington, Chadwick, Salisbury, White, and the mayor of the town. The sum of the paper not containing any exceptions against the governor himself, but against his power, and wholly denying that my Lord Fairfax had power to make a governor, or confer any such power on him, as his commission imported; the governor told them, it no further concerned him, but only to acquaint my Lord Fairfax, with whom he should leave it, to justify his own commission, and his authority to give one. But forasmuch as my lord was concerned in it, the gentlemen who had more respect for him disowned it, and these were the governor, the lieutenant-colonel, Mr. Pigott, Colonel Thornhagh, Major Ireton, Major Widmerpoole, Captain Lomax, and Alderman James. Then the governor told them, how he had been informed that this paper was of Chadwick's contrivance, and that when Mr. Millington saw it, he hugged Chadwick in his arms, with such congratulation, as is not to be imagined they could give to a fellow of whom they had

s 2

justly entertained so vile an opinion; and then before his face
he declared all their thoughts of indignation and contempt,
which they had formerly expressed of Colonel Chadwick, of
whom he asked, with what face he could question my lord's
authority to make him governor, when he had formerly used
such surreptitious cheats to obtain it for himself, by the same
authority? And he asked the committee, how it came to
pass, they now believed my Lord Fairfax had not authority
to make him governor, when they themselves at first wrote to
him for the commission? And to Mr. Millington he said, that
he had dealt very unfaithfully to those who trusted him to
compose differences, which he had rather made than found;
and very treacherously with him, making himself a party and
the chief of his adversaries, when he pretended only to be a
reconciler. Having at full laid them open one to another,
and declared all their treachery, malice, pride, and knavery,
to their faces, he went away, smiling at the confusion he had
left them in, who had not virtue enough in their shame to
bring them back to repentance, but having begun to persecute
him, with their spite and malice, were resolved to carry on
their wicked design; wherein they had now a double encouragement to animate them, Mr. Millington's sheltering them
in the parliament house, and obstructing all redress the
governor should there seek for, and the hopes of profit and
advantage they might upon the change of things expect from
the garrison, if they could wrest it out of the governor's hands,
either by wearying him with unjust vexations, or by watching
some advantage against him, to procure his discharge from
his office by the parliament; for they, knowing him to be impatient of affronts, and of a high spirit, thought to provoke him
to passion, wherein something might fall out to give them
advantages; but he, perceiving their drift, showed them that
he governed his anger, and suffered it not to master him, and

that he could make use of it to curb their insolency, and yet
avoid all excursions that might prejudice himself.* When
the governor undertook this employment, the parliament's
interest in those parts was so low, and the hazard so desperate, that these pitiful wretches, as well as others faithful-
hearted to the public cause, courted him to accept and keep
the place; and though their foul spirits hated the daylight of
his more virtuous conversation, yet were they willing enough
to let him bear the brunt of all the hazard and toil of their
defence, more willing to be secured by his indefatigable
industry and courage, than to render him the just acknowledgment of his good deserts. This ingratitude did not at all
abate his zeal for the public service, for as he sought not
praise, so he was well enough satisfied in doing well; yet
through their envious eyes, they took in a general good
esteem of him, and sinned against their own consciences in
persecuting him, whereof he had after acknowledgments and
testimonies from many of them. All the while of this contest, he was borne up by a good and honourable party of the
committee, and greater in number and value than the wicked
ones, whom Mr. Millington's power in the house only countenanced and animated to pursue their mischiefs. What it
was that drew Mr. Millington into their confederacy was
afterwards apparent; they hired him with a subscription of
losses, for which they gave him public credit double to what
he really had lost;† and they offered him a share of the

* To some the recital of these municipal broils may appear rather
tedious; but Whitelocke's Memorials show that these, and such like, in
various parts of the kingdom required the serious and frequent attention of
the parliament. Most readers will pity a man of Colonel Hutchinson's
exalted mind for being compelled to cope with such despicable adversaries,
but they will derive some pleasure from observing the address with which
he foiled their insidious attacks.

† Of this custom of applying to the parliament for reparation or com-
pensation, and of its being granted generally at the expense of their

governor's spoils, if he would help them to make him a prey, which would have been good booty to his mean family : for although the governor had hitherto got nothing but desperate hazard and vast expense, yet now, this garrison began to be in a more hopeful condition, by the late success in the north. After York was taken, the Earl of Manchester marched into our parts, upon whose coming Bolsover and Tickhill castles were delivered up to him, and Welbeck, the Earl of New-castle's house, which was given into Colonel Thornhagh's command, and much of the enemy's wealth, by that means, brought into Nottingham : Winkfield Manor, a strong garri-son in Derbyshire, was taken upon composition, and by this means a rich and large side of the country was laid open to help to maintain the garrison at Nottingham, and more hoped for by these gentlemen, who were now as greedy to catch at the rewards of another's labours, as unable to merit anything themselves.   But when the hopes of the harvest of the whole country had tempted them to begin their wicked plots, God, seeming angry at their ill use of mercy, caused the Earl of Manchester to be called back into the south, when he was going to have besieged Newark, and so that town, with the petty garrisons at Wiverton, Shelford, and Belvoir, were still left for further exercise to Nottingham.   Yet the hopes that these would in time be gained, made these gentlemen prosecute their design against the governor, whose party they endea-voured with all subtleties to weaken : and first they attempted Colonel Thornhagh, who having by his signalised valour arrived at a great reputation, they thought if they could gain him, he would be their best lever to heave out the governor, and that prop once removed they despaired not to make him contribute to his own ruin ; for they had discovered in him a

quents or cavaliers, there appear many instances in Whitelocke—no doubt many abuses crept in.   In Walker's Hist. of Independ. p. 81, Mr. Milling-ton is declared to have received in this manner £2000

facility of nature, apt to be deluded by fair pretences, and more prone to suspect the kind plain dealing of his friends, than the flattery of his enemies : but the governor, after they had displayed themselves, by his vigilancy prevented many of their malicious designs, and among the rest those they had upon this gentleman. During his sickness the governor took care of his regiment, and employed the troops that quartered .n the garrison : but through the wicked instigations of Captain White, being very refractory, and the regiment often called out on field-service, the governor sent for a commission, and raised a troop of horse, which the lieutenant-colonel commanded, and a troop of dragoons for the peculiar service of the garrison. These cunning sowers of sedition wrought, upon this occasion, Colonel Thornhagh into a jealous belief, that Colonel Hutchinson was taking the advantage of his sickness to work himself into his command. Colonel Thornhagh was grieved at it, but said nothing ; but the governor discovering the thing, notwithstanding his silence, when the lieutenant-colonel went to London, procured a commission for Colonel Thornhagh to be, next under Sir Thomas Fairfax, commander-in-chief of all the parliament's horse in Nottinghamshire, at all times ; which being brought to Colonel Thornhagh, when he knew nothing of it, cleared him of that suspicion. And now, although they were more inclined to delude than openly to oppose Colonel Thornhagh, yet they, having no exceptions against the governor in his own person, but only against his authority, were forced to deny Colonel Thornhagh's command as well as the governor's, they being both derived from the same power. The horse-captains, who were allured by fair colours of preferment, and indulged in their plunder, which they hoped to do with more freedom, if Captain White prevailed, were more obedient to Captain White and their own ambition, than to their colonel or the laws and customs of war. The committee hoped, by thus

disputing the colonel's powers, under a face of parliament
authority, to weary them out, and make them cast up their
commissions, when they had, by Mr. Millington, blocked up
the way of their complaint, so that they feared not being
turned out of the committee for the abuse of that trust: and
perhaps they had succeeded but that the governor scorned to
give up a good cause, either particular or public, for want of
courage to defend it amidst many difficulties; and then,
although he had many enemies, he had more friends, whom
if he should desert, would be left to be crushed by these
malicious persons; and more than all this, the country would
be abandoned into the hands of persons who would only make
a prey of it, and not endeavour its protection, liberty, or real
advantage, which had been his chief aim in all his undertakings.

The conspirators, as I may more justly term them, than
the committee, had sent Captain White to York, to my Lord
Fairfax, to get the governor's power defined; which the
governor understanding, the next day went thither himself,
and Mr. Pigott, who from the beginning to the ending showed
himself a most real and generous friend to the governor, and
as cordial to his country and the great cause, went along
with him, arriving a day after Captain White. When my
lord gave them a hearing together, he asked whether the
governor had done anything of consequence without consulting the committee, which White could not say he had; then
he asked White if he had any other misgovernment to
accuse him of, which when White could not allege against
him, the governor before his face told my lord all the business, whereupon White was dismissed with reproof and
laughter, and letters were written to the committee, to justify the governor's power, and to entreat them to forbear
disturbing him in his command, and to Mr. Millington, to
desire him to come over to York to my lord   both which the

governor delivered, but Mr. Millington would not go over, but, on the contrary, continued to foment and raise up the factions in the town against the governor, and by his countenance the committee every day meditated and practised new provocations, to stir up the governor to rage, or at least to weary him in his employment. The horse, without his knowledge, they frequently sent abroad; protections, tickets, and passes, they gave out; and, encroaching upon his office in all things whatsoever, wrought such a confusion in the garrison, that while all men were distracted and amazed, in doubt whose orders to obey, and who were their commanders, they obeyed none, but every man did what he listed; and by that means the public service was in all things obstructed and prejudiced. The governor, while the injury was only to himself, bore it, but when it extended almost to the destruction of the garrison, he was forced to endeavour a remedy. For about this time it happened that Salisbury, being treasurer, had given base terms and wilful delays to the soldiers who were assigned their pay, when the money was ready for them in the treasury; and when this base carriage of his had provoked them to a mutiny, the governor was sent for to appease it, which he did; but coming to the committee, told them he would no longer endure this usage of theirs, to have all things of power, honour, and command, wrested out of his hands, and all things of difficulty and danger put upon him; while they purposely stirred up occasions of rigour and punishment, and then expected he should be the executioner of it, by which he perceived they did these things only with design to render him contemptible and odious to all persons. Not long afterwards a command came for all the horse that could be spared in the garrison to go to Sir John Meldrum, to the relief of Montgomery Castle. The governor went to the committee to consult what troops should march, and they voted *none*. The governor told them, he

conceived when a command was given, they were to obey
without dispute, and that he came to advise with them wha
troops should be sent forth, not whether any or none ; therefore although they voted disobedience of the command, that
would not discharge him, especially the service being of great
consequence, and the troops lying here without other employment : wherefore at night he summoned a council of
war, and there almost all the captains, having no mind to
march so far from home, declared they conceived themselves
to be under the command of the committee, and would only
obey their orders.   Upon this the governor went to the committee and desired them that, since unanswerable things
were done, the public service neglected, and all the transactions of the garrison confused, they would unite with him in
a petition to parliament to define their several powers; and in
the meantime, either quietly to let him execute his duty, or
else to take all upon them and discharge him.   They presently made a motion, that he would call a muster, and put
it to all the soldiers, whether they would be governed by the
committee or the governor.   The governor told them his command was not elective, but of right belonged to him, and this
way was only the next occasion to cause a mutiny, which he
could not consent to.   But they persisting in their course, he
came again to them and desired they would discontinue these
affronts in his command, and also their underminings, whereby they endeavoured to alienate men's hearts from him, and
to raise a faction against him by close unworthy practices.
So after much debate it was on all hands agreed, that they
should not at all intermeddle with anything belonging to the
soldiery, nor interrupt the governor in his command, till the
house of parliament should decide it, and that the governor
and Captain White should both go to London, to procure a
speedy determination of the powers in a fair and open way.
This they all faithfully promised the governor, and made

many hypocritical professions to him, some of them with tears; whereupon he, who was of the most reconcilable nature in the world, accepted their fair pretences, and went to drink friendly with them in token of kindness. Yet was all this but hypocrisy and falsehood, for even at that very time they wearied many of the governor's officers out of the garrison, by the continued malice wherewith they persecuted all that had any respect for him. Among these was Mr. Hooper the engineer, a man very faithful to the cause, and very honest, but withal rough, who having to do with hateful businesses, was made odious to the common people, the priests too having a particular spite at him, as one they esteemed a leader of the separatists; yet he was very ingenious and industrious in his office, and most faithful as well to the governor himself as to the public service. The committee, to insinuate themselves with the common people, regarded him with an evil eye, and so discouraged him, that being offered much better preferment, and invited by Colonel Cromwell into other parts, he acquainted the governor with it, offering withal that, if he might yet be protected from affronts in his employment, he would stay and serve the governor for half the salary offered elsewhere. But the governor, although he was very sorry to part with him, and the service would much miss him, yet being so much injured himself, could not undertake the protection of any of his officers, and therefore would not hinder his preferment, but suffered him to go to Cromwell. Such was the envy of the committee to him, that that very day, just as he was going, they not willing to let him depart in peace, although they knew he had justly expended all the money he had received of them, yet they called for an account, from the beginning of his employment, which they had often seen in parcels; but believing he could not so readily give it them altogether, they then demanded it. He immediately brought it forth, and got by it twelve shillings due to him upon the foot thereof, which he intended not to have asked them for, but receiving it upon the exhibition of his account, went away smiling at their malice ; which yet would not let him go so, for then Henry Wandall came with a petition to the governor, that he would vindicate the honour of the Earl of Essex against Mr. Hooper, whom he accused of having spoken words against him, and done actions to his dishonour. The governor knowing this was but malice, accepted security for him, which was offered by Mr. Pigott and Major Watson, that he should answer what could be objected against him at any council of war he should be called to.*

Wednesday, September the 25th, 1644, Captain White went to London, to solicit the committee's business against the governor, for they pretended to put it upon a fair debate, as was promised. The next day the governor commanded Captain Barrett's troop to convoy him towards London; but just as he was going to horse, the committee, contrary to their engagements not to meddle with any mili tary affairs, commanded them another way, and so he was forced to go without a convoy, although the captain was afforded a whole troop to wait on him.

Two or three days before the governor went, Chadwick came privately to the governor's brother, and told him that his conscience would not suffer him to conceal the malicious designs, and that treachery, which he now discovered to be

* This Mr. Hooper was undoubtedly a person of singular abilities. Mr. Sprigge, in his Anglia Rediviva, mentions him as serving Sir Thomas Fairfax at the siege of Oxford and other places as engineer extraordinary, and greatly expediting all his enterprises, the rapidity and number of which were surprising : he was at the siege of Ragland Castle, the last garrison that surrendered ; he came again to Nottingham during Colonel Hutchinson's government, and, by the list of the garrison in Deering's Nottingham, appears to have continued with Captain Poulton.

in these men's oppositions to the governor; and with many insinuations, told him they were framing articles against the governor, whereof he gave him a copy, which the governor carried to London with him, and showed the lieutenant-colonel the originals in Mason's and Plumptre's own handwritings. Three days after the governor, Colonel Thornhagh went to London. That day the governor went, one of the presbyterian ministers, whose name was Goodhall, preached the lecture at the great church, with many invectives against governors and arbitrary power, so plainly hinting at the governor, that all the church well understood it; but of the committee he spoke fawningly, and told them he had nothing to say to them, but to go on in the good way they went. Some months afterwards, this poor man, preaching at a living the committee had put him into, was taken by the enemy, and much dejected at it, because he could not hope the governor would exchange him, after his unworthy pulpit railings at him; but the governor, who hated poor revenges when his enemy and one of his friends were both in the same prison, and he had but one exchange ready, first procured the minister's release, and let his own officer stay for the next exchange. Whereupon the man coming home, was struck with remorse, and begged the governor's pardon, with real acknowledgments both to himself and others of his sin, in supporting the faction against the governor, who was told that on his death-bed, for he died before the garrison was dissolved, he expressed to some of the governor's friends his trouble for having been his enemy. But not only to him, but to many others of his enemies, the governor upon sundry occasions, when they fell into his power to have requited their mischiefs, instead of vengeance rendered them benefits; so that at last his own friends would tell him, if they could in justice and conscience forsake him, they would become his adversaries, for that was the next way to engage him to obligations. But although his friends, who had greater animosities against his unjust persecutors than he himself, would say these things in anger at his clemency, his nature was as full of kind gratitude to his friends as free from base revenges upon his enemies, who either fell down to him from their own just remorse, or were cast under his power by God's just providence.

As soon as the governor was gone, the committee took all power upon them, and had the impudence to command the lieutenant-colonel, who was deputy-governor, and absolute in his brother's absence, to draw out his troop: he went to them and told them he was sorry they broke their agreement, but he could not break his trust of his brother's authority to obey them. Then they feigned a pretence and turned out the governor's quarter-master, who, by the governor's appointment had quartered soldiers at an ale-house Mr. Millington had given protection to, saying, that none should be quartered on account of some relation they had to him who married one of the daughters of the place. This occasioning some dispute, Cooke the quarter-master had uttered some words, for which they sent for him and cast out great threats, how they would punish him; which frighted his wife, big with child, in that manner, that her child died within her, and her own life was in great hazard. The committee then called a hall, and caused the townsmen to bring in horses for dragoons, whereof they voted a regiment to be raised, Chadwick to be the colonel, and Hall and Selby to be captains under him. They took upon them to command the soldiers, and made horrible confusion, by which they often put the garrison in great danger, if the enemy had known their advantage. Among the rest, one night after the guards were set, the captain of the guard, missing the deputy-governor to receive the word from him, gave them the same word they had before, t'll he had found out the governor to receive a new one. Mr. Millington coming by, half flustered, would have had the captain take a word from him, which when the captain refused, he being angry, commanded Captain Mason's drums to beat, and set a double guard. The lieutenant-colonel hearing the drums, and having no notice of his command, sent to Mason to command him to forbear drawing any men to the guard, but Mason would not obey him. Besides this, they did a thousand such like things, to provoke him to give them some colour of complaint, or some advantage against him and his brother, in order to carry on a wicked design, by which they were secretly managing to destroy them; but God, by a wonderful providence, brought it to light.

Their conspiracy was to accuse the colonel and his brother, as persons that had betrayed the town and castle, and were ready to surrender them to the enemy, which they would pretend to have discovered, and to have prevented their treachery, by a surprise of the lieutenant-colonel, the castle and the bridges, and all the officers that were faithful to the governor and his friends. Because they had not a force in town who would act this villany, they sent to Sir John Gell, in whom they had a great interest, and a man likely enough to promote their wickedness, had they even acquainted him with it, as black as it was in the cursed forge of their own hearts: but to carry on their business closely, they sent to tell him they had cause of suspicion that the lieutenant-colonel was false to his trust, and would deliver the castle to the enemy, to prevent which they desired him to assist them with some men and amunition; which ammunition was very secretly conveyed into the town, and the men were ready to march, and quarters taken up for them in Nottingham. The lieutenant-colonel dreamed nothing of the mischief that was natching against him, when, just at the very time of the execution, there came into Nottingham two gentlemen,

whom the parliament employed to carry intelligences · between the north and the south, and who used to meet at this
town.

Mr. Fleetwood, who came from the south, came immediately up to the castle, and was there familiarly and kindly
treated, as he used to be, by the lieutenant-colonel. This
was upon a Saturday night, in the month of October. Mr.
Marsh, his correspondent, who came from the north, passing
through Derby, was so cautioned by Sir John Gell, that he
durst not go up to the castle, but on the Lord's day sent for
Mr. Fleetwood to meet him in the town ; who coming to him,
he told him what information he had received from Sir John
Gell, and for that reason he durst not trust himself in the
castle. Mr. Fleetwood undertaking for his safety, brought
him up to the lieutenant-colonel, and finding the untruth
of their forgeries, told the lieutenant-colonel all the machinations against him ; whereupon, on the Monday morning, he
went away to London, and sent Mr. Millington word, that
having understood the suspicion they had of him, he was gone
to London, where, if they had anything to accuse him of, they
might send after him, and he should be ready to answer it,
and in his absence had left Captain Lomax governor of the
garrison. The committee, very much confounded that their
wickedness was come to light, resolved to outface the thing,
and denied that they had sent to Derby for any men. They
said indeed it was true, that having formerly lent Sir John
Gell some powder, they had sent for that back ; but this was
not all, for they had also persuaded the master of the magazine that was in the castle to convey, unknown to the lieutenant-colonel, two barrels of powder, with match and bullet
suitable, to such place as Chadwick should direct. This he,
not dreaming of their evil intention, had condescended to do,
and sent them to Salisbury's house ; but as soon as the lieutenant-colonel was gone, they took what care they could to

shuffle up this business, and presently despatched Captain Palmer to London and Lieutenant Chadwick to Derby, where he so wrought with Sir John Gell, that he brought back a counterfeit letter, pretended to have been all that was sent from the committee of Nottingham to him, and another of Sir John Gell's writing, wherein he disowned all that Mr. Marsh had related of his information. But God, who would not let them be hid, had so ordered that while matters were thus huddling up at Derby, Sir John Gell's brother came by chance to Nottingham, and affirmed that the committee of Nottingham had sent to his brother for three hundred men, to surprise Nottingham Castle; which, when the committee heard, they sent Captain Pendock after him the next day to charm him, that he might not discover the truth in that particular. Also the very day that these intentions of theirs were thus providentially brought to light, one of Sir John Gell's captains was known to be in town, whom Sir John had sent to discover the state of things, and the new quarter-master had been all that day taking billets for soldiers in several houses in the town.

When the governor came to London, the committee of both kingdoms had appointed a sub-committee to hear his business, whereof young Sir Henry Vane had the chair, Mr. William Pierrepont, Mr. Solicitor St. John, Mr. Recorder, and two of the Scotch commissioners, were nominated for the committee; before whom the governor's propositions and the committee's answers had been read, and when their solicitor, Captain White, saw they were likely to be cast out as frivolous, he produced some articles, which they had formed against the governor, lieutenant-colonel, and Mr. Pigott; but they proved as frivolous as the other, and the gentlemen answered them so clearly, that they appeared to be forged out of malice and envy, only to cause delays, there being scarcely anything of moment in them if they had been

s

true, whereas they were all false. And now after they had
trodden down the fence of shame, and impudently begun with
articles, there was not the least ridiculous impertinency that
passed at Nottingham, but they put into a scrip of paper and
presented it as an additional article to the committee; to each
of whom particularly Mr. Millington had written letters, and
given them such false impressions of the governor, and so
prepossessed them against him, who was a stranger to them all,
that they looked upon him very coldly and slightly, when he
made particular addresses to them. But he that scorned
to be discouraged by any men's disregard, from whom he
had more reason to have expected all caresses and thankful
acknowledgments of his unwearied fidelity and good services,
resolved to pursue his own vindication through all their
frowns and cold repulses: these he met with more from Mr.
William Pierrepont than from any of the rest, till Mr. Pierrepont perceived the injustice of their prosecution, and then
there was no person in the world that could demean himself
with more justice, honour, and kindness than he did to the
governor, whose injuries first became apparent to him, when
the lieutenant-colonel came and told his brother what combi-
nations had been discovered against him at Nottingham,
which the governor resenting with great indignation, complained of them to the committee. The Solicitor White
impudently denied the whole matter, or that ever the committee at Nottingham had had the least suspicion of the
governor or his brother, or the least ground of any. When
this had been with stiffness and impudence enough outfaced
before the committee, Mr. Pierrepont, then fully convinced
of their devilish malice, pulled a letter out of his pocket,
wherein Mr. Millington made this suggestion to him against
the governor and his brother, and desired that he might be
armed with power to prevent and suppress them. This
would have made others ashamed, but their solicitor was

notwithstanding impudent and rudely pressing upon the committee, who though they were persons of honour, and after they discovered the governor's innocence, were not forward to oppress him; yet as they were statesmen, so they were not so ready to relieve him as they ought to have been, because they could not do it without a high reflection upon one of their own members, who encouraged all those little men in their wicked persecution of him. They were such exquisite rogues, that all the while some of them betrayed one another to the governor, and told him, under pretence of honesty and conscience, the bottom of their whole designs, showed the foul original drafts of their articles, in the men's own hands that contrived them; and told him how, not so much dislike of him, as covetousness and ambition to advance themselves upon his ruins, had engaged them thus against him, and made them contrive that villainy to accuse him and his brother of treachery, and to have seized their garrisons, under that pretence, and gotten them to be made prisoners; and then Mr. Millington undertook to have so lodged their petitions in the parliament, that they should never have been heard and relieved.*   Colonel Thornhagh too was to have been wrought out of his command, and they had divided the spoil before they caught the lions.   Millington's son was designed to be governor of the castle; the ten pounds a week allowed for the governor's table, so many of the committee-men were to share by forty shillings a man; Chadwick was to be colonel of the town regiment, and Mason major; White colonel of the horse regiment, and Palmer. the priest, his major; and all the governor's friends were to

* It is averred in the History of Independency, " that the active speaking men pack committees who carry all the businesses of the house as they please, and when the matter is too bad, smother it with artificial delays."

be turned out, and their places disposed of to creatures of
their own, who drawn on with these hopes, were very active
to work the governor and his party out of the opinion of all
men.   They forgot the public interest in this private quarrel,
taking in all the malignant and debauched people that would
join with them, to destroy the governor, whom they hated
for his unmoved fidelity to his trust, and his severe restric-
tion of lewdness and vice.   But because he protected and
favoured godly men that were sober, although they separated
from the public assemblies, this opened wide the mouths of
all the priests and all their idolaters, and they were willing
enough to let the children of hell cry out with them to make
the louder noise; and as we have since seen the whole cause
and party ruined by the same practice, so at that time the
zealots for God and the parliament turned all the hate they
had to the enemies of both, and called on them to assist in
executing their malice upon the faithful servant and generous
champion of the Lord's and his country's just cause.   And
now the name of cavalier was no more remembered, Castilian
being the term of reproach with which they branded all the
governor's friends; and lamentable it was to behold how those
wretched men fell away under this temptation, not only from
public spiritedness, but from sobriety and honest, moral conversation; not only conniving at and permitting the wickedness of others, but themselves conversing in taverns and
brothels, till at last Millington and White were so ensnared
that they married a couple of alehouse wenches, to their
open shame and the conviction of the whole country of the
vain lives they led, and some reflection on the parliament
itself, as much as the miscarriage of a member could cast on
it, when Millington, a man of sixty, professing religion, and
having but lately buried a religious matronly gentlewoman,
should go to an alehouse to take a flirtish girl of sixteen;
yet by these noble alliances, they much strengthened their

faction with all the vain, drunken rogues in the town against
the governor. Now, that their first plot had, by God's pro
vidence, been detected, they fell upon others, and set on instruments every where, to insinuate all the lies they could,
that might render the governor odious to the town and to
the horse of the garrison, whom they desired to stir up to
petition against him, but could not find any considerable
number that would freely do it; therefore they used all the
strong motives they could, and told them that the governor
sought to exercise an arbitrary power over them, and to have
all their booties at his own disposal, and other such like
things, by which at length they prevailed with many of Col.
Thornhagh's regiment to subscribe a petition that they might
be under the command of the committee, and not of any
other person in the garrison.   This petition was sent up
by Captain Palmer, and he meeting Mr. Pigott at Westminster Hall, Mr. Pigott, in private discourse with him,
began to bewail the scandalous conversation of certain
persons of the committee, hoping that he, being familiar
with them, might be a means to persuade them to reformation.

After this the governor, Colonel Thornhagh, Mr. Pigott,
and some others, being in a tavern at Westminster, where
they dined, Captain Palmer came to the door, and they bade
him come in.   Upon discourse, the governor pulled out of
his pocket the articles which the committee had put in
against him, showed them to Captain Palmer, and asked him
whether he thought it possible that he should, after all his
toils and services, have been articled against for such things.
Palmer, who had been from the beginning with the committee,
and knew the falsehood of these accusations, professed he
was amazed at them, and that he had not till then heard anything of them.   Continuing in further discourse, the governor
mentioned an unchristian-like sermon, which Mr. Goodhall

had preached, with invectives against him in his absence.
Palmer undertook the justification of it with such saucy provocations, that the governor told him if it had not been more
in respect to his black coat than his grey, he would have
beaten him out of the room, which for his own safety he
advised him to leave ; so he went out very angry, and going
to Captain White, told him how Mr. Pigott called him a
whoremaster, Mr. Millington a drunkard, and Chadwick a
knave. White, meeting Mr. Pigott in the hall, challenged
him of these scandals. Mr. Pigott, seeing Palmer not far
off, led White to him, and told him he knew that person had
been his informer, repeating all he had said to him, and
added, that it was in a desire for their reformation, but he
would maintain that all the things he spoke were true.
Palmer further, in his rage, puts into the committee a paper
of reasons why he desired to be exempted from being under
the governor ; whereof one was, that he had cowardly and
unhandsomely behaved himself on an occasion when Palmer's
troop marched out with him to Elston. The governor sent
a copy of this paper down to Palmer's own troop, and the
lieutenant, cornet, and all the troopers sent up a certificate,
under their hands, of the falsehood of their captain's accusation. After this, Palmer came into the garrison, and made
a grievous exclamation all over the town against the governor
and Mr. Pigott for traducing the ministers, Mr. Millington,
and the committee ; adding a false report, that the governor
had thrown a trencher at his head ; and abused the pulpit
for persuading the people to vindicate them. Among other
things, he misapplied a place in Nehemiah, where Nehemiah
says, " I ate not the governor's bread, because the fear of
the Lord was upon me," to the governor ; that his accepting
a public table, was a mark of the want of the fear of God ;
and many other such malicious wrestings of scripture did he
and his fellow priests at that time practise. The committee

of Nottingham, on their side, taking this occasion, called a public hall in the town, where two orations were made by Mr. Millington and Colonel Chadwick.   Millington began with a large enumeration of Chadwick's worthy actions (known to no man), whereby he merited honour of all men, especially of this town ; and then mentioning his own good services for the town, told them how ungratefully they were repaid by Mr. Pigott, with the scandalous aspersion of being drunkards and knaves ; and that their singular affections and endeavours for the good of the town had exposed them to this calumny, wherefore they desired the town to join in their justification.   Chadwick made just such another speech, and both of them seemed to pass by their own particular, and only to desire the other's justification ; Chadwick, in his speech, saying that Mr. Pigott's abuse of Mr. Millington did not only asperse the committee, but even the parliament itself.   Captain Lomax, then deputy-governor of the garrison, after they had spoken, stood up, and advised the townsmen that they should forbear to entangle themselves in things they understood not, adding that Mr. Pigott, and the gentlemen at London, were persons of such honour and prudence, that they would maintain whatever they had spoken of any man.   Hereupon Captain Mason, and two malignant townsmen his soldiers, began to mutiny with high insolence, and to lay violent hands on him to thrust him out of the hall, giving him most reproachful terms ; but the man being very stout quieted them, and would not depart till the hall broke up.   After this, without acquainting the deputy-governor, they summoned another hall ; but Lomax, seeing their inclination to mutiny, forbade it.   Then, at ten o'clock at night, they got a common council together, at Mr. Salisbury's house, and there Mr. Millington again desired they would join in the vindication of himself, the ministers, and the committee, **and got about eight** of them to subscribe a blank paper.

Then the committee, with certain instruments of theirs, appointed rounds to walk the town, persuading some, and threatening others, to set their hands to a petition, which none of them that subscribed knew what it was, but they told them it was for the good of the town.

All this while these petty committee fellows had carried themselves as absolute governors, and Plumptre was now their intimate favourite, and began to vapour that he would have the castle pulled down to re-erect the church, and the fort at the bridges thrown down, and all the arms and soldiers brought into the town.

But at London, the governor being grown into acquaintance with the gentlemen of the sub-committee that were to hear his business ; and they perceiving with how much wicked malice he was prosecuted, Sir Henry Vane was so honourable as to give him advice to put his business in such a way, as might take away all colour from his enemies. Whereupon he put in some propositions to the committee of both kingdoms, for the composure of these differences, wherein he was willing to decline all things of his own right, which might be done without prejudice to the public service, and to pass by all the injuries that had been done him ; which condescension gave such satisfaction, that forthwith the whole business was determined at the committee of both kingdoms, and the governor sent back to his charge, with instructions drawn up for all parties, and letters written to the officers and soldiers, both of horse and foot, to be obedient ; and likewise letters to the mayor of the town and to the committee The governor returning, word was brought to Nottingham, that on Friday night he lay at Leicester, whereupon the committee, who had heard the determination of things above, got them ready to be gone, but the soldiers having notice thereof, went to the deputy-governor and entreated him to stop the treasurer ; whereupon he and the major of the regiment went to them, and entreated them to stay till the governor came, merely to see what instructions he brought with him from the powers above ; but when they would not be persuaded fairly, then the deputy peremptorily forbade the treasurer, as he would answer it, not to go.   But he refusing to obey, the deputy told him he should pass on his sword's point if he went, and accordingly went down to set guards at the Trent bridges ; which being told them, they made haste and fled out at the other end of the town.   Millington, Chadwick, Ayscough, Salisbury, and Mason (whom they had added to the committee to increase their faction), were the committee men, who took with them their new marshal and another of their created officers, Palmer, two more priests, and a town captain.   The governor was met on his way homewards by some of his officers, and told with what joy his garrison and regiment were preparing to entertain him, in all expressions they could possibly make, by volleys of cannon and muskets, and ringing of bells, and all such declarations as used to be made in a public and universal rejoicing ; but the governor, fearing his enemies might not bear such testimonies of love to him, without grief, sent into the town to desire them to forbear their kind intentions of giving him so loud a welcome.   When he was now near the town, another messenger came to acquaint him, that all those who would have been grieved at his joyful entertainment were fled, and that those who remained would be much grieved if he should not be pleased to give them leave to receive him with such demonstrations of their joy as they could make.   He now permitted them to do what they pleased ; which leave being obtained, every one strove to declare his gladness with all imaginable expressions of love and honour, and with all the solemnities the time and place would afford.   The governor on his side received them all with a cheerful obliging courtesy, and gave a large bounty to

his loving soldiers, who made that day as great a festival as
if themselves and their families had been redeemed from captivity.   The mayor of the town, with his brethren in their
scarlets, met him, and told him if he had been guilty of anything prejudicial to him, he was exceedingly sorry for it, for
he infinitely honoured him, and all his errors had been
through ignorance or misinformation, which he should be
most ready to repair.   That evening White came home pining
with spite and envy at the governor and the gentlemen that
joined with him, viz. Colonel Thornhagh, Mr. Pigott, Lieutenant-colonel Hutchinson, Major Widmerpoole, Captain
Lomax, and Alderman James ; for as to the mayor of the
town, notwithstanding his fair professions publicly to the
governor, White had the same night again turned about that
weathercock.

The next day the governor and the committee with him
sent a command to all the horse in town to march to the
assistance of Derby and Leicester, to fortify a house called
Coleorton ; which not being taken notice of, the governor
and Colonel Thornhagh summoned all the horse officers, and
declared to them the orders of the committee of both kingdoms, to which they cheerfully promised obedience ; but
White being sent for among them, insolently refused to come
up to the castle, and bade the governor come down to him to
the committee's chamber ; yet upon second thoughts he came
up, and the governor took no notice for that time.   On Monday the governor sent to the mayor to call a hall, but the
mayor entreated him to forbear till they saw whether the
committee-men that ran away would come back, and that he
might go with Captain White to persuade them ; both of
which the governor assented to ; but the men would not
return, but went from Derby to London.   Then the governor
called a general muster, and read to them the instructions he
had brought from the committee of both kingdoms, with

which all the men were exceeding well pleased. But Captain White all this while would not deliver the letters he had for the committee and the mayor of Nottingham.

Some few days afterwards word was brought the governor that the new dragoons were come for ammunition, to march out upon some design he was not acquainted with, whereupon he sent to the guards at the bridges not to suffer them to pass without his ticket. Immediately afterwards, White came along with them, and being denied to pass, gave the guards such provocative language that they were forced to send for the governor. He came down and found White in high rage, who gave him all the vile terms and opprobrious language he could invent, to provoke him to some anger upon which he might have taken his advantage; but the governor only laughed at his fogue,* and would not let him go till he showed a warrant from the council of war at London, and then he permitted him, after White had told him that he would not be commanded by him, and a thousand such mutinous speeches. As he went towards London he met the horse coming home from Coleorton, to whom he told such lies of the governor's usage of him, that they were frightened from coming into the garrison, but that Colonel Thornhagh prevailed with them to take his engagement, that the governor should give them no ill usage. So they came back, and that week their colonel charged the enemy's quarters with them and took eighty horse, two horse colours, a major and some other officers. The bridge troop also met with Colonel Stanhope, governor of Shelford,† who had two

* French—*Fougue,* fury or passion.

† Here, viz. in the end of the year 1644, Shelford clearly appears to be a garrison for the king; yet Whitelocke, p. 96, says that in July, 1644, Lord Grey of Groby, and Sir John Gell, had the thanks of the parliament for taking it. This is an evident inaccuracy of Whitelocke's, or a very successful puff of Sir John's. To put it out of doubt, Sprigge, in his

parties, each as many as they; his party where he himself was, routed, and he ran away, while the other party charged them in the rear, upon whom they turned, routed, and chased them out of the field, took Lieutenant-colonel Stanhope and his ensign, and many other prisoners, with many horse and arms. In the absence of the governor and his brother, the committee had done all they could to discourage and dissipate this troop, and would neither give them money nor provisions; yet, upon hopes of their captain's return, they kept themselves together, and when the governor came home he recruited them.

The committee of both kingdoms had sent down at this time an order for all the horse of Nottingham and Derbyshire to join with three regiments of Yorkshire, and quarter about Newark, to straighten the enemy there; and accordingly they rendezvoused at Mansfield, and from thence marched to Thurgarton, where Sir Roger Cooper had fortified his house, and lined the hedges with musketeers, who, as the troops passed by, shot and killed one Captain Heywood. Hereupon Colonel Thornhagh sent to the governor, and desired to borrow some foot to take the house. The governor accordingly lent him three companies, who took the house, with Sir Roger Cooper and his brother, and forty men in it, who were sent prisoners to Nottingham; where, although Sir Roger Cooper was in great dread of being put into the governor's hands, whom he had provoked before upon a private occasion, yet he received such a civil treatment from him, that he seemed to be much moved and melted with it. The foot had done all the service, and run all the hazard, in taking the house, yet the booty was all given to the horse; this they had very just reason to resent, but notwithstanding,

Anglia Rediviva, counts it among the king's garrisons, May, 1645; and Colonel Hutchinson, supported by Rossiter, took it in person and by storm a year after that.

they marched along with them to Southwell, and there were
most sadly neglected, and put upon keeping outguards for the
horse, and had no provisions, so that the governor was forced
to send them some out of his garrison, or else they had been
left to horrible distress.   Hereupon they sent to the governor
to desire they might come home, but upon Colonel Thornhagh's entreaty and engagement that they should be better
used, the governor was content to let them stay a little
longer, till more horse came up, which were sent for out of
Yorkshire.   In the meantime, those who were there already
did nothing but harass the poor country; and the horse
officers were so negligent of their own duty, and so remiss in
the government of their soldiers, that the service was infinitely prejudiced, and the poor country miserably distressed.
The Nottingham horse, being in their own country, and
having their families in and about Nottingham, were more
guilty of straggling than any of the rest; and Capt. White's
whole troop having presumed to be away one night when
they should have been upon the guard, the Newarkers beat
up our quarters, and took almost two whole troops of that
regiment.   White's lieutenant, without any leave from the
colonel, thereupon posted up to London, and contrived a
complaint against the governor, to make him appear guilty of
this disorder; but soon after Newark gave them another
alarm, and the parliament horse made so slender an appearance that the officers, thereupon consulting in a council of
war, concluded that the design could not to be prosecuted
without more force, and for the present broke up their
quarters.

The committee men that ran away when the governor returned had taken the treasurer away with them, and left
neither any money, nor so much as the rent rolls whereby
the governor could be instructed where to fetch in any;*

* Rent rolls of sequestrated or forfeited estates.

but by the prudence and interest of himself and his friends, he procured a month's pay for the foot, and twenty shillings a man for the horse,* as soon as he came home; and recruited all the stores, which the committee had purposely wasted in his absence, and fetched in a small stock of powder they had laid in at Salisbury's house. While he was thus industriously setting the things in order which they had confounded, they at London were as maliciously active to make more confusion. They contrived many false and frivolous articles and petitions against him, and proceeded to that degree of impudence in desiring alterations, and casting reflections upon the sub-committee itself, that they grew weary of them. Mr. Pierrepont and Sir H. Vane being now taken notice of as leaders of the independent faction,† when those gentlemen out of mere justice and honour discountenanced their envy and malice, they applied themselves to the presbyterian faction, and insinuating to them that the justice of those gentlemen was partiality to the governor, because he was a protector of the now hated separatists, they prevailed to have Sir Philip Stapleton and Sir Gilbert Garrett, two fierce presbyterians, added to the sub-committee, to balance

* One out of many instances of Colonel Hutchinson's generous devotion to the cause, which brought on him that load of debt, so oppressive to him in the reverse of affairs. In p. 623 and 624, of Rushworth, Thornhagh's Nottinghamshire horse state that they had served five years, and received barely six shillings a week in all ; and that there was £40,000 due to them. Judge, from these two corps, Colonel Hutchinson's being twelve hundred infantry, and two or three troops of dragoons, Thornhagh's about six hundred horse, what was the general state of the army as to pay ! Mr. Sprigge might well say of the troops as he does, " it was not their pay that pacified them, for had they not had more civility than money things had not been so fairly managed."

† Probably it was the experience these two excellent politicians had of Colonel Hutchinson's abilities and integrity on this trial which induced them afterwards to take him for their associate.

the other faction, and found this wicked invention not a little advantageous to them: yet Mr. Hollis, who was a person of honour, did not comply with their factious spirits, but gave the governor all just assistance against their malice which lay in his power.* But they quitting all modesty, and pressing the committee with false affirmations and forgeries, that all men would lay down their arms if the governor were not removed, at length prevailed, that he should be the second time sent for to London to justify himself against them. In that blank, to which they had by fraud and threats procured so many signatures, they wrote a petition, alleging that the governor was so generally detested, that if he were not removed all men would fling down their arms; and the subscriptions they thus abused were those they procured to vindicate Mr. Millington. Salisbury and one Silvester had, for their own profit, gotten a commission to set on foot the excise in the county, and joined with them one Sherwin. These two were such pragmatical knaves, that they justly became odious to all men; and although necessity might excuse the tax in other places, yet here it was such a burden that no man of any honesty or conscience could have acted in it. For when plundering troops killed all the poor countrymen's sheep and swine, and other provisions, whereby many honest families were ruined and beggared, these unmerciful people would force excise out of them for those very goods which the others had robbed them of; insomuch that the religious soldiers said they would starve before they would be employed in forcing it, or take any of it for their pay. The governor, being inclined in conscience to assist the poor country, was very active in his endeavours to relieve them

---

* Mrs. Hutchinson, who in other places speaks with much disapprobation of Mr. Hollis, here most candidly gives him his due.

from this oppression, which his enemies highly urged in their
articles against him.   These excisemen came very pressingly
to urge the governor to enforce the payment of it in the
town ; he told them before he would use compulsion he
would try fair means, and call a hall to see whether the
townsmen would be persuaded, which accordingly he did :
but when the day came the excisemen came to the governor
and advised him to take a strong guard with him, telling
him that the butchers had been whetting their knives, and
intended mischief, and had cast out many words, intimating
a dangerous design.   The governor told them he should not
augment his usual guard, and could fear nothing, having no
intent to do anything that might provoke them to mutiny.
They went again to the men and told them the governor intended to come with many armed men, to compel them to
pay it : whereupon when he came to the hall he found but a
very slender appearance, yet those who were there were all
fully resolved not to pay it; but the governor wrought with
them to represent their reasons, in a humble manner, to
the committee of both kingdoms, and that there should be
a fuller meeting for that purpose the next week, and that in
the meantime both parties should forbear any private addresses in this matter.   To this the excisemen agreed ; yet,
notwithstanding, the governor took a whole packet of their
letters going to London, which when he discovered, he also
wrote to his friends in London on behalf of the garrison.
The next week at a full meeting, a petition was signed,
which the governor offered the town to have carried, being
himself to go up, but they in a compliment refused to give
him the trouble, pitching upon Captain Coates and the town-
clerk to go up with it.   They accordingly went, about the
time that, after seven weeks' stay in the garrison, the governor was called again up to London to justify himself against
the malicious clamours of his adversaries.   When Captain

Coates and the other came to London they applied themselves to Mr. Millington, who, perceiving that the governor
stood for the ease of the garrison, put them into a way to
frustrate their own designs, and so they returned home;
and at the sessions, rendering the town an account of their
negotiations, they told them they found it an impossible
thing to get the excise taken off.   Yet the governor knew a
way how to ease them, but they feared he would be discouraged in it, because at his coming up he had found their
disaffections expressed against him in a petition to cast him
out of his command, "which," said the clerk, " you cannot do,
for he still is and must be governor; therefore, if any of you
have been cheated of your hands, contrary to your intentions
and desires, you would do well to testify your honesty, by
disclaiming what goes under your name."   Soon after, these
malignants stirred up the soldiers to mutiny, and there being
no governor in the garrison that could tell how to order them
otherwise, they were appeased with money; upon which occasion a general muster being called, the major told the
soldiers how they were injured at London by a petition, preferred in the name of the whole garrison, to cast the governor out of his command, which, if it were not their
desire, he wished them to certify to the contrary.   They all
with one voice cried, they desired no other governor; whereupon a certificate to that purpose was drawn up; but when
it came to be subscribed, certain of the committee faction
went up and down persuading the companies not to subscribe;
and when they found how little they prevailed, they foamed for
anger, and with such malicious railing, that one of the governor's soldiers, not able to bear them longer, cried out, " Why
do we suffer these fellows to vapour thus? let us clout them
out of the field:" but the major hearing it, committed him;
and the next morning the certificate went up, subscribed

T

with seven hundred townsmen's hands. After all was done, the major gave some small sum to the soldiers to drink, and the malicious faction, when they saw they could not hinder this certificate, made another false one of their own, that the major had with crowns a-piece hired all these subscriptions, with other such like lies, which when they could not make good, it is said they retracted their certificate at London.

The committee at London could never finish the business by reason of the impertinent clamours of the governor's enemies, therefore at length, wearied with the continual endless papers they had daily brought in, they made an order, wherein they assigned a certain day for the determination of their power, and in the meantime commanded all matter of crimination on both sides should be forborne. At the day they both appeared, but Mr. Millington presented a petition of a most insolent nature, and fresh articles against the governor, which gave the committee much distaste. The petition was, that whereas the committee had kept them ten weeks at great charges, they desired a speedy despatch now, according to their propositions. The committee were much offended at this, and told them they did them much injury to lay their stay upon them, who five weeks before desired them to return, and only leave a solicitor for each, and then they refused it; that they had broken their first orders, and given no satisfaction either for it nor for their last, in bringing in articles against the governor. They took it very ill that they, who were plaintiffs, should prescribe to them, who were judges, how to determine the business; wherefore they ordered that the governor should return and pursue his first instructions, till he received new ones, and that the business should be reported to the house. The governor sent his brother down to take care of the garrison, and stayed himself to receive the final determi-

nation of the house, where Mr. Millington, through his interest, kept off the report, by several tricks and unjust delays,
for about three or four months.

When the lieutenant-colonel came down, the captains were
wonderfully obedient, and all things pretty quiet, but the
governor's officers were discouraged at the countenance which
was given to his enemies, and the impunity of all the crimes of
that faction.   He having a certain spirit of government, in an
extraordinary manner, which was not given to others, carrying
an awe in his presence that his enemies could not withstand,
the garrison was much disordered by his absence, and in daily
peril ; although the lieutenant-colonel was as faithful and
industrious in managing that charge as any person could be,
and as excellent a person, but in a different way from his
brother.   Firmness and zeal to the cause, and personal valour
he had equally, but that vigour of soul which made him invincible against all assaults, and overcoming all difficulties he met
in his way, was proper to himself alone.   The lieutenant-col.
was a man of the kindest heart and the most humble familiar
deportment in the world, and lived with all his soldiers as if
they had been his brothers ; dispensing with that reverence
which was due to him, and living cheerful and merry, and
familiar with them, in such a manner that they celebrated him,
and professed the highest love for him in the world, and would
magnify his humility and kindness, and him for it, in a high
degree above his brother.   But with all this they grew so
presumptuous that, when any obedience was exacted beyond
their humours or apprehensions, they would often dare to fail
in their duty ; whereas the governor, still keeping a greater
distance, though with no more pride, preserved an awe that
made him to be equally feared and loved, and though they
secretly repined at their subjection, yet they durst not refuse
it ; and, when they came to render it on great occasions, they
found such wisdom and such advantage in all his dictates that,

their reason being convinced of the benefit of his government, they delighted in it, and accounted it a happiness to be under his command, when any public necessity superseded the mutiny of those private lusts, whereby all men naturally, but especially vulgar spirits, would cast off their bridle, and be only their own rulers.*

As the governor's absence was the occasion of many neglects in the government, not by his brother's fault, but the soldiers', who wanting their pay (which, while the committee should have been providing, they were spending in vexatious prosecutions of the governor), they were therefore discontented, and through that, careless of their duty; so, on the other side, the cavaliers, who were not ignorant of the dissensions in the garrison, took the advantage, and surprised the lieutenant-colonel's fort at the Trent bridges, while he was employed in keeping the castle. His soldiers in his absence lying out of their quarters, had not left above thirty men upon the guard, who were most of them killed, the ensign fighting it out very stoutly, after their entrance, till he died. The lieutenant-colonel was exceedingly afflicted with this loss, but presently applied himself to secure what remained. The whole town was in a sad uproar, and this happening upon a Lord's day in the morning, in May, 1645, all the people were in such a consternation that they could keep no sabbath that day. Then the lieutenant-colonel had an experiment of vulgar spirits, for even his own soldiers, who were guilty of the loss of the place by being out of their quarters, began to exclaim against him for a thousand causeless things; and although he laboured amongst them with as much courage and vigour as any man could use, to settle

* In the delineation of characters Mrs. Hutchinson remarkably excels. Nothing can be more amiable than that which she here draws of Mr. George Hutchinson, and this character he will be found to sustain with increased esteem to the er.: of the history.

their spirits and regain the place, yet they slighted him most unjustly, and all cried out now to have the governor sent for, as if he himself had been their castle.

Immediately after the unhappy surprise of the bridges, the lieutenant-colonel sent away to his brother a post, who by some of the lower fords got over the water, and carried the sad news to London. A trumpet was sent to the bridges, and obtained the dead bodies of the soldiers who were slain at the surprise, and they were brought up to the town in carts and buried. There were about twenty of them, very good and stout men, though it availed them not in their last need, when a multitude had seized them unawares. All that day a body of the enemy faced the town, which, through terrors without and discouragements and discontents within, was in a very sad posture. The malignant faction against the governor improved even this occasion, and suggested to the town that the castle would be the cause of their ruin; that the governor and his soldiers would secure themselves there, and leave the town undefended; and because the lieutenant-colonel was very strict that none of the castle-soldiers should lie out of their quarters, lest that place might be surprised as well as the other, the townsmen renewed their railings against the castle, and their malice to all that were in it; but the lieutenant-colonel, regarding none of their unjust railings, by God's blessing upon his vigilance, kept the town and castle till his brother's return.

As soon as the news came to the governor at London, he thought it time to throw off that patience with which he had hitherto waited at great expense, and went to the parliament-house before the house sat, and there acquainted the Speaker what had befallen at Nottingham, desiring he might be called to make a relation of it in the open house, or else he told the Speaker, though he died for it, he would press in and let them know how much the cause suffered by the indirect practices, which were partially connived at by some of their members. The Speaker seeing him so resolved, procured him, when the house was set, to be called in : and there he told them how their fort was lost, and, for ought he knew, the garrison, by that time ; which was no more than what he had long expected, through the countenance that was, by one of their members, given to a malignant faction, that obstructed all the public service, disturbed all the honest soldiers and officers in their duty, and spent the public treasury, to carry on their private malice. He further told them, how dishonourable, as well as destructive to their cause, it was, that their members should be protected in such unjust prosecutions, and should make the privilege of the house their shelter, to oppress the most active and faithful of their servants. This and many other things he told them, with such boldness, that many of the guilty members had a mind to have committed him, but he spoke with such truth and convincing reason, that all those of more generous spirits, were much moved by it, and angry that he had been so injuriously treated, and desired him to take post down and to use all means to regain the place, and gave him full orders to execute his charge without disturbance.*   From that time Mr. Millington so lost his credit, that he never recovered the esteem he formerly had among them ; and after that time, the governor's enemies perceiving they were not able to mate † him, made no more public attempts, though they continued that private malice which was the natural product of that antipathy there was between his virtues and their vices.‡   Neither was it his case

* How would a similar expostulation, made at the bar of the honourable house, be received at the present day ?

† Mate, conquer; Fr. matter, an expression taken from the game of chess.

‡ It must almost have exhausted the patience of the reader, and certainly have excited his highest indignation, to follow through all their

alone ; almost all the parliament-garrisons were infested and
disturbed with like factious little people, insomuch that many
worthy gentlemen were wearied out of their commands, and
oppressed by a certain mean sort of people in the house,
whom to distinguish from the more honourable gentlemen,
they called *Worsted-stocking Men.* Some as violently curbed
their committees, as the committees factiously molested them.*
Nor were there factions only in particular garrisons, but the
parliament house itself began to fall into the two great
oppositions of Presbytery and Independency : and, as if discord had infected the whole English air with an epidemical
heart-burning and dissension in all places, even the king's
councils and garrisons were as factiously divided. The king's
commissioners and the governor at Newark fell into such
high discontents, that Sir Richard Byron, the governor, was
changed, and Sir Richard Willis put into his place.† This
accident of the bridges put an end to that vexatious persecution wherewith the governor had had so many sore exercises of
his wisdom, patience, and courage, and so many experiences of
God's mercy and goodness, supporting him in all his trials,
and bearing him up against all discouragements, not only to
stand without the least dejection himself, but to be able to
hold up many others, who were ready to sink under the
burden of unrighteousness and oppression, where they ex-

mazes the crafty and atrocious persecutors of Colonel Hutchinson; at the
same time it must have been a great consolation to him to see integrity
supported by discretion thus work out its own preservation. We may now
congratulate him on emerging from these mists and intricacies, and finding
himself in open field and daylight, where the colonel's nobler virtues can
display themselves.

  * These men were but the natural consequences of a state of revolution.
Did these worsted-stocking men bear no likeness to the Jacobins of modern
days ?

  † The same who afterwards became a spy for Cromwell; a bad substitute
for the loyal Byron !

pected just thanks and rewards. It cost the governor above
three hundred pounds to defend himself against their calum-
nies, renewed forgeries, and scandals, laid upon him ; but
God was with him in all in a wonderful manner, bringing
truth to light through all the clouds of envy that sought to
obscure it, and making his innocence and uprightness to shine
forth as the noon-day, justifying him even in the eyes of his
enemies, and covering them with shame and confusion of face.
They maintained their prosecution of him out of the public
stock, and were not called to account for so mis-spending it.
Mr. Millington perceiving how much he had lost himself by
it, applied himself to seek a reconciliation by flattering letters,
and professions of conviction and repentance of his unjust
siding with those men. The governor, who was of a most
reconcileable nature, forgave him, and ever after lived in good
friendship with him.* Others of them also afterwards, when
they saw the governor out of their power, some through fear,
and others overcome with his goodness, submitted to him,
who lived to see the end of them all ; part of them dying
before any disgrace or great sorrows overtook him, and those
who survived, renouncing and apostatizing from their most
glorious engagements, and becoming guilty of those crimes
for which they falsely accused him, while he remained firm,
and dying sealed up the profession of his life ; in all the future
difficulties of which, he was still borne up with the experience
of God's goodness and manifold protections.

The governor being dismissed from the parliament, immediately took post, and coming through Northampton, met his
old engineer, Hooper, and brought him with him to Nottingham, where, by God's mercy, he arrived safe about three days

* As Mr. Millington will figure no more in this history, the reader is
here informed that he finished his career, after becoming one of the judges
who sentenced Charles the First, by coming in upon proclamation, making
a pitiful recantation, and being sentenced to perpetual imprisonment.

after the loss of the bridges. and was welcomed as if safety and victory, and all desirable blessings, had come in his train. His presence reinforced the drooping garrison, and he immediately consulted how to go about regaining the fort. To this purpose, and to hinder the enemy from having an inlet into the town by the bridges, he made a little fort on the next bridge, and put a lieutenant and thirty men into it, thereby enclosing those in the fort the enemy had surprised, whom he resolved to assault on the town side, having thus provided that their friends should not come from the other side*
to help them. But those of Newark understanding this, came as strong as they could one morning, and assaulted the little new fort, where Lieutenant Hall, failing of that courage which he had professed when he begged the honour of keeping it, gave it up, which the governor seeing from the other side, was exceedingly vexed at, and marched up to the bridge to assault them in that fort; but he found that they had only stormed the other little fort to make their own way to be gone, and that they had made shift to get to their friends upon the ribs of two broken arches, which, when they had served to help their passage, they pulled up, to hinder pursuit after them : and thus in a month's space God restored to the governor the fort which was lost in his absence ; and he newly fortified the place and repaired the bridges, whereby the great market out of the vale was again brought into the town, to their exceeding joy and benefit.

This summer there was a much greater progress made in the war than had been before, and the new parliament army prosecuted it so much in earnest, that they made a show to block up the king in his main garrison at Oxford, but he broke

* To understand this rightly it is necessary to be informed, that in approaching Nottingham from the south there is a very wide valley, through which the Trent and the Lene run in several branches, over which are bridges united by a causeway.

out, and joining Prince Rupert's horse, came, after several
attempts elsewhere, to Leicester, which he took by storm.
The loss of this town was a great affliction and terror to all
the neighbouring garrisons and counties, whereupon Fairfax
closely attended the king's motions, came within a few days
and fought with the king, and overcame him in that memorable battle at Naseby, where his coach and cabinet of letters
were taken; which letters being carried to London were
printed, and manifested his falsehood, how that, contrary to his
professions, he had endeavoured to bring in Danes and Lor-
rainers, and Irish rebels, to subdue the good people here,
and had given himself up to be governed by the queen in all
affairs both of state and religion.*   After this fight Fairfax
took again the town of Leicester, and went into the west,
relieved Taunton, took Bristol, and many other garrisons.
West Chester also and other places were taken that way. Meanwhile, the king, having coasted about the countries, came at
last to Newark, and there his commanders falling out among
themselves, he changed the governor, and put the lord Bellasis into the place, and went himself to Oxford, where he
was at last blocked up.

When Sir Thomas Fairfax was made chief general, Poyntz
was made major-general of the northern counties, and a committee of war was set up at York, whereof Colonel Pierrepont, by his brother's procurement, was appointed one, and
was pretty well satisfied, as thinking himself again set above
Colonel Hutchinson, because all the northern garrisons were

* The public is in possession of these, they having been printed by the
parliament, which some have thought a hardship, but surely without reason.   It is useless here to discuss the question as to what help it was allow-
able for the king to call in; but it is out of all question that the discovery of
that bitterness with which he was inclined to pursue the quarrel, and the
fraudulency with which he had managed treaties, and showed that he
meant to do others, cut up by the roots both compassion and confidence.

to receive orders from that committee : but the governor
heeding not other men's exaltations or depressions, only attended to his own duty.   About the latter end of this summer,
Poyntz came to Nottingham with all the horse that could be
gathered in the neighbouring counties.   He had before
marched with them and the Nottingham regiment into Cheshire, and brought several gentlemen prisoners into the garrison of Nottingham, who had been taken in divers encounters.   When he marched out, Palmer the priest, not daring
to venture himself in the field, laid down his commission,
when he saw that there was now no connivance to be found
at disobeying commands.

By reason of the rout at Naseby, and the surrender of
Carlisle and several other garrisons to the Scots, the broken
forces of the cavaliers had all repaired to Newark, and that
was now become the strongest and best fortified garrison the
king had, and Poyntz was ordered to quarter his horse about
it, till the Scots should come on the other side and besiege it.
At that time also the king himself was there.*   The governor having informed Poyntz how prejudicial it would be
to his design to suffer those little garrisons in the Vale at
Shelford and Wiverton to remain, it was agreed that all the
forces should take them in their way.   But the governor
having obtained permission of Poyntz, through a respect he
had to the family, sent a letter to Colonel Philip Stanhope,
governor of Shelford, to persuade him to surrender the
place he could not hold, and to offer to obtain honourable terms for him, if he would hearken to propositions.
Stanhope returned a very scornful, huffing reply, in which
one of his expressions was, that he should lay Nottingham

* Having come hither from Wales with a body of three thousand men
he stayed till fearing to be besieged by the Scots, who were approaching, he
went away by night to Oxford, November 6, 1645.

castle as flat as a pancake, and such other bravadoes, which had been less amiss, if he had done any thing to make them good. Hereupon the whole force marched against the place, and the several posts were assigned to the several colonels. The governor, according to his own desire, had that which seemed most difficult assigned to him, and his quarters that night were appointed in Shelford town. When he came thither, a few of the Shelford soldiers were gotten into the steeple of the church, and from thence so played upon the governor's men that they could not quietly take up their quarters. There was a trap door that led into the belfry, and they had made it fast, and drawn up the ladder and the bell-ropes, and regarded not the governor's threatening them to have no quarter if they came not down, so that he was forced to send for straw and fire it, and smother them out. Hereupon they came down, and among them there was a boy who had marched out with the governor's company, when he went first against Newark, and carried himself so stoutly, that Captain Wray begged him for a foot-boy, and when his troop was once taken by the enemy, this boy, being taken among them, became one of their soldiers. The governor making him believe he should be hanged immediately for changing his party, and for holding out to their disturbance, where he could not hope for relief, the boy begged he might be spared, and offered to lead them on to the only place where they could enter, where the palisade was unfinished. The governor, without trusting to him, considered the probability of his information, kept him under guard, and set him in the front of his men, and he accordingly proved to have told them the truth in all that he had said, and did excellent good service, behaving himself most stoutly. The governor being armed, and ready to begin the assault, when the rest were also ready, Captain White came to him, and, notwithstanding all his former malicious prosecutions, now pretended the most

tender care and love that could be declared, with all imaginable flattery; and persuaded the governor not to hazard
himself in so dangerous an attempt, but to consider his wife
and children, and stand by among the horse, but by no
means to storm the place in his own person.   Notwithstanding all his false insinuations, the governor, perceiving
his envy at that honour which his valour was ready to reap
in this encounter, was exceedingly angry with him, and went
on upon the place.   This being seated on a flat, was encompassed with a very strong bulwark, and a great ditch without,
in most places wet at the bottom, so that they within were very
confident of being able to hold it out, there being no cannon
brought against them; because also a broken regiment of the
queen's, who were all papists, were come in to their assistance.
A regiment of Londoners was appointed to storm on the other
side, and the governor at the same time began the assault at
his post.   His men found many more difficulties than they
expected, for after they had filled up the ditches with faggots
and pitched the scaling ladders, they were twenty staves too
short, and the enemy, from the top of the works, threw down
logs of wood, which would sweep off a whole ladderful of
men at once: the lieutenant-colonel himself was once or
twice so beaten down.   The governor had ordered other
musketeers to beat off those men that stood upon the top of the
works, which they failed to do by shooting without good aim;
but the governor directed them better, and the Nottingham
horse dismounting, and assailing with their pistols, and head-
pieces, helped the foot to beat them all down from the top of
the works, except one stout man, who stood alone, and did
wonders in beating down the assailants, which the governor being angry at, fetched two of his own musketeers
and made them shoot, and he immediately fell, to the great
discouragement of his fellows.   Then the governor himself
first entered, and the rest of his men came in as fast as

they could. But while this regiment was entering on this
side, the Londoners were beaten off on the other side, and
the main force of the garrison turned upon him. The cavaliers had half moons within, which were as good a defence
to them as their first works; into these the soldiers that were
of the queen's regiment were gotten, and they in the house
shot from out of all the windows. The governor's men, as
soon as they got in, took the stables and all their horses,
but the governor himself was fighting with the captain of the
papists and some others, who, by advantage of the half moon
and the house, might have prevailed to cut him off and those
that were with him, which were not many. The enemy being
strengthened by the addition of those who had beaten off
the assailants on the other side, were now trying their utmost
to vanquish those that were within. The lieutenant-colonel,
seeing his brother in hazard, made haste to open the drawbridge, that Poyntz might come in with his horse; which he
did, but not before the governor had killed that gentleman
who was fighting with him, at whose fall his men gave way.
Poyntz seeing them shoot from the house, and apprehending
the king might come to their relief, when he came in, ordered
that no quarter should be given. And here the governor
was in greater danger than before, for the strangers hearing
him called governor, were advancing to have killed him,
but that the lieutenant-colonel, who was very watchful to
preserve him all that day, came in to his rescue, and scarcely
could persuade them that it was the governor of Nottingham; because he, at the beginning of the storm, had pu.
off a very good suit of armour that he had, which being
musket-proof, was so heavy that it heated him, and so
would not be persuaded by his friends to wear any thing
but his buff coat. The governor's men, eager to complete
their victory, were forcing their entrance into the house:
meanwhile Rossiter's men came and took away all their

horses, which they had taken away when they first entered
the works and won the stables, and left in the guard of twu
or three, while they were pursuing their work. The governor
of Shelford, after all his bravadoes, came but meanly off; it
is said he sat in his chamber, wrapt up in his cloak, and
came not forth that day; but that availed him not, for how, or
by whom, it is not known, but he was wounded and stripped,
and flung upon a dunghill. The lieutenant-colonel, after the
house was mastered, seeing the disorder by which our men
were ready to murder one another, upon the command Poyntz
had issued to give no quarter, desired Poyntz to cause the
slaughter to cease, which was presently obeyed, and about
sevenscore prisoners were saved. While he was thus busied,
inquiring what was become of the governor, he was shown
him naked upon the dunghill; whereupon the lieutenant-
colonel called for his own cloak and cast it over him, and
sent him to a bed in his own quarters, and procured
him a surgeon. Upon his desire he had a little priest,
who had been his father's chaplain, and was one of the
committee faction; but the man was such a pitiful com-
forter, that the governor, who was come to visit him, was
forced to undertake that office: but though he had all the
supplies they could every way give him, he died the next
day.* The house which belonged to his father, the Earl of

* Thoroton, in his History of Nottinghamshire, says, "Shelford House
was a garrison for the king, and commanded by Colonel Philip Stanhope,
son of the first Earl of Chesterfield, which being taken by a storm, he and
many of his soldiers were therein slain, and the house afterwards burned ;
his brother Ferdinando Stanhope was slain some time before by a parliament soldier at Bridgford." This last happened in that skirmish with the
bridge soldiers recited in page 268, where he is said only to have been made
prisoner. Lady Catherine Hutchinson, who attested the remark to Colonel
Hutchinson her son-in-law's disadvantage, page 149, was the siste· of the
Earl of Chesterfield, and of course aunt of Colonel Stanhope, and as she

Chesterfield, was that night burned, none certainly knowing by what means, whether by accident or on purpose; but there was most ground to believe that the country people, who had been sorely infested by that garrison, to prevent the keeping it by those who had taken it, purposely set it on fire. If the queen's regiment had mounted their horses and stood ready upon them when our men entered, they had undoubtedly cut them all off; but they standing to the works, it pleased God to lead them into that path he had ordained for their destruction, who being papists, would not receive quarter, nor were they much offered it, being killed in the heat of the contest, so that not a man of them escaped.

The next day our party went to Wiverton, a house of the Lord Chaworth's, which, terrified with the example of the other, yielded upon terms, and was by order pulled down and rendered incapable of being any more a garrison.

Poyntz now quartered all his horse in the towns about Newark, and since he had no peculiar regiment of his own, the governor's regiment served him for his guards. The Scots also came and quartered on the other side of the town towards the north.

All that winter the governor lay at the Leaguer, and about Christmas time writs were sent down for new elections to fill up the parliament. There being a burgess-ship void at Nottingham, the town would needs, in a compliment, make the governor free, in order to elect him to the parliament. Mr. Francis Pierrepont hearing this, wrote to the governor to

takes no exception to it, we may safely give credit to this story of the storming of Shelford with all its circumstances: a very interesting one it certainly is, and told in the most unaffected, and therefore most affecting, manner; the scene with which it finishes is surely as striking and as singular as any that story or imagination can furnish, not excepting the death of Le Fevre in the Sentimental Journey.

desire that he would rather come into his father's place in
the county, and give him his assistance in this, as he should
engage his own and all his friends' interest for him in the
county. The governor, who was ever ready to requite injuries with benefits, employed his interest in the town to
satisfy the gentleman's desire, and having very many in his
regiment that had votes, he sent for them all home the
night before the day of election; which had like to have
been a very sad one, but that by the mercy of God, and the
courage of Poyntz and the lieutenant-colonel and Captain
Poulton, it had not so bad an event.* The Newarkers, hearing that so many of the regiment were away, fell upon their
quarters, and most of the men being surprised, were rather
endeavouring flight than resistance ; when the lieutenant-
colonel and Captain Poulton rallied all they could find, lined
some pales with musketeers, and beat the enemy again out of
their quarters, and Poyntz, mounting with as many horse as
were about him, which was very few, followed them in the
night up to the very works of Newark. Some loss there
was in the quarters, but nothing considerable ; some soldiers
ran away home, and brought the governor word they were all
cut off, but his brother sent a messenger to acquaint him with
the contrary. Hereupon, immediately after the election, he

* A fair and honest acknowledgment of a considerable oversight ! But
this passage leads us to observe of what sort of people the parliament
armies were composed, viz. the horse mostly of freeholders, the foot of
burghers. It will not probably be thought beside the purpose to quote
here Whitelocke's description of Cromwell's own regiment. " He had a
brave regiment of his countrymen, most of them freeholders and freeholders' sons, and who upon matter of conscience engaged in this quarrel;
and thus being well armed within by the satisfaction of their own consciences, and without by good iron arms, they would, as one man, stand
firmly and charge desperately." These circumstances must be allowed
their due weight, when we come to consider the right of the army to interfere in matters of state.

returned back again with his men. Not long after, the
elections were made for the county, who all pitched upon the
governor, in his father's room. White, whose envy never
died, used all the endeavours he could to have hindered it;
but when he saw he could do no harm, with a sad heart,
under a false face, he came and took his part of a noble
dinner the new knights had provided for the gentlemen of
the country. Without any competition Mr. Hutchinson had
the first voice in the room of his father, and Mr. Pigott the
second, in the room of Mr. Sutton, now a commissioner at
Newark. About the same time Colonel Thornhagh was
chosen burgess for the town of Retford; but none of them
went up to their places in parliament till the siege of Newark
was finished.

Poyntz drew a line about the town, and made a very regular entrenchment and approaches, in such a soldier-like
manner as none of them who had attempted the place before
had done. Most of that winter they lay in the field, and the
governor, carried on by the vigour and greatness of his mind,
felt no distemper then by that service, which all his captains
and the soldiers themselves endured worse than he. Besides
daily and hourly providences, by which they were preserved
from the enemy's cannons and sallies, there were some remarkable ones, by which God kept the governor's life in this
Leaguer. Once as Poyntz and he, and another captain, were
riding to view some quarter of the town, a cannon bullet
came whizzing by them, as they were riding all abreast, and
the captain, without any touch of it, said he was killed;
Poyntz bid him get off, but he was then sliding down from
his horse, slain by the wind of the bullet; they held him up
till they got off from the place, but the man immediately
turned black all over. Another time the governor was in
his tent, and by chance called out; when he was scarcely
out of it, a cannon bullet came and tore up the whole tent,

and killed the sentinel at the door. But the greatest peril wherein all on the English side were, was the treachery of the Scots, which they had very good reason to apprehend might have been the cutting off of all that force. Sir Thomas Fairfax had now besieged Oxford, and the king was stolen out of the town and gone in disguise, no man knew whither, but at length he came into the Scots' army. They had before behaved themselves very oddly to the English, and been taking sundry occasions to pick quarrels, when at the last certain news was brought to the English quarters that the king was come to the Scots, and by them received at South-well. The English could then expect nothing but that the Scots, joining with those that were in Newark, would fall upon them, who were far inferior in number to the other, and therefore they all prepared themselves, as well as they could, to defend themselves in their trenches. The governor had then very fine horses at the Leaguer, which he sent home to the garrison ; but while they were in expectation of being thus fallen upon, the king had more mind to be gone ; and because the Scots knew not how to break up their quarters while the town was not taken, the king sent to my Lord Bellasis, the governor of Newark, to surrender up the place immediately, which he did upon pretty handsome terms, but was much discontented that the king should have no more regard for them who had been so constant to his service.*
The governor with his regiment was appointed to receive the town and the arms, and to quarter in it ; where he now went and had the greatest danger of all, for the town was all over sadly infected with the plague ; yet it so pleased God that neither he nor any of the fresh men caught the infection, which was so raging there that it almost desolated the place.

* Among the names of those who signed the capitulation on the part of the parliament (as it appears in Rushworth) are those of Colonel Hutchinson and Colonel Twisleton.

Whether the king's ill council or his destiny led him, he was very failing in this action; for had he gone straight up to the parliament and cast himself upon them, as he did upon the Scots, he had in all probability ruined them, who were highly divided between the presbyterian and independent factions; but in putting himself into the hands of the mercenary Scotch army, rather than the parliament of England, he showed such an embittered hate to the English nation, that it turned many hearts against him. The Scots in this business were very false both to the parliament and to the king. For them to receive and carry away the king's person with them, when they were but a hired army, without either the consent or knowledge of the parliament, was a very false carriage in them; but besides that, we had *certain evidences* that they were prepared, and had an intent to have cut off the English army which beleaguered Newark,* but that God

* It has always been, and perhaps will always remain a mystery, what were the conditions or engagements on which the king relied in putting himself into the hands of the Scots. In Clarendon's State Papers there are several letters from the French ambassador, persuading him to this measure, and undertaking for the Scots to give him effectual support ; and the king wrote very positively to Ormond a letter, which was intercepted, and is produced by Rushworth, that the Scots had given him good security that they would join their forces to those of Montrose and the king's friends. On the other side, the general and committee of estates resident in the Scots army wrote, that "the king came privately into their camp, and that there had been no *treaty* or *capitulation* with him by them, nor any in their names, and that the assertion of the king in his letter to Ormond was a *damnable untruth.*" Heylin, in his Hist. of Presbyterianism, says, "The commissioners residing with the Scotch army, promised protection to the king and his friends, but broke their promise and sold him for £200,000, *as they would have done our Saviour for half the money.*" In another place he says, "Lowdon ranted to some tune about the disgrace of selling the king, but however the Presbyterians on both sides concluded the sinful bargain." Not to dwell upon what is elsewhere said on either side of the question, the symptoms of treachery discerned by Colone.

changed their counsels and made them take another course, which was to carry the king to Newcastle, where they again sold him to the parliament for a sum of money.

The country being now cleared of all the enemy's garrisons, Colonel Hutchinson went up to London to attend his duty there, and to serve his country as faithfully, in the capacity of a senator, as he had before in that of a soldier. When he came there he found a very bitter spirit of discord and envy raging, and the presbyterian faction (of which were most of those lords and others that had been laid aside by the self-denying ordinance), were endeavouring a violent persecution, upon the account of conscience, against those who had in so short a time accomplished, by God's blessing, that victory which he was not pleased to bestow

Hutchinson and others, before and at the time of the king's arrival, give ample reason to conclude that the Scots were aware of his coming, and that either there were two parties, one of which was devoted to the king and the other not so, and that the latter was prevalent, or else that the whole expected from the king conditions which he was unwilling to perform, and principally the signing the covenant, the refusal of which they afterwards openly resented, and this might be that " change God is said to make in their counsels."

There is much less doubt as to the justice of Mrs. Hutchinson's reflection, that, of all courses, that which he took was the worst: she, who had a truly British heart, well knew what effect ingenuous confidence would have had on the parliament, with the virtues as well as vices of which she was well acquainted. The parliament had asked him to " come to them with a royal, not martial, attendance, and promised to receive him well." The last message was passed on March 23, and in a few days after he went to the Scots army. *Quem Deus vult perdere prius dementat.* Those whom God destines to destruction he first deprives of their understanding. Artifice, which was Charles's greatest fault, was likewise his ruin, and he fell not like a conquered prince, as *præda victoris,* a noble prize for the victor, but *pretium sceleris,* the object of a scandalous traffic, apprehended and sold as a culprit and fugitive; and forfeited as his last resource, that respect and pity which the generous reserve for the unfortunate.

upon them. Their directory of worship was at length sent forth
for a three years' trial, and such as could not conform to it,
marked out with an evil eye, hated and persecuted under the
name of separatists.*   Colonel Hutchinson, who abhorred
that malicious zeal and imposing spirit which appeared in
them, was soon taken notice of for one of the independent
faction,† [whose heads were accounted Pierrepont, Vane,
          St. John's, and some few other grandees, being
men that excelled in wisdom and utterance, and the rest
were believed to adhere to them only out of faction, as if those
who did not vain-gloriously lay out themselves, without
necessity, but chose rather to hear and vote, had had no
understanding of right and wrong but from the dictates of
these great oracles.]   Though, to speak the truth, they very
little knew Colonel Hutchinson that could say he was of any
faction; for he had a strength of judgment able to consider
things himself and propound them to his conscience, which
was so upright that the veneration of no man's person alive,
nor the love of the dearest friend in the world, could
make him do the least thing, without a full persuasion
that it was his duty so to act.   He very well understood
men's gifts and abilities, and honoured those most whom he
believed to manage them with most uprightness of soul,
for God's glory and the good of his country, and was so far
from envying the just renown any man acquired that he
rejoiced in it.   He never was any man's sectary, either in

          * Mrs. Hutchinson differs from most of those who have written on the
subject respecting the rise and progress of the deadly feuds between the
presbyterians and independents; but she differs not from the truth and
reason.   Certainly the most impartial historian is Rapin; but he, though a
presbyterian, and labouring their defence, effects their condemnation.
Vol. ii. p. 624, he says, " They thought themselves in slavery if themselves
did not command."   What need of more words ?

          † All that is contained between these two brackets had lines struck
through it in the manuscript, and one of the names defaced.

religious or civil matters, farther than he apprehended them to follow the rules of religion, honour, and virtue; nor any man's antagonist, but as he opposed that which appeared to him to be just and equal. If the greatest enemy he had in the world had propounded anything profitable to the public, he would promote it; whereas some others were to blame in that particular, and chiefly those of the presbyterian faction, who would obstruct any good, rather than that those they envied and hated should have the glory of procuring it; the sad effects of which pride grew at length to be the ruin of the most glorious cause that ever was contended for. At the first, many gentlemen, eminent in gifts and acquirements, were as eminent in zealous improvement of them, for the advantage of God's and their country's interests, whereby they obtained just glory and admiration among all good men; but while the creature was so magnified, God, who was the principal author, was not looked upon, and gave them therefore up to become their own and others' idols, and so to fall.

And now it grew to be a sad wonder, that the most zealous promoters of the cause were more spitefully carried against by their own faithful armies, by whom God had perfected their victory over their enemies, than against the vanquished foe, whose restitution they henceforth secretly endeavoured, by all the arts of treacherous, dissembling policy, in order that they might throw down those whom God had exalted in glory and power to resist their tyrannical impositions. At that time, and long after, they prevailed not, until that pious people too began to admire themselves, for what God had done by them, and to set up themselves above their brethren, and then the Lord humbled them again beneath their conquered vassals.*

* To those, and they are not few, who, like Colonel Hutchinson, believe the peculiar interposition of Providence, this remark of the punishment inflicted on those who abused its gifts, will appear pleasing and

So long as the army only resisted unjust impositions, and remained firm to their first pious engagement, Mr. Hutchinson adhered to that party, which protected them in the parliament house.* His attendance there, changing his custom of life,

edifying ; to those who admit only a general dispensation, the fall of each party successively by their own malversation, will seem a signal mark of justice ; by both, this chain of causes and effects will be acknowledged to be drawn by the hand of a master.

* This history, which, as far as it relates to public affairs, is called only a summary, will nevertheless be found to redress many errors in larger histories, and to open a great field for reflection : in none, perhaps, more than in this question of the right of the army to interfere with the conduct of parliament or the business of the state : this is generally decided against them lightly and inconsiderately. The danger of admitting *armed* assemblies to *deliberate,* and the duty of a soldier to *obey,* but not *debate,* are very *boldly asserted ;* and as this doctrine suits the governors of every state, it will always be favoured ; but it goes on *a petitio principii,* a begging of the question that the military are the *hired servants* of the state : and military men have so far agreed to this unjust postulate, that they have consented to accept that which is a nickname, or term of reproach, as the generic one of their whole profession ; viz. soldier ; which is but a translation of the Italian *soldato,* mercenary or hireling. It has been repeatedly shown how ill this term agreed with the parliament troops in general, being mostly volunteers and freeholders or burghers, and ill, or sometimes not at all paid. Were such to be considered as mere machines, as having forfeited all right to an opinion of their own, and bound to support that of others ?—If so, then those who expected to maintain our constitution by putting arms into the hands of almost all whom patriotism or the preservation of their property animated to take them up, would have bereaved it of nearly all its defenders ! With good right did these men, who had taken a pious engagement to God and their country, and most manfully acquitted themselves of it, call on the parliament to complete it by a happy settlement. Their several petitions and remonstrances, preserved in Rushworth, vol. vii. p. 4, et infra, show that their views were just and rational, and such as have since in part been realised, in part are still wished for, viz. " The duration of parliaments to be limited; elections better regulated—the representation better distributed; improper privileges, and particularly that of being screened from creditors, given up; not

into a sedentary employment, less suitable to his active spirit, and more prejudicial to his health, he fell into a long and painful sickness, which many times brought him near the grave, and was not perfectly cured in four years. The doctors could not find a name for it; but at length resolved upon the running gout, and a cure, proper for that disease, being practised upon him, took effect.

The truth is, his great mind so far surmounted the frailty of his flesh, that it would never yield to the tenderness of his constitution, nor suffer him to feel those inconveniences of martial toils, which often cast down his captains, men of more able bodies and healthful complexions, while the business was in hand; but when that was finished, he found, what he had not leisure to consider before, that his body's strength was far unequal to the vigour of his soul.

After the surrender of Newark, Nottingham town and castle was continued a garrison for some time : between this and his greater employment at London, the governor divided himself. Meanwhile, upon the 15th day of July, 1646, propositions were sent to the king, then with the Scots at Newcastle, little higher than those which had been made him ι Uxbridge; but he wove out delays, and would not assent to them, hoping a greater advantage by the difference between the two nations, and the factions in the city and parliament, which both he and all his party employed their utmost in-

bishops, but their coercive power and civil penalties taken away; the king restored to his rights (but with some restrictions as to appointments for tι ι years); the laws simplified and lessened in expense; monopolies set aside ; tithes commuted, &c. But all this was interrupted by the domineering party." Who can help lamenting that there were not more found to unite with Colonel Hutchinson and this army to perfect the best system of government that ever did or will exist !

These proposals of the army are supposed to have been penned by Ireton.

lustry to cherish and augment. Both parliaments perceiving this, and not yet senseless of approaching destruction, from the common enemy, began to be cemented by the king's averseness to peace, and to consider how to settle the kingdom without him; and when they had agreed that the Scots should deliver up the English garrisons for a certain sum of money, it fell into debate how to dispose of the king's person; where the debate was, not who should, but who should not have him. At length, about January of the same year, two hundred thousand pounds was carried down by part of the army to Newcastle; and upon the payment of it, the Scots delivered their garrisons to the soldiers, and the king to certain commissioners of both houses of parliament, who conducted him honourably to his own manor of Holmeby, in Northamptonshire.

During this time Sir Thomas Fairfax himself lay at Nottingham, and the governor was sick in the castle. The general's lady was come along with him, having followed his camp to the siege of Oxford, and lain at his quarters all the while he abode* there. She was exceeding kind to her hus-

---

* Here is another of those paradoxes, with which historians have perplexed themselves and their readers, reduced to a very plain tale. It is generally said and believed, that Fairfax was a presbyterian, and much wonder is expressed that he should have so faithfully (it is even said *too faithfully*) served the independents; but it is impossible that any one could have a more clear and certain knowledge of his religious opinions than Colonel and Mrs. Hutchinson had, and they declare his chaplains to have been *independent ministers;* nor does it appear that he ever *changed his opinion,* but only that he suffered himself to be over-ruled by his wife. Heroes as great as he have been, both before and since, under the same dominion; as Horace sets forth in his facetious ode to Xanthias Phoceus, parodied by Rowe:

> *Nec sit ancillæ tibi amor pudori.*
> Do not, most fragrant earl, disclaim.

band's chaplains, independent ministers, till the army returned to be nearer London, and then the presbyterian
ministers quite changed the lady into such a bitter aversion
against them, that they could not endure to come into the
general's presence while she was there; and the general had
an unquiet, unpleasant life with her, who drove away from
him many of those friends, in whose conversation he had
found such sweetness. At Nottingham they had gotten a very
able minister into the great church, but a bitter presbyterian;
him and his brethren my Lady Fairfax carressed with so much
kindness, that they grew impudent enough to preach up their
faction openly in the pulpit, and to revile the others, and at
length would not suffer any of the army chaplains to preach
in the town.   They then coming to the governor and complaining of their unkind usage, he invited them to come and
preach in his house, which when it was known they did,
a great concourse of people came thither to them; and
the presbyterians, when they heard of it, were mad with
rage, not only against them, but against the governor, who
accidently gave them another occasion about the same time,
a little before the general came.   When formerly the presbyterian ministers had forced him, for quietness' sake, to go and
break up a private meeeting in the cannonier's chamber,
there were found some notes concerning pædobaptism, which
were brought into the governor's lodgings; and his wife
having then more leisure to read than he, having perused
them and compared them with the Scriptures, found not
what to say against the truths they asserted, concerning the
misapplication of that ordinance to infants; but being then
young and modest, she thought it a kind of virtue to submit
to the judgment and practice of most churches, rather than
to defend a singular opinion of her own, she not being then
enlightened in that great mistake of the national churches. But
in this year she, happening to be with child, communicated

her doubts to her husband, and desired him to endeavour her satisfaction; which while he did, he himself became as unsatisfied, or rather satisfied against it. First, therefore, he diligently searched the scriptures alone, and could find in them no ground at all for that practice; then he bought and read all the eminent treatises on both sides, which at that time came thick from the presses, and was still more satisfied of the error of the pædobaptists. After this, his wife being brought to bed, that he might, if possible, give the religious party no offence, he invited all the ministers to dinner, and propounded his doubt, and the ground thereof to them. None of them could defend their practice with any satisfactory reason, but the tradition of the church, from the primitive times, and their main buckler of federal holiness, which Tombs and Denne had so excellently overthrown. He and his wife then, professing themselves unsatisfied in the practice, desired their opinions, what they ought to do. Most answered, to conform to the general practice of other Christians, how dark soever it were to themselves; but Mr. Foxcraft, one of the assembly, said, that except they were convinced of the warrant of that practice from the word, they sinned in doing it: whereupon that infant was not baptized.* And now the governor and his wife, notwithstanding that they forsook not their assemblies, nor retracted their benevolences and civilities from them, yet were they reviled by them, called fanatics and anabaptists, and often glanced at in their public sermons. And not only the ministers, but all their zealous sectaries, conceived implacable malice against them upon this account; which was carried on with a spirit of envy and persecution to the last, though he, on his side, might well have said to them, as his Master said to the old Pharisees:

* Surely this shows an unbecoming propensity to speculate in religion: the story is, however, told with candour.

" Many good works have I done among you; for which of these do you hate me?" Yet the generality, even of that people, had a secret conviction upon them, that he had been faithful to them, and deserved their love ; and in spite of their own bitter zeal, could not but have a reverent esteem for him, whom they often railed at, for not thinking and speaking according to their opinions.

This year Sir Allen Apsley, governor of Barnstaple for the king, after the surrender of that garrison, came and retired to the governor's house, till his composition with the parliament was completed, the governor's wife being his sister, and the governor's brother having married the other sister;* and this was another occasion of opening the mouths of the malignants, who were ready to seize upon any one to his prejudice. Sir Allen Apsley had not his articles punctually performed, by which he suffered great expense and intolerable vexation ; and the governor, no less concerned in the injustice done to him than if he had suffered it himself, endeavoured to protect him only in that which was just, and for this was called a cavalier, and said to have changed his party, and a thousand more injuries ; in which none were so forward as those who had all the while been disaffected to the whole parliament party; but after they were conquered, burying their spite against the cause in their own bosoms, suffered that secret fire to rise up in a black smoke against the most faithful assertors of it.

When the commissioners went down to fetch up the king from the Scots, one of the lords coming to visit the governor, and finding him at that time very sick, persuaded him to

* Amongst the discords and distraction, public and private, which must have harassed the reader's mind, it is soothing for a moment to contemplate the harmony which reigned within Colonel Hutchinson's family, and the sincere friendship between them and Sir Allen Apsley, which will re-appear on many and frequent occasions to the very close of his life.

make use of one of the king's physicians that was with
them, that was called Dr. Wilson, and was a very able physician; but he mistook the method of his cure, and made issues
in both his arms, which rather wasted his strength than his
disease, which when he was cured were stopped up.   That
spring, growing a little better for the present, he went to
London, and having ineffectually tried several physicians,
Sir Allen Apsley persuaded him to make use of Dr. Frazier,
with whom he began a course of physic, in the midst of
which the doctor came and acquainted him that he was likely
to be imprisoned upon suspicion of carrying on designs
against the parliament underhand, for now the Scots were
threatening invasion and open war.   He professed his innocency with many protestations, and desired Mr. Hutchinson
to oblige him so far as to engage for him that he intended no
design beyond his calling ; which the colonel believing,
undertook for him to the committee of Derby-house.   When
the false Scot having thus abused him, left a letter of lame
excuse for him, and stole away out of England to the princes,
then beyond the seas, leaving a blot upon Mr. Hutchinson
for having undertaken for him ;* but he, acknowledging his
error in having been so abused, was thereby warned from cre-
dulity of any of that false nation any more.   That summer
he attended to the service of the house, being freed for a while
from his distemper during the summer, till the fall of the
leaf, when it returned again.   In the meantime jealousies
were sown between the parliament, the city of London, and
the army.   The presbyterian faction were earnest to have the
army disbanded ; the army resented the injury, and, being
taught to value their own merit, petitioned the general that
they might be satisfied, not only in things relating to them-

* This Dr. Frazier was afterwards employed by Charles the Second to
negotiate with the Scots.

selves particularly as an army, but the general concernments
and liberties of the good people of the nation which they
had fought for. The presbyterians were highly offended at
this, and declared it with such violence as gave the army
cause to increase their jealousies. The soldiers, led on to it
by one Cornet Joyce, took the king from Holmeby out of the
parliament commissioners' hands, and carried him about with
them. The parliament voted that the king should come to
Richmond, attended by the same persons that attended him
at Holmeby ; but the army, instead of obeying, impeached
eleven members of the house of commons of high treason,
and petitioned that those impeached members might be secluded the house, till they had brought in their answer to the
charge ; which being violently debated, they made a voluntary secession for six months. The general also entreated
that the king might no⁺ be brought nearer to London than
they would suffer the army to quarter. So he was carried
with them to Royston, Hatfield, Reading, and at last to
Woburn, till about July, 1647, when London grew into a
tumult, and made a very rude violation upon the parliament
house, which caused them to adjourn ; when, understanding
the fury of the citizens, the greatest part of the members,
with the Speaker, withdrew and went to the army, among
whom was Colonel Hutchinson.* The presbyterian members
who stayed behind chose new Speakers, and made many new
votes, and vigorously began to levy forces to resist the army,

* As did fourteen peers, among them the Earls of Manchester and Warwick, Lords Say and Sele and Mulgrave, and one hundred commoners, and
the palsgrave, or elector palatine, visited them. It would have been very
seasonable to have offered to the consideration of both parties Horace's
beautiful apologue of the Horse and the Stag.

Cervus equum bello melior, &c.

The calling in foreign aid to control their antagonists proved equally
destructive to both, but was begun by the presbyterians.

which were conducted by Massie and Poyntz. The parliament that was with the army made an order against the proceedings of the members at London, and advanced with the
general; which, when the city heard of, their stomachs
would not serve them to stand it out, but they sent commissioners, and, by the consent of the members with the general,
obtained a pacification, upon condition that the city should
disband all their new forces, deliver up their tower and their
forts to the general, and desert the members then sitting.
They daring to deny nothing, the general came triumphantly
to Westminster, and brought back both the Speaker and
the members, and put them again in their seats. The general
had solemn thanks from both houses, and then, with all his
chief officers, marched through the city, from the western
parts of it to the tower, where many commands were changed,
the presbyterian party depressed, and their generals, Poyntz
and Massie, with all the remaining officers of that faction,
forced to retire; who most of them then changed their party,
and never more appeared on the parliament side. Yet there
was still a presbyterian faction left in the house, of such as
were moderate, and who were not by the bitterness of their
zeal carried on to break their covenant with God and men,
and to renew a league with the popish interest, to destroy
that godly interest which they had at first so gloriously
asserted. After this tumult at London was quieted, about
August of that year the king was brought to one of his
stately palaces at Hampton Court, near London, and the army
removed to quarters about the city, their head-quarters being
at Putney. The king, by reason of his daily converse with
the officers, had begun tampering with them, not only then but
before, and had drawn in some of them to engage to corrupt
others to fall in with him; but to speak the truth of all,
Cromwell was at that time so incorruptibly faithful to his
trust and to the people's interest, that he could not be drawn

in to practice even his own usual and natural dissimulation
on this occasion. His son-in-law Ireton, who was as faithful
as he, was not so fully of the opinion (till he had tried it and
found to the contrary) but that the king might have beer
managed to comply with the public good of his people, after
he could no longer uphold his own violent will ; but, upon
some discourses with him, the king uttering these words to
him, " I shall play my game as well as I can," Ireton replied, " If your majesty have a *game* to play, you must give
us also the liberty to play ours." Colonel Hutchinson privately discoursing with his cousin about the communications
he had had with the king, Ireton's expressions were these :
" He gave us words, and we paid him in his own coin, when
we found he had no real intention to the people's good, but
to prevail by our factions, to regain by art what he had lost
in fight."

The king lived at Hampton Court rather in the condition of
a guarded and attended prince, than as a conquered and
purchased captive ; all his old servants had free recourse to
him ; all sorts of people were admitted to come to kiss his
hands and do him obeisance as a sovereign. Ashburnham
and Berkley, by the parliament voted delinquents, came to
him from beyond the seas, and others by permission of the
army, who had hoped they might be useful to incline him to
wholesome counsels ; but he, on the other side, interpreting
this freedom wherein he was permitted to live, not to the
gentleness and reconcilableness of his parliament, who,
after all his injuries, yet desired his restitution, so far as it
might be without the ruin of the good people of the land,
but rather believing it to proceed from their apprehension of
their own declining and his re-advancing in the hearts of the
people, made use of this advantage to corrupt many of their
officers to revolt from them and betray them ; which some
time after they did, and paid the forfeiture with their

lives.* When the king was at Hampton Court the lords who were formerly of his privy council at Oxford, also repaired to him, to be as a council attending him, but this gave so much disgust at London that they retreated again; but the Scotch lords and commissioners having free access to him, he drew that nation into the design of the second war; which broke out furiously the next summer, and was one of the highest provocations which, after the second victory, brought him to the scaffold. But I shall respite that, to return to his affairs whom I principally trace.

After the parliament was by the general restored to their seats, Colonel Hutchinson came down to his garrison at Nottingham, which, the war being ended, was reduced only to the castle; the works at the town and the bridges being slighted, the companies of the governor's regiment, all but two, disbanded, and he thinking, now in a time when there was no opposition, the command not worthy of himself or his brother, gave it over to his kinsman, Captain Poulton.

* This is one of the places where we find reason to regret Mrs. Hutchinson's being so summary in her account of public affairs. This matter of endeavouring to bring the king to reason, and his perverting the good intentions of friends as well as foes, is treated much at length by Ludlow, in his first volume, from p. 194 to 204, and he agrees with Mrs. Hutchinson in most particulars; but it seems extraordinary that he should attribute a very considerable and active part in this business to Sir Allen Apsley, and his sister should make no mention of him in it. The candour and benevolence of Ireton, who is so generally represented as a cynic, are equally apparent in both places, as likewise are the obstinacy and duplicity of the king. If Ireton is by any supposed to have been too favourably represented by Mrs. Hutchinson, it will not be thought that he is likewise favoured by Walker in his Hist. of the Independents, yet, p. 164, he reports thus. Ireton said the king had committed crimes enough to *depose and imprison him*, and crown the Duke of York, then a child, in his stead *(not to kill the king)*, and that if any thought their treatment of the king severe, they would applaud their clemency to the Duke of York.

With the assistance of his fellow parliament men he procured
an order from the parliament for five thousand pounds, that
had been levied for the Scotch army, but which they, departing with too much haste, had not received, to be distributed among the officers and soldiers of his regiment that
were at this time disbanded, in part of their arrears ; and,
that it might go the farther amongst them, he himself had
none of it.* The garrison at Nottingham being reduced,
Colonel Hutchinson removed his family back to his own
house at Owthorpe, but found that, having stood uninhabited,
and been robbed of everything which the neighbouring garrisons of Shelford and Wiverton could carry from it, it was
so ruined that it could not be repaired, to make a convenient habitation, without as much charge as would almost
build another. By reason of the debt his public employment
had run him into, and not being able to do this at present while
all his arrears were unpaid, he made a bad shift with it for
that year. At this time his distemper of rheum was very
sore upon him, and he was so afflicted with pains in his
head, which fell down also with violent torture upon all his
joints, that he was not able to go for many weeks out of his
chamber ; and here we had a notable example of the victorious power of his soul over his body. One day, as he
was in the saddest torture of his disease, certain horse came,
somewhat insolently and injuriously, exacting quarters or
moneys in the town ; whom he sent for, and telling them he
would not suffer such wrong to be done to his tenants, they
seeing him in so weak a condition, would not be persuaded to
forbear violent and unjust actions, but told him his government was expired, and they were no more under his command ;
with which, and some other saucy language, being provoked
to be heartily angry, he felt not that he was sick, but started

* Nota Bene.

x 3

out of his chair and beat them out of the house and town, and returned again laughing at the wretched fellows and at himself, wondering what was become of his pain, and thinking how strangely his feebleness was cured in a moment. But while he and those about him were in this amazement, half an hour had not expired before his spirits cooled, and that heat and vigour they had lent his members retired again to their noble palace, his heart; and those efforts, which had violently employed his limbs, made them more weak than before, and his pain returned with such redoubled violence, that we thought he would have died in this fit.

While he was thus distempered at home, Major-general Ireton sent him a letter, with a new commission in it, for the resuming his government of Nottingham Castle : for the principal officers of the army, foreseeing an approaching storm, desired to place it in his hands, by whom it had before been so prosperously and faithfully preserved : but the colonel sent them word, that as he should not have put his kinsman into the place, although he was assured of his fidelity, so he would never join with those who were so forgetful of the merits of men that had behaved themselves well, as to discourage them without a cause. Hereupon they suffered Captain Poulton to remain in his command ; but while the house was very busy in faction, they took no care of any of the garrisons, especially of such as were likely to continue firm to the cause ; the presbyterian faction having a design to weaken or corrupt them all, that they might be prepared for the great revolt from the parliament, which was now working in all countries. In Nottinghamshire, Colonel Gilbert Byron, a brother of Lord Byron's, meeting Captain Poulton, began to insinuate into him, and tempt him to betray Nottingham Castle; which proposition, when he heard, he thought fit not utterly to reject, lest the castle being then in a weak condition, and the soldiers discontented, some of

his under officers might be more ready to embrace it and betray
both the place and him.   He therefore took a little time to
consider of it, and came to Colonel Hutchinson and acquainted him with it.   He advised him to hold his cousin Byron
on in the treaty, till he himself could go to London and provide for the better securing of the place, which, his distemper
of health a little abating, he did: and when the place was
well provided, Captain Poulton, who was too gentle-hearted
to cut off Mr. Byron under a pretence of assenting to him,
sent to him to shift for himself, which Mr. Byron accordingly did; and now the insurrection began everywhere to
break out.

In the meantime, some months before, when the king had
laid the design of the second war with the Scots, and had employed all his art to bring the English presbyters to a revolt,
and was now full of hopes to bring about *his game,* and conquer those who had conquered him, while he was amusing
the parliament with expectations of a treaty, he privily
stole away from Hampton Court, by the assistance of Ashburnham and Berkley, no man knew whither; but these wise
men had so ordered their business, that instead of going beyond seas, which was his first intent, he was forced to give
himself up to Hammond, governor of the Isle of Wight,
who immediately gave notice to the parliament, and they sent
him thanks for his fidelity, and ordered that the king should be
honourably attended and guarded there in Carisbrook Castle.
The parliament were again sending him propositions there,
when they received a letter from him, urging that he might
come to a personal treaty in London.   Hereupon the two
houses agreed on four propositions to be sent him, to be passed
as bills; upon the passing of which, they were content he
should come to a personal treaty for the rest.   The four propositions were, 1st. That a bill should be passed for the settling
the militia of the kingdom.   2ndly. That all oaths, decla-

rations, &c., against the parliament and their adherents should
be called in.   3rdly. That the lords made by the great seal
at Oxford, should not thereby be capable of sitting in the
house of peers.   4thly. That the parliament might have
power to adjourn, as the two houses think fit.   The Scotch
commissioners opposed the sending these bills to the king,
and urged his coming to a personal treaty in London.
The king, understanding their mind and the factions in London, absolutely refused to sign them.   Wherefore the houses,
debating upon the king's denial, these votes were at length
passed by both houses, on the 17th day of January:—That
they would make no more addresses nor applications to the
king.   That no person whatever should make address or
application to him.   That whoever should break this order,
should incur the penalty of high treason.   That they should
receive no more messages from the king, and that no person
should presume to bring any to either house, or to any other
person.   Upon these votes the army put forth a declaration, promising to stand by the houses in them, which was
signed by the general and all his officers, at Windsor, January 19, 1647.   But in May following, tumults first began in
London; then the Surrey men came with a very insolent
petition, and behaved themselves so arrogantly to the parliament, killing and wounding some of the guards, that a troop
of horse was fetched from the Mews, and was forced to
kill some of them before they could quiet them.   After this,
the parliament was informed of another insurrection in
Kent, coming under the face of a petition, and sent out
General Fairfax with seven regiments to suppress them, who
pursued them to Rochester.   A great company of these Kentish men were gotten together about Gravesend, with fifteen
knights, and many commanders of the king's army to head
them; who, although they were more in number than Fairfax's men, yet durst not await his coming   Some of them

went to Dover Castle and besieged it, but the general ent
out Sir Michael Livesey, who happily relieved that place and
raised the siege; others went to Maidstone, and a few kept
together about Rochester. The general himself went to
Maidstone, where two thousand of them were gotten into
the town, and resolved to keep it; whom the general assaulted, and with difficulty entered the town, and fought for
every street, which were barricaded against him, and defended with cannon. Yet at length he killed two hundred,
and took fourteen hundred prisoners. Four hundred horse
broke away to an army of their friends, bigger than Fairfax's,
who saw the town taken, yet had not the courage to engage
against the general for the relief of it; but after they saw
his victory they dispersed. The Lord Goring then having
rallied about two thousand of these Kentish men, led them
to Greenwich, from whence he sent to try the affections of
the Londoners; but while he stayed there expecting their
answer, some troops of the army came, upon the sight of
whom, he and his men fled; the Kentish men, most of them
to their own houses, himself, with about five hundred horse,
getting boat, crossed the Thames into Essex, where the
Lord Capel with forces out of Hertfordshire, and Sir
Charles Lucas with a body of horse at Chelmsford, joined
him; to whom, in a short time, divers that had been the
king's soldiers, with many Londoners, and other malignants,
flocked in. General Fairfax, with part of his forces crossed
the Thames at Gravesend, and sending for all the rest out of
Kent and London, pursued the enemies, and drove them
into Colchester, where he besieged them, and lay before
them three months. At last, hearing of the defeat of Duke
Hamilton and the Scots, and others of the king's partisans,
and being reduced to eating horse-flesh, without hopes of
relief, they yielded to mercy. The general shot Sir Charles
Lucas and Sir George Lisle to death upon the place, and

reserved Goring, Capel, and others, to abide the doom of the parliament. While Fairfax was thus employed in Kent and Essex, Langhorne, Powell, and Poyer, celebrated commanders of the parliament side, revolted with the places in their command, and got a body of eight thousand Welshmen, whom Colonel Horton, with three thousand, encountered, vanquished, routed, and took as many prisoners as he had soldiers; but Langhorne and Powell escaped to Poyer, and shut up themselves with him in Pembroke Castle, a place so strong that they refused all treaty; and thereupon they were besieged by Lieutenant-general Cromwell, to whom at length, after some months' siege, it was surrendered at the conqueror's mercy. In divers other countries, at the same time, there were several insurrections and revolts; but those of the parliament party, as if they had lost courage and conscience at once, could no more behave themselves with that valour, which had before renowned them; and were slain or taken, losing the places they had betrayed, to their old companions, whose fidelity was crowned with success everywhere. Among the rest, Colonel Gilbert Byron had risen, with other gentlemen of Nottinghamshire and Lincolnshire, and had gotten together about five hundred horse; wherewith, after he had failed of his hopes of corrupting the governor of Nottingham, they intended to go and join themselves with others that were up in other countries; and this was so suddenly and secretly done, that they were upon their march before the rising was suspected. The governor of Nottingham had not time enough to send a messenger to be with Colonel Hutchinson at his house before them, and therefore shot off a piece of cannon; which Colonel Hutchinson hearing as he sat at dinner, and believing some extraordinary thing to be in it, commanded horses to be made ready, and went to Nottingham; but met the messenger who came to give him notice of the enemies' approach. The news being

sent home in haste, his arms and writings, and other things
of value, were put in a cart and sent away; which was not
long gone before the enemy marched by the house, and keeping their body on a hill at the town's end, only sent a
party to the house to fetch them what provisions of meat
and drink they found there; besides which, they took nothing
but a groom with two horses, who having ridden out to air
them, fell into their mouths, because he could not be readily
found when the rest of the horses were sent away.   The
reason why no more mischief was done by the cavaliers to
his family, at that time, was, partly because Colonel Gilbert Byron had commanded not to disturb them, if he were
not there, and partly because they were so closely pursued
by the Lincolnshire troops, that they could not stay to take,
nor would burden themselves with plunder, now they saw
it unlikely to get off without fighting.   This they did the
next day at Willoughby within three miles of Owthorpe,
and were there totally routed, killed, and taken by a party
under Colonel Rossiter's command, by whom Colonel Byron was
carried prisoner to Belvoir Castle.   Being in distress there,
although he was an enemy, and had dealt unhandsomely
with Colonel Hutchinson, in endeavouring to corrupt one for
whom he was engaged, yet the colonel sent him a sum of
money for his present relief, and afterwards procured him a
release and composition with the parliament.   The greatest
of all these dangers seemed now to be in the north, where
Duke Hamilton's faction being prevalent in Scotland, he had
raised an army, and was marching into England.   Sir Marmaduke Langdale and Glenham had already raised some men
in those parts, whom Lambert, with the assistance of some
Lincolnshire forces, joined to his Yorkshire brigade, kept in
ı lay ; but they reserved themselves to join with Hamilton.
Argyle and others of the kirk party, protested against him,
and many of the ministers cursed his attempt, but were

silenced for it, although God heard them. The presbyterians in London secretly prayed for his success, and hardly could the house of lords be brought to join with the house of commons in voting all the English traitors, that should join with the Scots, which yet at the last they did.

Colonel Hutchinson having been about this time at London, and wanting a minister for the place where he lived, and for which he had procured an augmentation, repaired to some eminent ministers in London,* to recommend a worthy person to him for the place. They, with a great testimonial, recommended a Scotchman to him, whom the colonel brought down; but having occasion to be with the committee at Nottingham, to take order for the security of the county in these dangerous times, while he was out the man made strange prayers in the family, which were couched in dark expressions; but Mrs. Hutchinson, understanding them to be intended for the prosperous success of those who were risen against the parliament, and of his nation that were coming to invade ours, told her husband at his return, that she could not bear with nor join in his prayers. The next day, being the Lord's day, the colonel heard his sermon, which was so spiritless and so lamentable, that he was very much vexed the ministers should have sent such a man to him; withal he publicly made the same prayers he uttered in the family for the success of the Scots; whereupon, after dinner, the colonel took him aside, and told him that he had done very sinfully to undertake an office for which he was so ill gifted, and desired him to depart in peace again the next day, and to forbear any further employment in his house.

---

* This entirely contradicts the opinion so generally propagated and believed, that all the independents were so fanatical as to decry and lay aside all regular ministry, and to give themselves up to the guidance of self-created teachers, pretending inspiration, i. e. impostors.

The man at first was very high, and told the colonel he was there by authority of the parliament, and would not depart; the colonel then dealt high with him, and told him he would declare to them the expressions of his prayers, which so confounded the man, that he besought him to have pity, and confessed that he was fled from his own country for having been of Montrose's party; and that covetousness, against his conscience, had drawn him to dissemble himself to be of the parliament's principles, but that God had judged him for his hypocrisy, and withdrawn his Spirit from him, since he practised it; he then submitted to go quietly and silently away, even begging it as a favour of the colonel, that he would permit him so to do.   He did it with such a counterfeit sorrow and conviction, that the colonel being of a most placable nature, freely forgave him, and sent him not away empty, for he had fifteen pounds for only a fortnight's service; yet this rogue, before he went out of the country, went to the presbyters at Nottingham, and told them his conscience would not permit him to stay in the colonel's house, because he and his wife were such violent sectaries, that no orthodox man could live comfortably with them; and this scandal those charitable priests were ready to receive and more largely to spread.   They themselves, with divers of their zealous disciples, whom they had perverted, among whom were Colonel Francis Pierrepont, Captains Rosse, White, Chadwick, and many others, were watching opportunity to break their covenant and rise against that parliament, under which they had served and sworn to assist, till all delinquents, as well greater as less, were brought to condign punishment.

At London things were in a very sad posture, the two factions of presbytery and independency being so engaged to suppress each other, that they both ceased to regard the public interest; insomuch, that at that time a certain sort of public-spirited men stood up in the parliament and the army, declaring against these factions and the ambition of the grandees of both, and the partiality that was in these days practised, by which great men were privileged to do those things which meaner men were punished for, and the injustice and other crimes of particular members of parliament, were rather covered than punished, to the scandal of the whole house. Many got shelter in the house and army against their debts, by which others were defrauded and undone. The lords, as if it were the chief interest of nobility to be licensed in vice, claimed many prerogatives, which set them out of the reach of common justice, which these good-hearted people would have equally to belong to the poorest as well as to the mighty; and for this and such other honest declarations, they were nicknamed levellers. Indeed, as all virtues are mediums, and have their extremes, there rose up afterwards with that name a people, who endeavoured the levelling of all estates and qualities; which these sober levellers were never guilty of desiring, but were men of just and sober principles, of honest and religious ends, and therefore hated by all the designing self-interested men of both factions. Colonel Hutchinson had a great intimacy with many of these; and so far as they acted according to the just, pious, and public spirit which they professed, he owned and protected them as far as he had power. These were they who first began to discover the ambition of Lieutenant-general Cromwell and his idolators, and to suspect and dislike it. About this time, he was sent down, after his victory in Wales, to encounter Hamilton in the north. When he went down, the chief of these levellers following him out of the town, to take their leave of him, received such professions from him, of a spirit bent to pursue the same just and honest things which they desired, that they went away with great satisfaction, till they heard that a coachful

of presbyterian priests coming after them, went away no
less pleased; by which it was apparent he dissembled
with one or the other, and by so doing lost his credit with
both.

When he came to Nottingham, Colonel Hutchinson went
to see him, whom he embraced with all the expressions of
kindness that one friend could make to another, and then
retiring with him, pressed him to tell him what his friends,
the levellers,* thought of him. The colonel, who was the

---

* The information Mrs. Hutchinson gives us on this subject is curious
and valuable, but differs from the tradition generally received respecting
the levellers; it is however well supported by Walker in his History of
Independency. He begins with describing two juntos of grandees, and
calls the rest the common people of the house; the former only feigned
opposition, but played into one another's hands, the latter were sincere and
earnest in it: he speaks of the *honest middlemen,* the same as Mrs. Hutchinson calls by that name, and likewise *levellers;* he declares levellers and
asserters of liberty to be synonymous terms: in a variety of places they
are treated as the only sincere patriots and opposers of the selfish schemes
of the grandees of both parties, peculiarly the independents, and above all,
of Cromwell; and the engrossers and monopolizers of oligarchy, desiring
to make themselves a corporation of tyrants, are said chiefly to dread the
opposition of these levellers; but the most remarkable passage is in p.
194. " Reader, let me admonish thee that the levellers, for so they are
miscalled, only for endeavouring to level the exorbitant usurpations of the
council of state and council of officers, are much abused by some books
lately printed and published in their names, much differing from their
declared principles, tenets, and practices, but forged by Cromwell and
others to make the sheep (the people) betray the dogs that faithfully
guard them." The mode here and before taken by Colonel Hutchinson,
of readily adopting a name which was intended him for a reproach, was
certainly the best way of disarming it of its sting. The principles held by
that party of the levellers which he supported, none venture openly to
oppose, but try to attach to them the absurd extreme of those he blames;
the modern philosophers who have stated that all men have equal rights,
but to unequal things, have not met with a much more candid construc-

freest man in the world from concealing truth from his friend,
especially when it was required of him in love and plainness,
not only told him what others thought of him, but what he
himself conceived ; and how much it would darken all his
glories, if he should become a slave to his own ambition,
and be guilty of what he gave the world just cause to suspect, and therefore he begged of him to wear his heart in
his face, and to scorn to delude his enemies, but to make
use of his noble courage to maintain what he believed to be
just, against all great opposers.   Cromwell made mighty professions of a sincere heart to him, but it is certain that
for this and such like plain dealing with him, he dreaded
the colonel, and made it his particular business to keep
him out of the army ; but the colonel desiring command,
not to serve himself but his country, would not use

tion. The abuses Colonel Hutchinson complained of, especially that of
the privilege of parliament, have since been a little diminished ; but many
families still continue to be defrauded and undone by the shelter which
members of parliament find from their debts, and which seems long likely
to continue a defect in our legislature, and a reproach to our morals.
Among a number of pamphlets published in Mr. Hutchinson's time, one
was found at Owthorpe, setting forth the views and desires of these inferior levellers.   They therein stated, that they were willing to acknowledge the proprietors of lands, and principally the lords of manors, as their
elder brothers, and rightfully possessed of the chief inheritance ; but
prayed to be allowed to cultivate the wastes and commons for their support.   Whether the permitting or even encouraging this under moderate
reservations might not have been conducive to the public good, is a question which seems to have been decided in the affirmative by the practice of
the French under the ancient government : a great share of the lands in
every parish having been thus granted out, and cultivated by small proprietors, who paid what was called *champarts,* fieldings or tithes, being
seven in the hundred ; the industry and population this produced is felt
by all Europe. The abrogating these payments to the lords, was one of the
grand *incitements* to, and *crimes* of, the revolution.

that art he detested in others, to procure himself any advantage.

At this time Colonel Thornhagh marched with Cromwell, and at his parting with Colonel Hutchinson, took such a kind leave of him, with such dear expressions of love, such brotherly embraces, and such regret for any rash jealousies he had been wrought into, that it took great impression in the colonel's kind heart, and might have been a presage to him that they should meet no more, when they parted with such extraordinary melting love ; but that Colonel Hutchinson's cheerful and constant spirit never anticipated any evil with fear.   His prudence wanted not foresight that it might come, yet his faith and courage entertained his hope, that God would either prevent it, or help him to bear it.

This summer the revolt was not greater at land than at sea.   Many of the great ships set the vice-admiral on shore, and sailed towards Holland to Prince Charles : to whom the Duke of York had come, having, by his father's advice, privately stolen away from London, where the parliament had received and treated him like a prince, ever since the surrender of Oxford.   To reduce these revolted ships, and preserve the rest of the navy from the like, the Earl of Warwick was made lord high admiral of England.   But at the same time his brother, the Earl of Holland, who had floated up and down with the tide of the times, rose also against the parliament, and appeared in arms, with the young Duke of Buckingham and Lord Francis Villars, his brother, and others, making about five hundred horse, at Kingston-upon-Thames. Here some of the parliament troops, assailing them before they had time to grow, totally routed and dispersed them. The Lord Francis Villars was slain ; the Earl of Holland, flying with those he could rally, was fought with at St. Neots; Dalbier and others of his associates were slain, and himself taken prisoner and carried to Warwick Castle.   Buckingham fled,

and at last got beyond seas, with a blot of base ingratitude
and treachery, which began then to appear, and hath since
marked out all his life. For these two lords being pupils,
and under the king's tuition, were carried with him to Oxford,
where they remained till the surrender of the place; and then
coming to London, as they were under age, they had all
their father and mother's great estates, freely, without any
sequestration or composition : and while they enjoyed them,
their secret intentions of rising being discovered to the parliament, the parliament would not secure them, as some
advised, but only sent a civil warning to the duke, minding
him how unhandsome it would be, if the information should
prove true. Whereupon the duke protested he had no such
intention, but utterly detested it, making all the expressions
of just gratitude to them that could be ; and yet, within a
very few days afterwards, he openly showed himself in arms,
to tell the world how perfidious a hypocrite he was ; for
which the parliament exempted him from pardon, and ever
afterwards detested his name, as one that rose only to fall
into contempt and obloquy.

And now was Cromwell advanced into Lancashire, where
Lambert, retreating from the invading Scots, joined with him
and made up an army of about ten thousand ; which were but
few to encounter five-and-twenty thousand, led by Hamilton,
Langdale, and other English joined with them. Yet near
Preston, in Lancashire, they fought, and Cromwell gained an
entire victory, about the end of August, and had the chase of
them for twenty miles, wherein many fell, and many were
taken prisoners. Hamilton himself, with a good party of
horse, fled to Uttoxeter, and was there taken by the Lord
Grey. But, in the beginning of this battle, the valiant Colonel
Thornhagh was wounded to death. Being at the beginning
of the charge on a horse as courageous as became such a
master, he made such furious speed to set upon a company of

Scotch lancers, that he was singly engaged and mortally wounded, before it was possible for his regiment, though as brave men as ever drew sword, and too affectionate to their colonel to be slack in following him, to come up time enough to break the fury of that body, which shamed * not to unite all their force against one man : who yet fell not among them, but being faint and all covered with blood, of his enemies as well as his own, was carried off by some of his own men. while the rest, enraged for the loss of their dear colonel. fought not that day like men of human race ; but deaf to the cries of every coward that asked mercy, they killed all, and would not that a captive should live to see their colonel die ; but said the whole kingdom of Scotland was too mean a sacrifice for that brave man. His soul was hovering to take her flight out of his body, but that an eager desire to know the success of that battle kept it within till the end of the day, when the news being brought him, he cleared his dying countenance, and said, " I now rejoice to die, since God hath let me see the overthrow of this perfidious enemy ; I could not lose my life in a better cause, and I have the favour from God to see my blood avenged." So he died, with a large testimony of love to his soldiers, but more to the cause, and was by mercy removed, that the temptations of future times might not prevail to corrupt his pure soul. A man of greater courage and integrity fell not, nor fought not, in this glorious cause ; he had also an excellent good nature, but easy to be wrought upon by flatterers, yet as flexible to the admonitions of his friends ; and this virtue he had, that if sometimes a cunning insinuation prevailed upon his easy faith, when his error was made known to him, notwithstanding all his great courage, he was readier to acknowledge and repair, than to pursue his mistake.† Colonel Thornhagh's regiment, in the reducing of

* Shamed not, used neutrally, instead of were not ashamed, blushed not.
† The valour of this gentleman seems to have been a favourite topic of

the garrison forces, had one Major Saunders (a Derbyshire man, who was a very godly, honest, country gentleman, but had not many things requisite for a great soldier) assigned them for their major, and with him he brought in about a troop of Derbyshire horse : but the Nottinghamshire horse, who certainly were as brave men as any that drew swords in the army, had been animated in all their service by the dear love they had to their colonel, and the glory they took in him, and their generous spirits could not take satisfaction in serving under a less man, which they all esteemed their major to be. But remembering their successes under Colonel Hutchinson, and several other things that moved them to pitch their thoughts upon him, the captains addressed themselves to Cromwell, and acquainted him with the discouragement and sorrow they had by the death of their colonel, for whom nothing could comfort them, but a successor equal to himself; which they could not hope to find so well as they might in the person of Colonel Hutchinson, with whose worth and courage they were well acquainted, and who was now out of employment.   Their only difficulty was, whether he would accept the command, which they hoped to prevail on him to do, if he would oblige them by sending to Lord Fairfax, to stop all other ways that might be thought of for disposing it, till they could know whether Colonel Hutchinson would accept it, for which they had prepared a messenger to send to his house.

admiration and praise among his brother warriors.   In Cromwell's letter (preserved by Whitelocke), wherein he gives an account of his victory, he laments " the death of this *too brave gentleman*."   Ludlow is full in his praises of him, and adds a very picturesque circumstance; " that as he lay wounded among his soldiers, he made them open to the right and left, that he might see the enemy run."   But it is doubtful whether at any time the pencil or the pen has consecrated any thing to the memory of a departed chief, so animated, so appropriate, as this character and description, which we may surely say Mrs. Hutchinson conceived in the very spirit in which her hero lived and 'ourished, fought and fell.

Cromwell, with all the assentation imaginable, seemed to rejoice they had made so worthy a choice, and promised them to take care the regiment should not be disposed of till they received Colonel Hutchinson's answer; whereupon the captains severally wrote to Colonel Hutchinson, with most earnest entreaties, that he would give them leave to procure a commission for him to conduct them, which the lieutenant-general had already promised to send for, if he pleased to accept it.

The colonel, though he had more inclination to rest at that time, by reason of the indisposition of his health, yet not knowing whether the earnest desires of his countrymen were not from a higher call, wrote them word that he preferred the satisfaction of their desires before his own, and if the commission came to him to be their leader, he would not refuse it, though he should not do anything himself to seek any command. Meanwhile Cromwell, as soon as the Nottinghamshire men had imparted their desires to him, sent for Saunders, and cajoling him, told him none was so fit as himself to command the regiment; but that all the regiment did not think so, but were designing to procure themselves another colonel, which he advised him to prevent, by sending speedily to the general, to whom Cromwell also wrote to further the request, and before the messenger came back from Owthorpe procured the commission for Saunders. When it came, he used all his art to persuade the captains to submit to it, and to excuse himself from having any hand in it; but they perceived his dissimulation, and the troops were so displeased with it, that they thought to have flung down their arms; but their captains persuaded them to rest contented until the present expedition were over. But they had not only this cheat and disappointment by Cromwell, but all the Nottingham captains were passed over, and a less deserving man made major of the regiment. The new colonel and major made it their business to discountenance and affront all

r 2

that had showed any desire for Colonel Hutchinson, and to weary them out, that they might fill up their rooms with Derbyshire men ; but as soon as they got to London, all that could otherwise dispose of themselves, went voluntarily off; and the rest that were forced to abide, hated their commanders, and lived discontentedly under them. The reasons that induced Cromwell to this, were two : first, he found that Colonel Hutchinson understood him, and was too generous either to fear or flatter him ; and he carried, though under a false face of friendship, a deep resentment of the colonel's plain dealing with him at Nottingham. He had besides a design, by insinuating himself with Colonel Saunders, to flatter him into the sale of a town of his called Ireton, which Cromwell earnestly desired to buy for Major-general Ireton, who had married his daughter; and when at last he could not obtain it, in process of time, he took the regiment away from him again.* Colonel Hutchinson was not at all displeased that the regiment was not given to him, but highly resented it that the men were ill used for their affections to him; and was sorry that this particular carriage of Cromwell's gave him such a proof of other things suspected of him, so destructive to the whole cause and party, as it afterwards fell out.

Sir Marmaduke Langdale, after the rout of Hamilton, came with two or three other officers to a little alehouse which was upon Colonel Hutchinson's land, and there were so circumspect, that some country fellows, who saw them by chance, suspecting they were no ordinary travellers, acquainted Mr. Widmerpoole, who lived within two or three miles, and had been major to the colonel in the first war: whereupon he

* This gentleman is mentioned in Granger's Biography; and there is a print of him in the hands of some curious collectors, peculiarly of John Townely, Esq. He is said to be of Ireton, in Derbyshire; but Ireton is believed to be in the Vale of Belvoir.

came forth, with some few others, and sent down to the
colonel to acquaint him that some suspicious persons were at
the lodge. The colonel, hearing of it, took his servants out,
and was approaching near the house, when Major Widmerpoole, being beforehand in the house, had given Langdale
ome jealousy that he might be surprised; thereupon one of
his company went out to fetch out his horses, which were
stopped for the present, and they seeing the colonel coming
up towards them, rendered themselves prisoners to Major
Widmerpoole, and were sent to Nottingham Castle, where
they continued some months, till at last Langdale finding an
opportunity, corrupted one of the guard, who furnished him
with a soldier's disguise, and ran away with him. The major,
who would have been baffled by these persons, if the colonel
had not come in, had all the booty, which the colonel never
took any share of whatever: but the major thinking the best
of his spoils justly due to him, presented him with a case or
two of very fine pistols, which he accepted.

About this time, the gentlemen that were commissioners
for the king at Newark, fell into disputes one with another;
nor only so, but suits were commenced in chancery upon this
occasion. One Atkins, and several other rich men at Newark,
when that garrison began to be fortified for the king, lent
certain sums of money, for the carrying on of that work, to
the commissioners of array, for which those gentlemen became
bound to the Newarkers. After the taking of that town by
the parliament, they, with other persons, coming in within
the set time, were admitted to composition. Having been so
cunning as to put out their money in other names, they ventured to leave out these sums, believing they were put into
such sure hands, that it would never be discovered. Mr.
Sutton, Sir Thomas Williamson, Sir John Digby, Sir Gervas
Eyre, the Lord Chaworth, Sir Thomas Blackwell, Sir Roger
Cowper, Sir Richard Byron, and others, had given bond for

this money, which Mr. Sutton, presenting to the king, as a sum that *he* had raised to signalize his loyalty, the king, to reward him, made him a baron. The whole sum thus taken up for the king's service, was eight or ten thousand pounds; fifteen hundred of it, that was lent by Atkinson, being demanded, would have been paid, but they would not take the principal without the interest. Sir Thomas Williamson was openly arrested for it in Westminster Hall; upon which Mr. Sutton and he, being maddened, put in a bill in chancery against Atkinson and others, praying that they might set forth to what ends and uses this money was lent to the said gentlemen, &c., &c.

The parliament had made a law, that all estates of delinquents, concealed and uncompounded for, should be forfeited, one half to the state, and the other half to the discoverer, if he had any arrears due to him from the parliament, in payment of them. There were clerks and solicitors, who in those days made a trade of hunting out such discoveries, and making them known to such as had any arrears due to them. Colonel Hutchinson at that time had received no pay at all. One of the clerks of that committee, which was appointed for such discoveries, sent him word that two officers of the army were upon this chancery bill, endeavouring to make a discovery of certain concealed moneys in Nottinghamshire, which being his own country, he thought might be more proper for him. Colonel Hutchinson, who had never any mind to disadvantage any of the gentlemen of the country, demurred upon this information, and did nothing in it, till some came to him, intimating a desire of my Lord Lexington's, that the colonel would pitch upon that for the payment of his arrears, that so they might fall into the hands of a neighbour, who would use them civilly, rather than of a stranger. After the colonel was thus invited by the gentlemen themselves, to pitch upon this money, he waived all the rest, and only entered as his discovery that money which these townsmen of Newark had lent; but upon full search and hearing at the committee, the money was found to be forfeited money, and the debtors were ordered to pay it into the committee, and Colonel Hutchinson had also an order to receive his arrear from that committee of Haberdashers' Hall. Hereupon Sir Thomas Williamson and Lord Lexington, who being the men of the best estates, were principally looked upon for the debt, applied themselves to Colonel Hutchinson, begging as a favour that he would undertake the management of the order of sequestration given out upon their estates; and would also oblige them, by bringing in several other gentlemen, that were bound to bear proportionable shares. The colonel, to gratify them, got the order of sequestration, and brought them to an accommodation, wherein every man, according to his ability, agreed upon an equal proportion; and the gentlemen, especially Mr. Sutton, acknowledged a very great obligation to the colonel, who had brought it to so equal a composition among them; and then, upon their own desires, the order of sequestration was laid upon their estates, but managed by one of their own bailiffs, in order to free them from inconveniences that otherwise would have come upon them. Some of them made use of it to get in arrears of rent, which they knew no other way of getting, and for which at that time they pretended the greatest sense of gratitude and obligation imaginable. The colonel also procured them days of payment, so that whereas it should have been paid this Michaelmas, 1648, it was not paid till a year after; and for these, and many other favours on this occasion, he was then courted as their patron, though afterwards this civility had like to have been his ruin. And now, about Michaelmas, 1648, he went to attend his duty at the parliament, carrying his whole family with him, because his house had been so ruined by the war that he could no longer live in it, till it was either repaired or newly built. On coming to London, he himself fell into his old distemper of rheumatism with more violence than ever, and being weary of those physicians he had so long, with so little success, employed, he was recommended to a young doctor, son of old Dr. Rudgely, whose excellence in his art was everywhere known; and this son being a very ingenious person, and considering himself, and consulting with his father, believed that all the other physicians who had dealt with him had mistaken his disease; which he finding more truly out, in a short space perfectly cured him of the gout, and restored him, by God's blessing on his endeavours, to such a condition of health as he had not enjoyed for two years before. When he was well again to attend the house, he found the presbyterian party so prevalent there, that the victories obtained by the army displeased them; and they had grown so hot in the zeal of their faction, that they from thenceforth resolved and endeavoured to close with the common enemy, that they might thereby compass the destruction of their independent brethren. To this end, and to strengthen their faction, they got in again the late suspended members; whereof it was said, and by the consequence appeared true, that Mr. Hollis, during his secession, had been into France, and there meeting with the queen, had pieced up an ungodly accommodation with her; although he was the man that at the beginning, when some of the more sober men, who foresaw the sad issues of war and victory to either side, were labouring for an accommodation, said openly in the house, that "he abhorred that word accommodation." After these were gotten in again, and encouraged by the presbyterian ministers and the people in the city, they procured a revocation of the votes formerly made; with such convincing reasons publicly declared for the same, why they had resolved on no more addresses to be made to the king. And now nothing was agitated with more violence than a new personal treaty, with honour and freedom ; and even his com'ng to the city, before any security given, was laboured for, but that prevailed not. Such were the heats of the two parties, that Mr. Hollis challenged Ireton, even in the house ; out of which they both went to fight, but that one who sat near them overheard the wicked whisper, and prevented the execution of it.*

Amidst these things, at last a treaty was sent to the king, by commissioners, who went from both houses, to the Isle of Wight ; and although there were some honourable persons in this commission, yet it cannot be denied, but that they were carried away by the others, and concluded, upon most dangerous terms, an agreement with the king. He would not give up bishops, but only lease out their revenues ; and upon the whole, such were the terms upon which the king was to be restored, that the whole cause was evidently given up to him. Only one thing he assented to, to acknowledge himself guilty of the blood spilt in the late war, with this proviso, that if the agreement were not ratified by the house, then this concession should be of no force against him.†
The commissioners that treated with him had been cajoled and biassed with promises of great honours and offices to every one of them, and so they brought back their treaty to be confirmed by the houses ; where there was a very high dispute about them, and they sat up most part of the night : when at length it was voted to accept his concessions, the dissenting party being fewer than the other that were carrying on the faction. Colonel Hutchinson was that night among them, and being convinced in his conscience that both

* Clarendon pretends Ireton would not fight. Surely Ludlow knew him best, and he says he would !

† Certainly there are many strange things to be found in the history o diplomacy, but perhaps none so strange as that an assertion should be admitted to be *provisionally true*.

the cause, and all those who with an upright honest heart asserted and maintained it, were betrayed and sold for nothing, he addressed himself to those commissioners he had most honourable thoughts of; and urged his reasons and apprehensions to them, and told them that the king, after having been exasperated, vanquished, and captived, would be restored to that power which was inconsistent with the liberty of the people, who, for all their blood, treasure, and misery, would reap no fruit, but a confirmation of their bondage ; and that it had been a thousand times better never to have struck one stroke in the quarrel, than, after victory, to yield up a righteous cause; whereby they should not only betray the interest of their country and the trust reposed in them, and those zealous friends who had engaged to the death for them, but be false to the covenant of their God, which was to *extirpate prelacy*, not to *lease* it.* They acknowledged to him that the conditions were not so secure as they ought to be; but in regard of the growing power and insolence of the army, it was best to accept them. They further said, that they who enjoyed those trusts and places, which they had secured for themselves and other honest men, should be able to curb the king's exorbitances ; and such other things they said, wherewith the colonel, dissatisfied, opposed their proceedings as much as he could. When the vote was passed, he told some men of understanding, that he was not satisfied in conscience to be included with the major part in this vote, which was contrary to their former engagements to God, but he thought it fit to testify their public dissent; he and four more, therefore, entered into the house-book a protestation

* There is, among Clarendon's State Papers, a letter from the queen to the king, assuring him that those with whom he had to deal were too penetrating to be duped by this artifice; if they were, or pretended to be, the queen was not.

against that night's votes and proceedings.* Whether it yet remains there, or whether some others of them got it out, he knew not, but he much wondered, after the change and scrutiny into all these things, that he never heard the least mention of it.

By this violent proceeding of the presbyterians they finished the destruction of him in whose restitution they were now so fiercely engaged, for this gave heart to the vanquished cavaliers, and such courage to the captive king that it hardened him and them to their ruin. On the other side, it so frightened all the honest people, that it made them as violent in their zeal to pull down. as the others were in their madness to restore, this kingly idol; and the army, who were principally levelled and marked out as the sacrifice and peace-offering of this ungodly reconciliation, had some colour to pursue their late arrogant usurpations upon that authority which it was their duty rather to have obeyed than interrupted; but the debates of that night, which produced such destructive votes to them and all their friends, being reported to them, they the next morning came and seized about† of the members as they were going to the house, and carried them to a house hard by, where they were for the present kept prisoners. Most of the presbyterian faction, disgusted at this insolence, would no more come to their seats in the house ; but the gentlemen who were of the other faction, or of none at all, but looked upon themselves as called out to manage a public trust for their country, forsook not their seats while they were permitted to sit in the house.‡

* Ludlow says he wished to do this very thing, but could not.

† Dugdale gives a list of the secluded members, forty-one in number, and hence we are furnished with some names which will serve to establish a peculiar fact stated at the latter end of the history of the republic.

‡ Whitelocke, who was exactly in the same predicament, acted in the same manner, and gives the same reasons for it.

Colonel Hutchinson was one of these who infinitely disliked
this action of the army, and had once before been instrumental in preventing such another rash attempt, which some
of the discerning and honest members having a jealousy of,
sent him down to discover.   When he came, going first to
commissary Ireton's quarters, he found him and some of the
more sober officers of the army in great discontent, for the
lieutenant-general had given order for a sudden advance of
the army to London, upon the intelligence they had had of
the violent proceedings of the other party, whereupon Cromwell was then in the mind to have come and broken them up;
but Colonel Hutchinson, with others, at that time persuaded
him that, notwithstanding the prevalency of the presbyteriar.
faction, there were yet many who had upright and honest
hearts to the public interest, who had not deserved to be sc
used by them, and who could not join with them in any
such irregular ways, although in all just and equitable things
they would be their protectors.   Whereupon at that time he
was stayed ;* but having now drawn the army nearer Lon-

* Mrs. Hutchinson does Ireton that justice which Whitelocke refuses
him, who seems to consider him in the light of an *instigator ;* but this is
clearly decided by Ludlow, who declares that "he himself, being sensible
that the presbyterian party were determined to sacrifice the common cause
to the pleasure of triumphing over the independents and the army, by
agreeing with the king, or by any means, went down to apprise Fairfax and
Ireton, then at the siege of Colchester, of this design, and to court the interposition of the army.   Fairfax readily agreed, but Ireton demurred to
interfering till the king and presbyterians should have actually agreed,
and the body of the nation been convinced of the iniquity of their coali-
tion."   Additional provocations and imperious circumstances afterwards
constrained him, but he acted no conspicuous part in the business.   In
this difference of opinion respecting the interference of the army we may
see the source of the dissension which more openly took place afterwards
between Colonel Hutchinson and Ludlow, and caused the latter to calum-
niate Colonel Hutchinson as he did.

don, they put this insolent force upon the house. Those who were suffered to remain, not at all approving thereof, sent out their mace to demand their members, but the soldiers would not obey. Yet the parliament thought it better to sit still and go on in their duty than give up all, in so distempered a time, into the hands of the soldiery; especially as there had been so specious a pretext for the necessity of securing the whole interest and party from the treachery of those men, who contended so earnestly to give up the victors into the hands of their vanquished enemies.   Many petitions had been brought to the parliament from thousands of the well-affected of the cities of London and Westminster and borough of Southwark, and from several counties in England, and from the several regiments of the army, whereof Colonel Ingolsby's was one of the first, all urging them to perform their covenant, and bring delinquents, without partiality, to justice and condign punishment, and to make inquiry for the guilt of the blood that had been shed in the land in both wars, and to execute justice ; lest the not improving the mercy of God should bring judgments in their room.

Then also a declaration to the same purpose was presented to the house from the Lord General Fairfax and his council of officers, and strange it is how men who could afterwards pretend such reluctancy and abhorrence of those things that were done, should forget that they were the effective answer to their petitions.

After the purgation of the house, upon the new debate of the treaty at the Isle of Wight, it was concluded dangerous to the realm and destructive to its better interest, and the trial of the king was determined.   He was sent for to Westminster, and a commission was given forth to a court of high justice, whereof Bradshaw, serjeant-at-law, was president, and divers honourable persons of the parliament, city, and army, nominated commissioners.   Among them Colonel

Hutchinson was one, who, very much against his own will was put in; but looking upon himself as called hereunto, durst not refuse it, as holding himself obliged by the covenant of God and the public trust of his country reposed in him, although he was not ignorant of the danger he run as the condition of things then was.

In January 1648,* the court sat, the king was brought to his trial, and a charge drawn up against him for levying war against the parliament and people of England, for betraying the public trust reposed in him, and for being an implacable enemy to the commonwealth. But the king refused to plead, disowning the authority of the court, and after three several days persisting in contempt thereof, he was sentenced to suffer death.† One thing was remarked in him by many of the court, that when the blood spilt in many of the battles where he was in his own person, and had caused it to be shed by his own command, was laid to his charge, he heard it with disdainful smiles, and looks and gestures which rather expressed sorrow that all the opposite party to him were not cut off, than that any were: and he

* Hume and Clarendon say January 1649.

† Without entering into the *merits* of the question, we may safely assert that the trial of the king was *without precedent*, though many sovereigns had been deposed and put to death *without trial*. It may appear fanciful to many to suggest that the precedent set at this period could have any influence on the fate of the unfortunate Louis XVI.; but those who have well observed the proneness of the French to mimicry (*singerie*), and peculiarly at the time of their first revolution, their *Anglomania*, or aping of the English (preferably in their foibles), will not be far from believing that this precedent emboldened them to the mockery of justice which they exhibited in his trial and condemnation. It is true that many, and even most circumstances were wanting to render the cases parallel, but they were determined to come up to the height of the English revolution (*à la hauteur des Anglais*), and therefore malice and invention supplied all deficiences.

stuck not to declare in words, that no man's blood spilt in this quarrel troubled him except one, meaning the Earl of Strafford. The gentlemen that were appointed his judges, and divers others, saw in him a disposition so bent on the ruin of all that opposed him, and of all the righteous and just things they had contended for, that it was upon the consciences of many of them, that if they did not execute justice upon him, God would require at their hands all the blood and desolation which should ensue by their suffering him to escape, when God had brought him into their hands. Although the malice of the malignant party and their apostate brethren seemed to threaten them, yet they thought they ought to cast themselves upon God, while they acted with a good conscience for him and for their country. Some of them afterwards, for excuse, belied themselves, and said they were under the awe of the army, and overpersuaded by Cromwell, and the like; but it is certain that all men herein were left to their free liberty of acting, neither persuaded nor compelled; and as there were some nominated in the commission who never sat, and others who sat at first, but durst not hold on, so all the rest might have declined it if they would, when it is apparent they would have suffered nothing by so doing. For those who then declined were afterwards, when they offered themselves, received in again, and had places of more trust and benefit than those who ran the utmost hazard; which they deserved not, for I know upon certain knowledge that many, yea the most of them, retreated, not for conscience, but from fear and worldly prudence, foreseeing that the insolency of the army might grow to that height as to ruin the cause, and reduce the kingdom into the hands of the enemy; and then those who had been most courageous in their country's cause whould be given up as victims. These poor men did privately animate those who appeared most publicly, and I knew several of them in whom I lived to see that saying of Christ fulfilled, "He that will save his life shall lose it, and he that for my sake will lose his life shall save it;" when afterwards it fell out that all their prudent declensions saved not the lives of some nor the estates of others. As for Mr. Hutchinson, although he was very much confirmed in his judgment concerning the cause, yet herein being called to an extraordinary action, whereof many were of several minds, he addressed himself to God by prayer; desiring the Lord that, if through any human frailty he were led into any error or false opinion in these great transactions, he would open his eyes, and not suffer him to proceed, but that he would confirm his spirit in the truth, and lead him by a right enlightened conscience; and finding no check, but a confirmation in his conscience that it was his duty to act as he did, he, upon serious debate, both privately and in his addresses to God, and in conferences with conscientious, upright, unbiassed persons, proceeded to sign the sentence against the king. Although he did not then believe but that it might one day come to be again disputed among men, yet both he and others thought they could not refuse it without giving up the people of God, whom they had led forth and engaged themselves unto by the oath of God, into the hands of God's and their own enemies ; and therefore he cast himself upon God's protection, acting according to the dictates of a conscience which he had sought the Lord to guide, and accordingly the Lord did signalise his favour afterwards to him.*

* The account here given of Colonel Hutchinson's motives in this great transaction is most ingenious, and lays his conduct fairly open to the discussion and decision of the reader, who, according to his own feelings, will determine it for himself to be *commendable, censurable,* or *venial.* The legislature unanimously voted it *venial.* It would be an invidious, but not a very difficult task, to point out the persons who, by their *politic declensions,* failed of saving their lives and estates ; but it is worthy of notice

After the death of the king it was debated and resolved to change the form of government from a monarchy into a commonwealth, and the house of lords was voted dangerous and useless thereunto, and dissolved. A council of state was to be annually chosen for the management of affairs, accountable to the parliament, out of which, consisting of forty councilors and a president, twenty were every year to go off by lot, and twenty new ones to be supplied. It is true, that at that time almost every man was fancying a form* of government, and angry, when this came forth, that his invention took not place; and among these John Lilburne, a turbulent-spirited man, who never was quiet in anything, published libels; and the levellers made a disturbance with a kind of insurrection, which Cromwell soon appeased, they indeed being betrayed by their own leaders.

But how the public business went on, how Cromwell finished the conquest of Ireland, how the angry presbyterians spit fire out of their pulpits, and endeavoured to blow up the people against the parliament, how they entered into a treasonable conspiracy with Scotland, which had now received and crowned the son of the late king, who led them in hither with a great army, which the Lord of hosts discomfited; how our public ministers were assassinated and murdered in Spain and Holland; and how the Dutch, in this unsettlement of affairs, hoped to gain by making war, wherein they wer

that Fairfax, after the restoration, with that ingenuousness which belonged to him, declared (Ludlow, vol. iii. p. 10), "that if any person must be excepted from pardon for the death of the king, he knew no man that deserved it more than himself, who being general of the army, and having power sufficient to prevent the proceedings against the king, had not thought fit to use it to that end." It is needless to multiply examples, one reasoning extending to the whole.

* A natural consequence of great popular revolutions, in which the modern French have had the glory of outdoing all the world !

beaten and brought to sue for peace,—I shall leave to the
stories that were then written; and only in general say that
the hand of God was mightily seen in prospering and preserving the parliament till Cromwell's ambition unhappily
interrupted them. Mr. Hutchinson was chosen into the
first council of state, much against his own will; for, understanding that his cousin Ireton was one of the commissioners to nominate that council, he sent his wife to him,
before he went to the house, that morning they were to be
named, to desire him, upon all the scores of kindred and
kindness that had been between them, that he might be left
out, in regard that he had already wasted his time and his
estate in the parliament's service; and having had neither
recompence for his losses, nor any office of benefit, it would
finish his ruin to be tied by this employment to a close and
chargeable attendance, besides the inconvenience of his
health, not yet thoroughly confirmed, his constitution being
more suitable to an active than to a sedentary life. These
and other things he privately urged upon him; but he, who was
a man regardless of his own or of any man's private interest,
wherever he thought the public service might be advantaged,
instead of keeping him out got him in, when the colonel
had prevailed with others to have indulged him with that ease
he desired. Mr. Hutchinson, after he had endeavoured to
decline this employment and could not, thought that herein,
as in other occasions, it being put upon him without his own
desire, God had called him to his service in councils as formerly in arms, and applied himself to this also, wherein he
did his duty faithfully, and employed his power to relieve the
oppressed and dejected, freely becoming the advocate of
those who had been his late enemies, in all things that were
just and charitable. Though he had now an opportunity to
have enriched himself, as it is to be feared some in all times
have done, by accepting rewards for even just assistances,

and he wanted not many who offered them and solicited him
therein, yet such was his generous nature that he abhorred
the mention of anything like reward, though ever so justly
merited ; and although he did a thousand highly obliging
kindnesses for many, both friends and enemies, he never had
anything in money or presents of any man.* The truth is,
on the contrary, he met with many that had not the good
manners to make so much as a civil verbal acknowledgment.
Among the rest one Sir John Owen may stand for a pillar of
ingratitude. This man was wholly unknown to him, and
with Duke Hamilton, the Earl of Holland, the Lord Capell,
and the Lord Goring, was condemned to death by a second
high court of justice. Of this, though the colonel was ro-
minated a commissioner, he would not sit, his unbloody
nature desiring to spare the rest of the delinquents, after the
highest had suffered, and not delighting in the death of men,
when they could live without cruelty to better men. The
parliament also was willing to show mercy to some of these,
and to execute others for example ; whereupon the whole
house was diversely engaged, some for one and some for
another of these lords, and striving to cast away those they
were not concerned in, that they might save their friends.
While there was such mighty labour and endeavour for
these lords, Colonel Hutchinson observed that no man spoke
for this poor knight ; and, sitting next to Colonel Ireton, he
expressed himself to him, and told him that it grieved him
much to see that, while all were labouring to save the lords,

* The lists of the first two councils, which embraced almost the whole
duration of the republic, are preserved by Whitelocke, and Colonel Hutchinson is in each of them ; he went out at the formation of the third. It
is extremely to be regretted, that Mrs. Hutchinson should have been so
concise in this part of her history, it being a period which naturally excites
much curiosity, but of which we have only indistinct, and, generally
speaking, invidious and partial accounts.

a gentleman, that stood in the same condemnation, should not find one friend to ask his life; " and so," said he, " am I moved with compassion that, if you will second me, I am resolved to speak for him, who, I perceive is a stranger and friendless." Ireton promised to second him, and accordingly, inquiring further of the man's condition, whether he had not a petition in any member's hand, he found that his keepers had brought one to the clerk of the house; but the man had not found any who would interest themselves for him, thinking the lords' lives of so much more concernment than this gentleman's. This the more stirred up the colonel's generous pity, and he took the petition, delivered it, spoke for him so nobly, and was so effectually seconded by Ireton, that they carried his pardon clear. Yet although one who knew the whole circumstance of the business, how Mr. Hutchinson, moved by mere compassion and generosity, had procured his life, told him, who admired his own escape, how it came about, yet he never was the man that so much as once came to give him thanks; nor was his fellow-prisoner Goring, for whom the colonel had also effectually solicited, more grateful.*

Some of the army, being very desirous to get amongst them a person of whose fidelity and integrity to the cause they had such good experience, had moved it to the general, my Lord Fairfax; who commanded to have it inquired in what way he would choose to be employed; and when he told

* This is differently represented by Whitelocke, Rapin, and Ludlow. Whitelocke simply says that he was reprieved; Rapin, that his sentence was suspended, because he should have been tried by an inferior court: and Ludlow, that Ireton moved the house in his favour, omitting Colonel Hutchinson either by negligence or design ; there is some reason to think it to nave been by the latter. Notwithstanding Colonel Hutchinson experienced ingratitude from many individuals, the general and collective sense of his justice and benevolence will be seen to have its full operation in his favour in the sequel.

them that, in regard of his family, which he would not willingly be much absent from, he should rather accept the government of some town than a field employment, four governments were brought to him, to select which he would have ;
whereof Plymouth and Portsmouth, and one more in the
west, being at a vast distance from his own country, he made
choice of Hull, in the north, though it was a less beneficial
charge than the other, thinking they had not offered him
anything but what had fairly fallen into their disposal.   Soon
after this, the lieutenant-general, Cromwell, desired him to
meet him one afternoon at a committee, where, when he
came, a malicious accusation against the governor of Hull
was violently prosecuted by a fierce faction in that town.
To this the governor had sent up a very fair and honest
defence, yet most of the committee, more favouring the adverse faction, were labouring to cast out the governor.   Col.
Hutchinson, though he knew him not, was very earnest in
his defence, whereupon Cromwell drew him aside, and asked
him what he meant by contending to keep in that governor ?
(it was Overton.)   The colonel told him, because he saw
nothing proved against him worthy of being ejected.   " But,"
said Cromwell, " we like him not."   Then said the colonel,
" Do it upon that account, and blemish not a man that is
innocent, upon false accusations, because you like him not."
" But," said Cromwell, " we would have him out, because
the government is designed for you, and except you put him
out you cannot have the place."   At this the colonel was
very angry, and with great indignation told him, if there was
no way to bring him into their army but by casting out others
unjustly, he would rather fall naked before his enemies, than
so seek to put himself into a posture of defence.   Then returning to the table, he so eagerly undertook the injured
governor's protection, that he foiled his enemies, and the
governor was confirmed in his place.   This so displeased

Cromwell that, as before, so much more now, he saw that as even his own interest would not bias him into any unjust faction, so he secretly laboured to frustrate the attempts of all others who, for the same reason that Cromwell laboured to keep him out, laboured as much to bring him in.

But now had the poison of ambition so ulcerated Cromwell's heart, that the effects of it became more apparent than before; and while as yet Fairfax stood an empty name, he was moulding the army to his mind, weeding out the godly and upright-hearted men, both officers and soldiers, and filling up their rooms with rascally turn-coat cavaliers, and pitiful sottish beasts of his own alliance, and other such as would swallow all things, and make no questions for conscience' sake. Yet this he did not directly nor in tumult, but by such degrees that it was unperceived by all that were not of very penetrating eyes; and those that made the loudest outcries against him lifted up their voices with such apparent envy and malice that, in that mist, they rather hid than discovered his ambitious minings. Among these, Colonel Rich and Commissary Staines and Watson had made a design even against his life, and the business was brought to the examination of the council of state. Before the hearing of it, Colonel Rich came to Colonel Hutchinson and implored his assistance with tears, affirming all the crimes of Cromwell, but not daring to justify his accusations, although the colonel advised him if they were true to stand boldly to it, if false to acknowledge his own iniquity. The latter course he took, and the council had resolved upon the just punishment of the men, when Cromwell, having only thus in a private council vindicated himself from their malice, and laid open what pitiful sneaking poor knaves they were, how ungrateful to him, and how treacherous and cowardly to themselves, became their advocate, and made it his suit that they might be no farther published or punished. This being permitted him, and tney thus rendered contemptible to others, they became beasts and slaves to him, who knew how to serve himself by them without trusting them. This generosity, for indeed he carried himself with the greatest bra very that is imaginable herein, much advanced his glory, and cleared him in the eyes of superficial beholders ; but others saw he creeped on, and could not stop him, while fortune itself seemed to prepare his way* on sundry occasions.   All this while he carried to Mr. Hutchinson the most open face, and made the most obliging professions of friend ship imaginable ; but the colonel saw through him, and forbore not often to tell him what was suspected of his ambition, what dissimulations of his were remarked, and how dishonourable to the name of God and the profession of religion, and destructive to the most glorious cause, and dangerous in overthrowing all our triumphs, these things which were suspected of him, would be, if true.   He would seem to receive these cautions and admonitions as the greatest demonstrations of integrity and friendship that could be made, and embrace the colonel in his arms, and make serious lying professions to him, and often inquire men's opinions concerning him, which the colonel never forbore to tell him plainly, although he knew he resented it not as he made show, yet it pleased him so to discharge his own thoughts.†

* By the admirers of Tacitus the development of this intrigue will be highly relished ; it aids likewise to confirm the remark that Cromwell's fort lay in watching and adroitly seizing opportunities, not in creating or inventing them. By the former method a man swims with the tide of human affairs, and is assisted by it; by the latter he must stem and encounter it.

† Men who think superficially will instantly proclaim the simplicity of Colonel Hutchinson and the shrewdness of Cromwell; those who think deeper, will in that simplicity see wisdom, in that shrewdness a more exquisite folly. In life, in death, and in reputation, which of these two was the happier !

The islanders of Jersey wanting a governor, and being acquainted, through the familiarity many of their countrymen had with him, with the abilities and honour of Colonel Hutchinson, they addressed themselves to my Lord General Fairfax, and petitioned to have him for their governor, which my lord assented to : and accordingly commanded a commission to be drawn up, which was done ; but the colonel made no haste to take it out. But my lord, having ordered the commission, regarded him as governor, and when the model of the castle was brought to my lord to procure orders and money for the repairing of the fortifications, he set it to the colonel, and all other business concerning the island.

In the meantime, the Scots having declared open war against the parliament of England, it was concluded to send an army into Scotland, to prevent their intended advance hither. But when they were just marching out, my Lord Fairfax, persuaded by his wife and her chaplains, threw up his commission at such a time, when it could not have been done more spitefully and ruinously to the whole parliament interest. Colonel Hutchinson and other parliament men, hearing of his intentions the night before, and knowing that he would thus level the way to Cromwell's ambitious designs, went to him and laboured to dissuade him; which they would 1ave effected, but that the presbyterian ministers wrought with nim to do it. He expressed his opinion that he believed God had laid him aside, as not being worthy of more, nor of that glory which was already given him.

To speak the truth of Cromwell, whereas many said he undermined Fairfax, it was false; for in Colonel Hutchinson's presence, he most effectually importuned him to keep his commission, lest it should discourage the army and the people at that juncture of time, but could by no means prevail, although he laboured for it almost all the night with most earnest endeavours.* But this great man was then as immovable by his friends as pertinacious in obeying his wife; whereby he then died to all his former glory, and became the monument of his own name, which every day wore out. When his commission was given up, Cromwell was made general, and new commissions were taken out by all the officers from him. He finding that Colonel Hutchinson's commission for the island was not taken out, and that he did **not** address himself to him, made haste to prevent the islanders, and gave a commission for the government to one of his own creatures. At this time the Lady Dormer being dead,

---

* Whitelocke tells the same story nearly in the same manner, but thinks Cromwell was not sincere : yet certainly he took all the same steps with those who were unquestionably so. How little soever Cromwell might wish to succeed, there was good policy in attending this conference, as it might in some degree serve to diminish the suspicions entertained of his own ambitious views, and prevent their being urged in argument to Fairfax, which if he had been absent they most likely would have been. Be this as it may, it may be truly said,

> *Ex illo fluere et retro sublapsi referri*
> *Res Danaum.*

for the true republicans or commonwealth's men,

> From thence the tide of fortune left their shore,
> And ebbed much faster than it flowed before.

For it was only with the co-operation of a man, who to his martial talents, which certainly exceeded all of his time, added that moderation and integrity, which will distinguish Fairfax to the end of time, that the great politicians of those days could have planned and finished such schemes of representation, legislation, and administration, as would have rendered the nation great and happy, either as a commonwealth or mixed government. They had in some respects such opportunities as never can again arise; and if the presbyterians have nothing else to answer for, the perverting the judgment of this excellent man was a fault never to be forgiven; if the ruin of their own cause could expiate it, they were not long before they made atonement.

had left to her grandchild, the Lady Anne Somerset, a papist,
daughter to the Marquess of Worcester, a manor in Leicestershire, which the lady, being more desirous of a portion in
money, had a great mind to sell, and came and offered it to
Colonel Hutchinson, with whom she had some alliance; but
he told her he was not in a purchasing condition, whereupon
she earnestly begged him, that if he would not buy it himself, he would procure of the parliament leave for her to sell
it. This he moved for and was repulsed, whereupon both the
lady, and one that was her priest, who negotiated for her,
and other friends, most earnestly solicited Colonel Hutchinson to buy it; who urging that he had not money for such a
purchase, they offered him time for payment, till he could sell
his own land, and assured him it should be such a pennyworth, that he should not repent the selling his own land to
buy it. He urged to them the trouble and difficulty it would
be to obtain it, and that it might so fall that he must lay a
weight upon it, more than the thing would be worth to him,
he having never yet made any request to the house, and
having reason to expect recompences for the loss of his estate,
as well as others. But my lady still importuned him, promising a pennyworth in it, that should countervail the difficulty and the trouble; whereupon, at the last, he contracted
with her, upon the desire both of her and her brother, the
Lord Herbert, who was her next heir, and was then at full
age, and he gave a release of all claim to it, under his hand
and seal; and my lady, being between nineteen and twenty
years old, then passed a fine, and covenanted at her coming
to full age to pass another, and absolutely bargained and sold
the land to Colonel Hutchinson, who secured the price of it
to the Marquess of Dorchester, whom the lady and her friends
had a great hope and desire to compass for a husband, and
had thoughts, that when the portion was secured in his hands,
it would be easily effected. This they afterwards entrusted

to Colonel Hutchinson, and desired his assistance to propound the business to my lord, as from himself, out of mutual well-wishes to both parties; but my lord would not hearken to it, though the colonel, willing to do her a kindness, endeavoured to persuade him, as much as was fitting. In the meantime the colonel could not, by all the friends and interest he had in the house, procure a composition and leave for my lady to sell her land, because they said it would be a precedent to other papists, and some moved, that what service he had done, and what he had lost, might be some other way con· sidered, rather than this should be suffered. But he vigorously pursuing it, and laying all the weight of all his merits and sufferings upon it, all that he could obtain at last was, to be himself admitted, in his own name, for taking off the seques-tration, after he had bought it, which he did; and they took two thousand pounds of him for his composition. By the interest of Sir Henry Vane and several others of his friends, powerful in the house, this too was with much difficulty wrought out, though violently opposed by several others. Of these Major-general Harrison was one, who, when he saw that he could not prevail, but that, through particular favour to Colonel Hutchinson, it was carried out by his friends; met the colonel after the rising of the house, and embracing him, desired him not to think he had acted from any personal opposition to him, but in his own judgment he had thought it fit the spoil should be taken out of the enemy's hands, and no composition admitted from idolaters. What-ever might be for a particular advantage to him, he envied not, but rejoiced in it, only he so dearly loved him, that he desired he would not set his heart upon the augmenting of outward estate, but upon the things of the approaching king-dom of God, concerning which he made a most pious and seemingly friendly harangue, of at least an hour long, with all the demonstrations of zeal to God and love to the colonel

that can by imagined.   But the colonel, having reason to fear
that he knew not his own spirit herein, made him only a short
reply, that he thanked him for his counsel, and should
endeavour to follow it, as became the duty of a Christian,
and should be glad to be as effectually instructed by his
example as by his admonition.   For at that time the major-
general, who was but a mean man's son, and of a mean
education, and of no estate before the war, had gathered an
estate of two thousand a year, besides engrossing great offices,
and encroaching upon his under-officers ; and maintained
his coach and family, at a height as if they had been born to
a principality.

About the same time a great ambassador from the King of
Spain was to have public audience in the house, and was the
first who had addressed them, owning them as a republic.
The day before his audience, Colonel Hutchinson was sitting
in the house, near some young men handsomely clad, among
whom was Mr. Charles Rich, since Earl of Warwick ; and
the colonel himself had on that day a habit which was pretty
rich but grave, and no other than he usually wore.   Harrison addressing himself particularly to him, admonished them all, that
now the nations sent to them, they should labour to shine
before them in wisdom, piety, righteousness, and justice, and
not in gold and silver and worldly bravery, which did not
become saints ; and that the next day when the ambassadors
came, they should not set themselves out in gorgeous habits,
which were unsuitable to holy professions.   The colonel,
although he was not convinced of any misbecoming bravery
in the suit he wore that day, which was but of sad-coloured
cloth trimmed with gold, and silver points and buttons ; yet
because he would not appear offensive in the eyes of religious
persons, the next day he went in a plain black suit, and so
did all the other gentlemen ; but Harrison came that day in
a scar'et coat and cloak, both laden with gold and silver lace,

and the coat so covered with clinquant (foil), that one scarcely
could discern the ground, and in this glittering habit he set
himself just under the speaker's chair; which made the
other gentlemen think that his godly speeches, the day
before, were but made that he alone might appear in the eyes
of strangers. But this was part of his weakness, the Lord at
last lifted him above these poor earthly elevations, which
then and some time afterwards prevailed too much with
him.*

After the colonel had bought my lady's land, some that
were extremely vexed at her having that sum of money, dealt
with the colonel to permit them to sequester it into his hands,
and offered him he should have it all himself; which, he told
them, he would be torn to pieces before he would do, and
that it was a treachery and villainy that he abhorred. Though,
notwithstanding this, he was much pressed yet he would not
yield, and to prevent force, which they threatened, after
moving in the house, how dangerous it was to suffer such
a sum of money to be in the hands of the daughter of an excepted person, especially at such a time (for now the king
was crowned in Scotland, and the Scots ready to invade,
and the presbyters to join with them), the colonel put the
money out of his own hands, to preserve it for my lady.
All that time both she and her brother, and other friends,
made all the acknowledgments of obligation that was possible. Not to confound stories, I finish the memorial of
this here.

After the parliament was broken up by Cromwell, and
after that my lady, seeing her project of marrying with my
lord Dorchester would not take, had embraced an offer of

* Ludlow gives very extraordinary accounts of his devotion to that which
he thought the cause of God, as well as of his readiness to suffer martyrdom
for it when it was in his power to avoid that severe trial.

Mr. Henry Howard, second son to the Earl of Arundel, and when, in the protector's time, the papists wanted not patrons, she began to repent the selling of her land, which before she thought such a blessing, and told her husband false stories, as he alleged, though his future carriage made it justly sus picious he was as unworthy as she.*

The colonel, presently after he had that land, had very much improved it, to a fourth part more than it was at when he bought it, and they, envying his good bargain, desired to have it again out of his hands, nor dealt fairly and directly in the thing, but employed a cunning person, Major Wildman, who was then a great manager of papists' interests, to get the land again, which he was to have four hundred pounds for, if he could do it. Whereupon he presently got money and came to the gentleman who had a mortgage upon it for three thousand pounds taken up to pay my lady, and tendered it. But Mr. Ash, a great friend of the colonel's, was so faithful that he would not accept it, and then Wildman began a chancery suit, thinking that the colonel, being out of favour with the present powers, would be necessitated to take any composition. When he had put the colonel to a great deal of vain charge, and found he could do no good, at last they desired to make up the business, and the lady and Mr. Howard passed a new fine to confirm the title, and the colonel was delivered from further trouble with them, till after the change and the return of the king. Then, when the parliament men began to come into question for their lives, my Lord of Portland and Mr. Howard came to Mrs. Hutchinson's lodgings three or four times, while she was out soliciting for her husband, and my lord left her a message,

---

* In the third vol. of Clarendon's State Papers, in a letter of his, dated August, 1655, he says, " Cromwell hypocritically pretends kindness to the catholics, but the levellers have real candour towards them, and are implacable enemies to Cromwell."

that he must needs speak with her, upon a business of much
concernment; whereupon she sought out my lord, knowing
that he had professed much kindness and obligation to her
husband, and thinking he might have some design now to
acknowledge it by some real assistance. But when she came
to him, he told her, her husband was in danger of his life,
and that if he would resign back Loseby to Mr. Howard, he
would help him to a good sum of money to fly, and Mr.
Howard would stand to the hazard of buying it; but she,
being vexed that my lord should interrupt her with this
frivolous proposition, told my lord that she would hazard it
with the rest of her estate, rather than make up such desperate bargains. When Mr. Howard saw this would not do,
he prepared a petition to get it excepted out of the act of oblivion, pretending that his wife being under age, the colonel
had by power and fraud wrested her out of her estate. But
when he showed this petition to his friends, they being informed of the falseness of the allegations, would none of
them undertake either to deliver or back it. Only one Sir
Richard Onslow, who was a violent man, and railed against
the colonel concerning it, but he not long afterwards died by
a blast of lightning. Others of his friends, when they understood that he himself had joined in the confirmation of
the fine, after the colonel had retired, in the protector's reign,
bade him for shame to make no more mention of his lady's
being fooled or frightened to an act which she had voluntary
done. Many told the colonel how unsafe it was to displease
a person who had so many powerful allies that might mischief him, but the colonel would neither be frightened nor
flattered to give away the estate, which when Mr. Howard found, he let fall his purpose, and made no more vain
endeavours.*

* How, when, or by whom this estate at Loseby was sold again, the

And now to return to his story where I left it. I shall not mention every particular action of his in the employment of a senator and councillor of the realms but only some which were more remarkable, to show the honour and excellency of his nature, among which this was one. His old opponents and enemies of the Nottingham committee had entered into the presbyterian conspiracy so deeply, that had they been brought to public trial, their lives would have been forfeited to the law, and this was discovered to him, and also that Colonel Pierrepont was the chief of them ; when he took care to have the business so managed, that Colonel Pierrepont was passed by in the information, and others so favourably accused, that they were only restrained from the mischief they intended, and kept prisoners till the danger was over, and afterwards, through his mediation released, without any further punishment on their persons and estates, though Chadwick's eldest son was one of these. For Colonel Pierrepont, he only privately admonished him, and endeavoured to reclaim him, which the man, being good-natured, was infinitely overcome with ; insomuch, that ever after, to his dying day, all his envy ceased, and he professed all imaginable friendship and kindness to the colonel. Indeed, his excellent gentleness was such, that he not only protected and saved these enemies, wherein there was some glory of passing by revenge, but was compassionately affected with the miseries of any poor women or children, who had been unfortunately, though deservedly, ruined in the civil war ; and

editor has not been able to discover, it never having come into the hands of his branch of the family, which purchased Owthorpe. One of the estates sold by Colonel Hutchinson in his lifetime, was that of Ratcliffe on Soar, which is spoken of in a note as given to Sir Thomas Hutchinson by his uncle Sacheverell ; the purchaser was Alderman Ireton, and it was, in all probability, sold to enable him jointly with the money borrowed of Mr Ash to purchase this estate.

without any interest of his own in the persons, whenever any
ruined family came to seek relief, when he was in power, he
was as zealous in assisting all such, as far as it might be
done with the safety of the commonwealth, as if they had
been his brothers. As it was a misery to be bewailed in those
days, that many of the parliament party exercised cruelty, injustice, and oppression to their conquered enemies; wherever
he discovered it he violently opposed it, and defended even
those enemies that were by might oppressed and defrauded
of the mercies of the parliament. Upon this account he had
contests with some good men, who were weak in these things,
some through too factious a zeal, and others blinded with
their own or their friends' interests. Among these Colonel
Hacker's father, having married my Lady Byron's mother,
was made a trustee for the estate of her son, which she had
by Strelley her first husband. He had about £1,800 of the
estate of young Strelley in his hands, which, he dying, his
eldest son and heir, Colonel Francis Hacker, was liable and
justly ought to pay. Young Strelley died in France, and
left his estate to his half-brother, the son of Sir Richard
Byron, who, all the time of the first war, was at school in
Colonel Hutchinson's garrison at Nottingham, and afterwards was sent into France. Being there, an infant, when
this estate fell to him, he returned and chose Colonel Hutchinson for his guardian, who overcame Colonel Hacker in the
right of his pupil, and recovered that money out of his
hands, which he would not have paid, if the infant had not
found a friend that was heartily zealous to obtain his just
right. Sir Arthur Haslerig was a great patron of Colonel
Hacker's, and laboured to bear him out against justice and
the infant's right in this thing; and when the colonel had
overcome him, they were both displeased; for Hacker, on
the other side, was such a creature of Sir Arthur's, that
without questioning justice or honesty, he was more diligent

2 A

in obeying Sir Arthur's than God's commands. Sir Allen
Apsley had articles at the surrender of Barnstaple, whereof
he was governor; and contrary to these he was put to vast
expense and horrible vexation by several persons, but especially by one wicked woman, who had the worst and the
smoothest tongue that ever her sex made use of to mischief.
She was handsome in her youth, and had very pretty girls
for her daughters, whom, when they grew up, she pros-
tituted for her revenge and malice against Sir Allen
Apsley, which was so venomous and devilish, that she stuck
not at inventing false accusations, and hiring witnesses to
swear to them, and a thousand other practices as enormous.
In those days there was a committee set up, for relief of such
as had any violation of their articles, and of this Bradshaw
was president; into whose easy faith this woman, pretending herself religious, and of the parliament's party, had so
insinuated herself, that Sir Allen's way of relief was obstructed.   Colonel Hutchinson, labouring mightily in his
protection, and often foiling this vile woman, and bringing
to light her devilish practices, turned the woman's spite into
as violent a tumult against himself; and Bradshaw was so
hot in abetting her, that he grew cool in his kindness to the
colonel, yet broke it not quite: but the colonel was very
much grieved that a friend should engage in so unjust an
opposition. At last it was manifest how much they were mistaken who would have assisted this woman upon a score of
her being on the parliament's side, for she was all this while a
spy for the king, and after his return, Sir Allen Apsley met
her in the king's chamber waiting for recompence for that
service.   The thing she sued Sir Allen Apsley for, was for a
a house of hers in the garrison of Barnstaple, which was
pulled down to fortify the town for the king, before he was
governor of the place.   Yet would she have had his articles
violated to make her a recompence out of his estate, treble

and more than the value of the house; pretending she was of the parliament's party, and that Sir Allen, in malice thereunto, had without necessity pulled down her house. All which were horrible lies, but so maliciously and so wickedly affirmed and sworn to by her mercenary witnesses, that they at first found faith, and it was hard for truth afterwards to over come that prepossession.

The colonel, prosecuting the defence of truth and justice in these and many more things, and abhorring all councils for securing the young commonwealth by cruelty and oppression of the vanquished, who had not laid down their hate, in delivering up their arms, and were, therefore, by some cowards, judged unworthy of the mercy extended to them,—the colonel, I say, disdaining such thoughts, displeased many of his own party, who in the main, we hope, might have been honest, although through divers temptations they were guilty of horrible slips, which did more offend the colonel's pure zeal, who more detested these sins in brethren than in enemies.

Now was Cromwell sole general, and marched into Scotland, and the Scots were ready to invade, and the presbyters to assist them in it. The army being small, there was a necessity for recruits, and the council of state, soliciting all the parliament-men that had interest to improve it in this exigence of time, gave Colonel Hutchinson a commission for a regiment of horse. He immediately got up three troops, well armed and mounted, of his own old soldiers, that thirsted to be again employed under him, and was preparing the rest of the regiment to bring them up himself; when he was informed, that as soon as his troops came into Scotland, Cromwell very readily received them, but would not let them march together, but dispersed them, to fill up the regiments of those who were more his creatures. The colonel hearing this, would not carry him any more, but rather employed himself in securing, as much as was necessary, his own country, for which he was sent down by the council of state, who at that time were very much surprized at hearing that the king of Scots was passed by Cromwell, and had entered with a great army into England.   Bradshaw himself, stouthearted as he was, privately could not conceal his fear ; some raged and uttered sad discontents against Cromwell, and suspicions of his fidelity ; they all considered that Cromwell was behind, of whom I think they scarce had any account, or of his intention, or how this error came about, to suffer the enemy to enter here, where there was no army to encounter him.   Both the city and country (by the angry presbyters, wavering in their constancy to them and the liberties they had purchased) were all amazed, and doubtful of their own and the commonwealth's safety.   Some could not hide very pale and unmanly fears, and were in such distraction of spirit, that it much disturbed their councils.   Colonel Hutchinson, who ever had most vigour and cheerfulness when there was most danger, encouraged them, as they were one day in a private council raging and crying out on Cromwell's miscarriages, to apply themselves to councils of safety, and not to lose time in accusing others, while they might yet provide to save the endangered realm ; or at least to fall nobly in defence of it, and not to yield to fear and despair.   These and such like things being urged, they at length re-collected themselves, and every man that had courage and interest in their counties, went down to look to them.*   Colonel Hutchinson came down into Nottinghamshire, and secured those

* The trepidation of the council of state, and the zeal with which they were supported, is well described by Whitelocke.   Whether Cromwell suffered the king to pass by him designedly or otherwise, is uncertain; but it is very likely that he did it by design, as knowing that those who did not like, for the same reason as Colonel Hutchinson, to send forces to him, would, for their own sakes, bring them forward to oppose the king.   Either his fortune or his judgment was great.

who were suspected as likely to make any commotion, and put the country into such a posture of defence as the time would permit. But it was not long before the king chose another way, and went to Worcester. Cromwell following swiftly after with his army, and more forces meeting him from several other parts, they fought with the king and his Scots, totally routed and subdued them, and he, with difficulty, after concealment in an oak, and many other shifts, stole away into France.

When the colonel heard how Cromwell used his troops, he was confirmed that he and his associates in the army were carrying on designs of private ambition, and resolved that none should share with them in the commands of the army or forts of the nation, but such as would be beasts, and be ridden upon by the proud chiefs. Disdaining, therefore, that what he had preserved, for the liberty of his country, should be a curb upon them, and foreseeing that some of Cromwell's creatures would at length be put in, to exercise him with continual affronts, and to hinder any man from standing up for the deliverance of the country, if the insolence of the army (which he too sadly foresaw) should put them upon it ; for this reason, in Cromwell's absence, he procured an order for the removal of the garrison at Nottingham, which was commanded by his kinsman Major Poulton, into the marching army, and for the demolishing of the place ; which accordingly was speedily executed.

When Major Poulton, who had all along been very faithful and active in the cause, brought his men to the army, he was entertained with such affronts and neglects by the general, that he voluntarily quitted his command, and retired to the ruined place, where the castle was which he had bought with his arrears.* When Cromwell came back through the country

* The machinations of Cromwell are spoken of in general terms by Rapin, Whitelocke, and others; but are nowhere so well detailed as here.

and saw the castle pulled down, he was heartily vexed at it, and told Colonel Hutchinson, that if he had been there when it was voted, he should not have suffered it. The colonel replied, that he had procured it to be done, and believed it to be his duty to ease the people of the charge, when there was no more need of it.

When Cromwell came to London, there wanted not some little creatures of his, in the house, who had taken notice of all that had been said of him when he let the king slip by ; how some stuck not in their fear and rage to call him traitor, and to threaten his head. These reports added spurs to his ambition, but his son-in-law, Ireton, deputy of Ireland, would not be wrought to serve him, but hearing of his machinations, determined to come over to England to endeavour to divert him from such destructive courses.*   But God

Of all things the most necessary to Cromwell was to obtain soldiers and subaltern officers perfectly subservient to his own purposes, but this he could hope to effect *then* and *then only*, when he had deprived them of such superior officers as would have preserved them from deception, and have kept them faithful to their country. The present and similar occurrences furnished him with the means so to do, which he employed most assiduously. Ludlow, vol. iii. p. 21. " And thus the troops of the parliament, which were not raised out of the meanest of the people and without distinction, as other armies had been, but consisted of such as had engaged themselves from a spirit of liberty in the defence of their rights and religion, were corrupted by him, kept as a standing force against the people, taught to forget their first engagements, and rendered as mercenary as other troops are accustomed to be." From about this period then we may date the change of sentiment of the army in general, and of course the change of opinion respecting them, in the minds of Colonel Hutchinson and others who before had sided with them.

* If this intention of Ireton is mentioned by any other person, it has escaped the search of the editor, it may have been known *with certainty* by Mr. Hutchinson alone; but something of the kind seems to have been in the *contemplation* of Whitelocke when he regrets his death, on account of the influence he had over the mind of Cromwell, which has been remarked in a former note; as likewise the probability that the prolongation of his

cut him short by death, and whether his body or an empty
coffin was brought into England, something in his name came
to London, and was to be, by Cromwell's procurement, mag-
nificently buried among the kings at Westminster.   Colonel
Hutchinson was, after his brother, one of the nearest kins-
men he had, but Cromwell, who of late studied to give him
neglects, passed him by, and neither sent him mourning, nor
particular invitation to the funeral, only the Speaker gave
public notice in the house, that all the members were desired
to attend it; and such was the flattery of many pitiful
lords and other gentlemen, parasites, that they put themselves into deep mourning; but Colonel Hutchinson that day
put on a scarlet cloak, very richly laced, such as he usually
wore, and coming into the room where the members were,
seeing some of the lords in mourning, he went to them to
inquire the cause, who told him they had put it on to honour
the general; and asked again, why he, that was a kinsman
was in such a different colour?   He told them, that because
the general had neglected sending to him, when he had sent
to many who had no alliance, only to make up the train, he
was resolved he would not flatter so much as to buy for himself, although he was a true mourner in his heart for his
cousin, whom he had ever loved, and would therefore go and
take his place among his mourners.   This he did, and went
into the room where the close mourners were; who seeing

life might have made a great difference in the conduct of Cromwell. What
is said of his funeral well agrees with what is said by Ludlow, who adds,
that " Ireton would have despised these pomps, having erected for himself
a more glorious monument in the hearts of good men, by his affection to
his country, his abilities of mind, his impartial justice, his diligence in the
public service, and his other virtues, which were a far greater honour to his
memory than a dormitory among the ashes of kings; who, for the most
part, as they had governed others by their passions, so were they as much
governed by them." For the rest, Colonel Hutchinson's reproof of Cromwell was a pithy one.

him come in, as different from mourning as he could make
himself, the alderman came to him, making a great apology
that they mistook and thought he was out of town, and had
much injured themselves thereby, to whom it would have
been one of their greatest honours to have had his assistance
in the befitting habit, as now it was their shame to have neglected him. But Cromwell, who had ordered all things, was
piqued horribly at it, though he dissembled his resentment
at that time, and joined in excusing the neglect; but he very
well understood that the colonel neither out of ignorance nor
niggardness came in that habit, but publicly to reproach their
neglects.

After the death of Ireton, Lambert was voted deputy of
Ireland, and commander-in-chief there, who being at that
time in the north, was exceedingly elevated with the honour,
and courted all Fairfax's old commanders, and other gentlemen; who, upon his promises of preferment, quitted their
places, and many of them came to London and made him up
there a very proud train, which still more exalted him, so
that too soon he put on the prince, immediately laying out
five thousand pounds for his own particular equipage, and
looking upon all the parliament-men, who had conferred this
honour on him, as underlings, and scarcely worth such a great
man's nod. This untimely declaration of his pride gave
great offence to the parliament, who having only given him
a commission for six months for his deputyship, made a vote
that, after the expiration of that time, the presidency of the
civil and military power of that nation should no more be
in his nor in any one man's hands again. This vote was
upon Cromwell's procurement, who hereby designed to make
way for his new son-in-law, Colonel Fleetwood, who had
married the widow of the late deputy Ireton. There went a
story that as my Lady Ireton was walking in St. James's
park, the Lady Lambert, as proud as her husband, came by

where she was, and as the present princess always hath presidency of the relict of the dead prince, so she put my Lady
Ireton below; who, notwithstanding her piety and humility,
was a little grieved at the affront.   Colonel Fleetwood being
then present, in mourning for his wife, who died at the
same time her lord did, took occasion to introduce himself,
and was immediately accepted by the lady and her father,
who designed thus to restore his daughter to the honour
she had fallen from.   Cromwell's plot took as well as he
himself could wish ; for Lambert, who saw himself thus cut
off from half his exaltation, sent the house an insolent
message, " that if they found him so unworthy of the honour
they had given him as so soon to repent it, he would not
retard their remedy for six months, but was ready to surrender their commission before he entered into his office."
They took him at his word, and made Fleetwood deputy,
and Ludlow commander of the horse ; whereupon Lambert,
with a heart full of spite, malice, and revenge, retreated to
his palace at Wimbledon, and sat there watching an opportunity to destroy the parliament.

Cromwell, although he chiefly wrought this business in the
house, yet flattered Lambert, and, having another ambitious
scheme in his breast, helped to inflame Lambert against those
of the parliament who were not his creatures, and cast the
odium of his disgrace upon them, and professed his own
clearness of it, and pity for him, that he should be drawn into
such an inconvenience as the charge of putting himself into
equipage, and the loss of all that provision ; which Cromwell,
pretending generosity, took all upon his own account, and
delivered him from the debt.   Lambert dissembled again on
his part, and insinuated himself into Cromwell, fomenting his
ambition to take the administration of all the conquered
nations into his own hands; but finding themselves not
strong enough alone, they took to them Major-general Har-

rison, who had a great interest both in the army and the church; and these, pretending to be piously tro bled that there were such delays in the administration of justice, and such perverting of right, endeavoured to bring all good men into dislike of the parliament, pretending that they would perpetuate themselves in their honours and offices, and had no care to bring in those glorious things for which they had so many years contended in blood and toil. The parliament, on the other side, had now, by the blessing of God, restored the commonwealth to such a happy, rich, and plentiful condition, that it was not so flourishing before the war, and although the taxes that were paid were great, yet the people were rich and able to pay them: they (*the parliament*) were in a way of paying all the soldiers' arrears, had some hundred thousand pounds in their purses, and were free from enemies in arms within and without, except the Dutch, whom they had beaten and brought to seek peace upon terms honourable to the English: and now they thought it was time to sweeten the people, and deliver them from their burdens. This could not be but by disbanding the unnecessary officers and soldiers, and when things were thus settled, they had prepared a bill to put a period to their own sitting, and provide for new successors. But when the great officers understood that they were to resign their honours, and no more triumph in the burdens of the people, they easily induced the inferior officers and soldiers to set up for themselves with them; and while these things were passing, Cromwell with an armed force, assisted by Lambert and Harrison, came into the house and dissolved the parliament, pulling out the members, foaming and raging, and calling them undeserved and base names; and when the Speaker refused to come out of his chair, Harrison plucked him out. These gentlemen having done this, took to themselves the administration of all things; a few slaves of the house consulted with them and would have

truckled under them, but not many. Meanwhile they and
their soldiers could no way palliate their rebellion, but by
making false criminations of the parliament-men, as that they
meant to perpetuate themselves in honour and office, that they
had gotten vast estates, and perverted justice for gain, and
were imposing upon men for conscience, and a thousand such
like things, which time manifested to be false, and truth
retorted all upon themselves that they had injuriously cast at
the others.*

At the time that the parliament was broken up Colonel

* Almost all the historical writers who have treated of these times concur in deprecating this parliament, and represent them as a small number
or junto whose principal view was to perpetuate themselves in the enjoyment of power and honours. Those readers who desire to form a true
judgment of this matter will be materially assisted by comparing the passages here before them with Whitelocke, and more particularly with the
first twenty pages of the second volume of Ludlow ; they will find that
sort of consonance which is the best mark of truth, viz. the recital of different circumstances tending to establish one and the same principal fact.
They will then be convinced that the great men who were at that time at
the head of affairs had conducted them in a manner worthy of themselves, and had brought the nation to a state of prosperity which nothing
less than a miracle can ever again bring it to, and which Mrs. Hutchinson
describes in few and simple, but impressive words ; *the people rich, the revenue great, debts paid, money in their purses, free from enemies within
and without.* They had concluded with reforming the abuses of the law,
and providing for their being succeeded by a fair and equal representation
of the people, which all confess still to be the grand desideratum of our
constitution. And it was the very circumstance of the act being on the anvil,
ready to receive the finishing stroke, that obliged Cromwell to act with
such precipitation as staggered his confederates.

From all which will arise these corollaries or deductions ; that a state,
however great, may be governed by a republican form, and every department properly filled and administered. But that no sufficient barrier has
yet been found against a military chief, who has popularity, address, and
ambition, to become the tyrant of it. And in the end, recourse must be
had to hereditary succession, from whence they at first departed.

Hutchinson was in the country, where, since his going in his course out of the council of state, he had for about a year's time applied himself, when the parliament could dispense with his absence, to the administration of justice in the country, and to the putting in execution those wholesome laws and statutes of the land provided for the orderly regulation of the people. And it was wonderful how, in a short space, he reformed several abuses and customary neglects in that part of the country where he lived, which being a rich fruitful vale, drew abundance of vagrant people to come and exercise the idle trade of wandering and begging; but he took such courses that there was very suddenly not a beggar left in the country, and all the poor in every town were so maintained and provided for, that they were never so liberally maintained and relieved before or since. He procured unnecessary alehouses to be put down in all the towns, and if any one that he heard of suffered any disorder or debauchery in his house, he would not suffer him to brew any more. He was a little severe against drunkenness, for which the drunkards would sometimes rail at him; but so much were all the children of darkness convinced by his light, that they were more in awe of his virtue than his authority. In this time he had made himself a convenient house,* whereof he was the

* Pained and disgusted as the mind of the reader must be with the tumults, anarchy, and crimes, it has witnessed, how welcome is the contemplation of this ease and leisure, devoted to elegant studies, virtuous pursuits, useful occupations, gentlemanlike amusements, rational converse, and conciliating hospitality ! How difficult will it be to him to believe that this *otium cum dignitate* is the honourable retreat of one of those *gloomy fanatics* whose tyranny, Rapin says, had become intolerable to the nation !

About thirty years ago it was the fate of the editor to visit this mansion of his ancestors, in order to bring away a few pictures and some books, all that remained to him of those possessions, where they had lived with so much merited love and nonour. Although he had not then read these

best ornament, and an example of virtue so prevailing, as metamorphosed many evil people, while they were under his roof, into another appearance of sobriety and holiness.

memoirs, yet having heard Colonel Hutchinson spoken of as an extraordinary person, and that he had built, planted, and formed, all that was to be seen there; the country adjoining being a dreary waste, many thousand acres together being entirely overrun with gorse or furze; he viewed the whole with the utmost attention.   He found there a house, of which he has the drawing, large, handsome, lofty, and convenient, and though but little ornamented, possessing all the grace that size and symmetry could give it. The entrance was by a flight of handsome steps into a large hall, occupying entirely the centre of the house, lighted at the entrance by two large windows, but at the further end by one much larger, in the expanse of which was carried up a staircase that seemed to be perfectly in the air.   On one side of the hall was a long table, on the other a large fire place; both suited to ancient hospitality.   On the right hand side of this hall were three handsome rooms for the entertainment of guests.   The sides of the staircase and gallery were hung with pictures, and both served as an orchestra either to the hall or to a large room over part of it, which was a ball room. To the left of the hall were the rooms commonly occupied by the family. All parts were built so substantially, and so well secured, that neither fire nor thieves could penetrate from room to room, nor from one flight of stairs to another, if ever so little resisted.

The house stood on a little eminence in the vale of Belvoir, at a small distance from the foot of those hills along which the Roman fosse-way from Leicester runs.   The western side of the house was covered by the offices, a small village, and a church, interspersed with many trees.   The south, which was the front of entrance, looked over a large extent of grass grounds which were the demesne, and were bounded by hills covered with wood which Colonel Hutchinson had planted.   On the eastern side, the entertaining rooms opened on to a terrace, which encircled a very large bowling-green or level lawn; next to this had been a flower-garden, and next to that a shrubbery, now become a wood, through which vistas were cut to let in a view of Langar, the seat of Lord Howe, at two miles', and of Belvoir Castle, at seven miles' distance, which, as the afternoon sun sat full upon it, made a glorious object : at the further end of this small wood was a spot (of about ten acres) which appeared to have been a morass, and through which an a rivulet: this spot Colonel Hutchinson had dug into a great number of canals, and planted the ground between them leaving room for walks, so

He was going up to attend the business of nis counsry
above, when news met him upon the road, near London, that
Cromwell had broken the parliament. Notwithstanding, ne
went on and found divers of the members there, resolved to
submit to this providence of God, and to wait till he should
clear their integrity, and to disprove those people who had
taxed them of ambition, by sitting still, when they had friends
enough in the army, city, and country, to have disputed the

that the whole formed at once a wilderness or bower, reservoirs for fish, and
a decoy for wild fowl.   To the north, at some hundred yards distance, was
a lake of water, which, filling the space between two quarters of wood land,
appeared, as viewed from the large window of the hall, like a moderate
river, and beyond this the eye rested on the wolds or high wilds which
accompany the fosse-way towards Newark.   The whole had been deserted
near forty years, but resisted the ravages of time so well as to discover the
masterly hand by which it had been planned and executed.   But the most
extraordinary and gratifying circumstance was the veneration for the family
which still subsisted, and which, at the period when the last possessor had
by his will ordered this and all his estates in Nottinghamshire to be sold,
and the produce given to *strangers*, induced the tenants to offer a large
advance of their rents, and a good share of the money necessary for purchasing the estates, in order to enable the remains of the family to come
and reside again among them.   It was too late ! the steward had contracted
with the executors, and resold the most desirable part, whereof the timber of
Colonel Hutchinson's planting was valued at many thousand pounds !   The
Editor could only retire repeating Virgil's first Eclogue :

> *Nos patriæ fines, nos dulcia linquimus arva.*
>   *   *   *   *
>
> *Impius hæc tam culta no—alia miles habebit ?*
> *Barbarus has segetes ?   En, quo discordia cives*
> *Perduxit miseros ! en, queis consevimus agros.*
>
> Round the wide world in banishment we roam,
> Forced from our pleasing fields and native home:
> Did we for these barbarians plant and sow,
> On these, on these our happy fields bestow ?
> Good heavens ! what dire effects from civil discord flow '
>
>   DRYDEN.

matter, and probably to have vanquished these usurpers. They thought that if they should vex the land by war among themselves, the late subdued enemies, royalists and presbyterians, would have an opportunity to prevail on their dissensions, to the ruin of both : if these should govern well, and righteously, and moderately, they would enjoy the benefit of their good government, and not envy them the honourable toil ; if they did otherwise, they should be ready to assist and vindicate their oppressed country, when the ungrateful people were made sensible of their true champions and protectors.   Colonel Hutchinson, in his own particular, was very glad of this release from that employment, which he managed with fidelity and uprightness, but not only without delight, but with a great deal of trouble and expense, in the contest for truth and righteousness upon all occasions.

The only recreation he had during his residence at London was in seeking out all the rare artists he could hear of, and in considering their works in paintings, sculptures, gravings, and all other such curiosities, insomuch that he became a great virtuoso and patron of ingenuity.   Being loth that the land should be disfurnished of all the rarities that were in it, whereof many were set for sale from the king's and divers noblemen's collections, he laid out about two thousand pounds in the choicest pieces of painting, most of which were bought out of the king's goods, which had been given to his servants to pay their wages : to them the colonel gave ready money, and bought such good pennyworths, that they were valued at much more than they cost.*   These he brought down into

* That the conduct of Colonel Hutchinson differed from that of most other men in power at that time, and brought a seasonable relief to the king's servants and creditors, appears from two passages in the History of Independency, p. 146 and 184.   " The king's servants and creditors starve for want of their own, while the members appropriate his furniture to their own use instead of selling it to pay debts."   " The king's servants and

the country, intending a very neat cabinet for them; and these, with the surveying of his buildings, and improving by inclosure the place he lived in, employed him at home, and, for a little time, his hawks employed him abroad; but when a very sober fellow, that never was guilty of the usual vices of that generation of men, rage and swearing, died, he gave over his hawks, and pleased himself with music, and again fell to the practice of his viol, on which he played excellently well, and entertaining tutors for the diversion and education of his children in all sorts of music, he pleased himself with these innocent recreations during Oliver's mutable reign. As he had great delight, so he had great judgment, in music, and advanced his children's practice more than their tutors: he also was a great supervisor of their learning, and indeed was himself a tutor to them all, besides all those tutors whom he liberally entertained in his house for them. He spared not any cost for the education of both his sons and daughters in languages, sciences, music, dancing, and all other qualities befitting their father's house. He was himself their instructor in humility, sobriety, and in all godliness and virtue, which he rather strove to make them exercise with love and delight than by constraint. As other things were his delight, this only he made his business, to attend to the education of his children, and the government of his own house and town. This he performed so well that never was any man more feared and loved than he by all his domestics, tenants, and hired workmen. He was loved with such a fear and reverence as restrained all rude familiarity and insolent presumptions in those who were under him, and he was feared with so much love that they all delighted to do his pleasure.

As he maintained his authority in all relations, so he en-

creditors may gape long enough before they sell the king's goods to pay debts."

deavoured to make their subjection pleasant to them, and
rather to convince them by reason than compel them to obedience, and would give way even to the lowest of his family
to make them enjoy their lives in sober cheerfulness, and not
to find their duties burdensome.

As for the public business of the country, he would not act
in any office under the protector's power, and therefore confined himself to his own, which the whole country about him
were grieved at, and would rather come to him for counsel as
a private neighbour than to any of the men in power for
greater help.

He being now reduced into an absolutely private condition,
was very much courted and visited by those of all parties, and
while the grand quarrel slept, and both the victors and vanquished were equal slaves under the new usurpers, there was
a very kind correspondence between him and all his countrymen.   As he was very hospitable, and his conversation no
less desirable and pleasant, than instructive and advantageous, his house was much resorted to, and as kindly open to
those who had in public contests been his enemies, as to his
continued friends ; for there never lived a man that had less
malice and revenge, nor more reconcilableness and kindness
and generosity in his nature, than he.

In the interim Cromwell and his army grew wanton with
their power, and invented a thousand tricks of government,
which, when nobody opposed, they themselves fell to dislike
and vary every day.   First he calls a parliament out of his
own pocket, himself naming a sort of godly men for every
county, who meeting and not agreeing, a part of them, in the
name of the people, gave up the sovereignty to him.   Shortly
after he makes up several sorts of mock parliaments, but
not finding one of them absolutely to his turn. turned them
them off again.   He soon quitted himself of his triumvirs,
and first thrust out Harrison, then took away Lambert's com-

mission, and would have been king but for fear of quitting
his generalship.   He weeded, in a few months' time, above a
hundred and fifty godly officers out of the army, with whom
many of the religious soldiers went off, and in their room
abundance of the king's dissolute soldiers were entertained;
and the army was almost changed from that godly religious
army, whose valour God had crowned with triumph, into the
dissolute army they had beaten, bearing yet a better name.
His wife and children were setting up for principality, which
suited no better with any of them than scarlet on the ape;
only, to speak the truth of himself, he had much natural
greatness, and well became the place he had usurped.   His
daughter Fleetwood was humbled, and not exalted with
these things, but the rest were insolent fools.   Claypole,
who married his daughter, and his son Henry, were two debauched, ungodly cavaliers.   Richard was a peasant in his
nature, yet gentle and virtuous, but became not greatness.
His court was full of sin and vanity, and the more abominable, because they had not yet quite cast away the name of
God, but profaned it by taking it in vain upon them.
True religion was now almost lost, even among the religious
party, and hypocrisy became an epidemical disease, to the
sad grief of Colonel Hutchinson, and all true-hearted Christians and Englishmen.   Almost all the ministers everywhere fell in and worshipped this beast, and courted and
made addresses to him.   So did the city of London, and
many of the degenerate lords of the land, with the poor-
spirited gentry.   The cavaliers, in policy, who saw that while
Cromwell reduced all by the exercise of tyrannical power
under another name, there was a door opened for the restoring of their party, fell much in with Cromwell, and heightened all his disorders.   He at last exercised such an arbitrary power, that the whole land grew weary of him, while
he set up a company of silly, mean fellows, called major-

generals as governors in every country. These ruled according to their wills, by no law but what seemed good in their own eyes, imprisoning men, obstructing the course of justice between man and man, perverting right through partiality, acquitting some that were guilty, and punishing some that were innocent as guilty. Then he exercised another project to raise money, by decimation of the estates of all the king's party, of which action it is said Lambert was the instigator. At last he took upon himself to make lords and knights, and wanted not many fools, both of the army and gentry, to accept of, and strut in, his mock titles.* Then the Earl of Warwick's grandchild and the Lord Falconbridge married his two daughters; such pitiful slaves were the nobles of those days. At last Lambert, perceiving him-

* The description given of the usurpations of Cromwell and his myrmidons, concise and contemptuous as it is, will be found perfectly just. With all his professions he did little else but deteriorate that state of things in which the parliament had left them: he patched up a much worse peace with the Dutch than the parliament would have made : to gratify or serve his personal views, he assisted the French against the Spaniards, and for ever weakened that power which would now have supported this nation against so dangerous a neighbour. Ireland he depopulated by encouraging the cavalier chiefs to emigrate with their adherents into foreign services. At home he rendered the very names of religion and liberty contemptible, and paved the way for the return of the Stuarts. Mrs Hutchinson mentions nothing of a circumstance which perhaps she did not know, or if she did, passed it over as beneath notice. The following letter shows the nature of it :—

Thurloe's State Papers, vol. iv. p. 299, Major-general Whalley writes to the protector : " For the town of Nottingham, I have a great influence upon it ; they will not choose any without my advice. The honest part of the county have of late, which I much wonder at, nominated Colonel Hutchinson to me, as not knowing upon whom better to pitch, to make up the fourth man, he having satisfied some of them concerning his judgment of the present government ; but I hope what I have hinted to them will cause them to think upon some other."

self to have been all this while deluded with hopes and promises of succession, and seeing that Cromwell now intended to confirm the government in his own family, fell off from him; but behaved himself very pitifully and meanly, was turned out of all his places, and returned again to plot now vengeance at his house at Wimbledon, where he fell to dress his flowers in his garden, and work at the needle with his wife and his maids, while he was watching an opportunity to serve again his ambition, which had this difference from the protector's; the one was gallant and great, the other had nothing but an unworthy pride, most insolent in prosperity, and as abject and base in adversity.*

The cavaliers, seeing their victors thus beyond their hopes falling into their hands, had not patience to stay till things ripened of themselves, but were every day forming designs, and plotting for the murder of Cromwell, and other insurrections, which being contrived in drink, and managed by false and cowardly fellows, were still revealed to Cromwell, who had most excellent intelligence of all things that passed, even in the king's closet; and by these unsuccessful plots they were only the obstructors of what they sought to advance, while, to speak truth, the Cromwell's personal courage and magnanimity upheld him against all enemies and malcontents. His own army disliked him, and once when sevenscore officers had combined to cross him in something he was pursuing, and engaged one to another, Lambert being the chief, with solemn promises and invocations to God, the

* A Life of Lambert has been very obligingly put into the hands of the editor, together with some other scarce tracts relating to those times by Mr. White, jun., of Lincoln's Inn, who had collected them in the north of England, where Lambert resided. He seems to have enjoyed a better reputation among his countrymen: his horticulture is therein much spoken of, and he is said to have *painted* flowers, not to have *embroidered* them.

protector hearing of it, overawed them all, and told them, " it was not they who upheld him, but he them," and rated them, and made them understand what pitiful fellows they were; whereupon, they all, like rated dogs, clapped their tails between their legs, and begged his pardon, and left Lambert to fall alone, none daring to own him publicly, though many in their hearts wished him the sovereignty. Some of the Lambertonians had at that time a plot to come with a petition to Cromwell, and, while he was reading it, certain of them had undertaken to cast him out of a window at Whitehall that looked upon the Thames, where others would be ready to catch him up in a blanket if he escaped breaking his neck, and carrying him away in a boat prepared for the purpose, to kill or keep him alive, as they saw occasion, and then to set up Lambert. This was so carried on that it was near its execution before the protector knew anything of it. Colonel Hutchinson being at that time at London, by chance came to know all the plot. Certain of the conspirators coming into a place where he was, and not being so cautious of their whispers to each other before him, but that he apprehended something ; by making use of which to others of the confederates, he at last found out the whole matter, without having it committed to him as a matter of trust, but which, carelessly thrown down in pieces before him, he gathered together, and became perfectly acquainted with the whole design; and weighing it, and judging that Lambert would be the worse tyrant of the two, he determined to prevent it, without being the author of any man's punishment. Hereupon, having occasion to see Fleetwood (for he had never seen the protector since his usurpation, but publicly declared his testimony against it to all the tyrants' minions), he bade Fleetwood wish him to have a care of petitioners, by whom he apprehended danger to his life. Fleetwood desired more particular information, but the colonel was resolved he would give him no more than to prevent that enterprise which he disliked. For indeed those who were deeply engaged rather waited to see the cavaliers in arms against him, which they thought would be the best time to arm for their own defence, and either to make a new conquest, or fall with swords in their hands. Therefore, they all connived at the cavaliers' attempts, and although they joined not with them, would not have been sorry to have seen them up upon equal terms with the protector, that then a third party, which was to be ready both with arms and men, when there was an opportunity, might have fallen in and capitulated, with swords in their hands, for the settlement of the rights and liberties of the good people : but God had otherwise determined things; and now men began so to flatter with this tyrant, so to apostatise from all faith, honesty, religion, and English liberty, and there was such a devilish practice of trepanning grown in fashion, that it was not safe to speak to any man in those treacherous days.

After Colonel Hutchinson had given Fleetwood that caution, he was going into the country, when the protector sent to search him out with all the earnestness and haste that could possibly be, and the colonel went to him; who met him in one of the galleries, and received him with open arms and the kindest embraces that could be given, and complained that the colonel should be so unkind as never to give him a visit, professing how welcome he should have been, the most welcome person in the land, and with these smooth insinuations led him along to a private place, giving him thanks for the advertisement he had received from Fleetwood, and using all his art to get out of the colonel the knowledge of the persons engaged in the conspiracy against him. But none of his cunning, nor promises, nor flatteries, could prevail with the colonel to inform him more than he thought necessary to prevent the execution of the design, which when the pro-

lector perceived, he gave him most infinite thanks for what
he had told him, and acknowledged it opened to him some
mysteries that had perplexed him, and agreed so with other
intelligence he had, that he must owe his preservation to
him : " But," says he, " dear colonel, why will not you come
in and act among us ?"   The colonel told him plainly, because
he liked not any of his ways since he broke up the parliament,
being those which would lead to certain and unavoidable
destruction, not only of themselves, but of the whole parliament party and cause ; and thereupon took occasion, with
his usual freedom, to tell him into what a sad hazard all
things were placed, and how apparent a way was made for
the restitution of all former tyranny and bondage.   Cromwell seemed to receive this honest plainness with the greatest
affection that could be, and acknowledged his precipitateness
in some things, and with tears complained how Lambert had
put him upon all those violent actions, for which he now accused him and sought his ruin.   He expressed an earnest
desire to restore the people's liberties, and to take and pursue
more safe and sober councils, and wound up all with a very
fair courtship of the colonel to engage with him, offering him
anything he would account worthy of him.   The colonel
told him, he could not be forward to make his own advantage, by serving to the enslaving of his country.   The other
told him, he intended nothing more than the restoring and
confirming the liberties of the good people, in order to which
he would employ such men of honour and interest as the
people would rejoice in, and he should not refuse to be one
of them.   And after he had endeavoured, with all his arts,
to excuse his public actions, and to draw in the colonel,
who again had taken the opportunity to tell him freely his
own and all good men's discontents and dissatisfactions, he
dismissed the colonel with such expressions as were publicly taken notice of by all his little courtiers then about

him, when he went to the end of the gallery with the colonel; and there, embracing him, said aloud to him, "Well, colonel, satisfied or dissatisfied, you shall be one of us, for we can no longer exempt a person so able and faithful from the public service, and you shall be satisfied in all honest things." The colonel left him with that respect that became the place he was in ; when immediately the same courtiers, who had some of them passed by him without knowing him when he came in, although they had once been of his familiar acquaintance, and the rest, who had looked upon him with such disdainful neglect as little people use to those who are not of their faction, now flocked about him, striving who should express most respect, and, by an extraordinary officiousness, redeem their late slightings. Some of them desired he would command their service in any business he had with their lord, and a thousand such frivolous compliments, which the colonel smiled at, and quitting himself of them as soon as he could, made haste to return to the country. There he had not been long before he was informed, that notwithstanding all these fair shows, the protector, finding him too constant to be wrought upon to serve his tyranny, had resolved to secure his person, lest he should head the people, who now grew very weary of his bondage. But though it was certainly confirmed to the colonel how much he was afraid of his honesty and freedom, and that he was resolved not to let him be any longer at liberty, yet before his guards apprehended the colonel, death imprisoned himself, and confined all his vast ambition and all his cruel designs into the narrow compass of a grave. His army and court substituted his eldest son, Richard, in his room, who was a meek, temperate, and quiet man, but had not a spirit fit to succeed his father, or to manage such a perplexed government.

The people, being vexed with the pocket-parliaments and the major-generals of the counties, who behaved like bashaws,

were now all muttering to have a free parliament, after the old
manner of elections, without pledging those that were chosen
to any terms.   Those at Richard's court, that knew his
father's counsels to prevent Colonel Hutchinson from being
chosen in his own country, advised Richard to prick him
for sheriff of the county of Nottingham, which as soon as
the colonel understood, he wrote him a letter, declaring his
resentment in such a civil manner as became the person.
Richard returned a very obliging answer, denying any intention in himself to show the least disfavour to him for former
dissents, but rather a desire to engage his kindness.   And
soon after, when the colonel went himself to London and
went to the young protector, he told him, that since God had
called him to the government, it was his desire to make men
of uprightness and interest his associates, to rule by their
counsels and assistance, and not to enslave the nation to an
army; and that if by them he had been put upon anything prejudicial or disobliging to the colonel in pricking him for sheriff,
he should endeavour to take it off, or to serve him any other
way, as soon as he had disentangled himself from the officers
of the army, who at present constrained him in many things;
and therefore if the colonel would please, without unkindness, to exercise this office, he should receive it as an obligation, and seek one more acceptable to him afterwards.   The
colonel, seeing him herein good-natured enough, was persuaded by a very wise friend of his to take it upon him, and
returned well enough satisfied with the courteous usage of
the protector.   This gentleman who had thus counselled the
colonel, was as considerable and as wise a person as any in
England, who did not openly appear among Richard's adherents or counsellors, but privately advised him, and had a
very honourable design of bringing the nation into freedom
under this young man; who was so flexible to good counsels,
that there was nothing desirable in a prince which might not

have been hoped for in him, but a great spirit and a just title ;
the first of which sometimes doth more hurt than good in a
sovereign ; the latter would have been supplied by the
people's deserved approbation. This person was very free
in imparting to the colonel all the designs of settling the
state under this single person, and the hopes of felicity in
such an establishment. The colonel, debating this with him,
told him, that if ever it were once fixed in a single person, and the army taken off, which could not consist with
the liberty of the people, it could not be prevented from returning to the late ejected family ; and that on whatever
terms they returned, it was folly to expect the people's cause,
which, with such blood and expense, had been asserted,
would not be utterly overthrown. To this the gentleman
gave many strong reasons, why that family could not be restored, without the ruin of the people's liberty and of all
their champions ; and thought that these carried so much
force with them, that it would never be attempted, even
by any royalist that retained any love to his country ;
and that the establishing this single person (Richard)
would satisfy that faction, and compose all the differences,
bringing in all those of all parties that were men of interest and love to their country. Although the business
was very speciously laid, and the man such a one whose
authority was sufficient to sway in any state, the colonel was
not much opiniated of the things he propounded, but willing
to wait the event; being in himself more persuaded that the
people's freedom would be best maintained in a free republic,
delivered from the shackles of their encroaching slaves in the
army.* This was now not merely muttered, but openly asserted

* The mention of this political discussion without the name of the principal speaker in it, naturally awakes curiosity and excites to conjecture.
The judicious writer of the critique on this work in the Annual Review

by all but the army: although of those who contended for it,
there were two sorts; some that really thought it the most
conducible to the people's good and freedom; others, who by
this pretence, hoped to pull down the army and the protec-
torian faction, and then restore the old family.   It is believed
that Richard himself was compounded with, to have resigned
the place that was too great for him; certain it is that his
poor spirit was likely enough to do any such thing.   The
army, perceiving they had set up a wretch who durst not
reign, and that there was a convention met, by their own
assent, who were ready, with a seeming face of authority of
parliament, to restore the Stewarts, they were greatly distressed; finding also that the whole nation was bent against
them, and would not bear their yoke, and having therefore no
refuge to save themselves from being torn in pieces by the
people, or to deliver themselves from their own puppets who
had sold and betrayed them, they found out some of the
members of that glorious parliament which they had violently
driven from their seats with a thousand slanderous criminations and untruths.   To these they counterfeited repentance,
and that God had opened their eyes to see into what a manifest hazard of ruin they had put the interest and people of
God in these nations, so that it was almost irrecoverable; but
if any hope were left, it was that God would sign it, with his
wonted favour, into those hands out of which they had injuriously taken it.   Hereupon they opened the house doors
for them; and the Speaker, with some few members. as many

combines this with a passage at p. 383, and supposes the secret there referred to, and which endeavours were in vain used to draw from Mrs.
Hutchinson, to be the same thing as is here hinted at : it is highly probable that it is so ; and as no evil could now result from a discovery, the
editor has taken pains to effect one, he believes with success—though when
the grounds of his conjecture are laid before the reader, he will judge for
himself.

as made a house, were too hasty to return into their seats, upon capitulation with those traitors who had brought the commonwealth into such a sad confusion. But after they were met, they immediately sent summons to all the members throughout England, among whom the colonel was called up,* and much perplexed, for now he thought his conscience, life, and fortunes were again engaged with men of mixed and different interests and principles ; yet in regard of the trust formerly reposed in him, he returned into his place, infinitely dissatisfied that any condescension had been made to the army's proposals, whose necessity rather than honesty had moved them to counterfeit repentance and ingenuity. This they did by a public declaration, stating how they had been seduced and done wickedly in interrupting the parliament, and that God had never since that time owned them and their counsels as before, and that they desired to humble themselves before God and man for the same, and to return to their duty in defending the parliament in the discharge of their remaining trust. According to this declaration, the army kept a day of solemn humiliation before the Lord ; yet all this, as the event afterwards manifested, in hypocrisy.†

Now the parliament were sat, and were no sooner assembled

---

* By this passage, that error which has become general, and which is to be found in Rapin, vol. ii. p. 605, is rendered palpable. He says they met in parliament to the number of forty-two; and again, p. 607, calls it a parliament of forty persons, but takes no notice of their sending summonses to all the members throughout England; but in the addition or suppression of this circumstance lies the total difference between truth and falsehood. Ludlow, who was one of them, says, vol. ii. p. 645, " That they amounted to a hundred and sixty, who had sat in the house since the seclusion of members in 1648."

† There are copies of this declaration extant, signed by Lambert, Fleetwood, &c., one particularly in the hands of John Townley, Esq., as likewise pamphlets written at that time, calling on the army to make the only amends they could to the nation, by restoring the parliament.

but they were invaded by several enemies.   The presbyterians had long since espoused the royal interest, and forsaken God and the people's cause, when they could not
obtain the reins of government in their own hands, and exercise dominion over all their brethren.*   It was treason, by
the law of those men in power, to talk of restoring the king ;
therefore the presbyterians must face the design, and accordingly all the members ejected in 1648, now came to claim
their seats in the house, whom Colonel Pride, that then
guarded the parliament, turned back, and thereupon there
was some heat in the lobby between them and the other
members.   Particularly Sir George Booth uttered some
threats, and immediately they went into their several counties,
and had laid a design all over England, wherein all the
royalists were engaged, and many of the old parliament
officers ; and this was so dexterously, secretly, and unanimously carried on, that before the parliament had the least
intimation of it, the flame was everywhere kindled, and small
parties attempting insurrections in all places ; but their main
strength was with Sir George Booth in Cheshire, who there
appeared the chief head of the rebellion.   The city, at that
time, was very wavering and false to the parliament, yet the
usual presence of God, that was with them in former times,

* Rapin, in a parallel passage, vol. ii. p. 611, says, that " the presbyterians, seeing no hopes of recovering the ground they had lost, agreed
with the king's party to deliver the nation from the servitude to which it
was reduced by an independent parliament, and an army whose officers
were mostly fanatics.   The particulars and terms of this union are not
known, because the historians who speak of it, being all royalists, have not
thought fit to do so much honour to the presbyterians.   But it cannot be
concealed, that from this time they not only ceased to be the king's enemies,
but very much promoted his restoration."   Behold the honour he asks for
them granted by their greatest enemy, an independent !   As was their
motive such was their reward ; beginning in rage and folly, it ended in
disgrace and ruin.

never appeared so eminent as now, miraculously bringing
to light all the plots against them, and scattering their
enemies before the wind, making them fly when there was
none to pursue them ; although even in the parliament-
house there wanted not many close traitors and abettors of
this conspiracy.   It was presently voted to send an army
down into Cheshire ; but then it fell into debate who should
lead.   Fleetwood, upon the deposing his brother Richard
(wherein he was most unworthily assistant), was made general,
but not thought a person of courage enough for this enterprize ; whereupon many of Lambert's friends propounded
him to the house, and undertook for his integrity and hearty
repentance for having been formerly assistant to the protector.
Colonel Hutchinson was utterly against receiving him again
into employment ; but it was the general vote of the house,
and accordingly he was brought in to receive his commission
from the Speaker ; who, intending to accept the humble submission he then falsely made, with high professions of fidelity,
and to return him an encouragement in declaring the confidence the house had in him,—through mistake made such a
speech to him, as afterwards proved a true prophecy of his
perfidiousness.   Many of the house took notice of it then only
to laugh, but afterwards thought that some hidden impulse, the
man was not then sensible of, led his tongue into those mistakes.   However, Lambert went forth, and through the
cowardice of the enemy obtained a very cheap victory, and
returned.   In Nottinghamshire Colonel White rose, only to
show his apostacy, and run away.   The Lord Byron also lost
himself and his companions in the forest, being chased by a
piece of the county troop.   And Mr. Robert Pierrepont, the
son of the late colonel, went out to make up the rout, and
ran away, and cast away some good arms into the bushes to
make his flight more easy.

During the late protectors' times Colonel Hutchinson, who

thought them greater usurpers on the people's liberties than
the former kings, believed himself wholly disengaged from
all ties, but those which God and nature, or rather God by
nature obliges every man of honour and honesty in to his
country, which is to defend or relieve it from invading tyrants,
as far as he may by a lawful call and means, and to suffer
patiently that yoke which God submits him to, till the Lord
shall take it off; and upon these principles, he seeing that
authority, to which he was in duty bound, so seemingly taken
quite away, thought he was free to fall in or oppose all
things, as prudence should guide him, upon general rules of
conscience.   These would not permit him in any way to assist
any tyrant or invader of the people's rights, nor to rise up
against them without a manifest call from God; therefore he
stayed at home, and busied himself in his own domestic
employments, having a very liberal heart, and a house open
to all worthy persons of all parties.   Among these the Lord
Byron, who, thinking that no gentleman ought to be unpro-
vided with arms, in such an uncertain time, had provided
himself with a trunk of pistols, which were brought down
from London; but some suspicion of it having reached the
protector's officers, he durst not fetch the trunk from the
carrier's himself, but entreated the colonel to send for them
to his house, and secure them there.   This the colonel did;
but afterward, when my Lord Byron had entered into a conspiracy with the enemies of the parliament, he knew that
Colonel Hutchinson was not to be attempted against them,
and was in great care how to get his arms out of the colonel's
house.   The colonel, being of a very compassionate and
charitable nature, had entertained into his service some poor
people who on the enemy's side had been ruined, and were
reduced from good estates to seek that refuge; and w o
counterfeited, so long as their party was down, such sobriety,
love, and gratitude, and sense of their sins and miscarriages

whilst on the other side, that he hoped they had been converts, but could not believe they would have proved such detestable, unthankful traitors, as afterwards they did. Among these, Lord Byron corrupted a gentleman who then waited on the colonel, as the man afterwards alleged ; my lord said he offered himself. However it was, the plot was laid that fifty men, near the colonel's house, should be raised for him, and he with them should first come to the colonel's house, and take away my lord's arms, with all the rest of the colonel's that they could find. To raise him these men, certain neighbours, who used to come to the house, were very busy, and especially two parsons, he of Plumptre and he of Bingham ; this one had an active, proud, pragmatical curate, who used to come to this traitor in the colonel's house and help to manage the treason, and the chaplain, the waiting woman, and two servants more, were drawn into the confederacy. The colonel was then at the parliament-house, and only his wife and children at home, when, the night before the insurrection, Ivie (that was the gentleman's name) came to a singing-boy who kept the colonel's clothes, and commanded him to deliver him the colonel's own arms and buff coat.

The boy was fearful, and did not readily obey him, whereupon he threatened immediately to pistol him, if he made the least resistance or discovery of the business ; so the boy fetched him the arms, and he put them on, and took one of the best horses and went out at midnight, telling the boy he was a fool to fear, for the next night, before that time, there would come fifty men to fetch away all the arms in the house.

As soon as the boy saw him quite gone, his mistress being then in bed, he went to the chaplain and acquainted him ; but the chaplain cursed him for breaking his sleep : then he went to the waiting gentlewoman, but she said she thought it would be unfit to disturb her mistress ; so the boy rested till next day, when Ivie, having failed of his men, was come

back again. Then the boy, finding an opportunity after
dinner, told his mistress, that though he had been bred a
cavalier he abhorred to betray or be unfaithful to those he
served; and that he had reason to suspect there was some
vile conspiracy in hand, wherein Ivie was engaged against
them, and told her his grounds. When Mrs. Hutchinson had
heard that, she bade him keep it private, and called immediately a servant that had been a cornet of the parliament's
party, and bade him go to the county troop's captain, and
desire him to send her a guard for her husband's house, for
she had intelligence that the cavaliers intended some attempt
against it. Mrs. Hutchinson, ashamed to complain of her
own family, thought of this way of security, till she could
discharge herself of the traitor, not knowing at that time how
many more such were about her. Then calling her gentlewoman, whom she thought she might trust, upon her solemn
protestations of fidelity, she took her to assist her in hiding
her plate and jewels, and what she had of value, and scrupled
not to let her see the *secret places in her house*, while the false
and base dissembler went smiling up and down at her mistress's simplicity. Meantime, the man that was sent for
soldiers came back, bringing news that the cavaliers had risen
and were beaten, and that the county troop was in pursuit of
them. Then also the coachman, who finding himself not
well, had borrowed a horse to go to Nottingham to be let
blood, came home, bringing with him a cravat and other
spoils of the enemy, which he had gotten. For when he
came to the town, hearing the cavaliers were up, he got a
case of pistols, and thought more of shedding than losing
blood, and meeting the cavaliers in the rout, it is said, he
killed one of them; although this rogue had engaged to
Ivie to have gone on the other side with him. Mrs. Hutchinson not being willing, for all this, to take such notice of
Ivie's treason as to cast him into prison, took him immedi-

ately to London with her, and said nothing till he came there. Then she told him how base and treacherous he had been ; but to save her own shame for having entertained so false a person, and for her mother's sake whom he had formerly served, she was willing to dismiss him privately, without acquainting the colonel, who, if he knew, must punish him. So she gave him something and turned him away, and told her husband she came only to acquaint him with the insurrection, and her own fears of staying in the country without him. He, being very indulgent, went immediately back with her, having informed the parliament, and received their order for going down to look after the securing of the country. His wife, as soon as she came down, having learned that the chaplain had been Ivie's confederate, told him privately of it, and desired him to find a pretence to take his leave of the colonel, that she might not be necessitated to complain, and procure him the punishment his treason deserved. He went away thus, but so far from being wrought upon, that he hated her to the death for her kindness.

The colonel having set things in order in the country, intended to have carried his family that winter with him tc London ; when just in that week he was going, news was brought that Lambert had once more turned out the parliament, and the colonel rejoiced in his good fortune that he was not present.

Lambert was exceedingly puffed up with his cheap victory, and cajoled his soldiers ; and, before he returned to London, set on foot among them their old insolent way of prescribing to the parliament by way of petition.

The parliament, after the submission of the army, had voted that there should no more be a general over them, but to keep that power in their own hands, all the officers should take their commissions immediately from the Speaker.* The

* It was a great oversight that they had not taken this course from the

conspiracy of the army, to get a leader in their rebellion, was laid, that they should petition for generals and such like things as might facilitate their intents.   Among others who were taken in arms against the parliament, Lord Castleton was one of the chief heads of the insurrection.   Him Lambert brought along with him in his coach, not now as a prisoner, but unguarded, as one that was to be honoured.   The parliament hearing of this, sent and fetched him out of his company and committed him to prison, and then the army's saucy petition was delivered, and, upon the insolent carriage of nine colonels, they were by vote disbanded.   Lambert being one of them, came in a hostile manner and plucked the members out of the house; Fleetwood, whom they trusted to guard them, having confederated with Lambert and betrayed them. After that, setting up their army court at Wallingford-house, they began their arbitrary reign, to the joy of all the vanquished enemies of the parliament, and to the amazement and terror of all men that had any honest interest: and now they were all devising governments; and some honourable members, I know not through what fatality of the times, fell in with them.*   When Colonel Hutchinson came into the

beginning: for although it is very difficult for a republic, which has need of considerable armies, to maintain its independence, which is for ever liable to be invaded by those who have the sword in their hands, yet the best chance it has lies in keeping the military under the direction of the civil power.   This method succeeded a good while with the French republic, and might have done still longer if some of the members of the executive power had not leagued with some of the military commanders.

* This was that committee of safety, or council of the *Stratocracy*, among the principal members of which were Sir Henry Vane, Ludlow, and Whitelocke, as mentioned by Whitelocke, p. 685.   He there says that he took his share in it reluctantly, and that all three were censured for it by the parliament at their return.   Ludlow was accused of treason; Vane made an ingenious excuse, but was banished to one of his country seats. Colonel Hutchinson evidently divided from Sir H. Vane on this occasion,

coun_ry some time before Lambert's revolt, Mr. Robert
Pierrepont, the son of the late Colonel Francis Pierrepont,
sent friends to entreat the colonel to receive him into his
protection.   Upon the entreaty of his uncle he took him into
his own house, and entertained him civilly there, whilst he
wrote to the Speaker, urging his youth, his surrender of himself, and all he could in favour of him, desiring to know how
they would please to dispose of him.   Before the letters were
answered Lambert had broken the parliament, and the colonel
told him he was free again to do what he pleased ; but the
young gentleman begged of the colonel that he might continue under his sanctuary till these things came to some issue.
This the colonel very freely admitted, and entertained him
till the second return of the parliament, not without much
trouble to his house, himself, and his servants, so contrary to
the sobriety and holiness the colonel delighted in, yet for
his father's and his uncle's sakes he endured it about six
months.

Some of Lambert's officers, while he marched near Nottinghamshire, having formerly served under the colonel's command, came to his house at Owthorpe and told him of the
petition that was set on foot in Lambert's brigade, and consulted whether they should sign it or not.   The colonel
advised them by no means to do it, yet notwithstanding, they
did, which made the colonel exceeding angry with them,
thinking they rather came to see how he stood affected, than

and, as Ludlow says, urged on the censure against him, which he considers
as inconsistent with Colonel Hutchinson's judgment passed on the king,
and as a proof of his treachery and underhand agreement with Monk. But
no conclusion can be more unwarranted than this: it was Col. Hutchinson's
anxiety to keep the king out, or at least to prevent his coming in with a
high hand and without limitation, that caused him so strenuously to oppose
these rash steps which made all wish for the king's return, to deliver them
from greater evils.

really to ask his counsel. When Lambert had broken up the house, the colonel made a short journey to London to inform himself how things were, and found some of the members exceedingly sensible of the sad estate the kingdom was reduced unto by the rash ambition of these men, and resolving that there was no way but for every man that abhorred it to improve their interest in their countries, and to suppress these usurpers and rebels. Hereupon the colonel took measures to have some arms bought and sent him, and had prepared a thousand honest men, whenever he should call for their assistance; intending to improve his posse comitatus when occasion should be offered. To provoke him more particularly to this, several accidents fell out. Among the rest, six of Lambert's troopers came to gather money, laid upon the country by an assessment of parliament, whom the colonel telling that in regard it was levied by that authority, he had paid it, but otherwise would not; two of them only who were in the room with the colonel, the rest being on horseback in the court, gave him such insolent terms, with such insufferable reproaches of the parliament, that the colonel drew a sword which was in the room to have chastised them. While a minister that was by held the colonel's arm, his wife, not willing to have them killed in her presence, opened the door and let them out, who presently ran and fetched in their companions in the yard with cocked pistols. Upon the bustle, while the colonel having disengaged himself from those that held him, had run after them with the sword drawn, his brother came out of another room, upon whom, the soldiers pressing against a door that went into the great hall, the door flew open, and about fifty or sixty men appeared in the hall,* who were there upon another business. For Owthorpe,

* The description of the house, contained in a former note, will give a just idea of the position of all the parties, and of the striking scene here described.

Kinolton, and Hicklin, had a contest about a cripple that was sent from one to the other, but at last, out of some respect they had for the colonel, the chief men of the several towns were come to him, to make some accommodation, till the law should be again in force. When the colonel heard the soldiers were come, he left them shut up in his great hall, who by accident thus appearing, put the soldiers into a dreadful fright. When the colonel saw how pale they looked, he encouraged them to take heart, and calmly admonished them for their insolence, and they being changed and very humble through their fear, he called for wine for them, and sent them away. To the most insolent of them he said, "These carriages would bring back the Stewarts." The man, laying his hand upon his sword, said, "Never while he wore that." Among other things they said to the colonel, when he demanded by what authority they came, they showed their swords, and said, "That was their authority." After they were dismissed, the colonel, not willing to appear because he was sheriff of the county, and had many of their papers sent him to publish, concealed himself in his house, and caused his wife to write a letter to Fleetwood, to complain of the affronts had been offered him, and to tell him that he was thereupon retired, till he could dwell safely at home.* To this Fleetwood returned a civil answer, and withal sent a protection, to forbid all soldiers from coming to his house,

* Probably this circumstance of Colonel Hutchinson concealing himself in his own home came at that time to be known at Nottingham, and gave rise to a tradition which is to be found in Throsby's edition of Thoroton, that he concealed himself in this manner after the restoration, but was taken in his return from church; both of which were untrue, as probably were some other tales, resembling the legends of romance, which the Editor heard of him at Owthorpe. But that there was an apartment so adapted for concealment, security, and convenience, as that he might have made a long residence in it without being discovered, the Editor had ocular demonstration.

and a command to Swallow, who was the colonel of these
men, to examine and punish them. Mrs. Hutchinson had sent
before to Swallow, who was then quartered at Leicester, the
next day after it was done, to inform him, who sent a letter
utterly disowning their actions, and promising to punish them.
This, Mrs. Hutchinson sent to show the soldiers who then
lay abusing the country at Colson; but when they saw their
officer's letter they laughed at him, and tore it in pieces.
Some days after he, in a civil manner, sent a captain with
them and other soldiers to Owthorpe, to inquire into their
misdemeanours before their faces; which being confirmed to
him, and he beginning to rebuke them, they set him at light,
even before Mrs. Hutchinson's face, and made the poor man
retire sneaped to his colonel; while these six rogues, in one
week's space, besides the assessments assigned them to gather
up within the compass of five miles, took away violently from
the country, for their own expense, above five-and-twenty
pounds. Notwithstanding all this pretended civility, Fleetwood and his counsellors were afraid of the colonel, and the
protection was but sent to draw him thither, that they might
by that means get him into their custody. But he, having
intimation of it, withdrew, while men and arms were preparing, that he might appear publicly in the defence of the
country, when he was strong enough to drive out the soldiers
that were left in those parts. Three hundred of them were
one night drawn out of Nottingham to come to Owthorpe for
him, but some of the party gave him notice, and he being
then at home, immediately went out of the house. Neither
wanted they their spies, who gave them notice that he was
gone again, so that they turned off upon the wolds and went
to Hickling; and the next day Major Grove, their commander,
sent to Mrs. Hutchinson to desire permission for himself only
to come down, which she gave, and so with only five or six
of his party he came. With him Mrs. Hutchinson so easily

dealt, that, after she had represented the state of things to him, he began to apologize that he had only taken this command upon himself to preserve the country, and should be ready to submit to any lawful authority; and he and his men were not come for any other intent but to prevent disturbance of the peace and gatherings together of men, who, they were informed, intended to rise in these parts. Mrs. Hutchinson smiling, told him it was necessary for him to keep a good guard, for all the whole country would shortly be weary of their yoke, and, no question, would find some authority to shelter them. At last he went so far as to desire her to let the colonel know he intended him no mischief, but he and all his men should be at her command to defend her from the insolencies of any others. She heard him without faith, for she knew the good will they pretended to her husband proceeded only from their fear. It is true that at that time the colonel had met with Colonel Hacker, and several other gentlemen of Northampton and Warwickshire, and at the same time Major Beque was to have reduced Coventry, and another colonel Warwick Castle. Two regiments of horse should have marched to a place within seven miles of Colonel Hutchinson's house, where his men should have rendezvoused, and the town of Nottingham at the same time to have seized all the soldiers there, and they of Leicester the like. These people had, through the spies that were about the colonel, gotten some little inkling of his rendezvous, but not right, neither could they have prevented it, had they desired.* But

---

* Perhaps this crisis was the most favourable to the cause of liberty of any that had occurred; for the genuine assertors of it would, at this moment, have found all the different factions weakened, and the body of the nation so tired of tumult and anarchy, that, had they now stood forth in any force, the voice of reason would in all probability have prevailed. But the fluctuations of power and party were at this time so frequent and sudden as hardly to leave sufficient interval for any enterprize that required

just before it should have been put into execution the parliament were restored to their seats, Lambert was deserted by
his men and fled, and Monk was marching on southwards,
pretending to restore and confirm the parliament; insomuch
that Colonel Hutchinson, instead of raising his country, was
called up to his seat in parliament. Here there were so
many favourers of Lambert, Fleetwood, and their partakers,
that the colonel, who used to be very silent, could not now
forbear high opposition to them; in whose favour things were
carried with such a stream, that the colonel then began to
lose all hopes of settling this poor land on any righteous
foundation.

It was the 26th of December, 1659, that the parliament
met again. The manner of it, and the contest and treaty in
the north between Monk and Lambert, are too well known to
be repeated; the dissimulations and false protestations that
Monk made are too public; yet the colonel and others suspected him, but knew not how to hinder him; for this insolent
usurpation of Lambert's had so turned the hearts of all men,
that the whole nation began to set their eyes upon the king
beyond the sea, and think a bad settlement under him better
than none at all, or than being under the arbitrary power of
such proud rebels as Lambert. The whole house was divided
into miserable factions, among whom some would then have
violently set up an oath of renunciation of the king and his
family. The colonel, thinking it a ridiculous thing to *swear
out* a man, when they had no power to defend themselves
against him, vehemently opposed that oath, and carried it
against Sir Ar. Haslerig and others, who as violently pressed
it; urging very truly that those oaths that had been formerly

combination. Moreover it is to be considered that the march of patriotism
is impeded by reserves and restraints which ambition overleaps in its career;
and after all it is perhaps justly observed, that Colonel Hutchinson *was too
unambitious* for his own glory or the public good.

imposed had but multiplied the sins of the nation by perjuries; instancing how Sir Arthur and others, in Oliver's time, coming into the house, swore on their entrance they would attempt nothing in the change of that government, which, as soon as ever they were entered, they laboured to throw down.   Many other arguments he used, whereupon many honest men, who thought till then he had followed a faction in all things, and not his own judgment, began to meet often with him, and to consult what to do in these difficulties, out of which their prudence and honesty would have found a way to extricate themselves; but that the end of our prosperity was come, hastened on partly by the mad rash violence of some that, without strength, opposed the tide of the discontented tumultuous people, partly by the detestable treachery of those who had sold themselves to do mischief, but chiefly by the general stream of the people, who were as eager for their own destruction as the Israelites of old for their quails.*

One observation of the colonel's I cannot omit, that the secluded members whom Monk brought in were, many of them, so brought over to a commonwealth that, if Sir Ar. Haslerig and his party had not forsaken their places because they would not sit with them, they would have made the strongest party in the house, but which by reason of their going off were afterwards outvoted in all things.†

* A frank acknowledgment that the independent parliament, however good the intentions of many of them might be, had become unpopular; but with the general mass of mankind the escape from any present evil is paramount to all future considerations.   Perhaps this reflux of the *public mind* was the most effectual cause of the counter revolution, without which Monk might have *plotted* in vain.   And thus perhaps in this, as in so many other instances, Mrs. Hutchinson's natural and rational way of tracing and unfolding the causes of great events will be found to bring us much nearer to the truth than all the subtleties employed by others!

† We do not know this circumstance to have been noticed by any other

Sir Anthony Ashley Cooper at that time insinuated himself into a particular friendship with the colonel, and made him all the honourable pretences that can be imagined ; called him his *dear friend*, and caressed him with such embraces as none but a traitor as vile as himself could have suspected ; yet was he the most intimate of Monk's confidants. Whereupon some few days before the rising of that house, when it began to be too apparent which way Monk inclined, the

historian; but it appears much more probable than that the secluded members should have been *unanimous*, and that in measures of such tran-scendant import as were now to be decided upon. For this secession Whitelocke blames and Ludlow commends Sir Arthur Haselrig and his friends ; their total ruin, which ensued, decides the question.

In support of the opinions and statements contained in this and the two next following pages, are adduced the following out of many extracts that might be made from the third volume of Clarendon's State Papers. Page 687, Broderick to Hyde, Dec. 30, 1659, ridicules the idea of its being possible to establish the Rump ; says Vane, Salway, and Whitelocke sit without blush or excuse; Haslerig must ruin them or be ruined. A. A. Cooper desires to establish these people. Haslerig would admit the se-cluded members provided they would renounce a single person and the line of the Stuarts.

Page 696, Do. to Do. March 9, 1659-60, " Of Monk I have much more reason to hope better than you apprehend, and would lose the hand with which I pay you this duty, that Mr. Edmondson (the king) had in-closed an answer to Howard by this conveyance, time being very precious, and what a day may produce known only to the prescience of Almighty God. All the progress that can be made without is carefully pursued, nor shall anything be wanting any care can supply. The last night's conference between the officers of the army and the members is so variously reported, even by themselves (with several of whom I have this morning discoursed), that it is hard to give a narrative of particulars; the main they agree in, viz. that the demands were, indemnity for all past actions, confirmation of all purchases, sale of what remains to the state in the king's houses, forests, &c. towards the payment of arrears; with some sharp reflections on the militia of several counties put into disaffected hands.

" Sir William Lewis" (one of the secluded members, as appears by Dug .

colonel, upon the confidence of his friendship, entreated him
to tell him what were Monk's intentions, that he and others
might consider their safety, who were likely to be given up
as a public sacrifice.   Cooper denied to the death any intention besides a commonwealth; "but," said he, with the
greatest semblance of reality that could be put on, "if the
violence of the people should bring the king upon us, let me
be damned, body and soul, if ever I see a hair of any man's
head touched, or a penny of any man's estate, upon this
quarrel."   This he backed with so many and such deep protestations of that kind, as made the colonel, after his treachery
was apparent, detest him of all mankind, and think himself
obliged, if ever he had opportunity, to procure exemplary

dale's list, and who evidently had joined Colonel Hutchinson's party since
his return), "Arthur Annesley, and Colonel Hutchinson, endeavoured their
satisfaction by repeating the acts already passed in their favour, justifying
many persons so chosen, promises of arrears, with whatever else they thought
reasonable to urge against the intrusion of military stipendiaries upon the
privilege of parliament.   Haslerig and some of his faction abetted the
soldiery, but all ended fairly, though far from satisfaction.   The general
had indeed before declared that he expected their obedience to the su-
preme authority, not their usurpation of it ; adding that it would be easier
to find officers in the room of those that remained obstinate, than for them
to find regiments if the house should deny pay.   Upon the whole, I am
commanded to tell you that we suffered nothing in the conference.   Haslerig concluded there was no other basis to build on than the parliament.
Colonels Rich, Scott, and the rest who hitherto refrained, now enter the
house with faint hopes of opposing the general current.   We make no
doubt of success every where.   All people cry out, the king ! the king !
some indeed add, he must come in on terms ; and why doth he not prevent the imposition by a fair offer published authentically, to release fears,
settle their minds, and render his entrance facile."

The same to the king, March 10, 1659-60, says, "Monk declared he
would acquiesce in the judgment of the parliament both as to king and
lords.   Another day he would spend the last drop of his blood rather than
the Stuarts should ever come into England; but he is in good temper again
the same night."

justice cn him, who was so vile a wretch as to sit himself and sentence some of those that died. And although this man joined with those who laboured for the colonel's particular deliverance, yet the colonel, to his dying day, abhorred the mention of his name, and held him to be a more execrable traitor than Monk himself. At this time the colonel, as before, was by many of his friends tempted every way to fall in with the king's interest, and often offered both pardon and preferment, if he could be wrought off from his party, whose danger was now laid before him: but they could in no way move him.* A gentleman that had been employed to tamper with him told me, that he found him so unmovable, that one time he and a certain lord being in the colonel's company, and having begun their vain insinuations, he, to decline them, seeing Cooper, went away with him; upon which this lord, that had some tenderness for the colonel, said to this gentleman, "The colonel is a ruined man; he believes that traitor, who will ruin him." When they could not work upon him one way, some, that were most kindly concerned in him, persuaded him to absent himself and not act for the parliament, and undertook with their lives to secure him, but he would not. He foresaw the mischief, and resolved to stay in his duty, waiting upon God, who accordingly was good to him. Some, when they saw Monk had betrayed them, would have

---

* It was hard for him, after this, to be accused by Ludlow of treachery and connivance with the king's friends; but Ludlow was at this time engaged in a different party, perhaps envious of him for escaping with impunity, when himself despaired of doing so, and went into voluntary exile: and besides Sir A. Ashley Cooper may have stipulated for Colonel Hutchinson's indemnity *gratuitously ;* while most people suppose that some conditions were imposed. His moderation in a time of phrenzy was surely a sufficient argument, and was probably that which Cooper used in support of the man whom he was forced to esteem, though he did not choose to imitate him.

fallen in with Lambert, but the colonel thought any destruction was to be chosen before the sin of joining with such a wretch.*

Now was that glorious parliament come to a period, not more fatal to itself than to the three nations, whose sun of liberty then set, and all their glory gave place to the foulest mists that ever overspread a miserable people.† A new parliament was to be chosen, and the county of Nottingham

* This was the point whereupon the heads of the republican party divided, but probably at this day the warmest friends of the liberties of the people will think that it was better to return to a monarchy, though not sufficiently limited and defined, than to fall under a stratocracy, or government of the army, which this would have been more completely than even that which existed under Cromwell: indeed it is not easy to see which way it would have differed from that of Algiers. Accordingly we do not find Mrs. Hutchinson ever to have repined that the king had been restored in preference to the establishment of such a power; but there were many other modes which might have been adopted, without flying to either of these extremes, had not their passions overpowered the reason of some of the great men of that day. In page 705 of the third volume of Clarendon's State Papers, a spy of Charles II. says to the Lords Bedford and Manchester, that Pierrepont, Popham, Waller, and St. John, made a junto to treat with the king before his restitution. But the most obvious method for obtaining a better settlement was that proposed by Whitelocke to Fleetwood, of an offer of their services to the king upon reasonable conditions: this opportunity was lost by hesitation, and an easy triumph left to Monk, whose determined conduct gave efficacy to the small force he possessed.

† If the change in politics was great, the change in morals was much greater: statutes have since retrieved the errors committed in the former; it is doubtful whether the national character in taste and morals has ever freed itself from the taint it then received.

Under the patronage and example of the king, wit put decency to flight; religion and patriotism, veneration of God and the love of our country, the two noblest affections of the mind, were dragged through the mire of doggrel rhymes, under the pretence of deriding hypocrisy; under the notion of gaiety and good fellowship, profligacy and sensuality gained a footing which they have never quitted, but still maintain their ground, by

had yet such respect for Colonel Hutchinson, that they fixed their eyes on him to be their knight, but Mr. William Pierrepont having a great desire to bring in his son-in-law, the Lord Haughton, to be his fellow knight, the colonel would not come into the town till the election was passed; which if he had, he had been chosen without desiring it; for many people came, and when they saw he would not stand, returned and voted for none, among whom were fifty freeholders of the town of Newark.

Some time before the writs for the new elections came, the town of Nottingham, as almost all the rest of the island, began to grow mad, and to declare themselves so, in their desires of the king. The boys, set on by their fathers and masters, got drums and colours, and marched up and down the town, and trained themselves in a military posture, and offered many affronts to the soldiers of the army that were quartered there, which were two troops of Colonel Hacker's regiment. Insomuch that one night there were about forty of the soldiers hurt and wounded with stones, upon the occasion of taking away the drums, when the youths were gathering together to make bonfires to burn the Rump,* as was the

the dangerous secret then taught them of reducing all by invidious surmises and unjust depreciations nearly to the level of their own baseness.

The plays and other writings of those days are tinctured with an air of rakishness which often appears affected and misplaced; it was the polite ridicule of the Spectators which put this folly out of countenance and practice. Some modern wits have attempted to revive it, and but for the general turn to philosophical inquiry they would probably have succeeded. Those who *reason* cannot but see that shameless depravity is a very bad substitute for even simulated virtue.

* The number of the members of the long parliament having been, by seclusion, death, &c., very much reduced, the remainder was compared to the rump of a fowl which was left, all the rest being eaten; and this coarse emblem was burnt in derision by the mob, to hail and flatter the rising power of the cavaliers.

custom in those mad days. The soldiers, provoked to rage, shot again, and killed in the scuffle two presbyterians, whereof one was an elder, and an old professor; and one that had been a great zealot for the cause, and master of the magazine of Nottingham Castle. He was only standing at his own door, and whether shot by chance or on purpose, or by whom, it is not certain; but true it is, that at that time the presbyterians were more inveterately bitter against the fanatics than even the cavaliers themselves, and they set on these boys. But upon the killing of this man they were hugely enraged, and prayed very seditiously in their pulpits, and began openly to desire the king; not for good will to him, but only for destruction to all the fanatics. One of the ministers, who were great leaders of the people, had been firmly engaged in Booth's rebellion, and led on very many of the godly, who, by the timely suppression of those who began the insurrection in Nottingham, were prevented from declaring themselves openly. Colonel Hutchinson was as merciful as he could safely be, in not setting on too strict inquisition; but privately admonished such as were not passed hopes of becoming good commonwealth's men, if it were possible that the labouring state might outlive the present storm. Upon this bustle in the town of Nottingham the soldiers were horribly incensed, and the townsmen ready to take part with the boys; whereupon the soldiers drew into the meadows near the town, and sent for the regiment, resolving to execute their vengeance on the town, and the townsmen again were mustering to encounter them. Mrs. Hutchinson by chance coming into the town, and being ac-quainted with the captains, persuaded them to do nothing in a tumultuary way, however provoked, but to complain to the general, and let him decide the business.

The men, at her entreaty, were content so to do, the townsmen also consented to restrain their children and serv-

ants, and keep the public peace; while it was agreed that
both of them should send up together a true information to
the general concerning the late quarrel.   But one of the
officers, more enraged than the rest, went away immediately
to Monk, and complained to him of the malice of the presbyterians and cavaliers against the soldiers.   He, without
asking more on the other side, signed a warrant to Colonel
Hacker, to let loose the fury of his regiment upon the town,
and plunder all they judged guilty; with which the officer
immediately went away.   Colonel Hutchinson being at that
time at the general's lodging, my Lord Howard told him
what order against the town of Nottingham had just been
sent down.   The colonel, who had been by his wife informed
of the disorders there, went to the general, and prevailed
with him for a countermand of all hostility against the town,
till he should hear and determine the business; which countermand the colonel sent immediately by one of the townsmen, who, though he rode post, came not till Colonel
Hacker, with all his regiment, were come into the town
before him, and the soldiers were in some of the houses
beginning to rifle them.   Wherefore the countermand coming
so seasonably from Colonel Hutchinson, they could not but
look upon him as their deliverer; and this being done a very
few days before the election for the next parliament, when
the colonel came to town and had waived the county, they
generally pitched upon him for the town.   But then Dr.
Plumptre laboured all he could to get the burgess-ship for
himself, and to put by the colonel, with the basest scandals he
and two or three of his associates could raise.   Mr. Arthur
Stanhope, in whose house the soldiers were entered to plunder,
being pitched upon for the other burgess, and having a great
party in the town, was dealt with to desert the colonel, and
offered all Plumptre's party; but he, on the other side, laboured more for the colonel than for himself, and at length,

2 D

when the election day came, Mr. Stanhope and the colonel were clearly chosen.*

The colonel and Mr. Stanhope went up to the parliament, which began on the 25th day of April, 1660; to whom the king sending a declaration from Breda, which promised, or at least intimated, liberty of conscience, remission of all offences, enjoyment of liberties and estates; they voted to send commissioners to invite him.† And almost all the gentry of all parties went, some to fetch him over, some to meet him at the sea side, some to fetch him into London, into which he entered on the 29th day of May, with a universal joy and triumph, even to his own amazement; who, when he saw all the nobility and gentry of the land flowing in to him, asked where were his enemies. For he saw nothing but prostrates, expressing all the love that could make a prince happy. Indeed it was a wonder in that day to see the mutability of some, and the hypocrisy of others, and the servile flattery of all. Monk, like his better genius, conducted him, and was adored like one that had brought all the glory and felicity of mankind home with this prince.

The officers of the army had made themselves as fine as

* Both Whitelocke and Ludlow assure us, that there were great solicitations in all parts to get to be parliament-men; and Rapin says, that almost all the elections were in favour of the presbyterians and royalists, peculiarly the former. This circumstance renders Colonel Hutchinson's popularity and personal merit so much the more conspicuous.

† That the parliament, and this, as Rapin calls it, a *presbyterian* parliament, should thus simply and unconditionally have invited the king, has always been matter of astonishment. The first to find out the error into which their precipitancy had led them were the royalists, and of them the *best*, the Earl of Southampton, who by Burnet, p. 89, is said to have laid the chief blame on Chancellor Hyde. But was it not equally in the power of the parliament *after* the king's arrival to have imposed any reasonable conditions, at least before they established for him such an income as to render him independent !

the courtiers, and all hoped in this change to change their condition, and disowned all things they before had advised. Every ballad singer sang up and down the streets ribald rhymes, made in reproach of the late commonwealth, and of all those worthies that therein endeavoured the people's freedom and happiness.

The presbyterians* were now the white boys, and according to their nature fell a thirsting, and then hunting after blood, urging that God's blessing could not be upon the land, till justice had cleansed it from the late king's blood. First that fact was disowned, then all the acts made after it rendered void, then an inquisition made after those that were guilty thereof, but only seven were nominated of those that sat in judgment on that prince, for exemplary justice, and a proclamation sent for the rest to come in, upon penalty of losing their estates.

While these things were debating in the house, at the first, divers persons concerned in that business sat there, and when the business came into question, every one of them spoke of it according to their present sense. But Mr. Lenthall, son to the late Speaker of that parliament, when the presbyterians first called that business into question, though not at all concerned in it himself, stood up and made such a handsome and

* It has been pretty generally reported and believed of the king, that he was more inclined to confirm and augment than disturb or diminish the extent of the amnesty he had proffered at Breda; and there are upon record very honourable instances of many of the royalists exhibiting a spirit of forgiveness and reconciliation ; perhaps the most rational way of accounting for the chief of the presbyterian party showing rigour, is to suppose that they did it in order to remove from themselves the odium of those violences of which they had been the original and remote cause, and to cast it on those who were the immediate and proximate ones. Be the cause or reasoning what it may, the fact is well established by the trials of the egicides.

2 D 2

honourable speech in defence of them all, as deserves eternal honour. But the presbyterians called him to the bar for it, where, though he mitigated some expressions, which might be ill taken of the house, yet he spoke so generously, that it will never be forgotten of him. Herein he behaved himself with so much courage and honour as was not matched at that time in England, for which he was looked on with an evil eye, and, upon a pretence of treason, put in prison; from whence his father's money, and the lieutenant of the tower's jealousy, delivered him. When it came to Ingoldsby's turn, he, with many tears, professed his repentance for that murder, and told a false tale, how Cromwell held his hand, and forced him to subscribe the sentence, and made a most whining recantation, after which he retired; and another had almost ended, when Colonel Hutchinson, who was not there at the beginning, came in, and was told what they were about, and that it would be expected he should say something. He was surprised with a thing he expected not, yet neither then, nor in any like occasion, did he ever fail himself, but told them, " That for his actings in those days, if he had erred, it was the inexperience of his age, and the defect of his judgment, and not the malice of his heart, which had ever prompted him to pursue the general advantage of his country more than his own; and if the sacrifice of him might conduce to the public peace and settlement, he should freely submit his life and fortunes to their disposal; that the vain expense of his age, and the great debts his public employments had run him into, as they were testimonies that neither avarice nor any other interest had carried him on, so they yielded him just cause to repent that he ever forsook his own blessed quiet, to embark in such a troubled sea, where he had made shipwreck of all things but a good conscience; and as to that particular action of the king, he desired them to believe he had that sense of it that befitted an Englishman, a Christian, and a gentleman."* What he expressed was to this effect, but so very handsomely delivered, that it took generally the whole house; only one gentleman stood up and said, he had expressed himself as one that was much more sorry for the events and consequences than the actions; but another replied, that when a man's words might admit of two interpretations, it befitted gentlemen always to receive that which might be most favourable. As soon as the colonel had spoken, he retired into a room where Ingoldsby was with his eyes yet red, who had called up a little spite to succeed his whinings, and embracing Col. Hutchinson, " O colonel," said he, " did I ever imagine we could be brought to this ? Could I have suspected it, when I brought them Lambert in the other day, this sword should have redeemed us from being dealt with as criminals, by that people for whom we had so gloriously exposed ourselves." The colonel told him he had foreseen, ever since those usurpers thrust out the lawful authority of the land to enthrone themselves, it could end in nothing else ; but the integrity of his heart, in all he had done, made him as cheerfully ready to suffer as to triumph in a good cause. The result of the house that day was to suspend Colonel Hutchinson and the rest from sitting in the house. Monk, after all his great professions, now sat still, and had not one word to interpose for any person, but was as forward to set vengeance on foot as any man.

Mrs. Hutchinson, whom to keep quiet, her husband had hitherto persuaded that no man would lose or suffer by this

---

* This speech will probably be considered as a specimen of art carried as far as a man of honour would permit himself to go, and managed with as much refinement and dexterity as the longest premeditation could have produced; accordingly it furnished his friends with a topic for his defence, without giving his adversaries grounds for reproaching him with tergiversation.

change, at this beginning was awakened, and saw that h.
was ambitious of being a public sacrifice, and therefore,
herein only in her whole life, resolved to disobey him, and
to improve all the affection he had to her for his safety, and
prevailed with him to retire; for she said, she would not live
to see him a prisoner. With her unquietness, she drove him
out of her own lodgings into the custody of a friend, in order
to his further retreat, if occasion should be, and then made
it her business to solicit all her friends for his safety. Meanwhile, it was first resolved in the house, that mercy should
be shown to some, and exemplary justice to others; then
the number was defined, and voted it should not exceed
seven; then upon the king's own solicitation, that his subjects should be put out of their fears, those seven were
named; and after that a proclamation was sent for the rest
to come in. Colonel Hutchinson not being of the number of
those seven, was advised by all his friends to surrender himself, in order to secure his estate, and he was very earnest to
do it, when Mrs. Hutchinson would by no means hear of it;
but being exceedingly urged by his friends, that she would
hereby obstinately lose all their estate, she would not yet
consent that the colonel should give himself into custody, and
she had wrought him to a strong engagement, that he would
not dispose of himself without her. At length, being accused of obstinacy, in not giving him up, she devised a way
to try the house, and wrote a letter in his name to the
Speaker, to urge what might be in his favour, and to let
him know, that by reason of some inconveniency it might
be to him, he desired not to come under custody, and yet
should be ready to appear at their call; and if they intended any mercy to him, he begged they would begin it
in permitting him his liberty upon his parole, till they
should finally determine of him. This letter she conceived

would try the temper of the house; if they granted this, she had her end, for he was still free; if they denied it, she might be satisfied in keeping him from surrendering himself.

Having contrived and written this letter, before she carried it to the colonel, a friend came to her out of the house, near which her lodgings then were, and told her that if they had but any ground to begin, the house was that day in a most excellent temper towards her husband; whereupon she wrote her husband's name to the letter, and ventured to send it in, being used sometimes to write the letters he dictated, and her character not much differing from his. These gentlemen who were moved to try this opportunity, were not the friends she relied on; but God, to show that it was he, not they, sent two common friends, who had such good success that the letter was very well received; and upon that occasion all of all parties spoke so kindly and effectually for him, that he had not only what he desired, but was voted to be free without any engagement; and his punishment was only that he should be discharged from the present parliament, and from all offices, military or civil, in the state for ever; and upon his petition of thanks for this, his estate also was voted to be free from all mulcts and confiscations. Many providential circumstances concurred in this thing. That which put the house into so good a humour towards the colonel that day, was, that having taken the business of the king's trial into consideration, certain committees were found to be appointed to order the preparation of the court, the chairs and cushions, and other formalities, wherein Colonel Hutchinson had nothing to do;* but when they had passed their

* In Nelson's Trial of Charles I., it appears, that on Friday, January 12, when a committee was appointed for ordering the trial, and many minute particulars agreed to for the management of it, Colonel Hutchinson

votes for his absolut e discharge and came to the sitting of
the court, he was found not to have been one day away. A
rogue that had been one of their clerks had brought in all
these informations; and above all, poor Mrs. Hacker, thinking to save her husband, had brought up the warrant for
execution, with all their hands and seals.*

Sir Allen Apsley too, who, with all the kindest zeal of
friendship that can be imagined, endeavoured to bring off the
colonel, and used some artifice in engaging his friends for
him.   There was a young gentleman, a kinsman of his, who
thirstily aspired after preferment, and Sir Allen had given
him hopes, upon his effectual endeavours for the colonel,
to introduce him; who being a person that had understanding enough, made no conscience of truth, when an officious lie
might serve his turn.   This man, although he owed his life
to the colonel, and had a thousand obligations to Mrs.
Hutchinson's parents, yet not for their sakes, nor for virtue,
nor for gratitude, but for his own hopes, which he had of
Sir Allen Apsley, told some of the leading men among the
court party, that it was the king's desire to have favour
shown to the colonel; whereupon Mr. Palmer, since Castlemain,† was the first man that spoke for the colonel, whom
Finch most eloquently seconded.   Then Sir George Booth

was absent, but attended most other days. On January 25, however, when
the sentence was suggested, he was absent, but was present at the signing,
and himself signed the warrant for execution.

* To those who have not read or not remembered the trials of the regicides, it may be useful to remark, that Colonel Hacker was tried for super-
intending the execution of the king in his military capacity, for which it
seems this warrant was expected to prove a sufficient justification : and
perhaps it ought to have been so considered : but it is extraordinary that
his wife, before she gave up an instrument which seemed so precious
to those who were seeking revenge, had not stipulated for her husband's
pardon.

† This Mr. Palmer was the husband of the celebrated Mrs. Palmer,

and his party all appeared for the colonel, in gratitude for his civility to them. For when the parliament had passed by the rebellion of Lambert and Fleetwood, and those who joined with them, and would not make their offences capital, he had told the house, they could not without great partiality punish these, and had moved much in their favour. Mr. Pierrepont, and all the old sage parliament men, out of very hearty kindness, spoke and laboured very effectually to bring him clear off; and there was not at that day any man that received a more general testimony of love and good esteem from all parties than he did, not one of the most violent hunters of blood opposing favour, and divers most worthy persons giving a true and honourable testimony of him. Although they knew his principles to be contrary to theirs, yet they so justified his clear and upright carriage, according to his own persuasion, that it was a record much advancing his honour, and such as no man else in that day received.*

Yet though he very well deserved it, I cannot so much attribute that universal concurrence that was in the whole house to express esteem for him and desire to save him, to their justice and gratitude, as to an overruling power of Him that orders all men's hearts, who was then pleased to reserve his servant, even by the good and true testimony of some that afterwards hated him and sought his ruin, for the perseverance in that goodness, which then forced them to be his advocates; for even the worst and basest men have a secret conviction of worth and virtue, which they never dare to persecute in its own name. The colonel being thus dis-

mistress to Charles II., afterwards created Lady Castlemain and Duchess of Cleveland. See Grammont's Memoirs.

* Mr. Lassels (probably Lascelles) enjoyed exactly a similar exemption, the peculiar reasons for it are not accurately known, but it is natural to suppose they were similar.

charged the house, retired to a lodging further from Westminster, and lay very private in the town, not coming into
any company of one sort or other, waiting till the act of oblivion were perfected, to go down again into the country ;
but when the act came to be passed in the house, then the
Lord Lexington set divers friends at work in the commons'
house to get a proviso inserted, that the Newarker's money,
which he paid into the committee of Haberdashers' Hall,
and was by that committee paid to the colonel for his pay,
might, with all the use of it, be paid out of the colonel's
estate. He forged many false pretences to obtain this ; but
it was rejected in the commons' house, and the bill going up
to the lords, it was passed without any provisoes. Only the
gentlemen who were the late king's judges, and who were
decoyed to surrender themselves to custody by the house's
proclamation, after they had voted only seven to suffer, were
now given up to trial, both for their lives and estates, and put
into close prison ; where they were miserably kept, brought
shortly after to trial, condemned, and all their estates con-
fiscated and taken away, themselves kept in miserable bondage under that inhuman, bloody jailor, the lieutenant of the
Tower, who stifled some of them to death for want of air ;
and when they had not one penny, but what was given them
to feed themselves and their families, exacted abominable
rates for bare, unfurnished prisons ; of some forty pounds
for one miserable chamber ; of others double, besides undue
and unjust fees, which their poor wives were forced to beg
and engage their jointures and make miserable shifts for ;
and yet this rogue had all this while three pounds a week
paid out of the exchequer for every one of them. At last,
when this would not kill them fast enough, and when some
alms were thus privately stolen into them, they were sent
away to remote and dismal islands, where relief could not

reach them, nor any of their relations take care of them: in this they were a thousand times more miserable than those that died, who were thereby prevented from the eternal infamy and remorse, which hope of life and estate made these poor men bring upon themselves, by base and false recantations of their own judgments, against their consciences; which they wounded for no advantage, but lived ever afterwards in misery themselves, augmented by seeing the misery of their wretched families, and in the daily apprehension of death, which, without any more formality, they are to expect whenever the tyrant gives the word. And these are the "*tender* MERCIES *of the wicked !*"* Among which I cannot forget one passage that I saw. Monk and his wife, before they were removed to the Tower, while they were yet prisoners at Lambeth House, came one evening to the garden and caused them to be brought down only to stare at them,—which was such a barbarism, for that man, who

* Almost all who have written any account of the transactions of those days show a desire to gratify the faction which then prevailed, and have endeavoured to establish a notion that great lenity was shown to all the regicides who were not of the seven excepted : what it was we here learn.

The English nation have long dealt on the hackneyed theme of French oppression, lettres de cachet, bastilles, &c., and have affected an ignorance of what has passed here, in full sight of a British parliament. Those who have viewed the matter near at hand know very well that *these* superlative powers were not at all more dangerous, nor so much abused in France as here, nor the treatment near so rigorous. The prisons of state there were always under the command of noblemen and military officers, who were little likely to practise the jailor's arts. The more any office is despised, the more vile hands will it fall into, and the more atrociously will it be executed ; this reasoning sufficiently establishes the necessity of watching with a jealous eye the conduct of these ministers of justice, if such they should be called, in a country like this. A more desolating picture of misery long drawn out can hardly be imagined. We shall again have to notice the conduct of this lieutenant of the Tower.

had oetrayed so many poor men to death and misery that
never hurt him, but who had honoured him, and had trusted
their lives and interests with him, to glut his bloody eyes with
beholding them in their bondage, that no story can parallel
this inhumanity.

Colonel Scrope, who had been cleared by vote as the
colonel was, was afterwards rased out for nothing, and had the
honour to die a noble martyr.

Although the colonel was cleared both for life and estate in
the house of commons, yet he not answering the court expectations in public recantations and dissembled repentance, and
applause of their cruelty to his fellows, the chancellor was
cruelly exasperated against him, and there were very great
endeavours to have rased him out of the act of oblivion.   But
then Sir Allen Apsley solicited all his friends, as if it had
been for his own life, and divers honorable persons drew up a
certificate, with all the advantage they could, to procure him
favour ; who in all things that were not against the interest of
the state had ever pitied and protected them in their distresses.*
The Countess of Rochester wrote a very effectual letter to the
Earl of Manchester, making her request that the favour to him
might be confirmed as an obligation to her, to quit some that
she, and, as she supposed, her lord had received from him.
This letter was read in the house, and Sir Allen Apsley's
candidate for preferment again made no conscience of deceiv -

* The Countess of Rochester was the wife of Wilmot, general of the
horse for the king, who upon disgust quitted his service, and, receiving a
passport, went abroad ; his wife expressed *loyalty to,* and received much
favour from, the parliament, as Whitelocke informs us; very likely by the
procurement of Colonel Hutchinson.   The passage before us (and many
others such like) may serve as a useful memento to those who are engaged
in civil broils, to maintain all they can of private kindness, consistently with
what they think their public duty.   For the honour of human nature let
due notice be taken of the steady friendship of Sir Allen Apsley.

ing several lords, that the preserving of the colonel would be acceptable to the king and the chancellor, who he now knew hated his life.   Many lords also of the colonel's relations and acquaintance, out of kindness and gratitude (for there was not one of them whom he had not in his day more or less obliged), used very hearty endeavours for him.   Yet Sir Allen Apsley's interest and most fervent endeavours for him, was that only which turned the scales, and the colonel was not excepted in the act of oblivion to anything but offices.

The provisoes to the act of oblivion were all cut off, and it was determined that those things should pass in particular acts ; when the Lord Lexington got one for that Newark money to be repaid out of the colonel's estate, with all the interest for fourteen years.   This act was committed, and the colonel had counsel to plead against it, and the Marquis Dorchester* having the chair, was wonderfully civil to the colonel. The adverse counsel, having been men that practised under the parliament, thought they could no way ingratiate themselves so well as by making invectives against those they formerly clawed with, and when, quite beside their matter, they fell into railings against the injustice of the former times and scandals of the colonel, the marquis checked them severely, and bade them mind their cause : but Mr. Finch, one of the colonel's counsel, after a lawyer had made a long

---

* The same whom, when Viscount Newark, Colonel Hutchinson rescued from the violence of the countrymen at Nottingham; to whom afterwards the colonel made, at the request of her friends, the offer of the hand and fortune of Lady Anne Somerset, and who so handsomely now evinces his candour and gratitude.   His character is well contrasted with that of Lord Lexington, who in the first place obtained a peerage for the sacrifice of this very money; next refused payment of it to the Newarkers, of whom he had borrowed it; then, upon being compelled to pay it, procured easy terms by the colonel's interference; and now attempts to plunder his benefactor of the whole !

railing speech, which held them a tedious while, he replied,
" My lord, this gentleman hath taken up a great deal of time
to tell your lordship how unjust that parliament was, how
their committees perverted judgment and right, which he sets
forth with all his power of language to make them odious,
and in conclusion would persuade your lordship therefore to
do the same things." After the hearing at the committee, a
report was made so favourable for the colonel that the bill
was cast aside, and the house being then ready to adjourn,
most of the colonel's friends went out of town, which opportunity Lexington taking notice of, the very last day in a
huddle got the bill past the lords' house.*

Then the colonel went down into the country, and found it
necessary to reduce and change his family, which were many
of them people he took in for charity, when they could no
where else be received; and they had been more humble and
dutiful while they were under hatches, but now that they
might find better preferments, they were not to be confided in;
yet he dismissed not any of them without bountiful rewards,
and such kind dismissions as none but that false generation
would not have been obliged by. But some of them soon
afterwards betrayed him as much as was in their power, whose
prudence had so lived with them, that they knew nothing that
could hurt his person.

When the colonel saw how the other poor gentlemen were
trepanned that were brought in by proclamation, and how the
whole cause itself, from the beginning to the ending, was
betrayed and condemned, notwithstanding that he himself, by
a wonderfully overruling providence of God, in that day was
preserved; yet he looked upon himself as judged in their
judgment, and executed in their execution; and although he

* The practice of parliament at that time must have differed from what
it now is, for such a bill to originate in the house of lords: we shall presently see it miscarry in the commons.

was most thankful to God, yet he was not very well satisfied in himself for accepting the deliverance. His wife, who thought she had never deserved so well of him, as in the endeavours and labours she exercised to bring him off, never displeased him more in her life, and had much ado to persuade him to be contented with his deliverance; which, as it was eminently wrought by God, he acknowledged it with thankfulness. But while he saw others suffer, he suffered with them in his mind, and, had not his wife persuaded him, he had offered himself a voluntary sacrifice; but being by her convinced that God's eminent appearance seemed to have singled him out for preservation, he with thanks acquiesced in that thing; and further remembering that he was but young at the time when he entered into this engagement, and that many who had preached and led the people into it, and many of that parliament who had declared it to be treason not to advance and promote that cause, were all now apostatised, and as much preached against it, and called it rebellion and murder, and sat on the tribunal to judge it; he again reflected seriously upon all that was past, and begged humbly of God to enlighten him and show him his sin if ignorance or misunderstanding had led him into error. But the more he examined the cause from the first, the more he became confirmed in it, and from that time set himself to a more diligent study of the scriptures, whereby he attained confirmation in many principles he had before, and daily greater enlightenings concerning the free grace and love of God in Jesus Christ, and the spiritual worship under the gospel, and the gospel liberty, which ought not to be subjected to the wills and ordinances of men in the service of God. This made him rejoice in all he had done in the Lord's cause, and he would often say, the Lord had not thus eminently preserved him for nothing, but that he was yet kept for some eminent service or suffering in this cause; although having been freely pardoned by the present powers, he resolved not to do anything against the king, but thought himself obliged to sit still and wish his prosperity in all things that were not destructive to the interest of Christ and his members on earth; yet as he could not wish well to any ill way, so he believed that God had set him aside, and that therefore he ought to mourn in silence and retiredness, while he lay under this obligation.

He had not been long at home before a pursuivant from the council was sent to fetch him from his house at Owthorpe, who carried him to the attorney-general. He, with all preparatory insinuations, how much he would express his gratitude to the king and his repentance for his error, if he would now deal ingenuously, in bearing testimony to what he should be examined, sifted him very thoroughly; but the colonel, who was piqued at heart that they should thus use him, to reserve him with an imagination that he would serve their turns in witnessing to the destruction of the rest, composed himself as well as he could, and resolved upon another testimony than they expected, if they had really called him to any. But the attorney-general was so ill satisfied with his private examination that he would not venture a public one. He dealt with him with all the art and flatteries that could be, to make him but appear, in the least thing, to have deserted his own and embraced the king's party; and he brought the warrant of execution to the colonel, and would fain have persuaded him to own some of the hands, and to have imparted some circumstances of the sealing, because himself was present. But the colonel answered him, that in a business transacted so many years ago, wherein life was concerned, he durst not bear a testimony, having at that time been so little an observer, that he could not remember the least tittle of that most eminent circumstance, of Cromwell's forcing Colonel Ingoldsby to set his unwilling hand, which, if his life had depended on that circumstance, he could not have

affirmed. " And then, Sir," said he, " if I have lost so great
a thing as that, it cannot be expected less eminent passages
remain with me."   Then being shown the gentlemen's
hands, he told him he was not well acquainted with them, as
having had commerce with but few of them by letters; and
those he could own, he could only say they resembled the
writings which he was acquainted with; among these he only
picked out Cromwell's, Ireton's, and my Lord Grey's.   The
attorney-general, very ill-satisfied with his private examination, dismissed him; yet was he served with a writ to appear
in the court the next day.   The colonel had been told that,
when they were in distress for witnesses to make up their
formality, Colonel Ingoldsby had put them upon sending for
him, which made him give that instance to the attorney.*
The next day the court sat, and the colonel was fetched in
and made to pass before the prisoners' faces, but examined in
nothing; which he much waited for, for the sight of the
prisoners, with whom he believed himself to stand at the bar;
and the sight of their judges, among whom was that *vile
traitor* who had sold the men that trusted him; and he that
openly said he abhorred the word *accommodation*, when
moderate men would nave prevented the war; and the
colonel's own *dear friend*, who had wished damnation to his
soul if he ever suffered penny of any man's estate, or hair of
any man's head, to be touched;—the sight of these† had so

* *Risum teneatis.* The subject is too serious for laughter, but an involuntary smile will be excited by this sarcasm, so well pointed. It is no
wonder the attorney-general did not wish to examine him further !

† Monk, Ashley Cooper, and Hollis. Does not every one feel his indignation roused at this wanton outrage upon decency ! Perhaps Colonel
Hutchinson's appearance in court may have been misconstrued by many,
as they might be ignorant that it was involuntary, and no one but himself
could know that he meant to give evidence contrary to what was desired of
him.

provoke: his spirit that, if he had been called to speak, he
was resolved to have borne testimony to the cause and against
the court; but they asking him nothing, he went to his lodging, and so out of town, and would not come any more into
their court, but sent the attorney-general word he could witness nothing, and was sick with being kept in the crowd and
in the press, and therefore desired to be excused from coming
any more thither.   The attorney made a very malicious report
of him to the chancellor and to the king, insomuch that his
ruin was then determined, and an opportunity only was
watched to effect it.*

When Sir A. Apsley came to the chancellor he was in a
great rage and passion, and fell upon him with much vehemence.   "O Nall," said he, " what have you done? you
have saved a man that would be ready, if he had opportunity,
to mischief us as much as ever he did."   Sir Allen was forced
to stop his mouth, and tell him, that he believed his brother
a less dangerous person than those he had brought into the
king's council, meaning Maynard and Glynne ;† but the truth
is, from that time, all kindness that any one expressed to the
colonel was ill resented, and the Countess of Rochester was
also severely rebuked for having appeared so kind to the
colonel.

When the parliament sat again, the colonel sent up his
wife to solicit his business in the house, that the Lord Lex-

* The king intimated to the lords, when there were disputes on foot
respecting the exceptions to the bill of indemnity, that " *other ways* might
be found to meet with those of turbulent and factious spirits :" thereby
showing that he had, like the rest of his family, secret reserves for rendering
insignificant his public acts.

† Maynard and Glynne had chimed in not only with the parliament but
with Cromwell, under whom both held offices.   The chancellor will hereafter find them dangerous inmates ;—in pushing the affair of his accusation
and exile.

ington's bill might not pass the lower house. At her first
coming to town a parliament-man, a creature of Worcester-
house, being in his coach, she out of hers called to him, who
was her kinsman, and desired his vigilance to prevent her
injury. " I could wish," said he, " it had been finished last
time, for your husband hath lately behaved himself so ill, that
it will pass against him." She answered, " I pray let my
friends but do their endeavours for me, and then let it be as
God will." He, smiling at her, replied, " *It is not now as
God will,* but as we will.*" However, notwithstanding many
other discouragements, she waited upon the business every
day, when her adversaries as diligently solicited against her.
One day a friend came out of the house and told her that they
were that day so engaged that she might go home and rest
secure that nothing would be done ; and that day most of her
friends were away, and her opposites took this opportunity to
bring it into the house, which was now much alienated,
especially all the court party, from the colonel ; but God, to
show that not friends, nor diligence, preserved our estates,
stirred up the hearts of strangers to do us justice, and the bill
was thrown out when we had scarce one of those friends we
relied on in the house.

Presently after Mrs. Hutchinson came to town, a kinsman
of hers, fallen into the wicked counsels of the court, came to
visit her one evening, and had been so freely drinking as to
unlock his bosom, when he told her that the king had been
lately among them where he was, and told them that they
had saved a man, meaning Colonel Hutchinson, who would
do the same thing for him that he had done for his father;
for he was still unchanged in his principles, and readier to
protect than to accuse any of his associates, and would not
discover any counsels or designs, or any party, though he was

* This well marks the change of style that had taken place.

2 E 2

known to have hated them.* Then this gentleman told her
how contemptuous a carriage it was, that he would only own
to the signatures of those who were dead, and how they were
resolved his pardon should never pass the seal, and what a
desperate condition he was reduced to. Having thus affrighted
her, then, to draw her in by examples, he told her how the
late statesmen's wives came and offered them all the informations they had gathered from their husbands, and how she
could not but know more than any of them ; and if yet she
would impart anything that might show her gratitude, she
might redeem her family from ruin ; and then he particularly
told her how her husband had been intimate with Vane,
Pierrepont, and St. John, whose counsels they knew had
gone far in this matter, and that if she would prevent others
in the declaring them, she might much advantage herself.
But she told him, she perceived that any safety one could
buy of them was not worth the price of honour and conscience ; that she knew nothing of state managements, or if
she did, she would not establish herself upon any man's blood
and ruin. Then he employed all his wit to circumvent her in
discourse, and to have gotten something out of her concerning
some persons they aimed at, which, if he could, I believe it
would have been beneficial to him : but she discerned his
drift, and scorned to become an informer, and made him
believe she was ignorant, though she could have enlightened
him in the very thing he sought for ; which they are now

* The king's satirical favourite, Rochester, reports of him that he never
said a foolish thing; but surely this was not a very wise one ! How could
he have faith in any such sudden changes ? What he did not mean to do
he did, which was to establish Colonel Hutchinson's steadiness and consistency beyond question. We know from this history that Colonel Hutchinson's sense of honour was a complete safeguard against him; but this
was a principle of which Charles felt not, and affected to disbelieve, the
existence.

never likely to know much of, it being locked up in the grave, and they that survive not knowing that their secrets are removed into another cabinet.* After all, natural affec-

* Any who are delighted with the discovery of a secret will be disappointed that Mrs. Hutchinson did not even here reveal hers, but resisted the bewitching vanity of showing the confidence that had been reposed in her by betraying it. She might perhaps, with great propriety, think it not prudent to commit it to writing, though it was to be read only by her own family. Of the persons here named, Sir H. Vane, it is well known, was sacrificed to the manes of Lord Strafford, whose attainder he was supposed in a great measure to have procured; but there seems not to have been any pretence for excepting him out of the amnesty. He viewed his fate, and the king who sentenced him to it, with equal contempt; and the passage before us is a proof of the fidelity he maintained towards his associates. St. John was excluded from all offices; but Pierrepont escaped untouched in all respects, and represented the county of Nottingham in the short parliament which restored the king, but appears not to have been rechosen in that which succeeded it. That he who was so *deeply engaged* should have come off so well, is matter of wonder, and the more so when we take into consideration the following particulars.

The ingenious writer of the critique of this work in the Annual Review, conjectures that the secret which this friend of Mrs. Hutchinson endeavoured to extort from her was, *the name of that considerable person who had formed the design of settling the state under Richard Cromwell*, as mentioned in p. 378 : this is highly probable, and still more so that this person was Mr. William Pierrepont, and that the royalists aimed peculiarly at his destruction, as will appear from many passages that are to be found in the third volume of Clarendon's State Papers. In one part the good will of Pierrepont to Richard Cromwell and Richard's respect for him is spoken of : in another Hyde instructs his spies to " gain Thurloe, whom he thinks considerable, and he would gain St. John and Pierrepont," adding significantly, " they have manifested that they have no inveterate objection to a *single person*, and the right heir is the best person." In another place it is said by one of the spies that " St. John, Pierrepont, and Thurloe, continue to cabal and press the general (Monk); *three such evil beasts do not exist.*" But when Pierrepont is reported to be ill, the most eager wishes are expressed for his death. No doubt but the *virtuous ministers* of Charles II. dreaded his abilities and integrity as they coveted his pro-

tion working at that time with the gentleman, he in great
kindness advised her that her husband should leave England.
She told him he could not conveniently, and the act of
oblivion being passed, she knew not why he should fear, who
was resolved to do nothing that might forfeit the grace he
had found.   But he told her it was determined that, if there
was the least pretence in the world, the colonel would be
imprisoned, and never be again let loose, which warning,
though others of her friends said it was but an effect of his
wine, the consequence proved it but too true.

She advertised the colonel and persuaded him, being also
advised to the same by other friends, to go out of England,
but he would not: he said this was the place where God had
set him, and protected him hitherto, and it would be in him
an ungrateful distrust of God to forsake it.*   At this time he
would have sold part of his estate to pay his debts, but the
purchasers scrupled, desiring to see his pardon, which he not
having, was fain to break off the treaty; and though all his
friends laboured for it, the chancellor utterly refused it.
There was a thousand pounds offered to one person to procure it, but it was tried several times and could not be passed,
by reason of which he lost the opportunity then of settling his
estate; yet a year afterwards a little solicitor shuffled it in

perty : but supported by such connexions as he was, they could not venture
to attack him without some clear and strong information against him.
That these harpies were disappointed in their project of extinguishing this
eminent patriot and his family, and pouncing on their possessions, may
then most likely be attributed to the constancy and discretion of Mrs.
Hutchinson.

* This is a pregnant instance of Colonel Hutchinson's strong belief in
the decrees of providence, and at the same time of his sincere conformity
to them : it is much to be regretted that he adhered so minutely and
literally to it, instead of making use of his own and his friends' discretion.
He might well have lived to see the happy Revolution, and have returned
and benefited his native country again by his spirit, wisdom, and experience

among many others, and managed it so dexterously that it passed all the seals.   The colonel's estate being in mortgage with a peevish alderman, who designed to have bought it for little or nothing, he had a great trouble with him; for having procured him his money, he would not assign the mortgage, and the others would not lend the money without assignment from him, so that it put the colonel to many inconveniences and great expense.

This parliament being risen, another was called by the king's writ, wherein the act of oblivion was again confirmed, not without some canvassing and opposition; and here again another act about that money of the Lord Lexington's was prepared and twice read in the house, through divers abominable untruths which they had forged and possessed the members withal.   The colonel himself solicited his own defence, and had all the injustice and foul play imaginable at the committee appointed to examine it, and it was so desperate that all his friends persuaded him to compound it; but he would not, though his enemies offered it, but he said he would either be cleared by a just, or ruined by an unjust sentence, and, pursuing it with his usual alacrity and vigour in all things, he at last removed that prepossession that some of the gentlemen had against him; and clearing himself to some that were most violent, it pleased God to turn the hearts of the house at last to do him justice, and to throw out the bill for evermore, which was a great mercy to him and his family, for it was to have thrown him out of possession of all the estates he had, and to have put them into his enemies' hands till they had satisfied themselves.   But the defending himself was very chargeable to him, and not only so, but this rumour of trouble upon his estate, and the brags of his enemies, and the cloud he lay under, hindered him both from letting and selling, and improving his estate, so that it very much augmented his debt.

Before this time, in December, 1660, Captain Cooper sent one Broughton, a lieutenant, and Andrews, a cornet, with a company of soldiers, who plundered his house at Owthorpe, while he was absent, of all the weapons they found in it, to his very wearing-swords, and his own armour for himself, although at that time there was no prohibition of any person whatsoever to have or wear arms. The colonel was not then at home, and the arms were laid up in a closet within his chamber, which they searched, and all the house over, to see if they could have found plate or any thing else; but when they could not, they carried these away, which one of his servants, whom he had dismissed with a good reward, betrayed to them. His eldest son went to the Marquis of Newcastle, lord lieutenant of the county, and complained of the violence of the soldiers, and my lord gave him an order to have the swords and other things back, and some pistols which were the Lord Byron's, but Mr. Cooper contemned my lord's order, and would not obey it. The arms were worth near £100.

Also an order came down from the secretary, commanding certain pictures and other things the colonel had bought out of the late king's collection, which had cost him in ready money between £1000 and £1500, and were of more value; and these, notwithstanding the act of oblivion, were all taken from him.

After these troubles were over from without, the colonel lived with all imaginable retiredness at home, and because his active spirit could not be idle nor very sordidly employed, he took up his time in opening springs, and planting trees, and dressing his plantations; and these were his recreations, wherein he relieved many poor labourers when they wanted work, which was a very comfortable charity to them and their families: with these he would entertain himself, giving them much encouragement in their honest labours, so that tney delighted to be employed by him. His business was serious revolving the law of God, wherein he laboured to instruct his children and servants, and enjoyed himself with much patience and comfort, not envying the glories and honours of the court, nor the prosperity of the wicked; but only grieved that the straitness of his own revenues would not supply his large heart to the poor people in affliction. Some little troubles he had in his own house. His son, unknown to him, married a very worthy person,* but with the manner of which he was so discontented that he once resolved to have banished them for ever, but his good nature was soon overcome, and he received them into his bosom; and for the short time he enjoyed her, he had no less love for her than for any of his own children. And indeed she was worthy of it, applying herself with such humble dutifulness and kindness to repair her fault, and to please him in all things he delighted in, that he was ravished with the joy of her, who loved the place not as his own wife did, only because she was placed in it, but with a natural affection, which encouraged him in all the pains he took to adorn it, when he had one to leave it to that would esteem it. She was besides naturalised into his house and interests, as if she had had no other regard in the world; she was pious and cheerful, liberal and thrifty, complaisant and kind to all the family, and the freest from humour of any women; loving home, without melancholy or sullenness, observant of her father and mother, not with regret, but with delight, and the most submissive, affectionate wife, that ever was. But she, and all the joy of her sweet, saint-like conversation, ended in a lamented grave, about a year after her marriage, when she died in childbirth, and left the sweetest babe behind her that ever was beheld, whose face promised all its mother's graces, but death within eight weeks after her birth, ravished

* The daughter of Sir Alexander Ratcliffe, of the Royalist party.

this sweet blossom, whose fall opened fresh the wounds of sorrow for her mother, thus doubly lost. While the mother lived, which was ten days after her delivery, the colonel and his wife employed all imaginable pains and cares for her recovery, whereof they had often hopes, but in the end all was in vain; she died, and left the whole house in very sensible affliction, which continued upon the colonel and his wife till new strokes awakened them out of the silent sorrow of this funeral.   Her husband having no joy in the world after she was gone, for some months shut himself up with his grief in his chamber, out of which he was hardly persuaded to go, and when he did, every place about home so much renewed his remembrance of her, that he could not think of her but with deep affliction; so, being invited by his friends abroad to divert his melancholy,* he grew a little out of love with home, which was a great damping to the pleasures his father took in the place: but he, how eager soever he was in the love of any worldy thing, had that moderation of spirit that he submitted his will always to God, and endeavoured to give him thanks in all things.

This winter, about October and the following months, the papists began to be very high, and some strangers were come into Nottingham, who were observed to distinguish themselves by scarlet ribbons in their hats; and one night, in a drunken humour, a papist fired a hay barn in a wood-yard in Nottingham, which, if not discovered and prevented by many providences, might have endangered much of the town: but it did £200 worth of mischief; but the matter was shuffled up and compounded, although on the same night several other towns were attempted to be fired.   A great papist, at Eastwold, was known to assemble two hundred men in arms in the night, and some of the Lord Carrington's tenants, who went to Arundel House to speak with their landlord, observed

* Mr. Thomas Hutchinson did not marry again, but died without issue.

very strange suspicious signs of some great business on foot among the papists, who, both in Nottinghamshire and Leicestershire, were so exalted, that the very country people everywhere apprehended some insurrection. Among the rest, there was a light-headed, debauched young knight, living in the next town to Owthorpe, who vapoured beyond all bounds, and had twelve pair of holsters for pistols at one time of the colonel's saddler, and rode at that time with half a dozen men armed, up and down the country, and sent them, and went himself, to several men who had been soldiers in the army, to offer them brave terms to enlist under him, telling them, that they, meaning the papists, should have a day for it. Besides, he, with the parson of the parish, and some other men, at an alehouse, began a health to the confusion of all the protestants in England; and one of the colonel's maids going to Colson, to have a sore eye cured by a woman in the town, heard there that he had vapoured that the papists should shortly have their day, and that he would not leave one alive in the colonel's house. He sent to the preacher of Cotgrove, to forbid him to preach on gunpowder treason-day, threatening to kill him if he did, insomuch that the town were forced to keep a guard all that day upon the steeple.

The men whom the papists had endeavoured to enlist, acquainted the colonel with it, whereof some being in Leicestershire, the colonel sent his son to Sir George Villiers, one of the deputy-lieutenants of that county, to acquaint him with it; but he slighted the matter, although at that time it could have been proved that Golding brought a whole coach laden with pistols, as many as they could stuff under the seats and in the boots, to the house of one Smith, a papist, dwelling at Quineborough, in Leicestershire. The colonel also sent to the deputy-lieutenants of our county to acquaint them with the public danger, and how he himself was threatened; and, by reason that his house had been

disarmed, desired that he might have leave to procure some
arms necessary to defend it; but they sent him word that the
insurrection of the papists was but a fanatic jealousy, and
if he were afraid, they would send him a guard, but durst
not allow him to arm his house.   He, disdaining their security who would not trust him with his own, would have taken
a house at Nottingham for his wife to lie in, who being then
big with child, was near her account; but although she was
fearful, yet when she found him resolved to stay in his own
house, she would not go; whereupon he made strong shut-
ters to all his low windows with iron bars; and that very
night that they sat up, the house was attempted to be broken
in, and the glass of one of the great casements broken, and
the little iron bars of it crashed asunder.   Mrs. Hutchinson being up late, heard the noise, and thought somebody
had been forcing the doors, but, as we since heard, it was
Golding who made the attempt.   The common people, everywhere falling into suspicion of the papists, began to be
highly offended at their insolence, and to mutter strange
words; whether it was this, or what else we know not,
but their design proceeded no further; yet there is nothing
more certain than that at that time they had a design of rising
generally all over England in arms.   But the colonel lived
so retired that he never understood how it was taken up,
and how it fell off, yet, although they would not take the
alarm from him, even the gentlemen of the county afterwards believed they were hatching some mischief, and
feared it.

The colonel continued his usual retirement all that winter
and the next summer, about the end of which he dreamt
one night that he saw certain men in a boat upon the Thames,
labouring against wind and tide, to bring their boat, which
stuck in the sands, to shore; at which he, being in the boat,
was angry with them, and told them they toiled in vain, and

would never effect their purpose; but, said he, let it alone and
let me try; whereupon he laid himself down in the boat, and
applying his breast to the head of it, gently shoved it along,
till he came to land on the Southwark side, and there, going
out of the boat, he walked into the most pleasant lovely fields,
so green and flourishing, and so embellished with the cheerful sun that shone upon them, that he never saw anything so
delightful, and there he met his father, who gave him certain
leaves of laurel which had many words written on them
which he could not read.   The colonel was never superstitious of dreams, but this stuck a little in his mind, and
we were therefore seeking applications of it, which proved to
be nothing in the event, but that having afforded one, I know
not whether the dream might not have been inspired.   The boat
represented the commonwealth, which several unquiet people
sought to enfranchise, by vain endeavours against wind and
tide, paralleling the plots and designs some impatient people
then carried on without strength, or council, or unity among
themselves; his lying down and shoving it with his breast,
might signify the advancement of the cause by the patient
suffering of the martyrs, among which his own was to be
eminent: and on the other side of the river his landing.
into walks of everlasting pleasure, he dying on that shore,
and his father's giving him these laurel leaves with unin-
telligible characters, foretold him those triumphs which he
could not read in his mortal estate.   But to let dreams pass,—

I cannot here omit one story, though not altogether so
much of the colonel's concern, yet happening this summer,
is not unworthy of mention.   Mr. Palmer, a certain non-
conformist preacher, was taken at his own house in Nottingham, by the mayor of the town, for preaching upon the
Lord's day, and some others with him (whereof one was
formerly a servant of the colonel's, and had married one of
his maids), and put into the town's gaol, where they continued

about two or three months. There being a grated window
in the prison, which was almost even with the ground, and
looked into the street, all people coming by might see these
poor people, kept in a damp, ill-favoured room, where they
patiently exhorted and cheered one another. One Lord's
day, after sermon time, the prisoners were singing a psalm,
and the people as they passed up and down, when they came
to the prison, stood still, till there were a great many gathered
about the window at which Mr. Palmer was preaching;
whereupon the mayor, one Toplady, who had formerly been a
parliament officer, but was now a renegade, came violently with
his officers, and beat the people, and thrust some into prison
that were but passing the street, kicked and pinched the men's
wives in his rage, and was but the more exasperated, when
some of them told him, how ill his fury became him who had
once been one of them. The next day, or a few days after,
having given order that the prisoners should every Lord's day
after be locked in the coal-house, he went to London and
made information, I heard on oath, to the council, that a
thousand of the country came into the town armed, and
marched to the prison window to hear the prisoner preach;
whereupon he procured an order for a troop of horse to
be sent down to quarter at Nottingham to keep the fanatics in awe. But one who had a relation to the town, being then at court, and knowing this to be false, certified to
the contrary and prevented the troop. After the mayor came
down, he was one night taken with a vomiting of blood, and
being ill, called his man and his maid, who also at the
same time fell a bleeding, and were all ready to be choked
in their own blood, which at last stopping, they came to assist
him; but after that he never lifted up his head, but languished
for a few months and died.

While these poor people were in prison, the colonel sent
them some money, and as soon as their time was expired,

Mr. Palmer came to Owthorpe to give him thanks, and preached there one Lord's day.* Whether this was taken notice of is not evident, but within a short time after, upon the Lord's day, the 11th of October, 1663, the colonel having that day finished the expounding of the Epistle to the Romans to his household, and the servants being gone off out of the parlour from him, one of them came in and told him soldiers were come into the house. He was not at all surprised, but stayed in the room till they came in, who were conducted by Atkinson, one of those Newark men, who had so violently before prosecuted him at the parliament, and he told the colonel he must go along with them, after they had searched

* This transaction is seemingly of small note; but will be found of the last importance to the parties concerned. By the declaration from Breda, —" Liberty was granted to tender consciences, and none were to be questioned for difference of opinion in matters of religion, which do not disturb the peace of the kingdom." But the parliament which was chosen after the restoration, and which consisted in a great degree of tories and high churchmen, encouraged and led on by the chancellor, passed several severe acts against all dissenters indiscriminately. Particularly one called the Act of Uniformity, and this they followed up with an act forbidding nonconformists to frequent conventicles, under which probably Mr. Palmer was seized. As it had been declared that those who differed from the church could not fail to be enemies to the state, and that the fanatics as they called them, resorted to these means under pretence of religion, but in reality to form and ripen plots and seditions, and that principally for this reason these acts were framed, this renegade very aptly introduced his thousand men in arms.

How far it was discreet in Colonel Hutchinson at such a juncture to let this man preach at Owthorpe, on whom a mark had been set, is doubtful; it seems that in general he confined his religious opinions and worship to his own house, and was of course inoffensive even to the captious government under which he lived.

The manner, time, and place of his being seized, demonstrate the falsehood of the legend contained in Throsby's edition of Thoroton's Nottinghamshire, of his long concealment in his own house, and at last being taken *coming home from church.*

the house ; for which the colonel required their commission,
which at the first they said they need not show, but afterwards they showed him an order from Mr. Francis Leke,
one of the deputy-lieutenants, forthwith to repair to his
house, to search for and bring away what arms they could
find, and to seize his person. All which they did, and found
no arms in the house but four birding-guns, that hung open
in the kitchen, which being the young gentleman's, they left
at that time. It was after sunset when they came, and they
were at least two hours searching every corner and all about
the house, and the colonel was not at that time very well
in health, and not having been on horseback for six months
before, had neither horses nor saddles at that time in the
house ; the coachman was also gone away, and the coach-
horses turned out, and it was as bitter a stormy, pitchy, dark,
black, rainy night as any that year ; all which considered,
the colonel desired that they would but stay for the morning
light, that he might accommodate himself; but they would
not, but forced him to go along with them then, his eldest
son lending him a horse, and also voluntarily accompanying
him to Newark, where, about four o'clock in the morning,
he was brought into the Talbot, and put into a most vile
room, and two soldiers kept guard upon him in that room.

And now what they ailed we knew not, but they were all
seized with a panic fear, and the whole country fiercely
alarmed, and kept at Newark many days at intolerable
charges, and I think they never yet knew what they were
sent for in to do, but to guard Colonel Hutchinson; who
being at first put into a room that looked into the street,
was afterwards removed into a back room, worse, if worse
could be, and so bad that they would not let the Duke of
Buckingham's footmen lodge in it ; and here he continued.
no man coming to him nor letting him know why he was
brought in. The next day Mrs. Hutchinson sent him some

linen, and as soon as the man came, Tomson, the host of the inn, would not suffer him to see his master, but seized him, and kept him prisoner two days. Mr. Thomas Hutchinson had a mare which the innkeeper had a desire to buy, and his father persuaded him to let him have her though worth more money, who thereupon agreed on the price, only Tomson desired him to let him try the mare six miles, which he condescended to, upon condition that if Tomson rode the mare above six miles he should pay the money for her, and furnish Mr. Hutchinson with a horse home, or to my Lord of Newcastle's, or for any other occasion he had while he was at Newark. Upon this bargain Tomson had the mare, but instead of going but six miles, he led a greater party of horse than those who had first seized the colonel, to Owthorpe, and coming in after sunset, to the affright of Mrs. Hutchinson and her children, again searched their house more narrowly if possible than at first, with much more insolent behaviour, although they found no more than at first ; but they took away the birding-guns they had left before, and from Owthorpe went to Nottingham, where they took one Captain Wright and Lieutenant Frank, who had been Lambert's adjutant-general, and brought the poor men to Newark, where they are yet prisoners, and to this day know not why.* Several others were taken prisoners, among the rest one Whittinton, a lieutenant, who, being carried to prison, " Col. Hutchinson," said he, " hath betrayed us all ;" such were the base jealousies of our own party over him, who, because he was not hanged at first, imagined and spoke among themselves all the scandals that could be devised of him, as one that had deserted the cause, and lay private here in the country to trepan all the party, and to gather and transmit

* This shows that the confinement of these persons lasted still longer than Colonel Hutchinson's, and likewise that this history was written while the events were still recent and fresh in the memory.

all intelligence to the court, and a thousand such things, giving each other warning to take heed of coming near him. Those who began to render him thus odious among his own party were the Lambertonians, in malice because he had openly opposed their rebellious insolencies against the parliament. Frank, Whittington, &c. were of these, but the colonel would not hazard himself to rectify their unjust thoughts, and had no resort of his own friends, the more sober and honest men of the party ; only, as much as the straights that were upon him would allow, he would send them relief when any of them were in distress. Hereupon some, convinced of the injuries they did him, about this time sought to do him right, in some meeting where one of the Buckingham's trepans was, and said he was unchanged in his principles, which was all that ever I could hear was informed against him, but anything would serve for those who sought a pretence.*

While the colonel was at Newark, Golding, the papist, was a very busy fellow in spying and watching his house at Owthorpe, and sending in frivolous stories, which amounted to nothing, but declaring his pitiful malice, as they that received them afterwards told the colonel.

When Tomson came back, Mr. Hutchinson, out of the window, spied his own gun, which some of the men brought in, and soon understood that this rogue had made use of his own horse to plunder him. At night Tomson, the host, came up

* The whole history of the reign of Charles the Second is filled with plots, real or imaginary, but mostly the latter. Of all the engines of state the most nefarious is that at this time much employed, of sham or pretended fomenters of sedition or *trepans*, who drew unwary persons either into some confederacy or expression of discontent, and then gave information, probably heightened by invention. Many have thought the information given against Lord Russell and Algernon Sidney, whereon they were tried and condemned, was no better.

into the colonel's chamber, and behaved himself most insolently, whereupon the colonel snatched up a candlestick and
laid him over the chaps with it; whereupon Mr. Leke, being
in the house, and hearing the bustle, with others, came in
with drawn swords, and the colonel took that opportunity to
tell him that he stood upon his justification, and desired to
know his crime and his accusers, and that till then he was
content to be kept as safe as they would have him, but
desired to be delivered out of the hands of that insolent
fellow, and to have accommodation fit for a gentleman ; which
when they saw he would not be without, for he would eat no
more meat in that house, two days after they removed him to
the next inn, where he was civilly treated, with guards still
remaining upon him.

It was not passion which made the colonel do this, for he
was not at all angry, but despised all the malice of his enemies; but he having been now four days in Newark, Mr. Leke
came every day to the house where he was kept by Leke's
warrant, and never vouchsafed so much as to look on him, but
put him into the hands of a drunken insolent host, who daily
affronted him; which, if he would have suffered, he saw would
be continued upon him, therefore knowing that Leke was
then in the house, he took that occasion to oblige him come
to him, and thereupon obtained a removal to an accommodation more befitting a gentleman.

While he was at the other inn, several gentlemen of the
king's party came to him, some whom he had known, and
some whom he had never seen, complimenting him, as if he
had not been a prisoner; which he very much wondered at, and
yet could never understand, for by his former usage he saw
it was not their good nature : but whether this carriage of his
had made them believe innocence was the ground of his confidence, or whether the appearance of his great spirit had
made them willing to oblige him, or whether even his virtue

2 F 2

had stricken them with a guilty dread of him, though a prisoner, certain it is, that some who had been his greatest
enemies began to flatter him ; whereupon, in a Bible he carried
in his pocket, and marked upon all occasions, he marked that
place, Prov. xvi. 7, " When a man's ways please the Lord, he
maketh his enemies to be at peace with him."

The 19th of October, Mr. Leke, with a party of horse, carried the colonel to the Marquis of Newcastle's, who treated
him very honorably ; and then falling into discourse with him,
" Colonel," saith he, " they say you desire to know your
accusers, which is more than I know." And thereupon very
freely showed him the Duke of Buckingham's letter, commanding him to imprison the colonel, and others, upon suspicion of a plot ; which my lord was so fully satisfied the
colonel was innocent of, that he dismissed him without a guard
to his own house, only engaging him to stay there one week,
till he gave account to the council, upon which he was confident of his liberty.* The colonel thus dismissed, came home,

* Here shines out the genuine spirit of a noble Briton ! This was the
same man, who, commanding a host, against which the forces Colonel Hutchinson had to defend Nottingham Castle with were but as a dwarf before
a giant, yet, saw his fidelity to be proof both against danger, and the temptation of great rewards, and had generosity enough to see and value virtue
in an adversary ; he well knew that such a person as the colonel, was safer
in the keeping of his own honour than of all the guards or prisons of his enemies. Who can fail to regret that such a man should have been so long
the dupe of his loyalty to the Stuarts, and above all that he should have to
receive mandates from the infamous sycophants of Charles the Second ? If
a man were inevitably to be persecuted, it made much for his honour, and
somewhat for his satisfaction, to have two men of such opposite characters
as Newcastle and Buckingham, the one for his protector, the other for his
persecutor.

Of Buckingham we shall again have occasion to speak.

As we shall not again see anything more of this *truly noble* man, the
Marquis of Newcastle, we take this opportunity to cite, from a tradition preserved by Deering in his History of Nottingham, that at the time of the

and upon the 22d day of October a party of horse, sent only
with a wretched corporal, came about eleven o'clock with
a warrant from Mr. Leke, and fetched him back to Newark,
to the inn where he was before, Mr. Twentyman's, who being
still civil to him, whispered him as soon as he alighted, that
it was determined he should be close prisoner; whereupon
the colonel said he would no more pay any sentinels that they
set upon him, yet they set two hired soldiers, having now dismissed the county, but the colonel forbade the inn to give
them any drink, or anything else upon his account. The
next day, being the 23rd, Mr. Leke came to him and showed
him a letter from my Lord Newcastle, wherein my lord wrote
that he was sorry he could not pursue that kindness he
intended the colonel, believing him innocent, for that he had
received a command from Buckingham to keep him a close prisoner, without pen, ink, or paper ; and to show the reality of
this, with the order he sent a copy of the duke's letter, which
was also shown the colonel; and in it was this expression,
" *that though he could not make it out as yet, he hoped he should*

---

great revolution, another Cavendish, Earl, and afterwards Duke of Devon-
shire, together with Lord Delamere, son of that Sir George Booth whose
life and fortunes Colonel Hutchinson preserved, together with Colonel Hutchinson's half-brother, and others of that country, set up their standard at
Nottingham ; there waked again the soul of liberty and patriotism, which
had slept ever since Colonel Hutchinson's days, and causing the trumpet to
sound to arms, and telling the inhabitants a Stuart was at hand with all his
army, saw the whole people fly to arms, some on horseback, some on foot,
with all the various weapons they could find, march all as one man to meet
him, and take their determined stand at that pass of the Trent where their
old governor had repeatedly fought and conquered, and whose spirit they
imagined to hover over and inspire them with its wonted energy. Having
thus tried their temper, he committed to the guard of these true-born sons
of freedom, that princess (Anne) who was to carry the British name to its
highest pitch of glory.

bring Mr. Hutchinson into the plot.''   Mr. Leke having communicated these orders to Mr. Hutchinson, told him he was to go to London, and should leave him in the charge of the mayor of Newark.

Because here is so much noise of a plot, it is necessary to tell what it hath since appeared.   The Duke of Buckingham set a work one Gore, sheriff of Yorkshire, and others, who sent out trepanners among the discontented people, to stir them up to insurrection to restore the old parliament, gospel ministry, and English liberty; which specious things found very many ready to entertain them, and abundance of simple people were caught in the net; whereof some lost their lives, and others fled.*   But the colonel had no hand in it, holding himself obliged at that time to be quiet.   It is true he still suspected insurrections of the papists, and had secured his house and his yards, better than it was the winter before, against any sudden night assaults.

After Mr. Leke was gone, the mayor, one Herring, of Newark, a rich, but simple fellow, sent the jailor to Mr. Hutchinson, to tell him he must go to his house; which the colonel refusing to do voluntarily, without a mittimus from some magistrate, the mayor sent five constables and two soldiers, who by violence both forced the colonel out of his quarters, and into the gaol without any legal commitment, although the colonel warned both the jailor and the men of the danger of the law, by this illegal imprisonment.   The colonel would not advance at all into the prison, into which the men would fain have entreated him; but when they saw they could not persuade, they violently thrust him in, where the jailor afterwards used him pretty civilly : but the room

* Rapin speaks slightly and cursorily of this, under the name of the Northern Plot; but plainly shows that some of the principal persons whom it was pretended had been concerned in it, neither were nor could be.

being unfit for him, he got cold and fell very sick, when, upon the 27th of October, Mr. Leke, with the marquis's secretary, came to him, and found him so, and acquainted him that the marquis had received express orders from the king, to send him up in safe custody to London. Mr. Leke finding him so ill, was so civil as to permit him to go by his own house, which was as near a road, that he might there take accommodations for his journey, and be carried up at more ease in his own coach ; Mr. Leke himself went away before, being necessitated to make more haste than he could have done if he had stayed for the party that was to guard the colonel, and left his orders for sending him away with Mr. Atkinson, who first seized him. The same 27th day, at night, his house at Owthorpe was again searched, and he and his wife being abroad, all their boxes and cabinets were broken open, and all their papers rifled, but yet for all this they could find nothing to colour their injustice to him.

Having been falsely and illegally imprisoned, from six o'clock on Friday night, the 23rd of October, till ten o'clock in the morning, October 28th, he was then, in order to his going to London, brought by Beek, the jailor, to Twentyman's inn, from whence he was hailed, to stay there till a commanded party of the county horse came to guard him to London. But one division of the county who had warrants sent them, not coming in, Atkinson sent into that part where the colonel lived, and his own neighbours coming slowly and unwillingly to that service, he was forced to stay there all that day till night in the custody of the jailor. At night, when he was in bed, the mayor being drunk, commanded him to be carried back to the jail, but the jailor, weary of his drunken commands, sat up with two soldiers, and guarded him in the inn.

The next day, the party not being come in, one Corporal Wilson, a mean fellow, who was appointed to command

the colonel's guard, came and told him that he must not go
by his own house, nor have the privilege of his coach, but he
carried up another way; whereupon the colonel sent to
Atkinson, to desire him he might not be denied that civility
Mr. Leke had allowed him; but he was so peevish and obstinate that the colonel was sending his son post to the
Marquis of Newcastle's to complain of his malicious inhumanity, who would have forced him on horseback without
any accommodation, when he was so taken ill that he could
not have ridden one stage without manifest hazard of his life :
and yet Mr. Cecil Cooper and Mr. Whally, though justices
and deputy lieutenants, could not prevail with him, till he
saw the colonel as resolute as himself: and then at last, by
their mediation (wherein Mr. Cecil Cooper did something to
redeem his former causeless hatred, which made him plunder
the house, and detain the plunder when it was ordered back),
the colonel, about sunset, was sent out of Newark, with
those horse that were come in, to stay for the rest at his own
house.   Being driven in the night by an unskilful coachman,
the coach was overturned and broken; but about twelve
o'clock at night they came safe home.   Thus the colonel
took his last leave of Newark, which being a place he had
formerly subdued, and replete with so many malicious
enemies to the whole party, and more particularly to him,
upon no other account but that he had been the most formidable protector of the other party in this country, he expected
far worse treatment from the generality of the town; who
were so far from joining in joy of his captivity, that when he
was forced through their streets, they gave him very civil
respect, and when he came away, civil farewells, and all
muttered exceedingly at their mayor, and said he would undo
their town by such simple illegal proceedings.   The colonel
regarded all these civilities from the town, who were generally
much concerned in his injuries, and from Cooper and others,

not as of themselves, but as from God, who at that time overawed the hearts of his enemies. as once he did Laban's and Esau's; and he was much confirmed in the favour of God thereby, and nothing at all daunted at the malice of his prosecutors, but went as cheerfully into captivity as another would have come out of it.

They were forced to stay a day at Owthorpe, for the mending of the coach and the coming in of the soldiers, where the colonel had the opportunity to take leave of his poor labourers, who all wept bitterly when he paid them off; but he comforted them and smiled, and without any regret went away from his bitterly weeping children, and servants, and tenants, his wife and his eldest son and daughter going with him, upon Saturday, the 31st of October.

Golding, the night before he went, had sent him a pot of marmalade to eat in the coach, and a letter to desire all grudges might be forgotten, and high flattering stuff, by his man who was to be one of the guard, whom, he said, he had chosen out from the best he had, and his best horse, and if he did not pay him all respect, he would turn him away; and as the colonel came by his door, he came out with wine, and would fain have brought him into the house to eat oysters, but the colonel only drank with him, and bid him friendly farewell, and went on, not guarded as a prisoner, but waited on by his neighbours. Mrs. Hutchinson was exceedingly sad, but he encouraged and kindly chid her out of it, and told her it would blemish his innocence for her to appear afflicted, and told her if she had but patience to wait the event, she would see it was all for the best, and bade her be thankful for the mercy that she was permitted this comfort to accompany him in the journey; and he with divers excellent exhortations cheered her who was not wholly abandoned to sorrow, while he was with her. who. to divert her, made himself sport with his guards, and deceived the way, till upon the 3rd of November he was brought to the Crown, in Holborn. From thence, the next day, he was carried by Mr Leke to the Tower, and committed there close prisoner, by warrant, signed by Secretary Bennett, the 20th of October, whereby he stood committed for treasonable practices, though he had never yet been examined by any magistrate, one or another. His wife, by his command, restrained herself as much as she could from showing her sadness, whom he bade to remember how often he had told her that God never preserved him so extraordinarily at first, but for some great work he had further for him to do or to suffer in this cause; and bade her be thankful for the mercy by which they had so long in peace enjoyed one another, since this eminent change; and bade her trust God with him, whose faith and cheerfulness were so encouraging that it a little upheld her; but, alas! her divining heart was not to be comforted: she remembered what had been told her of the cruel resolutions taken against him, and saw now the execution of them.

On Friday, November the 6th, he was sent for by Secretary Bennett, to his lodgings at Whitehall, which was the first time he was examined, and the questions he asked him were: 1st. "Where he had lived this four or five months?" To which he answered, "Constantly at home, at his own house in Nottinghamshire." 2nd. "What company used to resort to his house?" He told him, "None, not so much as his nearest relations, who scarcely ever saw him." 3rd. "What company he frequented?" He told him, "None; and that he never stirred out of his own house to visit any." Bennett said, "That was very much." 4th. "Whether he knew Mr. Henry Nevill?" He answered, "Very well." 5th. "When he saw him?" He said, "To his best remembrance never since the king came in." 6th. "When he wrote to him?" He said, "Never in his life." 7th. "When Mr. Nevill wrote to him?" He said, "Never." 8th. "Whether any messages

had past between them?" He said, "None at all." 9th.
"Whether none had moved anything to him concerning a
republic?" He answered, "He knew none so indiscreet."
10th. "What children he had?" He said, "Four sons and
four daughters." 11th. "How old his sons were?" He
said, "Two were at men's estate, and two little children."
12th. "Whether his sons had not done any thing to injure
him?" He replied, "Never that he knew of, and he was
confident they had not." 13th. "Where he went to church
to hear divine service, common prayer?" He said, "No
where, for he never stirred out of his own house." 14th,
"Whether he heard it not read there?" He answered, "To
speak ingenuously, no." 15th. "How he then did for his
soul's comfort?" He replied, "Sir, I hope you leave me that
to account between God and my own soul." Then Bennett
told him his answers to these had cut him off of many questions he should have asked, and he might return. So he was
carried back to the Tower with only two of the warders which
brought him thither.*

Not long afterwards one Waters was brought prisoner out

* What will the reader think of this examination when he is reminded,
or, if he knew it not before, is informed, that this gentleman who is so
anxious for the welfare of Colonel Hutchinson's soul, and so earnest for his
frequenting the church, was himself a concealed papist, and privy to the
king's being so too ! It is necessary to be here observed, that upon the
publication of the act of uniformity a very great number of the parochial
clergy quitted their benefices, and were replaced by others; it is highly
probable this would be the case at Owthorpe, and it was a very natural
consequence of it that Colonel Hutchinson should absent himself from his
church, where, although he had heretofore taken much pains to get a good
minister established and his salary augmented, he had now to expect,
instead of spiritual comfort, such pulpit railings as he had been assailed
with at Nottingham. Accordingly he performed the worship of God in his
own family, much as a protestant father of a family would have done in a
catholic country. And the history informs u he was so occupied when

of Yorkshire, a fellow of a timorous spirit, who, being taken, was in so great a fear, that he accused many, guilty and not guilty, to save himself; and caused his own wife to be put in prison, and hanged the dearest friend he had in the world, and brought his wife's brother into the same danger; some say through fear, others that he was a trepanner from the beginning, for he drew in all the people whom he accused. Whatever he was, he was so utter a stranger to colonel Hutchinson, that he never saw his face; yet the day he was examined at Whitehall, Colonel Hutchinson was in great haste fetched away from his dinner at the Tower, and told he should be examined in the king's own hearing; which he was very glad of, and, with great haste, and formality, and strictness he was carried by the deputy lieutenant and a strong guard by water from the Tower to Whitehall; and when he came to land at Whitehall Stairs, one Andrews, an officer, with two files of musketeers, was ready to receive him, and led him to Bennett's lodgings, where he observed a great deal of care to place the guard at the outward door in the court, and to keep the chamber door continually shut, that none might peep in, but a few gentlemen who were admitted to come now and then and stare him in the face at the door, but none were in the room for a long space but Andrews and himself, till at the last the keeper thrust himself in.   The colonel, having stayed two hours, concluded that he should now be confronted by some accuser, or at least have an examination more tending to treasonable practices than his first seemed to do, especially understanding that Mr. Waters had been many hours before in the house, and was yet there.   But at last,

the soldiers came to seize him : but it was prudent to say nothing of this to the *secretary confessor !*

Mr. Nevill, whom he speaks of, made a considerable figure in the latter times of the long parliament, as a staunch republican, a man of strict integrity, and a steady opposer of all the usurpations.

parturiunt montes! and out comes Secretary Bennett! who, taking him to a window apart from Mr. Andrews and the keeper, most formally begins thus : " Mr. Hutchinson, you have now been some days in prison, have you recollected yourself to say any more than when I last spoke to you ?" Mr. Hutchinson answered, " He had nothing to recollect, nor more to say." " Are you sure of that ?" said the secretary. " Very sure," said Mr. Hutchinson. " Then," said Bennett, " you must return to prison." And accordingly he was carried by the same guard back again to the Tower, where he was kept with a great deal of strictness, and some weeks passed before his wife was admitted to see him ; for whom, at the last, Sir Allen Apsley procured an order that she might visit him, but they limited it that it might not be but in the presence of his keeper. The lieutenant, in hopes of a fee, gave leave that her son and daughter might go into the room with her, who else must have stood without doors ; but he would not permit her to take lodgings in the Tower, which, being in a sharp winter season, put her to great toil and inconvenience, besides excessive charge of providing his meat at the Tower, and her company in another place : meanwhile he was kept a close prisoner, and had no air allowed him, but a pair of leads over his chamber, which were so high and cold, that he had no benefit from them ; and every night he had three doors shut upon him, and a sentinel at the outmost. His chamber was a room where it is said the two young princes, King Edward the Fifth and his brother, were murdered in former days, and the room that led to it was a dark great room, that had no window in it, where the portcullis to one of the inward Tower gates was drawn up and let down, under which there sat every night a court of guard. There is a tradition, that in this room the Duke of Clarence was drowned in a butt of malmsey ; from which murder this room, and that joining it, where Mr. Hutchinson lay, was called the Bloody Tower.   Between Mr. Hutchinson's chamber and the dark room there was a door, which Mr. Hutchinson desired the lieutenant might be left open in the night, because it left a little necessary house open to the chamber, which he and his man had occasion of in the night, having gotten fluxes with their bad accommodations and diet: but the lieutenant would not allow it him, although, when that was open, there were two doors more shut upon him, and he could not have any way attempted any escape, but he must, if it had been possible to work through the walls, have fallen upon a court of guard.

Notwithstanding all this strictness, which was also exercised on most of the other prisoners, yet their own sentinels hated the lieutenant, and his Cerberus, Cresset, because they cheated them, and had nothing of generosity or bounty to engage the hearts of their soldiers, who, seeing so much of their wickedness, abhorred them, and pitied the poor gentlemen that were so barbarously used by them; and whether out of humanity, or necessity, or villainy, I know not, but they would offer the prisoners many courtesies, and convey letters between them.   Mr. Hutchinson was never so imprudent to trust any of them with his, having within an hour of his imprisonment been instructed by another prisoner a safer and more convenient way; yet was it their interest to use courteously all those who offered themselves to do them service.   Among the rest, as he was one day sitting by the fire, the sentinel at the door peeped in his head and called to him: " Sir," said he, " God bless you! I have sometimes guarded you in another manner at the parliament house, and am grieved to see the change of your condition, and only take this employment now, to be more able to serve you, still hoping to see you restored to what I have seen you."   The colonel, not turning his head, told the man that language suited not the coat he wore, bade him mind his present duty,

and told him he had no employment of his service. " Well,"
said the soldier, " I perceive, sir, you dare not trust me, bu
my Lady Vane and my Lady Lambert know me, and if you
have any service to command me to them, I will bring you a
testimony from them." The colonel took no more notice of
him, but the fellow, officious, or hoping to get money, went
to my Lady Lambert's house, and told her that he had formerly been her husband's soldier, and that he wished his
restitution, and that he used sometimes to guard the prisoners, and would carry her letters to any of them, and that
he had lately been sentinel at Colonel Hutchinson's chamber,
and would carry anything she would send to him. She only
bade him remember her service to him, and tell him she
wished him liberty ; and the fellow flattering her with professing his love to her lord, she expressed some pleasure with
his speeches, and gave him some money ; which her daughter
considering, as soon as he was gone out told her that she had
done unwarily to open herself so much to one of the soldiers
in present employment, whom she did not know but he might
be set on purpose to trepan her. My lady, to prevent any
inconvenience of her error, thought it the best way to go
immediately and complain that one of the soldiers had come
to her to trepan her, under colour of a message from Colonel
Hutchinson, which she had not entertained ; and desired
they might not be allowed to do any such thing, protesting
her own loyalty and readiness to discover any that were
false to them. This was extremely well represented of her
at the court, and as ill of Colonel Hutchinson, that he had
not done the like ; and Colonel Leg, whose company it was
that then had the guard of the tower, was commanded to
find out and punish this soldier, who, as it proved afterwards,
was a good honest fellow, and was the only protestant in that
company, the rest being most of them Irish and papists, and
some rebels. This poor fellow, having been a pa l ament

soldier, enlisted among them to get a living, but was very tender-hearted to the prisoners, and had a desire to do them kindness. Hereupon he came to the colonel's man, and desired his master would not own him, and that he would send to my Lady Lambert to do the same, which the colonel did ; but when she was sent to by him, she sent a maid to see all the soldiers, who owned the man, and he was put in prison, and cashiered and undone, for nothing but offering his service to have done the prisoners slight services. And Colonel Hutchinson was ill thought of at the court, because when Colonel Leg brought his men under the window of his prison, and came up to Mr. Hutchinson and desired him to view them all, he would not accuse any of them ; which if he had, he would not only have cut off his own, but all the other prisoners' ways of sending to their friends abroad ; yet he never made use of this fellow, nor any of them, in any business of trust, although he thought it not good to discourage any that appeared to wish them well, among so many bloody murderers as they were given up to.

The colonel endured his prison patiently till the trial of those they called conspirators in Yorkshire was over ; but when he had lain from November till Candlemas term in prison, he sent his wife to Secretary Bennett to desire that such persons as had business with him might have liberty to come to him. She had before been with some of the privy council who were her husband's friends and allies, to complain of his unjust imprisonment, and his harsh usage there, contrary to all law from the beginning to the ending, even their own laws ; and they had told her that they were sensible of it, but that they only stood for cyphers, while the chancellor and Bennett managed all things without their privity, in most oppressive and illegal ways.* She, as she was

* It was thought better to bring together here several observations relating to Hyde, Earl of Clarendon, and chancellor Bennett, Earl of

advised, went therefore to Bennett and told him that. by reason
of some engagements for money her husband had upon his

Arlington, and secretary, and Villiers, second Duke of Buckingham. The
first is well known from his history and letters to have been an unreasonable
enemy to presbytery and presbyterians ; which prejudice induced him to
persuade his royal master, whose confidence for a great length of time he
almost entirely engrossed, to violate all his promises to them, though gratitude as well as honour should have made him keep them. About this
time his credit began to diminish by the introduction of Bennett to be
secretary of state instead of Nicholas, who was the particular friend of
Hyde. But at the period here spoken of, this had taken effect but partially, and not enough to furnish for those who were oppressed by the one,
a succour in the opposition of the other ; nor did there appear much
reason to hope for moderation in either. Who it was of the privy council
that gave Mrs. Hutchinson her information cannot be conjectured; but
there is no doubt that the too great ascendency of the chancellor did, no
long time after, cause him to be impeached in parliament, and accused of
all the misconduct of many years. It was in vain that he endeavoured, in
the written defence he sent to the parliament, to distribute the odium
among the council in general; the information here given to Mrs. Hutchinson obtained general belief ; he was condemned, and died in banishment.
He very justly, in the same writing, attributes a good deal of the hatred
and bitterness which prevailed against him to his many refusals of setting
the seal to pardons and other indulgences. When, among the speakers
against him, we see the names of Maynard, St. John, Hampden, and
Prynn,* we may well conclude that these men, though they had a little
temporized, were glad to assist in the downfall of the man who had persecuted the more zealous of their former associates, and pleased to see him
sue for that clemency which his own former severity gave him good reason
to despair of. Bennett was several years after impeached together with
Buckingham, the same who first entrapped and caused Colonel Hutchinson
to be seized, and whose infamous letter the Marquis of Newcastle showed
the colonel. On this occasion he employed his usual treachery, and cri-
minated the earl, who was fain to save himself from the indignation of the
parliament by a total change of conduct; by practising the hypocrisy he
had recommended to Colonel Hutchinson, of frequenting the commution
of a church he was averse to, and persecuting the papists, whom he had

* Rapin, vol. ii. p. 648.

2 G

estate, this very close imprisonment had been infinitely prejudicial to him, both his tenants and his creditors taking
advantage of his incapacity (by reason of his close restraint)
to defend himself, or to speak with lawyers or others about
affairs that nearly concerned his estate; besides the neglect
of all his business, and the intolerable charge and inconvenience of his disordered family, dispersed into three several
places, which would suddenly bring ruin upon his whole
family, besides the destruction of his health.   Bennett told
her, her husband was a very unfortunate person in regard of
his former crimes.   She told him she had rather hoped he
had been happy in being comprised in the act of oblivion,

protected, and wished to protect.   On account of his conduct a strict
inquiry was made by the commons concerning the commitment of persons
by order of council, and amendments were made in the Habeas Corpus
Act, which, if they had existed in the colonel's time, would have preserved
him from his long and unjust imprisonment.   Buckingham, after bringing
the family of Fairfax to extinction by marrying and slighting his daughter,
heightening and exposing his master's vices, and passing his whole life in
playing, by countless alternations, the parts of traitor and sycophant, died
in disgrace and beggary, and, to sum all up in that which to him would be
the greatest suffering, his memory remains hung up to ridicule in the chains
of never-dying satire by Pope, in some of the best lines he has written.

To those who believe in the peculiar interposition of God in human
affairs, as our author did, it must be very striking, and to her, if she lived
to witness it, highly gratifying, to observe this course of events.   Mr. Hutchinson's three great enemies, Buckingham, Clarendon, and Arlington,
ruin each other, and two of them, Clarendon and Arlington, without the
design of doing anything so good, laid the foundations of an alliance which
furnished the assertors of British liberty and toleration with a champion
who overthrew, it is hoped never to rise again, despotism in church and
state; for Clarendon recommended Charles the Second to constrain his
brother to marry his daughter, whom he had dishonoured; she brought
him the Princesses Mary and Anne, successively queens of England; and
Bennett, Earl of Arlington, to gain himself popularity in a moment of
need, first proposed the match between Mary and the Prince of Orange,
afterwards William the Third !

which allowed him not to be remembered as a criminal; and
that she had chosen to make her addresses to him on this
occasion, because some of the council had told her the king
left all the management of these things to him.   He was
very urgent with her to know who it was that informed her
that he was the sole actor in these businesses; but she desired to be excused from naming any author in that thing,
which she had not mentioned but that she thought it his
honour to own; but he told her he would not move for any
more liberty for her husband than he had, unless he could
be assured it might be done with more safety to his majesty
than he could apprehend from it.   " But," said he, " Mrs.
Hutchinson, I have some papers of yours which I would show,
not to examine you, but to see whether you will inform me
anything of them."   She told him she had curiosity enough
to see anything that passed under her name; whereupon he
called forth his man, who brought out a great bundle of
papers, called examinations, taken at Grantham, of passages
between Mrs. Hutchinson and Mrs. Vane.   First he showed
her a character which contained cyphers for the names of
many gentlemen and women who were not very distant
neighbours, with others whom she knew not at all.   She told
him she understood nothing at all of that paper; then he
turned down the rest, and showed her a letter, beginning,
" My dear Amaranta;" which she told him she knew not at
all.   " But," said he, " you will yet own your own hand;"
and showed her among these papers the copy of the letter
that was sent to the house of parliament in her husband's
name, written in her hand, which when she saw she was a
little confounded, wondering how it should come into his
hands; but she told him that she could not absolutely say
that was her writing, though it had some resemblance.   So
when she had again urged the business she came for, and
could obtain nothing from him, she went away, and left in

the room with the secretary, Sir Robert Byron, a cousin-german of her husband's, who had by chance come in thither upon some business of his own, and had stood by while she urged to the secretary the mischief and ruin her husband's imprisonment had brought upon his family and estate. As soon as she was gone, the secretary told Sir Robert that he had heard Mrs. Hutchinson relate the sad condition of her husband and his house; "and," said he, "you may here take notice how the justice of God pursues those murderers, that, though the king pardoned both his life and estate, yet by the hand of divine justice they were now likely to come to ruin for that crime;" which words being told Mr. Hutchinson, he laughed much at the simple folly of the man, who could call his own illegal persecutions and oppressions of innocence the judgments of God. The papers which he showed Mrs. Hutchinson she afterwards learned to have been some letters between Mrs. Vane, one of Sir Henry Vane's daughters, and one Mrs. Hutchinson, a gentlewoman who used to come thither, filled with such frivolous intelligence of private amours and intrigues as young people used to communicate to their confidants, and such as any wise statesman would have believed himself affronted to have had brought to him, and not made such politic inquiries, and imprisoned those with whom they were found, about so unconcerning a matter.

Mr. Henry Nevill and Mr. Salloway had been put into the Tower upon the same suspicion which they had of Mr. Hutchinson—a northern plot, for which there was a peculiar assizes, and some men were executed; and the judges, at their return, said that their confessions almost amounted to treason; but that almost served their turns. As soon as those assizes were past, Mr. Hutchinson sent to Mr. Nevill and Mr. Salloway, that he thought it now time for them to endeavour their liberty, and therefore desired to know what course they in-

tended to proceed in, that they might all take one way.   They
both sent Mr. Hutchinson word that they looked upon him as
the best befriended, and they were resolved to see first what
success he had, and to make him their leading card.   Hereupon he, fearful of doing anything which they could not, sat still
deliberating, while they, without giving him the least notice,
wrought their own liberties secretly, Mr. Nevill desiring to
travel, and Mr. Salloway making such a false, flattering petition, that no honest man could make such another, and a less
after his would have but more exasperated.   It took so, that
immediately he had his liberty, both of them taking some
oaths to confirm their loyalty, which were given them by the
clerk of the Tower.*   They had a mind at court that Mr.
Hutchinson should have made such another petition, and
therefore Salloway's was shown to a friend of his ; the words
of which were, " That since God by his miraculous providence
had set his majesty over us, he had acquiesced thankfully
under it, and never, not so much as in thought, made a wish
against it ;" and promises of the like nature : which perhaps
were no truer than his professions, for they were utterly false ;
for at his first coming into the Tower no man had muttered
more than he, who scarce refrained even from blasphemies
against God himself for bringing him into bondage.   After
his release he went to their common prayer, and pleased them
so well that it was said they would give him an office.   But
when they found that, notwithstanding their hint, Mr. Hutchinson would not follow his example, their malice grew very
bitter against him at the court, insomuch that a gentleman
having treated with Mrs. Hutchinson for a niece of his, to

* Mr. Nevill, as just before mentioned, had acted with steadiness and integrity; Mr. Salloway had been more valuable, and had been successively of
the council of state, of the Rump parliament, of the committee of safety
and council of officers.

whom he was guardian, that would have been a convenient fortune for her son, the Chancellor sent for the gentleman and peremptorily forbade him to proceed in the affair,* and openly said, " *he must keep their family down.*"

Mr. Hutchinson was not at all dismayed, but wonderfully pleased with all these things, and told his wife this captivity was the happiest release in the world for him; for before, although he had made no express engagement, yet, in regard that his life and estate had been freely left him when they took away others, he thought himself obliged to sit still all the while this king reigned, whatever opportunity he might have; but now he thought this usage had utterly disobliged him from all ties either of honour or conscience, and that he was free to act as prudence should hereafter lead him, and that he thought not his liberty out of prison worth purchasing by any future engagement, which would again fetter him in obligations to such persons as every day more and more manifested themselves to be enemies to all just and godly interests. He therefore charged his wife that she should not make applications to any person whatsoever, and made it his earnest request to Sir Allen Apsley to let him stand and fall by his own innocency, and to undertake nothing for him, which, if he did, he told him he would disown. Mrs. Hutchinson, remembering how much she had displeased him in saving him before, submitted now to suffer with him, according to his own will,† who, as he would do nothing that might en-

---

* What base and atrocious malice! yet this was the virtuous Lord Clarendon! This method of alternately persecuting those whom they suspect, and suspecting those they persecute, has for ever been the practice of bad ministers, and has for ever created rebels, and will for ever continue to create new ones in the place of those they destroy.

† There does not appear reason for supposing that Colonel Hutchinson had any distinct prospect of manifesting his sentiments with effect, nor can these declarations be accounted for upon any principle but that of general

tangle him for his freedom, so he patiently suffered their
unjust bondage, and had no guilt found in him; yet was he
cruelly and maliciously persecuted and hated; and criminals,
with threats and promises, were tried in all ways to see if
they could bring out any accusation against him, but all
they could arrive at was only that he was an unchanged person, yet they kept him still as close a prisoner as at the first.
After Salloway was released, Sir Allen Apsley asking the
Chancellor why his brother was not let out as well as Salloway;
" What," said the Chancellor," make you no difference between
your brother and Salloway?"   Sir Allen replied, he thought
his brother as innocent.   " Surely," said the Chancellor,
" there is a great difference ; Salloway conforms to the government, and goes to church, but your brother is the most
unchanged person of the party."

The colonel, at last, with some other prisoners were deliberating to sue out a habeas corpus, and in order thereunto sent
to the lieutenant of the Tower to desire a copy of the warrant
whereby he stood committed, which indeed was so imperfect,
that he could not legally be kept upon that, for there was
neither his Christian name nor any place of residence mentioned in it, so that any other Hutchinson might as well have
been kept upon it as he ; but the lieutenant refused to give
him a copy, and his jailor told the prisoner it was altered after
they had kept him four or five months in prison : then the
colonel wrote to Bennett, but neither from him could he
obtain any copy of his commitment.

After this a friend gave him notice that they had a design
to transport him to some island or plantation ; whereupon he
wrote a narrative of his imprisonment, and procured it to be
secretly printed, to have left behind him, if he had been sent

disdain.   The complete and generous attachment of Mrs. Hutchinson
deserves a higher term ; if our language would admit of it, as the French
does *dévouement,* we should call it *devotion.*

away, to acquaint the parliament, which was then shortly to assemble, and to leave with his friends; but he kept it in the mean time privately.*

At length, through the lies that the lieutenant of the Tower told of his prisoners, and the malice of their wicked persecutors, who envied even the bread which charity sent in to feed some of the men whose estates were wholly taken away, warrants were signed for carrying away most of the prisoners, some to Tangiers, and some to other barbarous and distant places: among the rest Colonel Hutchinson was destined to the Isle of Man, which Sir Allen Apsley hearing of, told the king he had some private business of trusts with the colonel concerning his own estate, for which he obtained a respite for him for three months, with liberty for lawyers to come to him But when the colonel heard of it, he was more displeased with this petty favour than with all their rigour, and had resolved to have done something to reverse it, but that his wife persuaded him to rest till she made a short voyage into the country to fetch him supplies, which he did.

As soon as she was gone, the lieutenant of the Tower sent his jailer, Mr. Edward Cresset, early in the morning, upon the 16th day of April, 1664, to fetch Mr. Hutchinson to his lodgings, whither being come, Cresset withdrew, and the lieutenant told Mr. Hutchinson that he had been civil to him in permitting his children to come to him with their mother, and yet he

---

* At the time of Colonel Hutchinson's imprisonment the parliament were so devoted to the views of the court, that they might very likely have taken little notice of his representations.   Many years elapsed before they animadverted as they ought upon such arbitrary and unjust proceedings. Probably the time will never arrive when parliaments will become sensible of the solecism of making good laws and then dispensing with the execution of them.   The fact is, that *governors* and *makers of laws* seldom feel the effects of them in their own persons: to the *governed*, any variableness destroys the benefit of all law.

had not paid him his fees and dues, although that warrant which allowed the access of his wife did not mention his children, and therefore he now demanded his dues. Mr. Hutchinson told him, " At his departure out of the Tower he should not be behind hand with him for the civility of suffering his children to come to him." Robinson replied, " That signified nothing, he expected his dues, and would have them." Mr. Hutchinson answered, " His was not every prisoner's condition, for he had been now twenty-four weeks kept close prisoner, and yet never knew accuser nor accusation against him, and therefore he should desire to consider before he parted with his money; but for any civilities he should repay them." Robinson said, " He meddled with no man's crimes, but whether guilty or not guilty, he expected his dues, which he could recover by law if they were refused." Mr Hutchinson asking, " What they were ?" He said, " Fifty pounds." Further demanding, " By what law they were due, whereby he could recover them?" Robinson answered, " By custom." Mr. Hutchinson told him, " He was confident that pretence would not recover them; and if he thought it would, he would go to a civil and fair trial with him the next term ; yet due or not due, what civilities he either had or should afford him, he would recompense at parting." Robinson answered, " He stood upon his right, and he would make Mr. Hutchinson, or somebody else, pay it." Mr. Hutchinson told him," He knew not whom he meant by somebody else, but if his liberty were taken from him without any reason that he knew of, he would not so part with his money, if he could help it." He then, in anger, said, " he would lock him up close, and let nobody come to him." Mr. Hutchinson told him, " He could be locked no closer than he had been all this time, and he hoped he would not forbid those coming to him who had warrant from the secretary ; for the rest he might use his pleasure " He, in fury, commanded Mr. Hutchinson to be taken away, and

locked him up, so that no person could come to him; and he
gave order at the Tower Gates to keep out his children and
all his relations that should come to inquire for him; and he
sent word to Serjeant Fountaine who had an order to come
in, that he should not be admitted, although his business was
of great concernment to others, and not to Colonel Hutchinson, who being a trustee for some of his relations, was to
have made some settlements in their affairs; which could not
be done, but they, to their prejudice, were forced to go without it.*   Although his commands were executed to the full,
yet Mr. Hutchinson's eldest son found means to steal into
the Tower, and to inform his father of a malicious lie which
the lieutenant had made of him at court, on that day that he

---

* The same respectable friend who, proceeding upon an intimation contained in the Annual Review, communicated to the editor the particulars
of the deliverance of George Fox, given in page 201, has upon a similar
intimation pointed out several passages in the life of William Penn, de-
monstrating the officious readiness of this same Sir John Robinson to act
as the minister of oppression and persecution. He first sends a serjeant
from the Tower to watch Penn; the serjeant finds him preaching to *friends*,
seizes him, drags him away to the Tower, and sends to Whitehall for Robinson—Robinson comes, sits as magistrate, overrules the just and legal
objections of Penn, and commits him to gaol. Penn, whilst in prison,
writes a very sensible and moderate letter to Bennett, Earl of Arlington,
complaining of coarse treatment in prison, although the secretary had pretended to give orders for his decent accommodation. At the trial of Penn,
Sir John Robinson sits as assessor to the recorder, and at the same time
obtrudes himself upon the court as an evidence, interferes to influence the
jury against the prisoner, and abuses the foreman because he will not suffer
himself to be browbeaten nor biassed. At last, when a verdict could not
be obtained conformable to the views of the judges, they fine the jury for that
which they have given, and Penn for contempt of the court. To enume-
rate, from the " Histories of the Sufferings of the Quakers," the instances of
his oppression and cruelty, would fill a volume. Suffice it to hold him up
here to infamy as lasting as the fame of those two virtuous men, in the hope
of deterring other ministers of injustice from doing the like.

fell out with him; which was this.—Robinson told the king, that when Mr. Henningham and others were carried out of the Tower to be shipped away, Mr. Hutchinson, looking out of his window, bade them take courage, for they should yet have a day for it. This lie coming to Mr. Hutchinson's knowledge on the 19th of April, moved him more than all his other base usage; whereupon he wrote a letter to Robinson, to tell him he should have taken care of provoking his prisoners to speak, who had so much exposed himself to every one of them; and to let him know what he himself had observed and could prove, he drew it up under certain heads, which he told him, if he continued his vile usage of him, he would publish. The articles were:—

1st. That Robinson had affirmed that the king gave no allowance to his prisoners, not so much as to those who had all their estates taken from them; and accordingly he gave them none, but converted what the king allowed them to his own use, and threatened some of the prisoners with death if they offered to demand it; and suffered others, at twelve o'clock at night, to make such a miserable outcry for bread, that it was heard in some parts of the city, and one was absolutely starved to death for want of relief; although the king at that time told a prisoner, that he took more care for the prisoners than for his own table.

2nd. That he set down to the king seven pounds a week for one prisoner, for whom he never laid out above twenty-seven or thirty shillings a week at the most.

3rd. That he not only kept back the prisoners' allowances, but exacted of them excessive rents for bare prison lodgings, and empty warders' houses, unfurnished; and if they had not punctually paid him, would have stifled them up by close imprisonment, without any order, although he knew they had not a penny to buy bread, but what came from the charity of good people.

4th That he received salary of the king for forty warders, and had not near so many, but filled up the list with false names, and took the pay to himself.

5th. That when he had received money for those warders he kept, he had detained it many months, to his own use, while the poor men were thereby in miserable wants.

6th. That he sold the warders' places, and let them houses at a dear rate, and yet took the most considerable prisoners, which ought to have been committed to them, into his own house, and made them pay him excessive rates for bed-rooms, and set his man, Cressett, over them, making them pay him for attendance, which the warders should have had.

7th. That he made many false musters in his own company belonging to the Tower, and though he had received the soldiers' money, yet it was run in arrears to them five or six pounds a man ; at which they cruelly murmured, because by this means their maintenance was straitened, and their duty brought more frequently upon them.

8th. That notwithstanding all his defrauding, oppressive, and exacting ways of raising money, he had ungratefully complained of the king's scanty recompense of his service.

9th. That after the starving of the poor prisoners and their miserable outcry, when shame forced him to allow about a a dozen poor tradesmen ten shillings a piece,* though at that time he received forty from the king for each of them, he and his man, Cressett, denied the king's allowance, and said it was his own charity.

10th. That he was frequently drunk, out of the Tower till twelve, one, and two o'clock, and threatened one of the war-

* It hence appears that many more in number, and persons of a different description from what other accounts mention, were made prisoners of state at this time.

ders, who came one night to fetch him home, with Newgate. and spited him ever after.

All these things being notoriously true, this letter put him into a great rage, and a no less dread that the colonel, as he had threatened him, would publish it; whereupon, as soon as these things were laid to his charge, within ten days he paid his soldiers fifteen months' pay out of twenty-two due to them when the letter was written, he having all that while kept back eighteen pence a week out of every soldier's pay; and the soldiers, understanding that Colonel Hutchinson's observations of his fraud had procured them this satisfaction, used to give him thanks when they came to stand sentinels at his door.

Presently after he received the letter, he went to Sir Allen Apsley and complained to him that the colonel had sent him a vile letter, but did not show it to Sir Allen, as he sent word to the colonel he would; whereupon Sir Allen Apsley sent Mr. George Hutchinson with a letter to Sir John Robinson, to tell him that if he would let him go to his brother, he doubted not but it would be a good means to persuade the colonel to pay him his fees, and to reconcile the differences between them. Sir John, upon the 21st of April, went along with Mr. George Hutchinson to his brother, and at his entrance, in a passion began to quarrel at the colonel's sour looks; who told him, if he had known they would not have pleased him, and had had notice of his coming, he would have set them in a glass for him. Then Robinson told him, in a rage, he had written him a libel. Mr. Hutchinson answered it was no libel, for he had set his name to it, and they were truths, which if he put him to it, he could prove by sufficient testimonies. Whereupon he fell into horrible railing and cruel language, but by Mr. George Hutchinson's interposition at length all was pacified, and he was fairly going out of the room with Mr. George

Hutchinson, when his man Cresset, reminding him that the
colonel had a foul copy of his letter, which he had said he
would send to Sir Allen, who had desired to see it; Robinson
resolved to take that draught away from him; but the colonel,
foreseeing that, had sent copies of it long before out of the
Tower, which Robinson's dull head not dreaming of, came
back and insolently commanded the colonel to give him the
first draught of the letter. The colonel desired to be excused, whereupon Robinson said he would have his pockets
searched, and accordingly bade Cresset feel in them. The
colonel, a little moved, took a bottle in his hand, and bade
Cresset forbear, if he loved his head, and told Sir John if
he had any warrant to search him from the king or council, he would submit to it, but otherwise he would not suffer
it, especially for a paper which was only of private concernment between them; for all this, when Sir John saw that
Cressett durst not approach the colonel, he commanded one
Wale, a warder, to search his pockets, who coming with entreaties to the colonel to permit it, he suffered him. And
then the lieutenant caused a little dressing box which the
colonel had to be opened, and took away all the papers he
found in it, among which there was one wherein the colonel
had written a verse out of the 43d Psalm; it was the first
verse, to be joined with the narrative of his imprisonment,
that he had provided to leave behind him for the satisfaction of his friends. This paper Robinson carried to court,
and said, that by the deceitful and unjust man the colonel intended the king, although the application was of his own
making. In the meantime, while they were ransacking his
box and pockets Robinson fell a railing at the colonel,
giving him the base terms of rebel and murderer, and such
language as none could have learned, but such as had been
conversant with the civil society of Picked-hatch, Turnbull-
street, and Billings-gate, near which last place the hero had

his education.* When the colonel patiently told him he transgressed the act of oblivion, he said he knew that well enough, and bade him sue out his remedy; then in fury and rage he turned the colonel's servant out of his chamber, who had been locked up with him all the time of his imprisonment, and left him altogether unattended, which having never been before in his whole life, put him into a cold and a flux, with a feverish distemper: but the greatness of his mind was not broken by the feebleness of his constitution, nor by the barbarous inhumanity of his jailers, which he received with disdain, and laughed at, but lost not anger on them.

After these things, Mrs. Hutchinson coming out of the country was, by the lieutenant's order, denied to see her husband, but at her lodgings she found letters from him conveyed to her every day, in spite of all his guards; and thereupon she wrote to Robinson to desire to know whether the secretary had countermanded his first order for her to see her husband, or whether he denied obedience to it; whereupon Robinson sent to her to come to him the next day, but when she came

---

* In a former note we remarked that the evils of imprisonment were considerably enhanced by the custody of prisons, and peculiarly prisons of state, being committed to persons of low education and sordid mind; it is here strongly exemplified, and doubly painful must it have been to Mrs. Hutchinson to witness the unworthy treatment her husband now received, and to compare it with that which the persons confined in this same place had experienced from her father, a man of liberal and noble mind. Considering the prejudice which reigns against prisons and prisoners, and therefore how few visit them, and how few prisoners dare make observations or remonstrances, it is to be feared many abuses pass unknown and uncorrected; it is but once, in ages, that there appears a Howard! These considerations ought to render the guardians of the public welfare extremely tender of the liberty of individuals: but if such things as state prisons be at all necessary, then careful to provide for their being superintended by gentlemen, and men of liberal and benevolent minds.

he was gone forth, and she was not admitted within the gates, and thereupon she went back to her lodgings and wrote him a smart letter, and sent him with it a copy of her husband's letter, which she told him she would publish, and not suffer him to be murdered to extort undue money from him. The next day, being the Lord's day, he sent one of the warders to entreat her to come to her husband, and the blood-hound Cressett met her at the gate, and led her to her husband, and left her all the day alone with him, which they had never done before during all the time of his imprisonment, and in the evening Sir John Robinson sent for her, and partly expostulated with and partly flattered her, and told her that her husband would have been sent to the Isle of Man,* but that he in kindness had procured a better place for him, and that he was not covetous, but since her husband would not pay him his fees, he might use his pleasure, and she and his children and relations might freely go to him. She received this as befitted her, being in his hands, and knowing that not good nature, but fear she would put him in print, moved him to this gentler course ; and this she understood, both by the inquiries his servants made of the colonel's warder concerning her intentions, and by Robinson's continuing, notwithstanding all his dissimulation, to make a thousand false insinuations against the colonel everywhere, and to do him all ill offices at court; even if there were not a more abominable wickedness than all this prac-

---

* An exile, for the second time, to the Isle of Man is mentioned. Had the colonel, or his friends, been properly informed, they would not have wished to exchange it for the flat coast of Kent. In our times, when it has become the retreat of the gay and imprudent, it must seem strange to hear it spoken of as a spot to be dreaded. Had he been sent there he would very likely have lived to see the downfall of his enemies, and have returned to shine in the autumn of his life as an evening sun, when his virtues would have been recognised and revered.

tised, namely, a lingering poison given him, which, though we had not wickedness enough to suspect then, the events that have since ensued make a little doubtful. It is certain that Cressett did make that attempt upon Sir Henry Vane and others, and two or three days before the colonel was sent away, he brought into his chamber, when he came to lock him up at night, a bottle of excellent wine, under pretence of kindness, which he, the colonel, and the warder drank together, and the warder and the colonel both died within four months; the colonel presently after fell sick, but was very unsuspicious, and we must leave it to the great day, when all crimes, how secret soever, will be made manifest, whether they added poison to all their other iniquity, whereby they certainly murdered this guiltless servant of God.

A few days after, at nine o'clock at night, after his wife was gone from him, Cressett brought the colonel a warrant, to tell him that he must, the next morning tide, go down to Sandown Castle, in Kent; which he was not surprised at, it being the barbarous custom of that place to send away the prisoners, when they had no knowledge of, nor time to accommodate themselves for their journey. But instead of putting him into a boat at the morning tide, about eight o'clock Sir Henry Wroth came with a party of horse to receive him of the lieutenant, and finding him sick, and not well able to endure riding in the heat of the day, he was so civil as to let him go by water in the evening tide to Gravesend, with a guard of soldiers in boats hired at his own charge, where the horse guard met him. By these means he got opportunity to take leave of his children which were in town, and about four o'clock he was sent out of the Tower, with one Gregory, designed to be his fellow prisoner; who, going over the drawbridge, turned back to the lieutenant, and told him he would have accepted it as a greater mercy if the king had commanded him to have been shot to death there, rather than have sent

him to a distant place to be starved, he having nothing but
his trade to maintain him, and his friends would now be so
far removed from him, that he could expect nothing.* The
lieutenant in scorn told him, he went with a charitable man
who would not suffer him to starve, whereby he exposed the
malice of their intentions to the colonel ; who thought it not
enough to send him to a far prison not much differing from
exile, but to charge him with a companion, whom however
his kindness might have rendered him charitable to, yet they
ought not to have put upon him ; neither would the colonel
take notice of their imposition, though he designed kindness
to the man, had he been worthy of it.

The colonel's wife and children got a boat and followed
him to Gravesend, whither also Gregory's wife, and one that
called him brother, went ; and that night all the company
and all the guards supped at the colonel's charge, and many
of the guards lay in the chamber with him, who, with the refreshment of the evening air, and the content he felt in being
out of Robinson's claws, found himself, or through the live-
liness of his spirit fancied himself, something better than he
was in the Tower. The next morning, very early, his guards
hurried him away on horseback ; but, to speak the truth, they
were civil to him. His son went along with him to see the
place he was sent to, and Sir Allen Apsley had procured an
order for his servant to continue with him in the prison ; his
wife went back to London, to stay there to provide him such
accommodation as she could hear he had need of.

When he came to the castle, he found it a lamentable old
ruined place, almost a mile distant from the town, the rooms
all out of repair, not weather proof, no kind of accommodation
either for lodging or diet, or any conveniency of life. Before

* This Gregory seems to have been a low man, but had probably commanded a company in some of the city regiments during the latter times of
the parliament.

he came, there were not above half a dozen soldiers in it, and a poor lieutenant with his wife and children. and two or three cannoniers, and a few guns almost dismounted, upon rotten carriages ; but at the colonel's coming thither, a company of foot besides were sent from Dover to help to guard the place, pitiful weak fellows, half-starved and eaten up with vermin, whom the governor of Dover cheated of half their pay, and the other half they spent in drink. These had no beds, but a nasty court of guard, where a sutler lived, within a partition made of boards, with his wife and family, and this was all the accommodation the colonel had for his victuals, which were bought at a dear rate in the town, and most horribly dressed at the suttler's. For beds he was forced to send to an inn in the town, and at a most unconscionable rate hire three, for himself, his man, and Captain Gregory ; he had to get his chamber glazed, which was a thoroughfare room, having five doors in it, one of which opened upon a platform, that had nothing but the bleak air of the sea, whilst every tide washed the foot of the castle walls. This air made the chamber so unwholesome and damp, that even in the summer time the colonel's hat-case and trunks, and every thing of leather, would be every day all covered over with mould,— wipe them as clean as you could one morning, by the next they would be mouldy again ; and though the walls were four yards thick, yet it rained in through the cracks in them, and then one might sweep a peck of saltpetre off of them every day, which stood in a perpetual sweat upon them. Notwithstanding all this, the colonel was very cheerful, and made the best shifts he could, with things as he found them ; when the lieutenant's wife, seeing his stomach could not well bear his food, offered to board him, and so he and his man dieted with her for twenty shillings a week, he finding wine besides, and linen, &c. Whilst the sutler provided his meat, Gregory ate with him ; but when he tabled with the captain.

2 H 2

Gregory's son coming to him, he had his meat from the
town, and soon after a woman came down who left not the
man destitute and comfortless. The worst part of the colonel's
sufferings in this prison, was the company of this fellow, who
being a fellow prisoner, and poor, and the colonel having no
particular retreat, he could not wholly decline his company;
and he being a carnal person, without any fear of God, or any
good, but rather scandalous conversation, he could take no
pleasure in him; meanwhile, many of his friends gave caution
to his wife concerning him, as suspecting him to be a trepanner, which we had afterwards some cause to fear.

The captain of the castle, one Freeman, had all this while
a chamber which was a little warmer, and had a bed in it,
but this he reserved, intending to set a rate upon it, and this
too was so dark that one could not have read by the fire or
the bedside without a candle at noon day.

When the colonel's wife understood her husband's bad
accommodation, she made all the means she could through her
friends to procure liberty that she might be in the castle with
him, but that was absolutely denied; whereupon she and her
son and daughter went to Deal, and there took lodgings,
from whence they walked every day on foot to dinner and
back again at night, with horrible toil and inconvenience;
and though they procured the captain's wife to diet them
with the colonel, when they had meat good enough, yet
through the poverty of the people, and their want of all necessaries, and the faculty of ordering things as they should be,
it was very inconvenient to them; yet the colonel endured it
so cheerfully that he was never more pleasant and contented
in his whole life. When no other recreations were left him,
he diverted himself with sorting and shadowing cockle-shells,
which his wife and daughter gathered for him, with as much
delight as he used to take in the richest agates and onyxes
he could compass, with the most artificial engravings, which

were things, when he recreated himself from more serious
studies, he as much delighted in as any piece of art.   But
his fancy showed itself so excellent in sorting and dressing
these shells, that none of us could imitate it, and the cockles
began to be admired by several persons who saw them
These were but his trifling diversions, his business and con
tinual study was the Scripture, which the more he conversed
in, the more it delighted him; insomuch that his wife having
brought down some books to entertain him in his solitude,
he thanked her, and told her that if he should continue as
long as he lived in prison, he would read nothing there but
his bible.   His wife bore all her own toils joyfully enough
for the love of him, but could not but be very sad at the sight
of his undeserved sufferings; and he would very sweetly and
kindly chide her for it, and tell her that if she were but
cheerful, he should think this suffering the happiest thing
that ever befell him; he would also bid her consider what
reason she had to rejoice that the Lord supported him, and
how much more intolerable it would have been if the Lord
had suffered his spirits to have sunk, or his patience to have
been lost under this.   One day when she was weeping, after
he had said many things to comfort her, he gave her reasons
why she should hope and be assured that this cause would
revive, because the interest of God was so much involved in
it that he was entitled to it.*   She told him she did not

* The notion of the revival of The Cause, and of the advancement of it
by their sufferings, seems to have been very prevalent with those who fell
in these times; accordingly they supported their fate with the true spirit of
martyrs.   The speech of Colonel Okey at the time of his execution, preserved in the Trials of the Regicides, maintains the style of prophetic
eloquence with so much dignity and firmness, as almost to captivate the
imagination of the coolest reasoner.   These sentences following are extracted
from it :—

"And truly, as to the Cause, I am as confident, even as I am of my

doubt but the cause would revive; but, said she, notwith-standing all your resolution, I know this will conquer the weakness of your constitution, and you will die in prison. He replied, I think I shall not, but if I do, my blood will be so innocent, I shall advance the cause more by my death hastening the vengeance of God upon my unjust enemies, than I could do by all the actions of my life. Another time, when she was telling him she feared they had but placed him on the sea-shore in order to transport him to Tangier, he told her, if they had, God was the same God at Tangier as at Owthorpe; prithee, said he, trust God with me, if he carry me away, he will bring me back again.

Sometimes when he would not be persuaded to do things wherein he had a liberty, for fear of putting a snare and stumbling-block before others that had not so, and when she would expostulate with him, why he should make himself a martyr for people who had been so censorious of him, and so unthankful and insensible of all his merits, he would say, he did it not for them, but for the cause they owned. When many ill usages he had received from godly people have been urged to him, he would say, that if they were truly the people of God, all their failings were to be borne; that if God had a people in the land, as he was confident he had, it was among them, and not among the cavaliers, and therefore

resurrection, that that cause which we first took up the sword for, which was for righteousness and justice, and for the advancement of a godly magistracy and a good ministry (however some men turned about for their own ends), shall yet revive again. I am confident, I say, that cause for which so much blood hath been shed, will have another resurrection, and that you will have a blessed fruit of those many thousands that have been killed in the late war. I would say to all good men, rather to suffer than take any indirect means to deliver themselves; and God, when it shall make most for his own glory and the good of his people, will deliver, and that in such a way that himself shall have glory in, and the gospel have no reproach by."

although he should ever be severe against their miscarriages
in any person in whomsoever he found them, yet he would
adhere to them that owned God, how unkindly soever they
dealt with him.   Sometimes he would say, that if ever he
should live to see the parliament power up again, he would
never meddle any more either in councils or in armies ; and
then sometimes again, when he saw or heard of any of the
debaucheries of the times, he would say, he would act only as
a justice of the peace in the country, and be severe against
drunkards, and suffer none in his neighbourhood.   Oftentimes he would say, that if ever he were at liberty in the world,
he would flee the conversation of the cavaliers, and would
write upon his doors,

Procul hinc, procul este, profani !

and that, though he had in his former conversation with
them never had any communication with their manners nor
vices, yet henceforth he would never, in one kind or other,
have any commerce at all with them ; and indeed it was a
resolution he would oftener repeat than any other, telling
us that he was convinced there was a serpentine seed in
them.   Yet he had many apprehensions of the rash, hot-
heated spirits of many of our party, and fears that their
pride and self-conceit of their own abilities would again
bring us into confusion, if they should ever have the reins
again in their hands ; and therefore he would bid us advise
his son, and would himself advise him, if ever we lived to
see a change, not to fall in with the first, how fair soever
their pretences were ; but to wait to see how their practices
suited them.   For he would say, that a hot-spirited people
would first get up and put all into confusion, and then a
sober party must settle things ; and he would say, let my son
stay to fall in with these.   He foresaw that the courses which
the king and his party took to establish themselves would be

their ruin, and would say, that whenever the king had an
army it would be his destruction.* Once when his wife was
lamenting his condition, having said many things to comfort
her, he told her he could not have been without this affliction, for if he had flourished while all the people of God
were corrected, he should have feared he had not been accounted among his children, as he had not shared their lot.
Then would he with thankfulness repeat the kind and gentle
dealings of the Lord at all times toward him, and erect a
firm and mighty hope upon it, and wonderfully encourage her
to bear it patiently, not only by words, but by his own admirable example.

After Mr. Hutchinson had been some time prisoner at
Sandown, the governor of the Castle came over, and would
fain have let him his chamber for 20s. a week, which Mr.
Hutchinson told him he would give him, if his wife might
come there to him ; but the governor refused that without
an express order, which was endeavoured but could not be
obtained. Then Freeman demanded a mark a week of the
colonel for fees, but the colonel told him, except he could
show how it was due by any known law, he would not pay
it. Some time after, the governor of Dover came over, with
the governor of Sandown and one Mr. Masters, and Freeman
consulting his master of Dover how he should get money of
the colonel, the governor of Dover advised him to put him into
a dungeon, but the fellow durst not attempt it. Yet some time
afterwards he came to the castle, and passing into his own
chamber, through Mr. Hutchinson's, who was there,—as he

---

* Is it permissible to extend this prediction to the time when James the
Second mustered his army near Salisbury, and in their almost general
defection received his irrevocable doom ? If it is, it will appear a very
signal instance of foresight. The king then reigning, Charles II. never
made but one, and that a very short-lived attempt to raise an army, which
was speedily disbanded.

went by with his Lieutenant, Moyle, at his heels, he called
out to Mr. Hutchinson's man, and bade him desire Hutchinson
to come to him, without the addition of so much as the title of
a gentleman.   Mrs. Hutchinson being then in the room with
her husband, desired that she might go in with him and
answer the captain's insolency, and that he would take no
notice of it; upon which he told her that he would not, neither
should she, and so they both went into the captain's chamber,
who had also called Gregory.   When they were both there,
the captain, turning to Moyle, said, " Captain Moyle, I ordain
you to quarter Hutchinson and Gregory together in the next
room; and if Hutchinson will make a partition at his own
charge, he may have that part of the chamber which has the
chimney, and for this you must expect a mark a week of
Hutchinson, and a noble of Gregory; and if they will have
any enlargement besides, they must pay for it."*   Mr. Hutchinson laughed at him, and bade his wife report his usage
of him to the secretary at London, to whom she immediately
wrote an account of it, and sent it to Sir Allen Apsley, desiring him either to procure an order for removal, or else for
better accommodation, and she showed this letter to Gregory
before it went, representing equally his condition with her
husband's.   Seeing she could not get admission into the castle,
she took a house in the town, to which she intended to have
brought her children for the winter, had not God prevented it.

Not † long after, the colonel's brother, Mr. George Hut-

---

* In speaking of the persons who had the command of the castle, and the
custody of the prisoners, there seems in some parts of the narrative to be a
little perplexity; but this passage shows clearly that Freeman was captain,
but did not reside at it; and that Moyle was his lieutenant, and did reside
at it.   The former was the person who, on this and some other occasions,
attempted to extort money from Colonel Hutchinson and his family; the
latter was the person whose wife boarded and accommodated them.

† We now hasten to the conclusion of our tragedy, and accordingly
here are all the principal characters in their proper places and attitudes,

chinson, came down, and brought with him an order, signed by the secretary Bennett, to allow the colonel leave to walk by the sea-side with a keeper, which order Sir Allen Apsley and his lady had at length procured with some difficulty and sent him; wherewith he was so well satisfied, that now he thought not his prison insupportable; neither indeed was it so to him before, for his patience and faith wonderfully carried him through all his sufferings. As it now drew nigh to the latter end of the year, Mrs. Hutchinson, having prepared the house, was necessitated to go to Owthorpe to fetch her children, and other supplies for her husband; whom, when the time of her departure came, she left with a very sad and ill-presaging heart, rather dreading that while he lay so ready on the sea-coast, he might some time or other be shipped away to some barbarous place in her absence, than that which afterwards ensued. The colonel comforted her all he could, and on the morning she went away said, " Now I myself begin to be loth to part with thee." But yet, according to his usual cheerfulness, he encouraged himself

---

our hero suffering with fortitude, calmness, and dignity; the kind-hearted brother, the idolizing devoted wife, the observant son and daughter, soothing him with their assiduities, and the constant friend procuring and sending alleviations. Evils so endured, so consoled, almost begin to partake of the nature of enjoyments; but even this state of things will prove very transient, and like the last gleams of departing day, and we must speedily descend into the vale of tears; those who solicited this exile as a mitigation of oppression, and this license of walking on the shore as a relief, little knew or thought of the effect this situation on this low shore would have on the constitution of a person tenderly brought up, and who had lived all his time in the centre of the kingdom ; or that walks by the sea-side, in the decline of the day and of the year, would add considerably to the danger. Those who are acquainted with these parts are well aware of it, and probably so were those who granted both.

> *Timeo Danaos et dona ferentes.*
> Trust not the fraudful present of a foe.

and her, and sent his son along with her. His daughter
and his brother stayed at Deal, who, coming to him every
day, he walked out with them by the sea-side, and would
discourse of the public concernments, and say that the ill-
management of the state would cause discontented wild
parties to mutiny and rise against the present powers, but that
they would only put things in confusion ; it must be a sober
party that must then arise and settle them. He would often
say to his son and his wife, as he did now to his brother,
" Let not my son, how fairly soever they pretend, too rashly
engage with the first, but stay to see what they make good,
and engage with those who are for settlement, who will have
need of men of interest to assist them ; let him keep clear
and take heed of too rash attempts, and he will be courted if
he behave himself piously and prudently, and keep free of all
faction, making the public interest only his own." He would
sometimes in discourse say, that when these people once had
an army, which they seemed to aim at, that army would
be their destruction, for he was very confident God would
bring them down ; he would often say they could not stand,
and that whoever had anything to do with them could not prosper. He once used this expression, " Although," said he,
" I am free from any truckling with them, yet even that con-
senting submission which I had, hath brought this suffering
upon me." And he would often say, he would never have so
much as a civil correspondence with any of them again ; yet
when he mentioned Sir Allen Apsley, he would say, he
would never serve any that would not for his sake serve the
person that had preserved him. When his wife went away
he was exceeding well and cheerful, and so confident of
seeing Owthorpe, that he gave her directions in a paper for
planting trees, and for many other things belonging to the
house and gardens. " You give me," said she, " these orders,
as if you were to see that place again." " If I do not," said

he, " I thank God I can cheerfully forego it, but I will not distrust that God will bring me back again, and therefore I will take care to keep it while I have it."

On the third of September, being Saturday, he had been walking by the sea-side, and coming home found himself aguish, with a kind of shivering and pain in his bones, and going to bed did sweat exceedingly: the next day he was a little better, and came down; but on the Monday, expecting another fit, which came upon him, he lay in bed all day, and rose again the next day, but went not down; and after that he slept no more till his last sleep came upon him, but continued in a feverish distemper, with violent sweatings, after which he used to rise out of his bed to refresh him, and when he was up used to read much in his bible. He had directed his wife, when she went away, to send him the Dutch Annotations on the Bible, and she had sent it down with some other things; which he presently caused to be brought him, though he was in his bed, and some places in the Epistle to the Romans read, which having heard, " these annotations," said he, " are short;" and then looking over some notes upon that Epistle, which his wife had gathered from him, and had written in a book; " I have," said he, " discovered much more of the mystery of truth in that Epistle, and when my wife returns I will make her set it down; for," said he, " I will no more observe their cross humours, but when her children are near, I will have her in my chamber with me, and they shall not pluck her out of my arms; and then, in the winter nights, she shall collect several observations I have made of this Epistle since I came into prison." The continual study of the Scriptures did infinitely ravish and refine his soul, and take it off from all lower exercise, and he continued it in his sickness even to the last, desiring his brother, when he was in bed and could not read himself, to read it to him. He found himself every day growing weaker, yet was not exceeding

sick, only he could not sleep at all, day nor night. There
was a country physician at Deal, who had formerly belonged
to the army, and had some gifts, and used to exercise them
among godly people in their meetings; but having been
taken there once by the persecutors, and being married to a
wicked unquiet woman, she and the love of the world had
perverted him to forsake all religious meetings; yet the man
continued civil and fair-conditioned, and was much employed
thereabouts.   He being sent for to Mr. Hutchinson, found
that on Friday his mouth grew very sore, whereupon he told
Mr. George Hutchinson that he distrusted his own skill in
looking to it, and apprehending some danger, advised him
to send for a very famous physician who was at Canterbury,
which they did, and he came on Saturday.   As he came along
he inquired of the messenger that fetched him what kind of
person the colonel was, and how he had lived; and what he
had been accustomed to, and which chamber of the castle he was
now lodged in?   Which when the man had told him, he said
his journey would be to no purpose, for that chamber had
killed him.   Accordingly, when he came, he told the colonel's
brother, on Saturday night, that he apprehended danger, and
appointed some remedies, and some applications to his temples,
and a cordial to procure rest, but it had no effect.   There
was a nurse watching in his chamber, and she told them after
his death, that she heard him pray in the night, with the
deepest sighs that ever she heard.   The next morning, before
the doctor and his daughter, and brother and servants came
to him, the gentlewoman of the castle came up and asked him
how he did?   He told her, incomparably well, and full of
faith.

Some time after, when the doctor came, he told his brother
that the fever had seized his head, and that he believed he
should soon fall into ravings and die, and therefore wished
him, if he had anything to say to him, to speak while he was

in his perfect senses. So Mr. George Hutchinson came to him, and told him he believed he could not live, and therefore desired him if he had anything to do, to despatch it, for he believed his end was approaching. The colonel, without the least dejection or amazement, replied, very composedly and cheerfully, " The will of the Lord be done: I am ready for it." And then he told them that he did now confirm the will he wrote in the Tower as his last will and testament, and all others were to be void. The doctor, who had, when religion was in fashion, been a pretender to it, came to him and asked him if his peace was made with God; to which he replied, " I hope you do not think me so ill a Christian, to have been thus long in prison, and have that to do now!" The doctor asked him concerning the ground of his hope; to which he answered, " There's none but Christ, none but Christ, in whom I have unspeakable joy, more than I can express; yet I should utter more, but that the soreness of my mouth makes it difficult for me to speak." Then they asked him where he would be buried? He told them, in his vault at Owthorpe; his brother told him it would be a long way to carry him: he answered, " Let my wife order the manner of it as she will, only I would lie there." He left a kind message to his wife, " Let her," said he, " as she is above other women, show herself, in this occasion, a good Christian, and above the pitch of ordinary women."* He commanded his daughter who was present to tell the rest, that he would have them all guided by her counsels; and left with his brother the same message to his eldest son. " I would," said he, " have spoken to my wife and son, but it is not the will of God;" then, as

* This is that command of her husband which Mrs. Hutchinson speaks of at the beginning of her narrative, where she says she has determined to employ her thoughts upon the preservation of his memory, not the fruitless bewailing of it.

he was going to utter something, " here's none but friends ;"
his brother reminded him that the doctor was present; " Oh,
I thank you," said he ; and such was their amazement in
their sorrow, that they did not think of speaking to the
doctor to retire, but lost what he would have said, which
I am confident was some advice to his son how to demean
himself in public concernments. He lay all the day very
sensible and very cheerful, to the admiration both of the
doctors and of all that saw him ; and as his daughter sat
weeping by him, " Fie, Bab," said he, " do you mourn for
me as for one without hope? There is hope." He desired
his brother to remember him to Sir Allen Apsley, and tell
him that he hoped God would reward his labour of love to
him. While he was thus speaking to them, his spirits
decayed exceedingly fast, and his pulse grew very low, and
his head was already earth in the upper part; yet he raised
himself in his bed, " And now," said he to the doctor, " I
would fain know your reason why you fancy me dying; I feel
nothing in myself, my head is well, my heart is well, and I
have no pain nor sickness any where." The doctor, seeing
this, was amazed ; " Sir," said he, " I would be glad to be
deceived ;" and being at a stand, he told Mr. George Hutchinson he was surprised, and knew not what to think, to see
him so cheerful and undisturbed, when his pulse was gone ;
which if it were not death, must be some strange working of
the spleen, and therefore advised him to send away for Dr.
Ridgely, which he would before have done, but that the
doctor told him he feared it would be in vain, and that he
would be dead before the doctor could come. While they
were preparing to write, the colonel spoke only these words :
" 'Tis as I would have it : 'tis where I would have it :" and
spoke no more, for convulsions wrought his mouth, yet did
his sense remain perfect to his last breath ; for when some
named Mrs. Hutchinson, and said, " Alas, how will she be

surprised!" he fetched a sigh, and within a little while departed; his countenance settling so amiably and cheerfully
after death, that he looked after he was dead as he used to do
when best pleased in life. It was observable that at the same
hour, and the same day of the month, and the same day of
the week, that the wicked soldiers fetched him out of his own
rest and quiet condition at home, eleven months before, the
Lord of hosts sent his holy angels to fetch him out of their
cruel hands up to his everlasting and blessed rest above;
this being the Lord's day, about seven o'clock at night, the
eleventh day of September, 1664; that, the same day and
hour, the eleventh of October, 1663.

The two doctors, though mere strangers to him, were so
moved that they both wept as if he had been their brother;
and he of Canterbury said, he had been with many eminent
persons, but he never in his whole life saw any one receive
death with more Christian courage, constancy of mind, and
stedfastness of faith, than the colonel had expressed from
the first to the last; so that, considering the height of his
fever, and his want of rest, there was an evidence of a divine
assistance that overruled all the powers and operations of
nature. This doctor, who was called Dr. Jachin, had most
curiously and strictly observed all his motions. I know not
by what impulse, but he afterwards said that, on account of the
colonel's former engagements, he knew he should be examined
of all these circumstances, and therefore was resolved diligently
to observe them; and as he guessed, it afterwards fell out.
for the gentlemen of the country, being of the royal party,
were busy in their inquiries, which the doctor answered with
such truth and clearness as made them ready to burst with
envy at the peace and joy the Lord was pleased to give his
servant, in taking him out of this wicked world. I am apt
to think that it was not tenderness of nature alone, but conviction of their own disturbed peace, which drew those tears

from the doctors, when they saw in him that blessed peace and joy which crowns the Lord's constant martyrs : whatever it was, the men were faithful in divulging the glory of the Lord's wonderful presence with his servant.

As soon as the colonel was dead, his brother sent away a messenger to carry the sad news to his house, and caused his body to be embalmed in order to his funeral, as he had thrice ordered. When he was disembowelled, all his inwards were found exceeding sound, and no taint in any part, only two or three purple spots on his lungs : his gall, the doctor said, was the largest that ever he saw in any man, and observed it to be a miracle of grace that he had been so patient as he had seen him.

Some two or three days before the colonel fell sick, Freeman, the captain of the castle, had sent down a very strict order that the colonel should carry nothing out of the castle; in pursuance of which the soldiers would not suffer them to take out his beds, furniture, or clothes, which Mr. Hutchinson forbore till an order came for them.

As soon as the news came to Owthorpe, the colonel's two eldest sons and all his household servants went up to London with his horses, and made ready a hearse, tricked with escutcheons and six horses in mourning, with a mourning coach and six horses to wait on it, and came down to Deal with an order from the secretary for the body ; but when they came thither, Captain Freeman, in spite, would not deliver it, because Mrs. Hutchinson herself was not come to fetch it; so they were forced, at an intolerable expense, to keep all this equipage at Deal, while they sent to the secretary for another order, which they got directed to the lieutenant in the absence of the captain, and as soon as it came they delivered it to him, who immediately suffered them to take away the body, which they did at that very hour, though it was night, fearing a further dispute with Freeman. For he, after

the body had been ten days embalmed, said he would have
a jury empannelled, and a coroner to sit upon it, to see
whether he died a natural death. Mr. Hutchinson asked him
why he urged that, when it lay on their side to have sought
satisfaction.   He said he must do it to clear the king's garrison.   Mr. Hutchinson told him he had slipped his time;
it should have been done at the first, before the embalming.
He said he would have it unlapped, and accordingly he sent
for a coroner and a jury, who, when they came, would not
unlap the body, but called those persons who had been about
him, and examined them as to the occasion of his death. They
made affidavit, which remains yet upon record, that the doctor said *that the place had killed him,* and, satisfied with this,
they did not unlap the body.   As it came into Deal, Freeman met it, and said, if he had been in the castle they should
not have had it till they had paid the money he demanded;
which, when he could not justify any right to it by any law,
he began to beg most basely and unworthily, but had nothing
given him for that.   However, though the secretary had also
ordered that the colonel should have his things out, yet he
detained all he found in the castle, his trunks, and beds,
and furniture, which could never be gotten out of his hands.
Although this spite of his put the colonel's family to an
excessive charge in staying so long in that cut-throat town
of Deal, yet there was a providence of the Lord in it; for
the colonel's daughter who was there, through grief had contracted a violent sickness, which took her with great severity, and wrought off of her stomach in black vomits, which
made her for the present desperately ill, and the doctor that
was with her said that if she had then been on her journey,
as she would have been had they not been delayed by Freeman's cruel spite, she could not have lived.

The next day after they had gotten out the body, they
brought it with a handsome private equipage to Canterbury,

and so forwards towards London, meeting no affronts in their way but at one town, where there was a fair, the priest of which place came out, with his clerk in his fool's coat, to offer them burial, and they laid hold of the horses to stop their nearse; but the attendants putting them by, the wicked rout at the fair took part with them, and set upon the horsemen ; but they broke several of their heads, and made their way clear, having beaten off all the town and the fair, and came on to London. They passed through Southwark, over the bridge, and through the whole heart of the city, in the day time, to their lodging in Holborn, and had not one reviling word or indignity offered them all the way but several people were very much moved at that sad witness of the murderous cruelty of the men then in power.

From London he was brought down to Owthorpe, very seriously bewailed all the way he came along by all those who had been better acquainted with his worth than the strangers were among whom he died ; and he was brought home with honour to his grave through the dominions of his murderers, who were ashamed of his glories, which all their tyrannies could not extinguish with his life.

AT OWTHORPE, IN NOTTINGHAMSHIRE,
(Supposed to have been written by Mrs. Hutchinson.)

Quousque Domine !

In a vault under this wall lieth the body of

JOHN HUTCHINSON,

Of Owthorpe, in the county of Nottingham, Esq.,
Eldest sonne and heire of Sir Thomas Hutchinson, by his first wife, the
Lady Margaret, daughter of Sir John Biron, of Newsted,
in the said county.

This monument doth not commemorate
Vaine ayrie glorious titles, birth, and state ;
But sacred is to free, illustrious grace,
Conducting happily a mortal's race ;
To end in triumph over death and hell.
When, like the prophet's cloake, the fraile flesh fell,
Forsaken as a dull impediment,
Whilst love's swift fiery chariot climb'd th' ascent.
Nor are the reliques lost, but only torn,
To be new made, and in more lustre worn.
Full of this ioy he mounted, he lay downe,
Threw off his ashes, and took up his crowne.
   Those who lost all their splendor in his grave,
   Ev'n there yet no inglorious period have.

He married Lucy, the daughter of Sir Allen Apsley, lieutenant of the Tower of London, by his third wife, the Lady Lucy, daughter of Sir John St. John, of Lidiard Tregos, in the county of Wilts, who dying at Owthorpe, October 11, 1659, lieth buried in the same vault.

e left surviving by the sayd Lucy 4 sons; Thomas, who married Jane, the daughter of Sir Alexander Radcliffe, buried in the same vault : and Edward, Lucius, and John : and 4 daughters ; Barbara, Lucy, Margaret, and Adeliza ; which last lies buried in the same vault.

He died at Sandowne Castle, in Kent, after 11 months' harsh and strict imprisonment,—without crime or accusation,—upon the 11th day of Sept. 1664, in the 49th yeare of his age, full of joy, in assured hope of a glorious resurrection.

VERSES WRITTEN BY MRS. HUTCHINSON,

In the small Book containing her own Life, and most probably compos'd
by her during her Husband's retirement from public business
to his seat at Owthorpe.

———————

ALL sorts of men through various labours press
To the same end, contented quietness ;
Great princes vex their labouring thoughts to be
Possessed of an unbounded sovereignty ;
The hardy soldier doth all toils sustain
That he may conquer first, and after reign ;
Th' industrious merchant ploughs the angry seas
That he may bring home wealth, and live at ease.
These none of them attain : for sweet repose
But seldom to the splendid palace goes ;
A troop of restless passions wander there,
And only private lives are free from care.
Sleep to the cottage bringeth happy nights,
But to the court hung round with flaring lights,
Which th' office of the vanished day supply,
His image only comes to close the eye,
But gives the troubled mind no ease of care,
While country slumbers undisturbed are ;
Where, if the active fancy dreams present,
They bring no horrors to the innocent.
Ambition doth incessently aspire,
And each advance leads on to new desire ;
Nor yet can riches av'rice satisfy,
For want and wealth together multiply :
Nor can voluptuous men more fulness find,
For enjoyed pleasures leave their stings behind.
He's only rich who knows no want ; he reigns
Whose will no severe tyranny constrains ;

And he alone possesseth true delight
Whose spotless soul no guilty fears affright.
This freedom in the country life is found,
Where innocence and safe delights abound.
Here man's a prince ; his subjects ne'er repine
When on his back their wealthy fleeces shine :
If for his appetite the fattest die,
Those who survive will raise no mutiny :
His table is with home-got dainties crowned,
With friends, not flatterers, encompassed round ;
No spies nor traitors on his trencher wait,
Nor is his mirth confined to rules of state ;
An armed guard he neither hath nor needs,
Nor fears a poisoned morsel when he feeds ;
Bright constellations hang above his head,
Beneath his feet are flow'ry carpets spread :
The merry birds delight him with their songs,
And healthful air his happy life prolongs ;
At harvest merrily his flocks he shears,
And in cold weather their warm fleeces wears ;
Unto his ease he fashions all his clothes ;
His cup with uninfected liquor flows :
The vulgar breath doth not his thoughts elate,
Nor can he be o'erwhelmed by their hate.
Yet, if ambitiously he seeks for fame,
One village feast shall gain a greater name
Than his who wears the imperial diadem,
Whom the rude multitude do still condemn.
Sweet peace and joy his blest companions are :
Fear, sorrow, envy, lust, revenge, and care,
And all that troop which breeds the world's offence,
With pomp and majesty, are banish'd thence.
What court then can such liberty afford ?
Or where is man so uncontroll'd a lord ?

A JOURNAL

OF

THE SIEGE OF LATHOM HOUSE,

IN LANCASHIRE,

DEFENDED BY

CHARLOTTE DE LA TREMOUILLE, COUNTESS OF DERBY

AGAINST

SIR THOMAS FAIRFAX, KNIGHT,

AND OTHER

PARLIAMENTARIAN OFFICERS.

1644.

Y⁺ never was sene their Captayne being STANLEYE,
That Lancashyre, Cheshyre, and Wales ran aweye.

MS. Metrical Hist. of the Stanley Family. By
Tho. Stanley, Bp. of Man. Fitt. III. L. 652

ADVERTISEMENT

THE following luminous and accurate account of the Siege of Lathom House will form an appropriate sequel to the Memoirs of Colonel Hutchinson, as not only referring to the same eventful and debatable period of our history, but as contrasting, in a striking point of view, the highly culti-vated and intellectual qualifications of the lady of the Governor of Nottingham Castle, with the intrepid valour and heroic spirit displayed by the Countess of Derby—the worthy de-scendant of the renowned Count William of Nassau.

The Journal of this memorable Siege is one so full of chivalrous and dramatic effect, that it is gratifying to find that Sir Walter Scott has conferred on it new and addi-tional interest, by setting his own impress upon it in his popular and interesting novel of " Peveril of the Peak."

Two manuscript copies of the Siege of Lathom House are still in existence—one in the Ashmolean Museum, Oxford (A. Wood, MSS. D. 16), written by Capt. Edward Halsall ; and the other among the Harleian Manuscripts (No. 2043) in the British Museum, probably a transcript of the former by Mr. Cole, a diligent collector of documents relating to Lancashire.

Captain Halsall bore the name of an ancient family at Halsall, near Ormskirk, Lancashire, and although he must have been very young at the time of the siege, was evidently an eye-witness of it, and an inmate of the mansion. In a letter dated June, 1650, recounting the means used to dis-cover the murderers of Anthony Aschaw, Cromwell's late resident at Madrid, it is mentioned that five persons had been arrested, and among these, in the official report of the Li-centiate de Guevara, we find, " Dom Edward Halsall, En-glishman, of the Duchy of Lancaster, of twenty-three years of age, knight."*

* Rymer, vol. xx. Thurloe, vol. i. pp. 151, 204.

Lathom is a township in the parish of Ormskirk, hundred of West Derby, Lancashire. Lathom House, once the chief seat of the Stanleys, was originally built by the De Lathoms; and at the time the great civil war broke out, James, the seventh Earl of Derby, and his wife Charlotte, were living in princely hospitality at this place. The mansion was so spacious and noble that it is said three kings and their trains could receive accommodation at one time in it. According to a poem, written in the reign of Henry VIII., Thomas, the second Earl of Derby, represents it as having eighteen towers; for in quitting that place in 1513, he says :—

> " Farewell, Lathom, that bright bower,
> Nine towers thou bearest on high,
> And other nine thou bearest in the utter walls,
> Within thee may be lodged kings three."*

The following description of the mansion from Bishop Rutter's † manuscripts, printed in Seacome's Historical Account of the House of Stanley, will be found more minute than the one given in the Journal :—

" Lathom House stands upon a flat, upon a moorish, springy, and spumous ground, and was encompassed with a strong wall of two yards thick; upon the walls were nine towers, flanking each other, and in every tower were six pieces of ordnance, that played three one way, and three the other: without the wall was a moat eight yards wide, and two yards deep; upon the back of the moat, between the wall and the graff, was a strong row of palisades around. Besides all these, there was a high, strong tower, called the Eagle Tower, in the midst of the house, surmounting all the rest; and the gate-house had also two high and strong buildings, with a strong tower on each side of it; and in the entrance to the first court, upon the top of these towers, were

* Weber's Flodden Field, from Harl. MSS. 293, 367.

† Samuel Rutter was the favourite companion and chaplain to the Earl of Derby, as well as tutor to his eldest son. He was appointed archdeacon of Man, and " governed the church with great prudence," says Sacheverell, " during the late unhappy civil wars." At the Restoration he was raised by the young earl to the bishopric of the island. He died in the year 1663, and was buried under the uncovered steeple of St. Germain's, then in ruins.

placed the best and choicest marksmen, who usually attended the earl in his hunting and other sports, as huntsmen, keepers, fowlers, and the like ; who continually kept watch, with screwed guns and long fowling-pieces, upon those towers, to the great annoyance and loss of the enemy, especially of their commanders, who were frequently killed in their trenches, or as they came or went to or from them. Besides all that has hitherto been said of the walls, towers, moat, &c., there is something so particular and romantic in the general situation of this house, as if nature herself had formed it for a strong-hold, or place of security; for, before the house, to the south and south-west, is a rising ground so near it, as to overlook the top of it, from which it falls so quick, that nothing planted against it on those sides can touch it further than the front wall ; and on the north and east sides, there is another rising ground, even to the edge of the moat, and then falls away so quick, that you can scarce, at the distance of a carbine shot, see the house over that height; so that all batteries placed there, are so far below it, as to be of little service against it : and, let us observe, by the way, that the uncommon situation of it may be compared to the palm of a man's hand, flat in the middle, and covered with a rising round about it, and so near to it, that the enemy, during the siege, were never able to raise a battery against it, so as to make a breach in the wall practicable to enter the house by way of storm."

The officers engaged in this memorable siege were,—under the command of General Sir Thomas Fairfax, Colonels Rigby, of Burgh ; Egerton, of Shaw ; Moor, of Moor Hall ; Ashton, of Middleton ; Holcroft, of Holcroft ; and Holland, of Denton ; with Major Morgan as officer of engineers :— On the side of the Countess of Derby, who acted as governess, were Major William Turner, Captains William Farrington, of Wearden ; Charnock, of Charnock ; Chisenhall, of Chisenhall ; Edward Rawstorne, of New Hall ; Henry Ogle, of Prescot ; Richard Fox, and Molineux Radcliffe ; and Lieutenants Penketh, Worrill, and Walthew.

A JOURNAL

OF THE

SIEGE OF LATHOM HOUSE.

THE Earl of Derby, having, on the rise of this rebellion, at his own charge, brought up near 3000* of the best men and arms to the king's standard, purposing to have attended his sacred majesty in person, was, at the request of the truly noble Sir Gilbert Haughton and others, sent back into Lancashire by his majesty's express command, where, with naked or thinly armed men, he sustained the fury of the rebels, and kept the field against them for seven months together, storming several of their towns, and defeating them in sundry battles ; himself, in every assault and skirmish, charging in the front, and encouraging his soldiers with exemplary resolution, when the multitude of the enemy exceeded his own number by the advantage of two or three to one, till his lordship, unhappily called to crush the thriving sedition in Cheshire, withdrew his horse into that county.

The enemy now spying an opportunity for action in his absence, drew out their garrisons, and with their whole strength assaulted the town of Preston, which, not yet fortified, and being suddenly surprised, notwithstanding the endeavours and resolute resistance of Sir Gilbert Haughton, the mayor, and other gentlemen, was lost to the enemy. Upon his lordship's return he found himself straitened within a narrow compass ; yet, opposing loyal thoughts to dangers, and endeavouring to throw life in the business by speedy

* The Lord Molineux's and Sir Gilbert Gerard's regiments out of Lancashire, Sir Thomas Salisbury's out of Wales.

action, he drew into the field, and marched above twenty
miles into the enemy's country, taking Lancaster, and regaining Preston by assault, when the rebels, who were within
six hours' march, were pursuing him with a more numerous
army.   After this his lordship gave two or three days to
refresh his soldiers, toiled out with three days' restless
service.   The enemy also got fresh supplies from Yorkshire,
Cheshire, Staffordshire, and Derbyshire, so that, now again
swelled into a numerous body, they attempt an assault on
Wigan, which, with little service, was unfortunately lost ere
his lordship could come to its relief; whereof her majesty,
then at York, having intelligence, sent an express command
to his lordship not to engage his army in any service till she
sent him aid, which his lordship expected every day ; but, in
a fortnight, being disappointed in his hopes, and the enemy
growing insolent by his stillness, he was moved by the Lord
Molineux, Sir Thomas Tildsley, and other gentlemen with
him, to repair to the queen in person, to hasten the promised
supplies ; when, after a fortnight's attendance, there happened
that unfortunate surprise of the Lord Goreing in Wakefield,
which utterly disenabled her majesty to spare him any relief;
which the governor of Warrington (Colonel Norris) understanding, after five days' siege, gave up the town, the greatest
key of the county, to the enemy, and all his lordship's forces,
then with the Lord Molineux and Colonel Tildsley, marched
down to York.

At the same time her majesty received intimation of the
Scottish design for the invasion of England, and his lordship
being signified of their intention to ship from Scotland for
the Isle of Man, and so for England ; it was therefore the
queen's pleasure expressly to command him to the island, to
prevent their passage that way.

Upon his arrival there, he found the whole country in
sedition and insurrection ; some turbulent spirits, tutored by
their brethren the Scots, having taught the commons the new
trick of rebellion, under the mask of defensive arming for the
preservation of their religion and liberties ; and indeed this
subtle poison had so wrought in that little body, that the
whole country was swelled into one tumult, which, by all
symptoms, would have broken out in three days, with the
death of the bishop-governor, and the loss of the island.

To prevent this rupture, his lordship presently raised the

horse of the country, apprehended the persons of their seditious agents, doing execution upon some, imprisoning others,
and striking a general terror into all, which suddenly calmed
the madness of the people, and threw a face of quiet upon
the country.

Yet to remove the ground of this disease required both
skill and time, as well to prevent the relapse of the countrymen, as an invasion of the Scots, who still promised, for con-
science-sake, to abet them in their rebellion, it being the
good fortune of that ungrateful nation to be esteemed angels
for troubling and poisoning all waters.

His lordship, by the queen's command, having spent
much time in this unhappy business, is at last called back
by his majesty to attend his parliament at Oxford, and on
his return to England, is welcomed with the news of a siege
against his lady, which had been long in consultation, and
which was now matured for action.

Upon the surrender of Warrington, May 27, 1643, a summons came from Mr. Holland, governor of Manchester, to
the Lady Derby, to subscribe to the propositions of the parliament, or yield up Lathom House; but her ladyship denied
both—she would neither tamely give up her house, nor purchase her peace with the loss of her honour. But being
then in no condition to provoke a potent and malicious
enemy, and seeing no possibility of speedy assistance, she
desired a peaceable abode in her own house, referring all her
lord's estate to their disposal, with promise only to keep
so many men in arms, as might defend her person and house
from the outrages of their common soldiers, which was hardly
obtained.

From this time she endured a continued siege, being, with
the exception of her gardens and walks, confined as a prisoner within her own walls, with the liberty of the castle-
yard, suffering the sequestration of her whole estate, besides
daily affronts and indignities from unworthy persons, and
the unjust and undeserved censures of some that wore the
name and face of friends; all which she patiently endured,
well knowing it to be no wisdom to quarrel with an evil she
could not redress. Therefore, to remove all pretences of
violence or force against her, she restrained her garrison
soldiers from all provocation and annoyance of the enemy,
and so by her wisdom kept them at a more favourable dis-

tance for tne space of almost a whole year. Rigby, all this time, restless in his malice, sought all occasions to disturb her quiet, sending out his troops to plunder her next neighbours, and to surprise such of the king's good subjects as had fled unto her for safety. In the beginning of February, her garrison soldiers had a skirmish with a troop of his horse, commanded by Captain Hyndley, wherein they rescued some of her friends, taking prisoners Lieutenant Dandy, first wounded, his cornet, and some troopers. By his unjust report of this action, and some other visitations of musket-shot from her house, he wrought on Sir Thomas Fairfax and the rest of the parliament forces to his own purpose.

On Saturday, the 24th of February, it was resolved in a council of the holy states at Manchester, after many previous debates and consultations to the same purpose, that three parliament-colonels, Mr. Ashton of Middleton, Mr Moor of Bank-hall, and Mr. Rigby of Preston, should with all speed come against Lathom, of which her ladyship had some broken intelligence on Sunday morning, and therefore despatched a messenger to her secret friend, one acquainted with their secret determinations, to receive fuller information: in the meantime she used all diligence and care to furnish her house with provisions and men, which was a hard work, considering that she had been debarred of her estate for a whole year. Yet in these straits she used not the least violence to force relief from any of her neighbours, though some of them were as bad tenants as subjects; but with her own small stock, by the charity of some few friends, and by the industry of her careful servant, Mr. Broome, she provided herself to bear the worst of a cruel enemy.

The messenger returned on Monday. She had assurance of their design, who were then on their march as far as Bolton, Wigan, and Standish, under pretence of going into Westmoreland, but were carrying the multitude blindfold against a house which their fathers and themselves, whilst their eyes were open, had ever honoured, reputing Lathom, in more innocent times, to be both for magnificence and hospitality, the only court in the northern parts of this kingdom; when good men would in mere love vent their harmless treason, saying, "God save the Earl of Derby and the king."But their factious ministers, very dutiful sons of the church of England, made the pulpit speak their design aloud; one of whom,

Bradshaw, to the dishonour of that house (Brasenose) which had given him more sober and pious foundations, took occasion, before his patrons in Wigan, to profane the fourteenth verse of the fiftieth chapter of Jeremiah, from thence by as many marks and signs as ever he had given of antichrist, proving the Lady Derby to be the scarlet whore and the whore of Babylon, and Lathom to be Babel itself, whose walls he made as flat and as thin as his discourse. Indeed, before he despatched his prophecy, he thumped them down, reserving the next verse to be a triumph for the victor.

February 27, 1643-44. On Tuesday the enemy took their quarters round the house, at the distance of a mile or two, or three at the farthest.

February 28. On Wednesday Captain Markland brought a letter from Sir Thomas Fairfax, and with it an ordinance of parliament, the one requiring her ladyship to yield up Lathom House upon such honourable conditions as he should propose ; and the other declaring the mercy of the parliament to receive the Earl of Derby, if he would submit himself, in which business Sir Thomas Fairfax promised to be a faithful instrument. To which her ladyship gave answer, "She much wondered that Sir Thomas Fairfax should require her to give up her lord's house, without any offence on her part done to the parliament; desiring, that in a business of such weight, which struck both at her religion and at her life, and that so nearly concerned her sovereign, her lord, and her whole posterity, she might have a week's consideration, both to resolve the doubts of conscience, and to have advice in matters of law and honour." Not that her ladyship was unfixed in her own thoughts, but endeavoured to gain time by demurs and protractions of the business, which the good knight, happily suspecting, denied her the time desired, moving her ladyship to come to New Park, a house of her lord's, a quarter of a mile from Lathom, and to come thither in her coach (no mean favour, believe it), where himself and his colonels would meet her for a full discourse and transaction of the business.

This her ladyship flatly refused, with scorn and anger, as an ignoble and uncivil motion, returning only this answer, "That, notwithstanding her present condition, she remembered both her lord's honour and her own birth, conceiving it more knightly that Sir Thomas Fairfax should wait upon her than she upon him."

Thursday, February 29, and Friday. March 1, were spent in letters and messages; his generalship at last requiring free access for two of his colonels, and assurance of their safe return, unto which her ladyship condescended.

On Saturday, Mr. Ashton and Mr. Rigby vouchsafed to venture their persons into Lathom House. being authorised by the general to propound the following conditions :—

1. That all the arms and ammunition of war shall be forth-with surrendered into the hands of Sir Thomas Fairfax.

2. That the Countess of Derby, and all the persons in Lathom House, shall be suffered to depart, with all their goods, to Chester, or any other of the enemy's quarters, or, upon submission to the orders of parliament, to their own houses.

3. That the countess, with all her menial servants, shall be suffered either to inhabit Knowsley House, and to have twenty muskets allowed for her defence. or to repair to her husband in the Isle of Man.

4. That the countess for the present, until the parliament be acquainted with it, shall have allowed her for her main-tenance all the lands and revenues of the earl her husband within the hundred of Derby, and that the parliament shall be moved to continue this allowance.

These conditions her ladyship rejected, as being in part dishonourable, and in part uncertain; adding withal, she knew not how to treat with them who had not power to per-form their own offers, till they had first moved the parlia-ment, telling them it were a more sober course, first to acquaint themselves with the pleasure of the parliament, and then to move accordingly; but for her part, she would not trouble the good gentlemen to petition for her; she would esteem it a greater favour to be permitted to continue in her present humble condition.

The two colonels, being blank in their treaty, spent their stay in wise instructions to her ladyship, and in unjust ac-cusations of her friends and servants, from which she not only cleared them, but which she also nobly and sharply re-turned upon their religious agents ; so that the grave men, being disappointed both of their wit and malice, returned as empty a; they came.

Sunday was their sabbath.   On Monday Mr. Ashton came again, alone, with power to receive her ladyship's propositions, and to convey them to his general (a notable and trusty employment), which came in these terms :—

1. Her ladyship desired a month's time for her quiet continuance in Lathom ; and then for herself and children, her friends, soldiers, and servants, with all her goods, arms, and ordnance, to have free transport to the Isle of Man, and in the meantime that she should keep a garrison in her house for her own defence.

2. She promised that neither during her stay in the country, nor after her coming to the Isle of Man, should any of the arms be employed against the parliament.

3. That during her stay in the country, no soldier should be quartered in the lordship of Lathom, nor afterwards should any garrison be put into Lathom or into Knowsley House.

4. That none of her tenants, neighbours, or friends, then in the house with her, should, for assisting her, suffer in their persons or estates, after her departure.

In the first of these she struck at more time ; in the second, she understood *the parliament of the three Estates at Oxford*, knowing no other ; in the third, she laboured to remove impediments that might hinder the victualling of her house ; in the fourth, she gave a colour to her departure, and content to her soldiers, of whom in her treaty she showed an honourable care.

These propositions, returned by Mr. Ashton, were interpreted in their right sense, being apprehended too full of policy and danger to be allowed, as only beating for more time and means, that her ladyship might use that opportunity to confirm herself in her fastness ; and therefore in his answer Sir Thomas thus qualified them to a better understanding.

1. That the Countess of Derby shall have the time she desires, and then liberty to transport her arms and goods to the Isle of Man, excepting the cannon, which shall continue there for the defence of the house.

2. That her ladyship, by ten o'clock to-morrow, disband all her soldiers, except her menial servants, and receive an officer, and forty parliament soldiers, as her guard.

This, as the last residue of all their councils, with some terrible presages of the danger she stood in, was delivered to her ladyship by one Morgan, one of Sir Thomas's colonels, a little man, short, and peremptory, who met with staidness and judgment to cool his heat ; and had the honour to carry back this last answer, for her ladyship could screw them to no more delays.

" That she refused all their articles, and was truly happy that they had refused hers, protesting she had rather hazard her life, than offer the like again. That though a woman and a stranger, divorced from her friends, and robbed of her estate, she was ready to receive their utmost violence, trusting in God both for protection and deliverance."

Being now disappointed in their plot, who expected a quick dispatch with the afflicted lady, by a tame surrender of her house, and having scattered very fearful apprehensions of their great guns, their mortar-piece, their fire-works, and their engineers, after all their consultations, they prepare for action. But they find her ladyship as fearless of their empty terrors, as, careful to prevent a real danger, she is willing to understand the power of the enemy, and studious to prevent it ; leaving nothing with her eye to be excused afterwards by fortune or negligence, and adding to her former patience a most resolved fortitude. " Ne minimo quidem casui locum relinqui debuisse." Cæs. Com. lib. 6. Otho, in Tacit. lib. 1.

All treaties being now broken off, and Rigby, being of the same opinion with the historian,* " That no delay should be suffered in that enterprise which none will commend before it be ended," proceeds forthwith to action.

The next morning discovered some of the enemy's night-works, which were begun about musket-shot from the house, on a sloping, declining ground, that their pioneers, by the nature of the place, might be secured from our ordnance on the towers, and so in an orb or ring-work they cast up much earth every day, by the multitude of country people forced to the service.

March 7, 8, 9, 10. After three days, finding a fixedness and resolution in her ladyship still to keep her house for the service of his majesty against all his enemies, on Sunday they employ six neighbours of the best rank to take a petition to her ladyship ; having thrust a form into their hands, and prepared their heads with instructions, as by confession now

* Tacitus.

appears; " That in duty to her ladyship, and love to their country, they most humbly beseech her to prevent her own personal dangers, and the impoverishing of the whole country, which she might do if she pleased to slacken something of her severe resolution, and to condescend in part to the offers of the gentlemen."

These her ladyship received with all courtesy, discoursing unto them the nature of former treaties, and the order of her proceedings, and this so smoothly and agreeably, that the good men were satisfied, and had little more to say, but " God save the king and the Earl of Derby." In answer to their paper, she told them it was more fit for them to petition the gentlemen who robbed and spoiled their country, than she, who desired only a quiet stay in her own house, and the preservation not the spoil of her neighbours. One of the six, of more ability and integrity than the rest, reported the whole business of the answer, and of their entertainment, as a true subject of his majesty and a faithful friend to her ladyship; upon which the noble colonels were moved to new propositions, in mere mercy, if you might believe them, to her ladyship and her children. The next day, therefore, Captain Ashurst, a man who deserves a fairer character than the rest, for his civil and even behaviour, brought a new message to her ladyship in these terms :—

1. That all former conditions be waived.

2. That the Countess of Derby, and all persons in the House, with all arms, ordnance, and goods, shall have liberty to march to what part of the kingdom they please, and yield up the House to Sir Thomas Fairfax.

3. That the arms shall never be employed against the parliament.

4. That all in the House, excepting 100 persons, should immediately leave it, and the rest within ten days.

The message read, her ladyship perceived they began to cool in their enterprise, and therefore, to lend them some new heat, returned this answer by the captain ;—that she scorned to be a ten days' prisoner in her own house, judging it more noble, whilst she could, to preserve her liberty by her arms, than to buy a peace with slavery :* " And what assurance," said she, " have I either of liberty, or of the per-

* Pax servientibus gravior quàm liberis bellum. Liv. lib. 3.

formance of any condition, when my strength is gone? I have received, under the hands of some eminent personages, that your general is not very conscientious in the performance of his subscriptions, so that from him I must expect an unsinewed and faithless agreement.* It is dangerous treating when the sword is given into the enemy's hands;" and therefore her ladyship added, " that not a man should depart from her house ; that she would keep it, whilst God enabled her, against all the king's enemies ; and, in brief, that she would receive no more messages without an express of her lord's pleasure, who, she now heard, was returned from the Isle of Man, and to whom she referred them for the transaction of the whole business, considering that frequent treaties are a discouragement to the soldiers besieged, as exhibiting some want or weakness within, and so commonly become the first key that opens the gate to the enemy."

To second and confirm her answer, the next day, being Tuesday, a hundred foot, commanded by Captain Farmer, a Scotchman, a faithful and gallant soldier, with Lieut. Bretergh ready to second him in any service, and some twelve horse, our whole cavalry, commanded by Lieutenant Key, sallied out upon the enemy ; and because the sequel of every business dependeth much upon the beginning, the captain determined to do something that might remind the enemy that there were soldiers within. He marched up to their works without a shot, and then firing upon them in their trenches, they quickly left their holes ; when Lieutenant Key, having wheeled about with his horse from another gate, fell upon them in their flight with much execution. They slew about thirty men, took forty arms, one drum, and six prisoners. The main retreat was that day made good by Captain Ogle, a gentleman industrious to return the courtesy which some of their party showed to him when he was taken prisoner at the battle of Edgehill. The other passage was carefully secured by Captain Rawstorne. Not one of our men was that day slain or wounded.

By the prisoners we understood the purpose of the enemy was to starve the house ; the commanders having courage to pine a lady, not to fight with her.

The four days following (13, 14, 15, 16), passed without

* Pax Samnitica, pax infida, pax incerta.

much action on either side, saving that the garrison gave them some night alarms, which ministered to some an occasion of running away, and to others of belying their own courage, that they had repulsed the garrison soldiers, and slain thousands out of hundreds.

March 17. On Sunday night the commanders under her ladyship resolved to try their watches, and therefore, at three o'ciock in the morning, Captain Chisenhall, a man of known courage and resolution, Lieutenant Bretergh, and Lieutenant Heape, with only thirty musketeers, issued out of the back gates to surprise the enemy in their new trenches ; but they, discovering that some of the light matches ran faster than the captain or his soldiers could pursue, securing their flight in a wood close by ; where, not willing to engage his soldiers in unnecessary dangers, he left them, only killing two or three, and chasing the rest in flight.

These sallies and frequent alarms so diseased the enemy that their works went slowly on, they having been there three weeks and not having yet cast up one mount for ordnance ; but now, for their own security, to keep off our men with their cannon, they hasten the business, with the loss, however, of many men's lives, compelled to do so desperate a service. It moved both wonder and pity to see multitudes of poor people so enslaved to the reformer's tyranny, that they would stand the musket and lose their lives to save nothing ; so near are these to the times complained of by the historian, when they would no less fear men for their vices, than they once honoured them for their virtues.*

March 19, 20. On Tuesday night they brought up one piece of cannon. On Wednesday morning they gave us some sport. They then played their cannon three shots, the ball a twenty-four pounder. They first tried the wall, which being found proof, without yielding or showing the least impression ; they afterwards shot higher to beat down the pinnacles and turrets, or else to please the women that came to see the spectacle. The same day Sir Thomas Fairfax sent her ladyship a letter which he had received from the Earl of Derby, wherein his lordship desired an honourable and free passage for his lady

* Tacit. lib. 1.

and children, if she so pleased, being loth to expose **them to** the uncertain hazard of a long siege, especially considering the roughness and inhumanity of the enemy, who joined pride and malice, ignorance and cruelty, against her; not knowing, by reason of his long absence, either how his house was provided with victuals and ammunition, or strengthened for resistance; he was therefore desirous to leave only the hardy soldiers for the brunt, till it should please his majesty to yield him relief, and so to preserve his lady and children from the mercy of cruel men, which indeed was the desire of all her friends. But she had more noble thoughts within her, which still kindled and increased at the apprehension of danger; and, returning an acknowledgment of that first courtesy of Sir Thomas Fairfax, after some discourse with the messenger, one Jackson, a savage and zealous chaplain to Mr. Rigby, gave back this answer: " She should willingly submit herself to her lord's commands, and therefore willed the general to treat with him; but till she was assured that such was his lordship's pleasure, she would neither yield up the house, nor desert it herself, but wait for the event according to the good will of God." And with the like signification she despatched a messenger to his lordship in Chester, who was sent out by an alarm which opened a passage through their guards and sentries.

March 21, 22, 23, 24. These four following days were spent in alarms and excursions, without doing business of much service.

March 25. On Monday they gave us seven shot from their culverins and demi-cannons, one whereof, by some check in the way, entered the great gates, which were presently made good by the opposition of beds, and such like impediments, to stay the bullet from ranging the court.

March 28. On Thursday five cannons. This day, the enemy, capable of any impression of fear, took a strong alarm, fighting one against another, and in the action fired off two pieces of cannon in the air.

March 29. The next day, one of our men, foolishly provoking danger with his body above a tower, was at once shot to death. In the afternoon, they played four cannons, one whereof, levelled **to** dismount one of our ordnance upon the **great gates, struck** the battlements near one of our **marks** men, ready to discharge at the cannoneer, and crushed him to death.

March 31. On Sunday night, two cannons were mounted at the lodging chambers, intending, most likely, to catch us napping, as our men had often caught them.

April 1. On Monday, during the day and night, six cannon were fired, charged with chain-shot and bars of iron.

April 2. The next day they played their mortar-piece three times, loaded with stones, thirteen inches in diameter, eighty pounds in weight. It was planted about half a musket-shot south-west from the House, on a rising ground, conveniently giving the engineer a full prospect of the whole building. Their work for securing it was orbicular, in the form of a full moon, with two yards and a half of rampart above the ditch.

April 4. On Thursday they shot one stone and one grenado, which overplayed the house. We had chosen men upon guard, standing ready with green and wet hides, to quench any burning, had their skill, for they did not want malice, enabled them to have cast fire-works.

April 5. Having hitherto met with such unprosperous success in their holy work, the two colonels, Mr. Ashton and Mr. Moor, threw a show of religion over their execrable actions, and, like those devout men in the poets,* by public and private supplications, called God to assist them in their merciless practices, for which purpose they issued their commands to all their ministers, for a general and humble supplication, in the following form :—

* . . . . Nocturnus adulter,
Tempora Santonico velans adoperta cucullo.
Juv. viii. 145.

Tacito mala veta susurro
Concipimus.
Lucan (Pharsal. v. 104).

. . . . . . Pulchra Laverna,
Da mihi fallere, da justum sanctumque videri.
Horat. (Ep. xvi. lib. 1. l. 60.)

Quæ nisi seductis nequeas committere Divis.
Persius (Stat. ii. l. 4).

To all Ministers and Parsons in Lancashire, well-wishers to our successe against Lathom House, theise.

Forasmuch as more then ordinary obstructions have from the beginning of this present service agaynst Lathom House interposed our proceedings, and yet still remaine, which cannot otherwise be removed, nor our successe furthered, but onely by devine assistance; it is therefore our desires to the ministers, and other well-affected persons of this county of Lancaster, in publike manner, as they shall please, to commend our case to God, that as wee are appoynted to the said imployment, soe much tending to the settleing of our present peace in theise parts, soe the Almighty would crowne our weake endeavours with speedy successe in the said designe.

RAPH ASHTON,
JOHN MOOR.

Ormskirk, April 5, 1644.

The four following days were on their parts slept out in this pious exercise.

On Wednesday our men resolved to waken them. About ele en o'clock, Captain Farmer and Captain Molineux Radcliffe, Lieutenant Penketh, Lieutenant Worrill, with 140 soldiers, sallied out at a postern gate, beat the enemy from all their works and batteries, which were now cast up round the house, nailed all their cannon, killed about fifty men, took sixty arms, one set of colours, and three drums. In this action Captain Radcliffe deserves this remembrance, that with three soldiers, the rest of his squadron being scattered with the execution of the enemy, he cleared two sconces, and slew seven men with his own hand. Lieutenant Worrill, engaging himself in another work among fifty of the enemy, bore the fury of them all, till Captain Farmer relieved him, who, to the wonder of us all, came off without any dangerous wound.*

The sally port was this day warded by Captain Chisenhall, who with fresh men stood ready to succour our men had they been put to any extremity; but they bravely marched round the works, and came in at the great gates, where

---

* Plus animi est inferenti quam periculum propulsanti.—*Cæs. Com.*

Captain Ogle, with a party of musketeers, kept open the passage. Captain Rawstorne had the charge of the musketeers upon the walls, whom he placed to the best advantage to vex the enemy in their flight. Captain Fox, with colours in the Eagle Tower, gave signals when to march and when to retreat, according to the motions of the enemy, which he observed at a distance. In all this service we had but one man mortally wounded, and we took only one prisoner, an officer, for the sake of intelligence. In former sallies some prisoners had been taken, and were released by exchange. Colonels Ashton and Rigby had promised to set at liberty as many of the king's friends who were then prisoners in Lancaster, Manchester, Preston, and other places, as her ladyship proposed; but they most unworthily broke their conditions, it suiting well their religion neither to observe faith with God nor with men; and this occasioned a greater slaughter than either her ladyship or the captains desired, because we were in no condition to keep many prisoners, and knew their commanders would never release them but upon base and dishonourable terms.

The same night they played a saker twice, to tell us they had cannon that would speak, though our men had endeavoured to steel up all their lips. This whole night was one continued alarm with them, there being nothing but shouts and cries amongst them, as if the cavaliers had still been upon them.

April 12. On Friday they sent us two shots from their mortar-piece, which our men had nailed and battered with smiths' hammers, but it had too wide a mouth to be stopped. This day a chance bullet from their saker passing through the clay walls, entered the windows of my lady's chamber, but was too weak to fright her from her lodging.

April 13. On Saturday their demi-cannon opened again, yet spake but once, and then very low, some of the steel nails yet sticking in her teeth, and the gunners also suspecting poison in her belly.

April 15. On Monday they played their mortar-piece five times with stones, and once with grenado, which fell short of the house in a walk near the chapel tower. Some pieces of the shell, two inches thick, flew over the walls, and were taken up in the furthest part of the house.

April 16. On Tuesday morning they had a hot alarm, not

having yet quitted themselves of the fright they took at the last
sally. They played their cannon twice, and their muskets
for half an hour. In addition to which, at about eleven
o'clock, they played their mortar-piece with stone, and perceiving it struck within the body of the house, they cast a
grenado at the same level, which fell into an old court, striking above half a yard into the earth, yet it rose again with
such violence in bursting, that though its strength was much
lessened, and deadened by the earth, yet it shook down the
glass, clay, and weaker buildings near it, leaving only the
carcase of the walls standing about it, yet without hurting any
person, except that two women in a near chamber had their
hands scorched, to put them in mind hereafter that they had
been in the siege at Lathom.

The mortar-piece was now more terrible than formerly, insomuch that the captains, to prevent the soldiers' fears,
lodged them in upper rooms, within clay walls, as not fearing there the force of the grenado : and one thing which
now happily lent more courage to our men, was this, that one
of their engineers, mounting the rampart to see the fall
of the grenado, was slain by a marksman from one of our
towers.

On Saturday, they made thirty shots from their demi-cannon and culverin, to batter a postern-tower, some part whereof stood without the moat and palisades, yet it was so fenced
in by a rising ground, that their ordnance took only the battlements and a yard of wall, which was made good again the
same night, with greater strength and safety for our musketeers than formerly. It was some requital for the breach
of a few stones that their cannonier was slain through a port-
hole by one of our men on the tower. Having done either
with the cannon or cannonier, they now begin with the
mortar-piece, which during that afternoon they played
five times, in the night twice with stones and once with
grenado ; which also, by the change in the gunner, fell short
of the house.

April 22. On Easter Monday they must needs show the
people some pastime, and therefore they gave us the bullets,
and then the noise of nine cannons and two periers, in order
to hear the rabble shout. That night, being too dark for action, the captain sent out two or three firelocks, which struck
them into alarm for the whole night, so that to their muskets

hey added one mortar-piece, and two cannon wi h chain
and small shot.

April 23. The next day was the second wakes, when
Rigby must gratify the country for their £2,000 with the
battery of the Eagle Tower at Lathom, against which they
played their culverin and demi-cannon twenty-three times,
which, unhappily striking against a stair-case, forced a large
breach.   Two of the bullets entered her ladyship's chamber,
which at length made her ladyship seek a new lodging, with
this protest, however, that she would keep the house, while
there was a single building to cover her head.

This action must needs have proceeded either from pride
or malice, as it could be no furtherance to the taking of
the house to batter a tower that stood in the midst of it:
but sure it was their plot either to strike off one of the
horns of the whore of Babylon, or else to level one of her
hills ; the seven towers, in the divine's sermon, being easily
found to be the seven hills of Rome.   It saved the tower
some buffets that day, that two of their gunners were discharged from their employment by our marksmen from the
top of the same tower which they were battering.   The
same night a strong alarm beat all their men to their
cannon, not to defend them, but themselves, which they
bravely discharged, twice loaden with cartridge and chain,
against two lighted matches cast near their works in balls
of clay.

April 24. On Wednesday they only gave us three periers
and two cannon.   But now Mr. Rigby, who undertook the
management, and expected the glory of this enterprise, having
wearied his soldiers, wasted his powder, and emptied himself of a good part of his exacted and plundered monies,
finding her ladyship inclined to yield nothing to his great
guns, but daily to beat and baffle his soldiers, is now for
present fire and ruin.   He has provided a new stock of
grenadoes, and intends to spend the rest of his powder and
malice in them.

April 25. On Thursday he sends his last message, as he
calls it, a furious summons to her ladyship to yield up
Lathom House, and all the persons, goods, and arms within
it, into his hands, to receive the mercy of the parliament,
and to return her final answer the next day before two o'clock.
Her ladyship having read this, with a brave indignation calls

for the drum, and tells him that, " a due reward for his pains is to be hanged up at her gates; but," says she, " thou art but the foolish instrument of a traitor's pride; carry this answer back to Rigby," (with a noble scorn tearing the paper in his sight), " and tell that insolent rebel, he shall neither have persons, goods, nor house; when our strength and provision is spent, we shall find a fire more merciful than Rigby's, and then, if the providence of God prevent it not, my goods and house shall burn in his sight; and myself, children, and soldiers, rather than fall into his hands, will seal our religion and loyalty in the same flame;" which being spoken aloud in her soldiers' hearing, they broke out into shouts and acclamations of joy, all closing with this general voice, " We will die for his majesty and your honour—God save the king !"

The drum returned. Her ladyship and the captains fell into consultation for a further answer to that proud message. Something must be done, and now was the nick and joint of time, according to the observation of the historian, " that the changes of times are the most fit for brave attempts, and delays are dangerous, and that softness and quietness draw more danger than hazarding rashly."*

The mortar-piece was that which troubled us all. The little ladies had stomachs to digest cannon, but the stoutest soldiers had no hearts for grenadoes; and why might they not at once free themselves from the continual expectation of death ? " 'Tis a hard choice for any good man," says young Diso, " either to kill or be killed," and this was exactly our present condition —either sheepishly to receive death, when they would send it upon our heads, or manfully to return it upon their own. At last it was resolved, notwithstanding that there was a battery and ordnance planted against every passage, to sally out the next morning and venture for all.

April 26. All things being prepared, about four o'clock the next morning Captain Chisenhall and Captain Fox, Lieut. Bretergh, Lieutenant Pencket, Lieutenant Walthew, and Lieutenant Worrill, are designed for the service. Captain Ogle had the main guard to secure a retreat at the southern gate; Captain Rawstorne had the charge of the sally gate, to secure our retreat on the east side; Captain Radcliffe had

* Transitus rerum.—Tacit. iib. 1.   Necem desperes nunc posse fien quod jam toties actum est.—*Cæs. Comm.*

the care of the marksmen and musketeers upon the walls, to attend the approaches or vex the flight of the enemy.   Capt. Farmer, with a reserve of fresh men, was to stand ready at the parade to relieve either captain in case of necessity.

All things being thus disposed, Captain Chisenhall, with his eighty men and two lieutenants, issued out at the eastern gate, and before he was discovered had got under their cannon, marching straight upon the stones, where they had planted their great guns.   It cost him a slight skirmish to gain the fort; at last he entered; many being slain, some being taken prisoners, and some escaping.   Now, by having the command of that battery, their retreat being assured, Captain Fox, according to orders, seconds him with much bravery, beating up their trenches from the eastern to the south-west point, till he came to the work which secured the mortar-piece, which being guarded by fifty men, he found sharp service in forcing his way through musket and cannon, and in beating the enemy out of the sconce with stones, his muskets, by reason of the high work, being unserviceable. After a quarter of an hour's hard service, his men got the trench, and scaled the rampart, whereupon many of the enemy fled, and the rest were slain.   The sconce, thus won, was made good by a squadron of musketeers, who much annoyed the enemy, who were attempting to come up again. The two main works being thus obtained, the two captains walked the rest of the round with ease; whilst Mr. Broome, with a company of her ladyship's servants and some fresh soldiers, took care to level the ditch, and by a present device, lifting the mortar-piece on with ropes to a low drag, by strength of men drew it into the house,—Captain Ogle defending the passage against another company of the enemy which played upon their retreat.   The like endeavour was used to gain their great guns; but they lying beyond the ditch, and being of such bulk and weight, all our strength could not bring them off before the whole army would have fallen upon us; however, our men took time to poison all the cannon round, if anything will do this feat; Captain Rawstorne still defending the first pass against some attempts of the enemy to come up from the wood.

This action continued for an hour, with the loss of only two men on our part, who, after they were mortally wounded, still fired upon the enemy till all retreated.   What number of the enemy were slain it is not easy to guess.   Besides the execution done to them in their works and trenches, the reserves of Captain Farmer and Captain Radcliffe, with the best marksmen, played upon them from the walls with such slaughter as to make them quit their holds.   Our men brought in many arms, three drums, and but five prisoners, preserved by Captain Chisenhall, to show that he had mercy as well as valour.   One of these was an assistant to their engineer Browne, who discovered to us the nature of their trench, in which they had laboured for two months to draw away our water.

Their first design was to drain and open our springs, not considering their rise from a higher ground south-east of the house, which must needs supply our deep well, wherever they might sink their fall.   This invention failing, they bring up an open trench in a worm-work, the earth being indented and sawn, for the security of their miners, and the ditch being two yards wide and three deep, for the fall of the water.

But now neither ditches nor aught else troubled our soldiers, their grand terror, the mortar-piece, which had frightened them from their meat and sleep, lying like a dead lion quietly among them ; every one had his eye and his foot upon it, shouting and rejoicing as merrily as they used to do with their ale and bagpipes.   Indeed, every one had this estimation of the service, that the main work had been done, and that what was yet behind was but a mere pastime.

The house, though outwardly well fenced against the shot of cannon, had many internal buildings of wood, especially one ancient and weak fabric, in which many men's lives had been nakedly exposed to the periers, but by this day's action was now preserved, in respect of which, of all other occurrences in the siege, we may say what Livy speaks of the battle at Nola—" Ingens eo die res, ac nescio an maxima illo bello gesta sit—Circa Alesiam tantæ res gestæ, quantas audere vix hominis, perficere nullius, nisi Dei sit."—Paterculus.   It was the greatest and most fortunate exploit.   Her ladyship, though not often overcarried with any light expressions of joy, yet religiously sensible of so great a blessing, and desirous, according to her pious disposition, of returning acknowledgments to the right author, God alone, commanded her chaplains to make a public thanksgiving.

The enem , terrified by this defeat, durst not venture into their works again till midnight ; towards morning removing some of their cannon, and the next night stealing away all the rest, save one piece left for a memorandum. This one escaped nailing, which the colonels did not venture to place on its own mount, but planted at a distance, for fear of the madmen in the garrison.

One thing should not be here omitted. The day on which our men gave Rigby that shameful defeat, he had destined for the execution of his utmost cruelty. He had invited, as it is now generally confessed, all his friends, the holy abettors of this mischief, to come to see the house either yielded or burned, he having purposed to use his mortar-gun with fire-balls or grenados all the afternoon ; but her ladyship, before two o'clock (his own time), gave him such a very scurvy satis-fying answer, that his friends came opportunely to comfort him, who was sick of shame and dishonour, in being routed by a lady and a handful of men.

After this he was hopeless of gaining the house by any other means than starving us out, or withdrawing the water ; which our captains perceiving, immediately sunk an eye, to meet them in their works, to discover any mines to blow up the towers or walls, in which we had diligent observers to hearken to any noises from their trench, by which our men might thereby direct their countermines.

From this time to the 25th of May we had a continued calm, Mr. Rigby's spirit being laid within our circle, so that we were scarcely sensible of a siege, except by the restraint upon our liberty. But our men continually vexed their quiet, either by the excursion of a few in the night, or by frequent alarms, which the captains gave the soldiers leave to invent and execute for their recreation. Sometimes, in spite of their perdues, they would steal a cord round some tree near the enemy's works, and, bringing the end round, would make it terrible with many ranks and files of light matches ; some-times dogs, and once a forlorn horse, handsomely starred with matches, being turned out of the gate, appeared in the dark night like some huge constellation. But the enemy were so diseased and beaten both in jest and in ear-nest, that many of them quitted their charge, and the rest cried out for pay, ready to take any occasion to leave the plunder of Lathom House to others. Colonel Rigby, per-ceiving them ready to crumble into mutinies, endeavoured to cement the breaches with some small pittance of their pay, declaring that the siege had cost him £2000 of his own money. He was never known to have been worth one till he became a public robber by law; but you must remember that he had been a lawyer, and a bad one.

All this cheap talk would not keep his soldiers from defection; many ran away, one of whom, having escaped from the enemy's works at mid-day, came to us, from whom we received this intelligence. Our men, not judging it safe to trust a fugitive enemy, would not venture upon another sally, imagining that some treachery might have been weaved in with all these plain webs, and been covered by the artifice of this strange convert; but Rigby, hearing of this renegade, presently smelled a plot, and every day and night doubled his guards. His men, wearied out with extraordinary duty, and he himself being perplexed with fears and jealousies, was forced to call Colonel Holland to come from Manchester to his assistance.

About this time we discovered a cessation in their mine-works, the abundance of rain so slackening and loosening the earth, that all their trench fell in, with the death of three of their miners.

May 23. On Thursday, Captain Edward Mosley brought another summons to her ladyship from his colonels, Holland and Rigby, something fuller than the former (it not befitting Mr. Rigby's greatness to remit anything of his former rigour), that her ladyship should forthwith yield up her house, her arms and goods, all her servants, and her own person and children, into their hands, to be submitted to the mercy of the parliament; which being read, her ladyship smiled, and in a troubled passion challenged the captain with a mistake in the paper, saying *mercy* instead of *cruelty*. " No," says he, " the mercy of the parliament;" when her ladyship quickly and composedly replied, " The mercies of the wicked are cruel. Not that I mean," says she, " a wicked parliament, of which body I have an honourable and reverend esteem, but wicked factors and agents, such as Moor and Rigby, who, for the advantage of their own interests, labour to turn kingdoms into blood and ruin. That unless they would treat with her lord, they should never have her, nor any of her friends, alive;" which the soldiers seconded with a general acclamation.

The captain finding her still resolute in her first intention, in his discourse with her ladyship and some others, gave a tacit intimation (most likely not without instructions from the colonels), that her ladyship might now have her own first conditions for quitting the house; but she returned the captain with the first answer, that she would never treat without commands from her lord.

The same night, one of our spies, sent out for news, approached the enemy's works, and taking the opportunity of a single sentry, pistolled him, and entered the house with intelligence from his lordship, that his highness Prince Rupert was in Cheshire, on his march to her ladyship's relief, which gave us a joyful occasion that night to pray for the prince's happy and victorious approach.

May 24, 25. Friday and Saturday were passed over in a hopeful ignorance, for while we knew nothing, we had good cause to hope well.   It being the custom of the enemy to storm us with most hideous tales from their trenches, when they had the least foundation for a lie.

May 26. On Sunday night, our sentries discovered a weakness in the enemy in the thinness of their relief, wherefore the captains agreed to sally out the next morning at three o'clock with 200 men.

Captain Ogle and Captain Rawstorne were allotted for this action; but the enemy, like good provident fellows, thrifty of their own lives, prevented the captain this honour; for, hearing of the prince's victorious entrance into the country (by the defeat of Colonels Duckenfield, Mainwaring, Buckley, and others, who kept the pass at Stockport, the second key of the county), they stole away betwixt twelve and one o'clock in the morning.

The next day Rigby drew up his companies, and what fresh supplies he could raise, in all about three thousand men (Mr. Holland having returned to Manchester, and Mr. Moor to Liverpool), unto Eccleston Green, six miles from Lathom, standing there in a great suspense which way to turn.   At last, imagining that the prince would either march through Blackburn or Lancaster to the relief of York, he determined not to come in his way, but diverts to Bolton, formerly a garrison, and still fortified.

In this town the prince also intended to take up his quarters, having been truly certified by his scouts that it was without an enemy; but being happily prevented by Rigby

2 L

with some other auxiliaries from Colonel Shuttleworth, to
the number of four or five thousand in all, his highness on
Tuesday drew up his army before the town, being truly happy
of an occasion to fight with the merciless besiegers of a princess in misery, and forthwith with all gallantry and resolution
led on his men to an assault.

The Earl of Derby desiring to be one of the first avengers
of that barbarity and cruelty displayed to his lady, with a
part of the prince's own horse charged a troop of the enemy,
which had bravely issued out of the town to disorder and
vex our foot in the assault. These he chased to the very
walls, where he slew the cornet, and with his own hand took
the colours, being the first ensign taken that day, and which
he sent to his highness. On his first passing into the town,
closely following the foot on their entrance, his lordship met
with Captain Bootle, formerly one of his own servants, but
now the most virulent enemy against his lady in the siege.
Him he did the honour of too brave a death of dying by
his lord's hand, with some others of his good countrymen,
who had for three months thirsted for his lady's and his chil-
drens' blood.

May 29. The prince this day not only relieved but revenged the most noble lady his cousin, leaving 1600 of her
besiegers dead in the place, and carrying away 700 prisoners.
For a perpetual memorial of his victory, as a brave expression of his own nobleness, and a gracious respect to her
ladyship's sufferings, the next day he presented her ladyship,
by the hands of the valiant and truly noble Sir Richard
Crane, with twenty-two of those colours, which three days before were proudly flourished before her house, which gift
will give honour to his highness and glory to the action, so
long as there lives one branch of that ancient and princely
family which his highness that day preserved.

A VIEW OF THE GARRISON, THEIR STRENGTH AND DISCI-
PLINE.—Her ladyship commanded in chief; whose first care
was the service of God, which, in sermons and solemn prayers,
she saw duly performed. Four times a day was she commonly present at public prayer, attended by the two little
ladies her children, the Lady Mary and the Lady Catherine,
for piety and sweetness truly the children of so princely a
mother: and if daring in time of danger may add anything

to their age and virtues, let them have this testimony, that though truly apprehensive of the enemy's malice, they were never startled by any appearance of danger.

HER CAPTAINS.—Capt. Henry Ogle, Capt. Edward Chisenhall, Capt. Edward Rawstorne, Capt. Wm. Farmer, Capt. Molineux Radcliffe, Capt. Richard Fox, assisted in their consultations by William Farrington of Wearden, Esq., who, for executing the commission of array, and for attending her ladyship in her troubles, had suffered the seizure of all his personal estate, and the sequestration of all his lands.

THE SOLDIERS were three hundred in number, proportioned to every captain. Their duty was to have one hundred and fifty men upon the watch every second night, excepting sixteen select marksmen out of the whole, who kept the towers all day. The sallies were by lot. The captains drawn by her ladyship chose their own lieutenants. Without the walls is a deep ditch, fenced on each bank with strong pallisades; upon the walls were seven towers, conveniently flanking one another. Within, the walls are lined with earth and sods, two yards thick, by the industry of the soldiers in the siege.

THE ORDNANCE consisted of six sakers and two slingpieces; in every tower one or two murderers to scour the ditches.

Our greatest fear was from the want of powder, which would have been soon spent, had not the captains dispensed it frugally, and prohibited the soldiers from waste of shots.

Every sally brought us in some new stock to augment our magazine, which the soldiers found in the enemies' trenches.

This fear made the captains sparing in their sallies and their ordnance, who would else have prevented the enemy's near works.

In the whole siege we spent but seven barrels, besides what we took from the enemy. During the whole time they gave us neither assault nor alarm.

The provisions would have lasted two months longer, notwithstanding the soldiers had always sufficient, whom her ladyship took care oftentimes to see served herself.

We lost but six men in the whole siege, four in service, and two by their own negligence, or over-daring in appearing above the towers.

A VIEW OF THE ENEMY.—Sir Thomas Fairfax commanded in chief; under him Col. Ashton, Col. Holland, Col. Moor, and Col. Rigby, by turns assisting one another.

The common soldiers, continually in league, were between two or three thousand, which, divided in tertias, made seven or eight hundred watching every third day and night.

THEIR ARTILLERY.—One demi-cannon, one culverin, a mortar-piece, and three sakers.

Their works were an open trench round the house, a yard of ditch, and a yard raised with turf, at the distance of sixty, one hundred, or two hundred yards from the walls.

They had eight sconces raised in such places as might most annoy our men in the sally, built *directis lateribus;* with two yards of rampart and a yard of ditch, in some places staked and palisaded to keep off a violent assault.

Their pioneers were first sheltered by baskets and hurdles, and afterwards by a kind of testudo, a wooden engine running on wheels, roofed towards the house, with thick planks, and open for the enemy to cast up the earth.

They shot one hundred and seven cannon, thirty-two stones, and four grenados. They spent, by the confession of their own officers. nearly one hundred barrels of powder; and they lost about five hundred men, besides one hundred and forty who were maimed and wounded.

The Oxford MS. contains the following formal terminations, which have been omitted in the MS. Journal in the British Museum :—

" Finis of a brief Journal of the Siege against Lathom House."

And on a fly-leaf is written in the same hand as the MS. ' Wherein I was wounded, EDWARD HALSALL."

POSTSCRIPT.

AFTER the siege of Lathom House, so vividly described in the preceding Journal, the Countess of Derby, with her children, under the protection of the earl, retired to the Isle of Man, leaving Lathom House to the care of Colonel Rawstorne, who furnished the garrison with provisions and ammunition for sustaining another siege.

In the month of July, of the following year (1645), the siege was renewed by General Egerton, at the head of four thousand men, who fixed his head quarters at Ormskirk. Colonel Rawstorne immediately ordered out a strong party of horse and foot, under the command of Major Munday and Captain Molineaux Radcliffe, who gallantly attacked the enemy's quarters with so much courage, resolution, and bravery, as made them to retreat for a few weeks from the neighbourhood.

The defeat of the Royalists about this time at Marston Moor, and the flight of Prince Rupert to Chester, prevented the king from rendering his loyal garrison at Lathom any further assistance; which having now become reduced to extremities for want of the munitions of war, his majesty advised that a commission should be appointed by both parties to treat of a surrender. This intended compromise, however, was defeated through the treachery of an Irish soldier connected with Lathom, and on the 2nd of December, 1645, Colonel Rawstorne, after a gallant and successful stand, surrendered into the hands of the parliamentary forces, upon bare terms of mercy, the ancient, noble, and almost invincible House of Lathom, "whose antiquity, famous siege, and most heroic defence," says Seacome, "can never be forgotten whilst history remains in the world."

At the time of the surrender, the mansion contained twelve pieces of ordnance, besides a large store of arms and ammunition. The besiegers soon converted the most valuable effects of the house into booty; the rich silk hangings of the beds were rent in pieces; the towers, from whence so many fatal shots proceeded, were demolished, and the sun of Lathom seemed for ever to have set.

On the 8th of December, 1645, the "Perfect Diurnall," a newspaper of the day, gave the following intelligence of its fall :—" On Saturday, December 6, after the house was up, there came letters to the Speaker of the Commons' House of the surrender of Lathom House in Lancashire, belonging to the Earl of Derby, which his lady, the Countess of Derby, proving herself the better soldier of the two, hath above these two years kept in opposition to our forces."*

* Peck's Desiderata Curiosa, 449

At the Restoration, Lathom House returned into the possession of the Earl of Derby; but having been almost destroyed, the family residence was fixed at Knowsley. William Richard George, the ninth Earl of Derby, however, intending to rebuild this seat, erected in the same situation a sumptuous and lofty front, which composes a part of the south front of the present house, but did not live to complete his design. After his death it devolved to his eldest daughter, Henrietta, married first to the Earl of Anglesey, and secondly, to Lord Ashburnham, who sold it to Henry Furnese, Esq., from whom it was purchased in 1724, by Sir Thomas Bootle, Knight of Melling, in this county, afterwards chancellor to Frederick Prince of Wales, whose niece and heiress married Richard Wilbraham, Esq., of Rode Hall, in Cheshire. The estate is now possessed by Lord Skelmersdale, the eldest son of that marriage.

For the Earl of Derby and his consort, after the fall of Lathom House, a gloomy prospect of troublous days was still before them. Cooped up in their diminutive kingdom, the Isle of Man, where they were honoured as patriarchal princes, they bade defiance to the fleets, the threats, and the persuasions of parliament. On the faith of a safe conduct from Fairfax, they sent their children into England for their education; who, however, were seized and sent as prisoners to Liverpool. Though repeated offers were made to restore them, and the whole of his estates, if the earl would give up his island, he remained firm to his royal master, and boldly replied—" That he was greatly afflicted at the suffering of his children; that it was not in the nature of great and noble minds to punish innocent children for the offences of their parents; that it would be a clemency in Sir Thomas Fairfax either to send them back to him, or to their mother's friends in France and Holland; but if he would do neither, his children must submit to the mercy of Almighty God, but should never be released by his disloyalty."

In 1651, when Charles the Second made an attempt to recover the throne of his father, the Earl of Derby was among the first to join his standard, leaving the government of the Isle of Man, as he had formerly trusted the defence of Lathom, to his heroic countess. After the loss of the battle of Worcester, the earl nobly provided for the safety of his young sovereign at the expense of his own. On the borders of Chester he was overtaken by a party under Major Edge, to whom he surrendered his sword, under a promise of being treated with honour as a prisoner of war· but his enemies—especially Bradshaw, Rigby, and Birch—were resolved on his downfall. The execution was fixed for the 15th of October, in his own town of Bolton-le-Moors, where a scaffold was erected with the timbers of the ruins of Lathom House. Just before he suffered he calmly requested that the block might be removed so as to face the church, saying, " I will look toward thy sanctuary while here, as I hope to live in thy heavenly sanctuary for ever hereafter."

Colonel Birch soon after attacked the Isle of Man, when, through the treachery of a false friend, the countess and her children were betrayed into the hands of their enemies. During their incarceration in an unhealthy dungeon two of her children fell victims to the small-pox. She remained in prison till the Restoration of Charles the Second, when she returned with her remaining children to Knowsley Hall, in the neighbourhood of Lathom House, where she departed this life in the year 1663

INDEX.